Peasant Uprisings

IN SEVENTEENTH-CENTURY FRANCE, RUSSIA, AND CHINA

By Roland Mousnier

Translated from the French by Brian Pearce

HARPER TORCHBOOKS
Harper & Row, Publishers
New York, Evanston, San Francisco, London

This work was first published in French under the title *Fureurs Paysannes:
Les paysans dans les Révoltes du XVIIe Siècle (France, Russie, Chine)*. ©
Calmann-Levy, 1967.

Contents

Maps

Chart

Translator's Note

PROFESSOR MOUSNIER ASSUMES his French reader to possess a familiarity with the agrarian relationships and with the administrative and fiscal structures of seventeenth-century France which is not to be expected in many of those who will read this English version of his book. He therefore uses, as a matter of course, a number of technical terms belonging to these fields. It would be as futile to try to translate some of these in the text as it might be, in a translation from English into some other language of a book in which cricket matches are described, to try to translate terms like "cover point," "mid off," or "long stop." Instead, a note is here offered on some aspects of the French scene in the period covered by this book, composed so as to bring out the significance of those terms that have been left in the original language in the text. For the sake of brevity and clarity some generalizations and unqualified statements have been risked which readers who know the subject already may find rather daring: but this note is not meant for them.

First, some points about agrarian relationships. Here confusion may arise from the use of the word *domaine* (Latin, *dominium*) to mean both "ownership" and the physical area of land subject to ownership in one form or another. A lord possessed *domaine direct* (or *domaine éminent*) over all his land; it meant that he had the right to homage or dues from all who occupied it. In practice, a lord often, if not usually, granted out most of his land to other people. Those to whom he granted it were said to possess the *domaine utile* of the land assigned to them: in other words, after rendering to their lord that which it was their duty to render, they could keep for themselves whatever they could make out of the land they cultivated. The land thus granted out by the lord was called his *directe seigneuriale*.

Some of this *directe seigneuriale* was granted out in the form of *fiefs nobles*, in return for noble services. (The person who received such a fief was normally himself a nobleman, though, as mentioned in the text, a peasant or bourgeois could obtain one on condition of paying what was called *franc-fief*, "frank-fee.") One of the obligations incurred by the recipient was the rendering of *aveu et dénombrement*—literally, "acknowledgment and enumeration"—a formal record and description of the holding and all the responsibilities connected with it. If such a fief was sold, the purchaser had to pay the lord *quint et requint*—literally, "a fifth, and a fifth of that"—which meant, e.g., that if the fief changed hands for 100,000 livres, the purchaser had to pay the lord 20,000 livres plus 4,000 livres, i.e., 24,000 livres. Should the fief be bequeathed to someone who was not a relative in the direct line of succession, he had to pay *rachat* (or relief) to the lord, usually amounting to one year's income from the fief.

That part of the *directe seigneuriale* that was granted out in *fiefs roturiers*, or "commoners' fiefs," and was usually cultivated by peasants, owed the lord first and foremost the annual payment called *cens*. This might in itself be a very small quit-rent, fixed long before and bearing no relation to the present economic value of the land, but payment of it entailed obligation to pay *lods et ventes* in the event of the holding (*censive*) changing hands by sale. That meant a payment to the lord of around 10 percent of the purchase price, and *lods et ventes* have been described as "the most important and productive of seignorial rights." In addition, the peasants were often obliged to pay their lord a kind of tithe, called *champart* (or *agrière*, or *terrage*), which was a definite proportion of their crops. On the average it was about 12 percent, but it could be much higher in some areas: if it amounted to one-third, the land thus heavily burdened was called a *tiercerie*.

That part of his estate which the lord did not grant out in noble fiefs or to *censitaires* (*cens*-payers) was called the *domaine proche,* or *réserve seigneuriale.* Some of this he might exploit through his own steward as a "home farm," but a large part of it he would probably lease out—to capitalist farmers, so to speak, in contrast to the feudal tenants, noble and non-noble, of his *directe seigneuriale.* Whereas the obligations of the latter were supposed to be governed by custom and tradition, those of the former were frankly determined by economic considerations alone. These tenants were either *fermiers*—"farmers" in the strict sense—who paid an economic rent in money, or *métayers,* "sharecroppers," who paid a fixed proportion of the crops they raised, in kind—often as much as 50 percent.

Other dues, services, and rents besides those mentioned are alluded to in the text, but do not involve the use of special French terms, so they are ignored here. The special system of *domaine congéable* which prevailed in part of Brittany is adequately explained by the author.

Second, an outline of the relevant parts of the administrative and fiscal regime should be offered. Here, it has to be realized that the king's hierarchy of officials was paralleled by a corresponding hierarchy, who often bore the same titles, within the feudal lordships: and also that the normal practice when a new institution was created was to leave nominally intact the one that it replaced, in whole or in part, so that a great deal of overlapping, duplication, rivalry, and conflict occurred. The position was therefore extremely confused and irrational.

The provinces of France were, in principle, each headed by a governor, who was always a great nobleman, and whose functions were military. The functions of administration and justice, so far as the king fulfilled these, were carried out by *baillis* and *sénéchaux.* These ruled over areas called *bailliages* and *sénéchaussées* respectively—there was no difference between them, each of the names being "customary" in particular parts of France. A small province might consist of a single *bailliage* (or *sénéchaussée*) while a large one might be divided into several. The *baillis* (or *sénéchaux*) were always members of the hereditary "nobility of the sword"; that is, they belonged to the *noblesse de robe courte,* in contrast to the

noblesse de robe longue, which meant that they had no legal
training. To look after their judicial functions as representatives of
the king's justice, they were assisted by a *lieutenant-général.* (Confusion may be caused by the fact that the provincial governors
were, from Henry IV's time onward, assisted, and held in check,
by a royal representative called *lieutenant-général du roi* appointed
to work with them.) These *lieutenants-généraux de bailliage* were
lawyers; they were in their turn assisted by *lieutenants particuliers,*
who divided among themselves responsibility for civil cases,
criminal cases, and the maintenance of law and order. Each
bailliage and *sénéchaussée* was divided into a number of *prévôtés
royales,* each headed by a king's judge called the *prévôt* (in
Normandy, the *vicomte*), or *châtellenies,* headed by a similar
official of lower rank, the *châtellan* ("castellan").

Thus, for example, the province of Angoumois, a relatively small
one, of 400 parishes, was united at one stage with another small
province, Saintonge, under a single governor. Angoumois itself
formed a single, self-contained *sénéchaussée,* divided into three
prévôtés royales (centered at Angoulême, Châteauneuf, and
Boutteville), and thirty-one *châtellenies principales.*

At Angoulême, chief town of the *sénéchaussée,* there was a court
called a *présidial.* The courts called *présidiaux* had been created in
the middle of the sixteenth century by giving additional powers to
the *lieutenants-généraux* in certain *bailliages* and *sénéchaussées,* of
which Angoumois was one, the purpose being to provide a
reasonably accessible court of appeal for regions that otherwise
would have had no nearer court of appeal than their very distant
parlement. There were only eight of the supreme courts called
parlements: at Paris, Rouen, Rennes, Bordeaux, Toulouse, Aix-en-
Provence, Grenoble, and Dijon—and the area of competence of
the *Parlement de Paris* was extremely large, reaching down into
Auvergne: it was no accident that about half out of all the
présidiaux were created in *bailliages* within the "territory" of the
Parlement de Paris. The *présidial* court was composed of the
lieutenants-général et particulier, civil et criminel, together with
seven *conseillers.* (The title of *conseiller du roi*—"king's councillor"—was sold rather widely, so that a great many officials of
various courts all bore it.)

Attached to every *parlement* and *présidial*, and to every *bailliage* and *sénéchaussée*, were a group of lawyers—a procurator and a number of advocates—whose duty it was to see to the safeguarding of the king's interests in all cases that came before the courts. These were the *gens du roi*, the "king's men": they corresponded to the "procurators-fiscal" whom the lords who held courts on their own fiefs maintained there as watchdogs for *their* interests. The royal courts, at every level, also had a staff of *enquêteurs et examinateurs*, who functioned as examining magistrates, carrying out inquiries and interrogating witnesses on behalf of the courts.

The *baillis* and *sénéchaux* themselves, their administrative and judicial powers having been taken over, in effect, by all these lawyers who were nominally their assistants and subordinates, were left with, as their chief practical task, the organizing of the *ban et arrière-ban*, i.e., the musters of the noblemen in their territory who owed military service to the king.

Originally, the kings of France, like other feudal monarchs, were expected to live "of their own," that is, mainly from the resources of their royal domains. From the time of the Hundred Years' War onward, however, it was accepted that the king must be helped to meet the cost of the defense of the country through a special tax called the taille, payable by all commoners. The original taille was eventually found inadequate, and a series of additional taxes were imposed, all, nominally at least, for paying the soldiers—*taillon*, *creue* (or *crue*), *subsistance*. The separate organizations for collecting domain dues and for collecting the taille and its supplements came to be merged. Those provinces that did not possess assemblies of estates ("states") which retained the power to discuss and vote on taxation were divided into *généralités* for tax-collection purposes. Each *généralité* usually covered several *bailliages* or *sénéchaussées*. At the head of a *généralité* was a *bureau de finances*, made up of officials called *trésoriers de France*, who were responsible for the revenues of the royal domain, and *généraux de finance*, who were in charge of the taille. Later, the two sets of officials were united as *trésoriers-généraux* ("treasurers-general"). The *généralités* were divided into smaller districts called *élections*, because the officials at the head of them were called *élus*: they had indeed been "elected" in the early days of the institution, but soon came to be appointed from above, though the name was retained. To take again our example of the province of Angoumois, this was divided into two *élections*, with centers at Angoulême and Cognac, and these *élections* were subordinate to the *généralité* centered at Limoges, outside the province. There were about 150 *élections* in France in the 1620s and about 180 forty years later. The *élu* was responsible for allotting the share of the burden of the taille to be borne by each parish within his *élection*; he was usually a rich man who had bought this position, which gave him many opportunities for money-making as well as exempting him personally from paying the taille. Other officials of the *élection* were called *receveurs* and *collecteurs*.

The administrative framework constituted by the *généralités*—set up in the first place for a merely fiscal purpose—was increasingly utilized by the kings of France during the seventeenth century for all the work they assigned to their *intendants de provinces*. These were special "commissaries," recruited initially from among the *maîtres de requêtes* ("masters of requests") attached to the State Council, who were sent *en chevauchée* ("on circuit") to carry out special inquiries and missions for the central government in the provinces, and who encroached more and more on the powers of the older-established officials.

A number of indirect taxes—broadly known as *aides*—also had to be paid, the most controversial of these being the gabelle, a tax on salt enforced by making the sale of this essential commodity a quasi-monopoly of the Crown. After a revolt in 1548 a large area of southwestern France was exempted from gabelle in return for a redemption payment; part of Normandy enjoyed a special, modified salt-tax regime called *quart-bouillon*, explained in the text; and Brittany was exempt altogether. These anomalies resulted in much smuggling of salt from one area to another. The extreme unpopularity of the gabelle led to this term being used for any new tax regarded by the people as outrageous, and *gabeleur* for the official who came to assess or collect it. Minor taxes mentioned in this book include the charges levied by the official *courtiers* ("brokers") who had to take part in all transactions in the wine trade; the *contrôle*, an obligation for all deeds drawn up by notaries and process servers to be entered in a special register, with corresponding payment of fees; and the *fouage,* a local tax levied in Brittany. The latter was so called because it was charged upon the *feu,* which did not mean a "family hearth" or "household," as might be supposed, but was a quite arbitrary fiscal unit. Each village was declared to consist of a certain number of *feux,* and when the amount to be raised from each *feu* had been decided centrally, responsibility for payment was divided among the inhabitants so as to ensure that the village's quota was fulfilled. The number of *feux* tended to remain the same regardless of increases, decreases, or shifts of population in the province.

Of the coins mentioned in the book, an *écu* was made up of three livres, a livre of twenty sols, and a sol of four liards (or twelve deniers). The tax called the *sol pour livre* was an addition of one-twentieth to an already existing tax, imposed in order "to make up for the decline in the value of money."

B.P.

Introduction:
A Century of Revolts All Over the World

I HAVE BEEN ASKED TO DISCUSS the part played by the peasants in some of the revolts of the seventeenth century. The latter was a great period of revolts and revolutions, in which all social groups participated. In Europe, in the first place, where the high point of these crises occurred between 1640 and 1660, the following may be mentioned: the English Revolution, which culminated between 1648 and 1653 and which was perhaps the first great bourgeois revolution of modern times; that attempt at reaction against monarchical innovations called the Fronde, in France between 1648 and 1652; the revolt of Catalonia (1640–1652), and that of Portugal (1640–1668), both against Spain; in 1647 the Neapolitan revolt of Masaniello, who was killed on July 16 but whose supporters fought on until February, 1648, against the Spanish troops of the Viceroy Arcos and the fleet of Don John of Austria; the attempted coup d'etat by William II, in Holland in 1650; the Ukrainian insurrection between 1648 and 1654. These were the most outstanding episodes, but throughout Europe there were disturbances in both town and country—in Ireland (in 1641), in Switzerland, in Germany, and in Russia: popular riots in 1648 in Moscow, Ustyug, Kozlov, Solvychegodsk, Tomsk, and other towns; in 1649, a debtors' revolt in Moscow; in 1650, riots in Pskov and Novgorod-Veliky; in 1653, a peasants' war in Switzerland; in 1662, a revolt in Moscow caused by the minting of copper currency.

Moreover, the period 1640–1660 had no monopoly on disturbances. It was both preceded and followed by long periods of riot and upheaval. In France the revolts in town and country were innumerable from the 1630s onward: revolts at Dijon and Aix-en-Provence in 1631, in Bordeaux in 1635, the revolt of the *Croquants* in 1636 and of the *Nu-Pieds* in 1639, the revolt in Rouergue in 1643, and at Montpellier in 1645. These are merely a few examples. Under the personal rule of Louis XIV there occurred the revolt in the Boulonnais in 1662, the rebellion of Audijos in Chalosse, which lasted from 1664 to 1670, the revolt in Lower Vivarais in 1670, the "stamped paper" revolt in Bordeaux and in Brittany in 1675, and finally the religious uprising of the *Camisards*. In Russia there were the insurrections of the "Troubled Times" of 1601 to 1613, the great revolt of the Cossack Stenka Razin in 1670–1671, the rebellion of the Solovetsky monastery in 1668–1676, directed against the revision of the liturgical books. In Ireland there was the revolt of 1689, and in Bohemia the peasant uprising of 1670.

Not only Europe was affected. In China from 1620 onward rebellions spread and grew until the Ming dynasty collapsed in 1644. They began again on an enormous scale with the great rising of General Wu San-Kwei, which began in 1673 and went on until his death in 1681. These Chinese revolts were more or less contemporary with the great European movements. In Japan the Christians rebelled against the Tokugawa shoguns, who were Confucian, Shintoist, and intolerant. Even though they were primarily religious in character, revolts did occur, the chief one being that of Amakusa, in 1637; the Japanese Christians rose up at the same time as the *Croquants* in Périgord. In India the Hindu national rising against the Mogul conquerors began with the Mahrattas in 1648. The Sikh rebellion against the Moslem persecutors had begun earlier, in the time of the Great Mogul Jahangir (1605–1627). These two movements continued to grow and intensify, especially from 1675 onward, the year of the troubles in Brittany and Bordeaux. Professor Charles Gibson, author of that fine book *The Aztecs under Spanish Rule (1519–1810),* told me last year, in Iowa City, that in Mexico too the seventeenth century was an epoch of social disorders and outbreaks.

Contemporaries were aware that they lived in particularly difficult times. Robert Mentet de Salmonet, in the preface to his *Histoire des troubles de la Grande Bretagne*, published in Paris in 1649, expresses this feeling very well: "I will pass no Judgment upon the Manners of the Age wherein we live, only that 'tis none of the best, being an Iron Age, which is a bad reformer of Men's Lives, an Excess of Vice, with the Desolation of Countries commonly attending War. However, 'tis famous for the great and strange Revolutions that have happen'd in it. Men have been seen to mount Thrones possess'd by great and powerful Kings, without striking a Stroke, and to take Possession of them, with as much Ease, as if they had been but small Estates. We have seen Princes humbled, and some even reduc'd to the last Degree of Affliction, which Holy Scripture calls *breaking the Bands of Kings asunder*. And in other Places, Subjects who durst not look their Sovereign in the Face, have been seen to have the Boldness to summon him to appear before a Tribunal, where formerly they trembled when they spoke to him . . . Revolts have been frequent both in the East and West. . . ." (*History of the Troubles of Great Britain*, by Robert Monteth of Salmonet, London, 1735, p. ii)

Revolts flared up all round the world, and it would require a collective enterprise by historians of all countries to investigate the characteristics of such movements, in accordance with the different types of social structure involved and the reasons for their coincidence in time. To undertake such a task is too much for one man, or for one book. My subject will be a much more modest one. I shall focus my attention on the peasants, as, moreover, I have been asked to do, without losing sight of the fact that in western Europe the peasant revolts were not isolated and cannot be understood without taking account of the activities of the towns and the help rendered by other social groups. I am going to study them in three countries which I have chosen because their social structures are very different. Leaving aside England, whose revolution is to be examined in another volume in this collection, I shall apply myself to France, Russia, and China. Needless to say, I shall not study every single peasant rising in each of these countries. That is ruled out alike by the limited size of the book and by consideration for the reader. Furthermore, I intend to devote a special study, not forming part of this series, to French popular risings as a whole, the characteristics of which have been matters of controversy among historians. So far as France is concerned, I shall therefore restrict myself to the three revolts of the *Croquants*, the *Nu-Pieds*, and Lower Brittany. As for Russia, I shall deal only with the peasant risings of the Troubled Times, around the first Dmitri and Bolotnikov, and, in the second half of the century, with Stenka Razin. Regarding China, I shall discuss the rebellions of Chang Hsien-chung and Li Tzu-Cheng against the Ming emperors. Then I shall compare these specimens and try to ascertain whether they show differences which can be explained by differences in social structure and resemblances which may be due to similar conjunctions of circumstances. It is, of course, not a matter of finding definitive solutions or of working out a theory of these rebellions, but only of making more precise, if one can, a few hypotheses for use in research.

PART ONE

FRANCE: PEASANT REVOLTS

[1]

The Social Structures
of the Kingdom of France

ONE CANNOT STUDY PEASANT REVOLTS without first describing, however briefly, the social stratification of the countries where they occur. This is not to say that such revolts can be reduced merely to struggles between different social strata. Unfortunately, matters are not so simple. There were instances in which the rebel grouping was formed by way of a sort of vertical split running through all social strata, as in France during the Fronde. In any case, these movements do not make sense unless one has at least a rough knowledge of the stratification of society. What is meant by "social stratification"? A society like that of seventeenth-century France was made up of many and various social groups: in the first place, families which in this society often took the form of "dynasties," especially in the higher strata; their corporations and colleges, such as craft guilds, corporations of "officials" (that is, of persons carrying out public functions which had been raised to the status of "offices" and which entailed, along with fixity of tenure, a certain social status and some of the characteristics of pieces of property), universities, academies, religious orders, etc.; different territorial communities, such as villages, towns, lordships, and provinces. Each of these corporations, colleges, or communities had its own organs, which gave voice to its will and made it a moral personality—variously, as-

3

semblies, councils, provincial estates, presidents, syndics, municipal magistrates, consuls, lords; each had its own privileges, based perhaps on established fact, on custom which was immemorial and therefore sacred according to a way of thinking in which everything old-established in society seemed ipso facto good and worthy of veneration. These privileges corresponded to social functions; those who held them considered them the necessary conditions of their existence and also as conferring status, and therefore saw them as absolute, inviolable rights, whereas the royal government preferred to see them as matters of grace and favor, temporary and subject to recall.

Nevertheless, the social groups most important for our understanding of the revolts do seem to be the social strata. In most societies, as soon as the division of labor appears, differentiations take place which lead men to think of the society in which they live as being made up of groups of men forming social "layers," so to speak, strata placed one above the other in a hierarchical order. Where the France of the sixteenth, seventeenth, and eighteenth centuries is concerned, historians like to call these strata variously castes, orders, or classes, which gives rise to confusion.[1] Actually, in a caste society, the social groups called castes are arranged in a hierarchy neither according to their members' riches or consuming capacity nor according to the role they play in the production of material wealth, but in hereditary fashion, on the basis of their degree of religious purity or impurity. Relations between individuals and between groups are based on religious and ritualistic notions. Society is thus fragmented into groups which live segregated from each other, in separate little worlds, as it were. Society is divided according to a principle of segregation based on degree of religious purity. Strict rules tell each group with whom its members may associate, whom they may touch, from whom they may accept food or drink, and what sort of food and drink, and also tell them whom they must avoid, who are the untouchables. A morbid fear of defilement keeps the groups at a distance from one another. Membership of a caste is hereditary, a matter of race

1. See R. Mousnier, J.-P. Labatut, Y. Durand, *Problèmes de stratification sociale. Deux cahiers de la noblesse (1649–1651)* (Paris, Presses Universitaires de France, 1964).

and blood. The individual is bowed beneath the irresistible pressure of this iron law. There was a stratification like this in India, but never in France.

In a class stratification, in a market economy, the social groups known as classes are arranged hierarchically in accordance with the role played by each in the production of material wealth, and with the money obtained in the exercise of this role by the individuals who make up these groups. Thus, a class is formed of those who have the same source of income, who possess wealth or income of the same approximate amount, and who share the same way of life and common interests. A class is complete if it also possesses consciousness of all that is common to its members, and carries out action in common. This is the type of stratification which was increasingly predominant in the nineteenth century, in Europe and in America. It was not the general and main type of stratification in France before the middle of the eighteenth century.

The France of the sixteenth, seventeenth, and eighteenth centuries was a society of orders, or estates, which themselves were subdivided. In a stratification by orders, or estates, these social groups are, in principle, arranged hierarchically not according to the wealth and consuming capacity of the members and not according to their role in the production of material goods, but according to the respect, honor, and dignity attached by society to social functions which may have nothing to do with the production of material goods. In France in the times under consideration, social respect, honor, and dignity were associated first and foremost with the profession of arms and what results from it, namely, fitness for command and the protection of others. There is thus a consensus which, owing to the circumstances in which society once found itself, decides what the most important social function is, and places a given social group at the top of the hierarchy. The principle of classification can then survive even after the circumstances that gave rise to it have passed, through the interest shared by all in maintaining the social order; through the fear of those dangers which always appear when a society is overturned, even when this is being done in order to change it for the better; through the force of habit which makes it hard to imagine a different social order; through the association between every

established social order and a whole system of ideas which provide
it with a rational justification; through the tendency of groups
(including, of course, the dominant group) to make the circumstances that gave rise to this type of stratification renew themselves
endlessly—for example, in this military society, the taste for war,
and repeated wars.

Each social group was assigned by this consensus of opinion its
rank, honors, privileges, rights, duties, obligations, social symbols,
dress, diet, arms, way of life, education, expenditure and recreation,
its functions, the occupations open to its members and those
closed to them, the behavior appropriate for them in relation to
other groups on various occasions, what treatment they must expect from other groups, the persons they must normally mix with
and treat as equals and comrades, and those they must merely
coexist with, having with them only those relations necessitated by
their social function or the inevitable requirements of life, and so
on. This was the social charter which laid down, in principle, the
level of wealth, of affluence or poverty, appropriate to everyone,
because it was this charter that entitled one to receive a larger or
smaller share of the income of society—in the form, so far as the
higher strata were concerned, of salaries, bounties, grants, pensions,
rents, services rendered by the lower strata, and exemptions from
taxation or common burdens.

Within each "estate" the corporations, colleges, and professional
communities formed groups engaged in common action, each with
its own social charter, resulting from a consensus of opinion, a
degree of social esteem, and its legal or customary body of rights.
Within each "estate," groups with a common mode of existence
brought together the "dynasties," linked together by marriage and
forming circles of related families which tended to become exclusive.

On the other hand, corporations, colleges, and communities
were divided horizontally by the "estates," and the territorial communities each embraced several estates. Some villages and towns
included only a few estates of the lowest order, the so-called Third
Estate, and some lower estates of the highest order, the clergy. As
a rule, however, the territorial communities embraced some estates
belonging to each of the three orders.

In all of the estates making up the orders of society there was a tendency to endogamy, that is, for the men to marry within their own estate or even within their own corporation or professional community—a tendency mitigated, however, by hypergamy on the part of the women, that is, the possibility that existed for a woman to marry a member of a higher estate. Moreover, endogamy was much less rigorous in this society than in caste societies, and was a noticeable tendency rather than an absolute rule.

In each of the estates which made up the orders of society, and even in each of the corporations or professional communities, there was a tendency to heredity. In the higher section of the nobility, the nobility "of the sword," and by imitation also in those estates which sought to draw close to this section, there was even a tendency to become a caste, in the sense that concern for purity of blood played an important part. Here too, however, there was more a tendency in this direction than an absolute rule, and it was not the same as caste because purity of blood was not a condition of religious purity.

Finally, in contrast to caste societies, a certain amount of social mobility was possible, though this applied in contrast to what happens in class societies, to families, to "dynasties," rather than to individuals, for, as a rule, three generations were usually needed for a person to pass from the Third Estate into the nobility, and even sometimes merely to rise from one subdivision of an estate to another. This social mobility was supervised and restricted by society. In the first place, the newcomer had to secure recognition of his status by his new estate, this being given tacitly through the behavior of the members of this group toward him. But social mobility was also supervised and restricted by the state or by those to whom the state had entrusted a share of public authority, and whose task it was to consecrate change of status by an official act.

Most of these rules were enforced only by social pressure, by the consensus of opinion. Some of them, however, received legal sanction, by custom and statute.

These features of the social system need to be described precisely. It is important to know what the French themselves thought of them, since any social stratification is, after all, a phenomenon of collective psychology, the picture that people have in their minds of how they ought to behave to each other. This is the nature of it, even if, in the last analysis, its cause is material and to be sought, for example, in the interplay of economic or military influences. What seventeenth-century Frenchmen thought about it is known to us from the work of a magistrate named Charles Loyseau, who, in 1610, published a sort of anatomy of French society, in particular from his *Traité des ordres et simples dignitez*.[2] That Loyseau correctly described the views of the higher strata at least is shown by two facts: his book was reissued again and again until, in the following century, attention came to be turned toward the class society then being formed; and it was to be found in a considerable number of libraries belonging to seventeenth-century personages. These facts measure the duration and universality of the book's success.

For Loyseau, the whole of French society is stratified into orders arranged in a hierarchy. An order, he explains, is "a rank, with a particular fitness for public authority . . . and in French it has the special name of *estat* ('estate' or 'state') since it is the rank and quality which is a man's most stable and inseparable feature." Officially, the whole population of France is grouped in three main orders. At the top is the ecclesiastical order, the clergy, since, by rights, the "ministers of God" should possess "the first place of honor." Then the nobility, both the "gentlefolk, ancient and immemorial," descended "from old families," and also those nobles who owe their rank to the offices and lordships they have acquired, which confer upon them the same privileges. Last, the Third Estate, embracing all the rest of the people.

Each of these main orders, however, is subdivided into "particular orders," hierarchically arranged in "ranks," "degrees," or "subordinate orders." The ecclesiastical order consists of a hierarchy, from the top downward, or cardinals, primates or patriarchs, archbishops, bishops, the three holy orders of priests, deacons and subdeacons, the four minor orders of acolytes, exorcists, readers and doorkeepers, and finally those who have merely taken the tonsure, since "the tonsure . . . is the way into all the

2. C. Loyseau, *Cinq livres du droit des offices suivis du livre des Seigneuries et de celui des Ordres* (Paris, 1610). Cf. the analysis and commentary in R. Mousnier *et al.*, *op. cit.*, pp. 25–43.

orders of the church, that which makes a man a cleric and distinguishes the clergy from the people." The order of the nobility is subdivided, from above downward, into princes of the blood; princes; more distant relations of the sovereign; the higher nobility of chivalry, distinguished among themselves by their fiefs of rank, from dukes at the top down through marquises, counts, and barons to castellans; and, finally, the ordinary nobility of gentlemen of family, engaged in the profession of arms. The Third Estate actually includes the officials administering justice and government finance, though some of these men are ennobled by their offices, so that they are noble in rank. In principle, this order is headed by the "men of letters"—doctors, licentiates, bachelors of the faculties of theology, law, medicine, and arts (grammar, rhetoric, philosophy). Then come the advocates. After them follow the financiers, meaning "all those who concern themselves with the management of finance, that is, of the king's revenues." Next, the "practitioners or men of affairs," those of the long robe, registrars, notaries, attorneys; then those of the short robe, bailiffs, trumpeters, valuers and sellers of confiscated property. Then, the merchants, both because of the utility and even necessity of trade . . . and because of the wealth these men usually possess, which brings them esteem and respect, together with the fact that the means they enjoy of employing craftsmen and laborers gives them a great deal of power in the towns; accordingly, the merchants are the lowest group of the common people that possess the quality of honor, being called "honorable men" or "worthies" (honnêtes personnes) and "bourgeois of the towns." Grouped with them are the crafts of apothecary, goldsmith, jeweler, "wholesale" haberdasher, draper, hatter, and furrier, men who are engaged in trade rather than in manual work. All these can be styled "bourgeois" if they live in privileged towns which have the right to constitute corporations and communities, if they share in the honors of their city, its rights and privileges, and vote in its assemblies. Next below the merchants come all those who in their occupations "depend more upon manual labour than on trade or on the sharpness of their wits, and whose occupations are therefore the basest." This means, first and foremost, the laboureurs, "those whose normal occupation is ploughing the land for others, as tenant-farmers." They, like all

country people or "peasants," are "base persons." Beneath them,
however, are the craftsmen "who practise the mechanical arts,
which are so called in contrast to the liberal arts . . . We give
the name mechanical to whatever is base and contemptible . . ."
in their several ranks of master craftsmen, journeymen, and ap-
prentices. Still lower stand "those who have neither craft nor trade
and earn their living by the strength of their arms, the people we
everywhere call hands, or hired men, such as porters, builder's
labourers, carters and other workers hired by the day, who are all
the basest of this same people" of town and country. Finally, at the
very bottom of the social scale, the order of "sturdy beggars,"
"vagabonds and tramps" who live "in idleness and without care, at
the expense of others."

Each order has "its special mark, sign or outward ornament,"
that is, its social symbol. The members of the ecclesiastical order
wear the long robe, the tonsure and various other distinguishing
marks, such as the miters, croziers, gloves, and rings of the bishops,
and the cardinals' hats and scarlet robes. "Among the nobles, the
mere gentlemen have their coats of arms surmounted by helmets,
the knights have their spurs and gilded armour . . . the princes
have their princely cloaks . . . Among the commoners, the doctors,
licentiates and bachelors have their different kinds of hood,
corresponding to the different faculties, besides the long robe
which they share with the churchmen; the advocates have their
distinctive hats, while the attorneys have only the long robe which
marks them off from the mere legal practitioners who have no
status in court."

The orders possess "two other prerogatives of honour, namely,
title and rank." Titles are those of chevalier for the great nobles,
the high officers of the Crown, the members of the State Council,
the presidents and king's men of the Parlement de Paris, the first
presidents of the other sovereign courts; of *noble homme* for the
officers of justice and advocates who are not nobles, with that of
demoiselle for their wives; of "King's councillor" for a number of
officials, members of the parlement, *baillis* and *sénéchaux* with
their lieutenants, and treasurers-general of France.

There are "honorific epithets": "illustrious and excellent" for
princes, "high and mighty lord" for knights and great lords, "most

illustrious" for cardinals, "most reverend" for bishops, "reverend father in God" for abbots, "venerable and discreet person" for other minor ecclesiastics, "noble man" (*noble homme*) for officials, "honorable man" or "worthy person" (*honnête personne*) for "bourgeois."

There are "forms of address": "Sire" for kings, "Monseigneur" for princes, "Messire" for knights, "Monsieur" for ordinary nobles; "Maistre" for men of letters, "Sire so-and-so" for merchants or craftsmen; "Madame" for wives of knights, "Mademoiselle" for noblemen's wives, Dame so and so (or, by usurpation, Madame) for burgesses' wives.

Each order has its "rank, that is to say, its precedence in sitting and walking"; for example, the ecclesiastical order is the first, that of the nobility second, and the Third Estate is last—though there is no "ordinance" to this effect, and the precedence is observed through "voluntary respect." Thus, the humblest of priests should precede the greatest of gentlefolk. "But because the ecclesiastical order is regarded as being outside secular affairs, our Redeemer Himself having said that his kingdom is not of this world . . . it is commonly seen nowadays that those who possess some secular rank do not choose to give way to priests unless the latter hold some high rank in the church." "The least of the gentlefolk must go before the richest and most honourable member of the Third Estate." A difficulty arises, however, when a member of the Third Estate is a royal official. In such a case, the princes "do not yield precedence to any official, whoever he may be"; knights (chevaliers) and other members of the higher nobility give way only to those officials who are knights themselves, ex officio ("since the latter belong to the same order as they do and in addition have their offices"), such as the chancellor of France, the councillors of the State Council, the heads of the sovereign courts; ordinary nobles, gentlemen, squires, give way to royal officials who are magistrates, that is, to the principal officers of government and justice, "in the area of their jurisdiction," even if these officers are commoners.

The orders as such have no authority, no public administrative organization. Some of them, though, "have corporations and colleges, which sometimes possess the right to make regulations

and elect higher officers who have power over the whole body," or
else they include a number of corporations and colleges of this
kind, like the crafts. The orders have their specific privileges. The gentry alone hold
the right to bear coats of arms surmounted by a helmet or other
"head-armor." A certain number of offices are in principle reserved
for the gentry: the headships of the offices of the royal household,
many military offices, positions as gentlemen of the bedchamber,
gentlemen of the bodyguard, waiting-gentlemen, equerries of the
stable, gentlemen of the stag-hunt and of the falcon-house; "all
the principal military appointments, whether in command of
fortresses or of companies, and in particular all cavalry commands;
and even for the command of ordnance and infantry companies
gentlemen are given preference."

As for ecclesiastical appointments, "*plusieurs*" cathedrals and
"*plusieurs*" abbeys have their positions of rank, canonries and
monks' seats reserved for gentlemen. *Plusieurs*, in those days,
meant not "several" but "many." In general, the gentry are
favored in the church by being given dispensations that privilege
them as regards age limits, pluralism, or the amount of time to be
devoted to study.

As regards lordships, fiefs are reserved for gentlefolk, Commoners may acquire them, but only if given a dispensation to do so
and then on payment to the king of the due of frank-fee. Only
gentlemen may hold great lordships—dukedoms, marquisates,
countships—and also medium ones—viscountships, baronies, appointments as *vidame* or castellan. Commoners are allowed to
acquire only ordinary lordships, with rights of high, middle, and
low justice.

Gentlemen, to the exclusion of nobles of the long robe, alone
have the right to wear the sword, "this being the sign and ornament of nobility, and in France they wear it even in the King's
chamber." All members of the higher nobility have the right to be
saluted by commoners. Since they risk their lives for the defense
of the state, paying with their blood, gentlemen are "exempt from
paying the tailles or other personal taxes levied for war purposes . . .
and from having men-at-arms billeted on them." "Gentlemen
furthermore possess the privilege of hunting . . . so that in peace-

time they may be able to exercise themselves in a way that re-
sembles the practice of war."

For an ordinary crime gentlemen are not punished so severely as
commoners and are never condemned to shameful punishments
such as whipping or hanging. While they are punished more
leniently so far as corporal penalties are concerned, they are
punished more severely when it is a matter of fines. Also they
suffer harsher punishment for crimes which are repugnant to their
quality as nobles, and which are therefore aggravated by the rank
of the offender, such as treason, theft, perjury, fraud.

Gentlemen enjoy the privilege of seeking satisfaction for an
insult by fighting a duel. Dueling is reserved to the members of
their order, and they are not obliged to fight duels with commoners.

Those members of the Third Estate who are engaged in the
production of material goods enjoy as a community an enormous
privilege, namely, that gentlemen, with the exception of glass-
makers and a few others, are not allowed to take part in gainful
activity in trade or crafts, and so cannot compete with these
members of the Third Estate, who thus possess the exclusive right
to make money at the expense of the clergy, the nobility, and the
officials.

Membership of an order is acquired. The ecclesiastical order is
entered by way of the tonsure, which is the public acknowledgment that a man is dedicating himself to God. The noble order
is entered by birth or by letters patent from the king, "distributor
ordained by God of the tangible honours of this world," or by
appointment to and acceptance and installation in offices, royal or
municipal, which confer nobility on the holder. Thus, knighthood
is conferred on members of the higher nobility, the great officers
of the Crown, the heads of the offices of the royal household, the
heads of the sovereign courts, the king's governors and lieutenants
in the provinces. Since they belong to the higher nobility, their
children are automatically gentlefolk. Secretaries to the king, the
Household and Crown of France have the status of nobles of four
generations and their nobility passes to their children, provided
they bequeath their offices to sons or sons-in-law. The councillors
of the sovereign courts are personally noble, and if grandfather,

father, and son have held office without a break, then their
descendants are ipso facto noble. By royal privilege, the municipal
offices of certain towns confer nobility on their holders. Finally,
anyone can claim nobility by virtue of a decision of the *Cour des
Aides* (administering indirect taxation) if he can prove that he,
his father, and his grandfather have lived "in noble style," pref-
erably on a lordship or fief, exercising the profession of arms, and
without committing any base action that would forfeit their rank.
Later these conditions were made stricter. The royal declaration
of June 22, 1664, made it necessary to prove by incontestable
evidence that one's family had been noble before 1560.[3]

Membership in the different sections of the Third Estate is
acquired by the grant of university degrees, by appointment to,
and acceptance and installation in, various offices which do not
confer nobility, by registration as an advocate or as an attorney in
the various courts of justice, or by acceptance into the craft guilds.

Membership in an order can be lost. One ceases to be a member
of the priestly order if one is unfrocked for infamous conduct.
Membership of the nobility of office is forfeited as a result of
ignominy entailing removal from office. Nobility of blood is lost
if one is guilty of *lèse-majesté* or treason, when a gentleman is
declared infamous and deprived of his nobility by the sentence
passed upon him. Other crimes, and the practice of base or
mechanical arts for gain, do not, however, annul the noble quality
of the gentlemen concerned, but merely suspend it temporarily,
since nobility of blood is "as though part of a man's nature." "The
employments incompatible with nobility are those of attorney
acting for another, registrar, notary, bailiff, clerk, merchant and
craftsman of any craft . . . . This is understandable, since all
these employments are carried on for profit; for it is profit, base
and sordid, that takes away nobility, the characteristic of which is
to live on one's rents, or at least not to sell one's labour-power.
And yet judges, advocates, doctors and professors of the humani-
ties do not forfeit any nobility they possess, although they earn
their living by means of their occupation; this is because, besides
the fact that their occupation involves mental rather than manual

3. L.-N.-H. Cherin, *Abrégé chronologique sur la noblesse* (1788), pp.
139–140.

work, it is honorary rather than mercenary . . . . Agricultural work is not incompatible with nobility . . . since nothing that a gentleman does for himself, and without receiving money from others for it, is incompatible . . . Nobles are not forbidden to take up share-cropping leases (*métairies*) in perpetuity, for lõng periods or for life, since in such leases the *dominium utile* of the land is transferred to the tenant . . . so that the gentleman is then said to be cultivating his own land and not that of another."

That is the picture that Loyseau draws of the stratification of French society into orders. This lawyer describes to us, above all, whatever had been given legal significance, whether by custom, edict, ordinance, or decision of the council or the parlements. Though his book is scattered with observations taken from reality, things this penetrating observer noted in everyday life, the magistrate Loyseau does not furnish us with a complete sociological description. This was not his aim. Besides, in general, the idea that contemporaries have of the society in which they live, and to which they give expression, is incomplete and sometimes mistaken. There are facts, even important ones, of which contemporaries are unaware, others that they prefer not to admit or confess to, and others again that are so basic that they seem commonplace to such a degree that contemporaries do not take the trouble to describe them, and they come to our notice only through a few words dropped in passing in some document. The historian's task is to bring out these forms of social behavior by analyzing a substantial number of accounts, offered in the form of memoirs, letters, and chronicles, and a substantial number of legal transactions, revealed by notaries' records and the proceedings of courts.

We must therefore add to Loyseau's description the endogamous tendencies that existed at every level of the two lay orders, offset by the cases of hypergamy on the part of women; the general tendency to heredity in a given order or estate, and the caste tendencies which showed themselves among the gentry; the restrictions on social mobility resulting from the manners and customs of society, since it often required several generations of "living as gentlefolk" for the families of ennobled persons to be accepted by gentlefolk as belonging to their social group. What is essential is the principle that a family cannot acquire a place in the higher levels of this hierarchy by virtue of money obtained in activities aimed at the production of material wealth (whether agriculture, industry, or trade) if these are carried on for the purpose of selling the product. The order to which one belongs is, in principle, what decides the quantity of the riches of this world that one receives, and for the clergy and the nobility, together with the higher strata of the Third Estate, this income is received in the form of feudal dues, land rents, state bonds, pensions, emoluments, salaries, honoraria (including magistrates' fees), proportional allowances or taxations (especially in the case of finance officials). The income obtained even from productive activities was sometimes regulated by custom rather than by the state of the market. There were, as a matter of fact, gentlemen, graduates and magistrates who were poor but who were, nevertheless, as a rule, held in higher respect than the richest of merchants.

From the legal standpoint, the noble order was the second of the three orders. Socially it was the first and the one which everybody strove to enter. Officials, "bourgeois," merchants, all called themselves "Sieur," and took the title of "esquire" (écuyer), the first title that a gentleman could assume. Their wives awarded themselves the name of demoiselle. The husbands also put helmets on their coats of arms, though this was forbidden by the ordinances of Orléans and Blois; they wore swords and dressed like gentlemen. By exercising the profession of arms, by living "nobly" on lordships and fiefs, above all by filling those offices which conferred nobility on their holders, members of the higher strata of the Third Estate succeeded in obtaining legal recognition as nobles, with all the privileges of gentility. But, socially, these nobles were not regarded as gentlefolk. The nobility of the sword refused to acknowledge them as nobles at all, even denying them the quality of "nobles by virtue of office, function or robe." For the gentlemen of the sword, these officials were mere bourgeois.[4] The son of an ennobled person, who was himself accepted in 1649 by the gentry of Angoumois as having the "quality" of gentility, Jean-Louis Guez de Balzac, wrote to Chapelain on December 20, 1636: "I hold our

4. R. Mousnier, La Vénalité des offices sous Henri IV et Louis XIII (Rouen, Maugard, 1945), pp. 501–506.

friend in very high esteem and would greatly like to link my family with his. But . . . the young lady's head is full of her noble rank . . . . From that comes . . . this disdain of every sort of *bourgeoisie*, even though it be arrayed in crimson and seated on the Fleurs de Lys. Her mother seems to have less exalted notions, more favourable to the long robe . . . [but] she is approached every day by many persons of standing, and in the state of mind in which I left her yesterday a councillor of the Great Council would not be good enough for her daughter."[5] *Bourgeoisie!* That was what the "nobility of the robe" amounted to, in the eyes of a gentleman. The Abbé François-Timoléon de Choisy, member of the French Academy, goes even further: "My mother, who came of the family of Hurault de l'Hospital, often said to me: 'Listen, my son, do not be vainglorious, remember that *you are only a bourgeois*. I know very well that your fathers and grandfathers were Masters of Requests and Councillors of State; but take it from me that in France the only nobility that counts is that of the sword. This nation, wholly warlike, has identified glory with arms."[6] This military essence of nobility was further stressed by the Archbishop of Embrun, *messire* Georges d'Aubusson de La Feuillade, presiding over the assembly of the clergy in the midst of the Fronde, when he replied on March 15, 1651, to the deputies of the assembly of the nobility: "And so it is this nobility, not of blood but of your heroic spirits, which is not buried in the tombs of your ancestors but lives again in the sequence of your generous actions, that has inspired you with the idea of *assembling to safeguard your privileges*. It is this ancient glory . . . *that has been unable to tolerate any longer* that all the affairs of a State *which is military by its very foundation* and of which you form the most brilliant and most powerful section *should be decided without your votes*."[7]

The gentry thrust the nobles of the robe, so far as they were concerned, out of the nobility, and in consequence French society

---

5. *Lettres familières de Balzac à M. Chapelain* (Amsterdam, Elzevier, 1661), Letter XXX, pp. 55–56.
6. Choisy, *Mémoires*, edited by Michaud and Poujoulat, p. 554.
7. *Journal de l'Assemblée de la noblesse* (no place or date, Bibliothèque Nationale), L.b 37–1858, 79.

was dominated by the conflict between these orders. It was notable that at the States-General of 1614–1615 the majority of the nobles of the robe sat with the Third Estate. The conflict between the orders, between the officials and the gentry, was what enabled the king to emerge as the arbiter, what caused the failure of the States-General and the triumph of royal absolutism.[8]

The nobility complained that the members of the higher strata of the Third Estate left their allotted sphere and competed with nobles for the social functions of command and defense. They complained that, using money acquired in trade or government finance, members of the Third Estate obtained fiefs and lordships from debt-ridden nobles and monopolized offices in the king's service, which, from the time of Francis I had been officially sold, or granted in return for loans "not to be repaid," and which reversions—and especially, since 1604, the annual due or *paulette*, an insurance premium—were said to have rendered hereditary. The gentry demanded abolition of the *paulette* and of salability of offices generally. They demanded that certain specific offices be absolutely reserved for gentlefolk, together with at least one-third of the rest. Thus they were endeavoring quite plainly to keep up their preeminence in society by securing access to positions of rank—for office is "rank with a public function attached"—and also access to the emoluments, salaries, fees, and taxations that were associated with offices. They went even further, and the members of the Third Estate expressed indignation at the fact that the nobles were asking permission to engage in large-scale trade without forfeiting their nobility, in order to make money by profit.

But, with conditions like these, is it not profit that gives access to fiefs, lordships, and offices, and determines one's position in the social hierarchy? Do we not see here *classes* in process of formation, struggling against the old orders? Is not the struggle of the officials against the gentry the struggle of a rising class society against a declining society of orders, and even, fundamentally, a class struggle? Apparently not. It seems to be still a matter of

8. R. Mousnier, *La Vénalité* . . . (*op. cit.*), Book III, Ch. 4, pp. 569–587. *Idem, L'Assassinat d'Henri IV: le problème du tyrannicide et l'affermissement de de la monarchie absolue* (Paris, Gallimard, 1964), Ch. 3, "Les états-généraux de 1614–1615."

orders and conflicts between orders. Here are some reasons why
this is so. First, it appears quite clear that it is the dignity, the
social esteem, if you like, attached to one's quality or occupation
that determines where one stands in the social hierarchy, much
more than one's wealth or income, right down to the "worthy
persons," inclusive, that is, down to the merchants and higher
levels of the crafts embraced in this category. Below that level,
among the *laboureurs* and the masters of the middle-ranking
crafts, and a fortiori, among the masters of the less-productive
crafts, the shoemakers, sword-furbishers, and makers of pewter, or
among the unskilled workers, it seems normal for the degree of
wealth or poverty, the amount of one's profits or one's wages, to
decide one's social rank. More searching investigations than have
been made so far, however, will be needed before we can be sure
that even at this level the degree of "dignity" or "baseness" attached to an occupation did not play a big part.

Then again, whatever the gentry might allege, money alone did
not enable a man to acquire offices in the judiciary, nor money
regardless of its origin. A grain merchant who had become rich
would not have been able to purchase an office as councillor in the
parlement, the sovereign court of justice, either for himself or, as
a rule, for his son. Even if he got round the chancellor, he would
not have been accepted by the sovereign court. The baseness of
his origins would not have allowed it. Generally speaking, one had
to rise by degrees, from trade to finance, from finance to a minor
judicial office or an office as one of the king's secretaries. After
that, one might hope to make one's way into the magistracy, into
the offices of *lieutenant-général de bailliage* or into the offices of
the sovereign courts, the parlements, Chambres des Comptes,
Cours des Aides, the Great Council, then to those of master of
requests and the State Council. In most instances, two, three, or
four generations were needed—generally four—to complete the
ascent. It was the quality ascribed by a consensus of opinion to the
way of life of each social stratum that made it possible for a man
to rise from stratum to stratum, by means of resources obtained
through the activities appropriate to each of these strata in turn.
From the moment when a man gave up "trade," these resources
had to come to him in the form of rents, salaries, fees, and not in
the form of profits. The gentry were not kept out of offices in the

judiciary by their lack of profits, since these were not absolutely
necessary, and they were kept out, less by the inadequacy of their
rents than by the extravagant way of life characteristic of them,
and by their contempt for education.
The same can be said of lordships and fiefs. A grain merchant
could certainly compel a gentleman who owed him money to sell
him a fief in order to pay off his debt (though it was more often
to officials, persons higher up in the hierarchy of orders, that
gentlemen applied when they wanted loans). But the merchant
had to pay the king the due of frank-fee. Ownership of the fief
did not ennoble him: he was merely tolerated there. He still had
to pay the taille. And it was only if he adopted the "noble" way
of life on his fief that, after many years, he, or rather his son, or
more probably still his grandson, would succeed in persuading the
king's tax collectors to remove his name from the list of those
subject to the taille on the grounds that, over a long period, the
head of the family had been living like a noble, wearing a sword
and not "engaging in trade."

Finally, it is very striking to observe that what the nobles of the
robe wanted was not so much to adopt the way of life of a gentleman, to assume the ruinous profession of arms and undertake
boundless liberalities. Some did this, and came to experience the
financial difficulties of the gentry, often, as a result, setting their
families on the downward path. In general, though, it was rare for
anyone to enter, by deliberate choice, into the nobility of the
sword by way of the profession of arms and access to the higher
ranks of the army and governorships of fortresses or districts. What
was more frequent among those who reached the office of master
of requests and the commission of state councillor was to settle
their eldest sons in positions in the State Council, with, for
certain families like the Phélypeaux, access to the highest places,
as secretary of state, comptroller-general of finance, or minister.
What was usual was to consolidate eldest sons in the offices of the
parlements, those supreme courts of justice which have "something
sacred and venerable about them,"[9] or in those of the other
supreme courts—like the Nicolai family in the Chambre des

9. État de la France de 1642, ed. E. Griselle, Formulaire de Lettres et État
de la France (Paris, 1919), p. 245.

Comptes. The sovereign courts also offered, besides the advantages of public esteem and of leisure in the exercise of calmer, more regular, and more routine functions, opportunities to save money and to carry out profitable operations—royal commissions, loans, farming of taxes and demesne dues, and sometimes speculations in land—that were not to be encountered in the king's army. Accordingly, most of the ambitious lawyers preferred to get into civil offices, the king's council and the sovereign courts, the higher magistracy. The members of all these bodies comprised the same social stratum, the same "estate," sharing a nobility of function which was legally similar to that of the gentry but was socially distinct from it. Connections by marriage were formed between gentry and officialdom, especially through hypergamy by the womenfolk of the latter. What matters, however, in this patrilineal society is the fate of the men, and in particular that of the eldest sons. One must not be misled by the examples that can be found of younger sons of officials who chose the profession of arms, or of junior branches of official families in which, from father to son, the men served that profession. So long as one had not risen above the rank of *mestre de camp,* or colonel, and until one had acquired important governorships, it was hard to enter the gentry if one was not a gentleman by blood. A family in which the eldest sons and the senior branch continued to be officials was a family of officials. As in everything, of course, there might be exceptions.[10]

As a rule, the officials remained in their order. But there was a steady and stubborn struggle, revealed by the attitude and declarations of the Third Estate in the States-General of 1614–1615, by the policy of the Parlement de Paris, by the role that it and the other parlements played during the Fronde, not to transform the society of orders into a class society but to change the hierarchy of orders, so that the order of magistrates, "the gentlemen of pen and ink," might be recognized as the first order—to alter the principle of society and cause to be acknowledged as the most worthy, not the service of arms but the civil service of the state. The magistracy was to become the real nobility. Loyseau gives very simple expression to this tendency on the part of the officials. He arranges so-

10. R. Mousnier, *Lettres et Mémoires adressés au chancelier Séguier (1633–1649)* (Paris, P.U.F., 1964), I, pp. 169–170.

ciety in accordance with fitness to exercise public authority. Accordingly, he divides society into two parts, those who command and those who obey. Those who command are the king and his officials. Those who obey, "the people," are all the rest: ecclesiastics, nobles, and Third Estate: "The sovereign has close to his person his officials of general competence, who convey his orders to the magistrates of the provinces, who in turn convey them to those of the towns,[11] and these magistrates cause them to be carried out by the people. So much for those who command, and as for the people who obey, they, being a body with many heads, are divided into orders, estates and particular occupations . . . These are our three orders, or States-General of France, namely, the clergy, the nobility and the Third Estate." And Loyseau stresses that, leaving aside the princes who are related to the king, what is involved here is not merely a political and administrative authority enjoyed by the magistrates in the exercise of their functions, but a claim on their behalf to social ascendancy, to preeminence in rank, to "precedence in sitting and walking," even outside the realm of their functions.

Loyseau attacks the intellectual foundations of the primacy of the nobles, the notion of superiority of family and purity of blood, an obstacle that the claims of the officials could not overcome. He makes use, in favor of the officials, of the old myth that explains French society by a conquest—for him this is not a myth, moreover, but history itself. The origin of the social stratification of France was the Frankish conquest. The victorious Franks were the nobles; the conquered Gauls were the commoners. The Frankish conquerors reserved to themselves the use of arms, public authority, possession of fiefs and exemption from all taxes. But Loyseau does not draw the usual conclusion, namely, that this social stratification is just and reasonable because it is derived from the right of conquest, a sacred right. The conclusion he draws is quite different: it is that nobility is born of "public and general law," that it belongs to "common law," that it originates not "from natural law, like freedom, but from the ancient law and disposition

11. He means the king's officials residing in the towns, the *lieutenants-généraux de bailliages* and their *lieutenants particuliers*, for example, in contrast to the provincial governors, and *not* the municipal magistrates.

of the state." One can see what this reflexion suggests: something that is a natural right is unchangeable, but something that is a right established by the state may be changed. Accordingly, if a law of the state made the warrior a noble, another such law can make the magistrate a noble, and this not only alongside the warrior but even above him. In a society which is still a society of orders, with the same forms of nobility, the magistrate may become the noble par excellence, in place of the warrior.

The gentry fought against this tendency on the part of the officials. They called these nobles by office and function "bourgeois." What makes difficulties for us today is that things were a little more complicated than Loyseau says, because the words *bourgeois* and *bourgeoisie* had more than one meaning for his contemporaries. Often they stood for "the totality of the people living in a town," the townspeople as against the countrypeople. Often also they stood for all the people belonging to the Third Estate, in contrast to the gentry and the churchmen. Or, again, a bourgeois could be anyone who employed workmen.[12] The epithet bourgeois is frequently a mere legal title used to indicate someone whose domicile is in a town, who contributes to the town's financial expenditure, belongs to its militia, and has been acknowledged as a "bourgeois" by the town corporation. In this sense, a humble shoemaker—or a gentleman—may be a bourgeois of a given place. Some gentry and even some members of the higher nobility were proud of their title of "bourgeois de Bordeaux." In a number of towns it was necessary to fulfill certain conditions relating to wealth, income, and residence. The chief masters of craft guilds and the merchants might even be considered a town's only bourgeois. There is, however, one meaning which is frequent among the authors of histories of towns written in the sixteenth and seventeenth centuries, and which is very striking: a "bourgeois" is a commoner who resides in a town and there lives "nobly" on his *rentes*, without engaging in the business of any craft or form of trade, and who, moreover, has the right to the title of bourgeois of his town, which means that he shares in its honors and privileges, votes in its assemblies, and may have the opportunity of be-

12. Furetière, *Dictionnaire*.

coming a municipal magistrate. These bourgeois are not at all a
social group consisting of capitalist entrepreneurs engaged in
producing material goods. In any case, it is certain that the terms
bourgeois ˙and bourgeoisie, terms of contempt when spoken or
written by gentlemen, do not take us outside of the framework of
a society of orders. But this variety of meanings, mostly so different
from the meaning that came to prevail in the nineteenth century,
invites us, when we come upon these terms in a document, to
examine the context closely in order to try to make out exactly
what social group is meant in the given instance. This precaution
is even more necessary when we are studying popular revolts.

Can one call this society "feudal"? To do so undoubtedly brings
with it the risk of much confusion. True, in the legal sense, the
feudal system was still in being, and would go on existing down to
the Revolution. True, probably nine-tenths of the landed property
in the kingdom consisted of fiefs and censives, and important
social relationships followed from this form of property. It is even
possible that its social and economic role became more important
during the great economic recession of the seventeenth century.
But we are no longer, by any means, dealing with the sort of
society which was in process of development between about 850
and about 1250, in the area between the Loire and the Meuse, the
society properly called feudal. In French society of the seventeenth
century, while the social relations resulting from fiefs and censives
were still important, they were no longer the dominant relations.
Social relations were now dominated by the hierarchy of ranks and
by fealties (fidélités). The latter had no legal sanction, which is
why official documents do not mention them and why one can
easily underestimate their importance. Within the order of the
nobility, and also as between the Third Estate and the nobility,
men offer themselves to a "protector," a patron, and become his
"fidèles," his "créatures." They give themselves to him, swearing
full allegiance and absolute devotion, dedicate their services to
him, fight for him, in duels, brawls, and pitched battles, speak,
write, and intrigue for him, follow him in his misfortunes, even
afar, abroad, go to prison for his sake, and kill on his behalf. In
exchange for all this, the master, the "protector," clothes and feeds
them, trusts them and takes them into his confidence, promotes

their worldly advancement, arranges marriages for them, secures appointments for them, protects them, gets them out of prison and, if he is a prince, makes stipulations in their interest in the treaties with the king that conclude revolts. The king himself is able to make himself obeyed only through the agency of such *fidèles* who are "his men" and who in turn have their own *fidèles*, their own *créatures*. Louis XIII had Richelieu and Richelieu had Séguier, Bouthillier, Sublet de Noyers, who in turn had their own *fidèles*. The *fidèle* does not commit himself by an act of faith and homage and does not expect in return to be given a fief to support him, so that this is not feudalism. It is certainly true that these "fealties" were derived, in the France of this period, from feudalism and from the period of vassalage which preceded feudalism. But we must not confuse the nature of an institution with its origins. Fealties are not necessarily bound up with feudalism. They have existed in societies which did not know and had never known a feudal regime. They are something different and are features of another type of society, or at least another species of the great genus of societies of orders.[13]

The French peasants, some of whose revolts we propose to examine, were caught in the hierarchy of ranks which made up the social stratification of France, and we have glimpsed in passing the place that the peasant strata occupied in this total hierarchy. An individual is always, however, a member of more than one social group, and in order to understand the revolts we must define the position occupied by the peasants in two territorial communities, the village and the lordship. Let us first recall some general features of these communities. The village, with the land attached to it, forms part of a lordship, or is perhaps divided among several lordships. The village also forms part of a church parish. A number of orders or sections of orders are usually represented in a village. There will be one or more lords, who may be gentlemen, officials, advocates, town merchants, courtiers. Many

---

13. See the documents in R. Mousnier, *La Vénalité* . . . (*op. cit.*), pp. 497–501. See also O. Ranum, *Richelieu and the Councillors of Louis XIII* (Oxford, Clarendon Press, 1963), and J. R. Major, "The crown and the aristocracy in Renaissance France," *American Historical Review*, LXIX, 3 (April, 1964), pp. 631–645.

of the gentlemen are countrymen, resident squires. The village often has a priest, if it is the center of the parish. The village may possess a notary or a scrivener, and one or more "practitioners" (legal consultants) to deal with any matters of law that arise. There are usually a barber-surgeon, some craftsmen—a blacksmith, a carpenter, a wheelwright, a mason, a tailor—all of whom spend half their time working the land, and one or more tavern keepers. The bulk of the population consists of agriculturists. Among these we must briefly distinguish a number of social strata differentiated mainly on economic lines. There are the *laboureurs*, that is, the cultivators who own plow teams; these may be found in fertile plain areas near large towns or rivers and seas which provide facilities for transport and export by farmers of large-scale farms; they are by way of being capitalist entrepreneurs cultivating very large farms of 100 to 150 hectares and employing several hands, or else sharecroppers with smaller holdings, of 30 to 60 hectares, more in the nature of family farms. Below these come the *haricotiers* (to use for the whole group the name given them in the Beauvaisis) or *bordiers*, who possess small holdings which provide subsistence for themselves and their families in good years but who often need to find other work as well in order to live. Below these again are the *brassiers* or *manouvriers*, who usually own a house and a small bit of land but who can live only by hiring themselves out to the *laboureurs* and the lords. The village craftsmen are on their level socially, or not much above them. Some peasants who call themselves merchants are in a higher category; their work as peasants is combined with trade in grain, wine, or cattle. The *blatiers*, who own one, two, or three horses, buy grain from the peasants in the local market in order to take it to a regional market. Other peasants, *haricotiers* or *laboureurs*, can own fiefs, for some of the latter are extremely small, only two hectares of land, for instance. The *laboureurs* farm from the lords the task of collecting "feudal" and seignorial dues from their lordships—competing for this work with notaries and advocates. Status, however, among the commoners of the countryside, is associated with the cultivation of land; this is the activity that "places" a man. The aggregate of inhabitants of a village constitute a community, which possesses communal property and traditional rights (to use the forest land of the lordship, for example), and which runs its own affairs through an assembly of heads of families—the husbands or their widows—meeting under the chairmanship of the lord's judge or, where the king is the immediate lord, under that of a royal judge. The village assembly elects its syndic, its communal shepherd, its watchmen for protecting the crops and other officers, decides on the rotation of crops and on when the fields will be made available for common pasture, and settles all matters of common interest. In these assemblies the richest of the *laboureurs*, the "cocks of the parish," wield preponderant influence, after that of the lord himself, because they are the ones who can offer work, and their plow teams are needed by the other peasants if the latter are to cultivate their land.

Lordship is a form of landed property which includes social status together with public authority. In principle, only gentlemen may own lordships. Actually, since the time of Louis XI, commoners, officials, advocates, merchants, and even peasants have been allowed to own them and to exercise all the rights of lords, on condition that they pay the king the due of frank-fee, amounting to one year's income out of every twenty. The lordship is usually itself a fief, forming part of the feudal hierarchy and owned on conditions of faith and homage, of *aveu et dénombrement*, and of noble service, in relation to the owner of a superior fief. But it may, though less frequently, be an alodium, the owner of which is subject to the king, to his authority as head of state and to the laws of the realm, but is not the vassal of any superior fief-holder standing between him and the king.

A lordship embraces, in principle, three main elements: the lord's demesne, one or more fiefs, and the lord's rights to administer justice. Nevertheless, the law long since agreed to the dismemberment of lordships, and it was sometimes the case, in a number of regions, that one person owned the demesne and the fiefs while another owned the right to administer justice. The demesne is the château or manor house of the lordship, with the lands, woods, meadows, and ponds that the lord keeps for himself. He either gives the land out to be cultivated by farmers or sharecroppers, or else cultivates it himself, through the agency of a steward and farm-servants, helped by hired agricultural workers.

The noble fiefs belonging to the lordship are property which is granted to others on condition of faith and homage, *aveu et dénombrement*, and held by them in return for allegiance and services. The act of faith and homage includes, indeed, an oath of allegiance which makes of the vassal who swears it the "man" of the suzerain to whom it is sworn. The vassal henceforth owes respect, obedience, and noble services, rendered by arms or by counsel, to his lord. He owes him *aveu et dénombrement*, that is, an exact description of the fief. If he sells his fief, the purchaser must pay the suzerain a *quint*, one-fifth of the price and a *requint*, one-fifth of this fifth. Should the holder of the fief change through collateral succession, the incoming vassal must pay the suzerain one year's revenue from the fief, the due of relief or *rachat*.

But the lordship also includes a large number of commoners' fiefs, land that can be granted not on condition of faith and homage and noble services but on condition of allegiance, cultivation of the soil, service and payment of *droits recognitifs* and *droits utiles*. In accordance with a distinction which was clearly formulated in the second half of the fifteenth century, the estate or lordship was divided into two parts. The lord retained the *dominium directum* over the tenure, while the purchaser, who was usually a peasant but might also be a notary, an advocate, an attorney, or a merchant who himself then leased the land to a peasant, acquired the *dominium utile*. By force of his *dominium directum* the lord was entitled to, first, an acknowledgment from the tenant, a declaration by deed to his lord, that he possessed such and such a piece of land belonging to the lord's *dominium directum*, subject to such and such dues which he undertook to pay. The lord was further entitled to a *cens*, an annual payment which implied and denoted the *dominium directum*, a recognition of their obedience and subjection on the part of the *censitaires*, and of the superiority of the lord, a symbolic payment of a few sols or deniers. The *cens* implied the *lods et ventes* corresponding in the *censive* to the *quint* and *requint* in the fief; the owner of the *dominium directum* was entitled to seignorial rents, *champart*, *terrage*, or *agrière*, a share of the fruits of the soil which varied a great deal from one region to another; sometimes to land rent, in kind or in money; generally to demesne rights which were not seignorial in nature and were not derived from the *cens*—tallage, *corvées* (that is, days to be spent in work and cartage, the number of these being fixed by custom), and obligation to use only the lord's oven, mill, and winepress. Finally, the lord was in general entitled to respect, obedience, and service, for the *censitaires* were his subjects, his "men." In return for all this, the *censitaire* enjoyed the entire *dominium utile*, that is, he could cultivate the land, enjoy its produce, sell this, sell the land itself, mortgage it, bequeath it to his children or to others, and use it in practice as though it were his own. The *censitaire* was, moreover, except in very rare and narrowly localized cases, not a serf but a freeman who was a legal person, could marry, own property, act as head of a family, initiate a lawsuit if he wished, and who was allowed, if he found the conditions of the *dominium directum* too severe, to move out (*déguerpir*), that is, to give up his tenure and go away, provided he paid any arrears outstanding to the lord.

Finally, as a rule, and in fact very often, the lordship also included the right of high, middle, or low justice. In principle, the right to administer justice was a concession from the king. The sovereign reserved to himself the right to deal with a certain number of crimes, called *cas royaux* or *cas prévotaux*. The king's judges could "forestall" the lords' judges, that is, could deal with cases which were within the competence of the latter, if they had failed to undertake investigations within twenty-four hours. Naturally, those who came under the lords' judges could appeal to the king's judges; but within the limits of his competence and subject to this right of appeal, the lord exercised instead of the state, and on the state's behalf, the public power of justice, together with the powers of authority and maintenance of order which resulted from it. All this part of public power was regarded as belonging to the lord's patrimony, salable and inheritable, a real hereditary property held on condition of faith and homage to the king, mediately and immediately. The lord dispensed justice through his judges and his procurator-fiscal, who acted for him. Subordinate officers carried out arrests: process servers and bailiffs who conveyed and enforced the decisions and orders of the court, jailers who took charge of prisoners. In principle, only the lord who possessed the right of high justice, but in practice many another lord too, published the edicts and proclamations of the king, passed on administrative regulations and executed them, made bylaws governing markets, prices, weights and measures, highways, procedure for accepting new masters of crafts, practice of crafts and cultivation of the land. In practice, too, many lords exercised justice over agrarian matters, in order to safeguard their seignorial rights and their *cens*.

Regarding relations between the lord and his men, between the lord and the land—that is, the role he played in the exploitation of the soil—differences were many and marked between one region and another. The social relations resulting from the seignorial form of property were very different in the Paris region, in Burgundy, in Brittany, and so on. Around Paris, in a region of large-scale trade and capitalist enterprises, the lord's justice operated much like that of the justices of the peace of the Third Republic, and in practice, in everyday life, *censitaire* property was little different from the absolute private property of post-Revolutionary times. In this region and in similar ones, fiefs and *censives* brought comparatively little income to the owner of the *dominium directum*. They were an unprofitable form of ownership. Probably they served above all as a social symbol, and were mainly matters of dignity and prestige, in consequence of sentimental survivals.[14] Things were not like this in Burgundy, a province which had retained its provincial estates, as an organ of the lords confronting the king, a province broken up into small districts, harder to get about, with less exchange between one place and another; a province which, moreover, was ravaged in the seventeenth century by wars and epidemics. Here the lords exercised very extensive powers. Furthermore, they gave protection to their men. Here the lordship really was a community, an association. The lord's authority might be oppressive, interfering, or burdensome, but on the other hand it meant organization, arbitration, and protection. The lord was even a rampart against the state and against the soldiery, who behaved in a friendly country just as in a conquered one. The lord intervened frequently in the drawing up of the list of persons due to pay the taille, the principal royal tax, so as to protect the

14. R. Mousnier, "L'Évolution des Institutions monarchiques en France et ses relations avec l'état social," *XVII siècle*, 58–59 (1963), pp. 68–71.

interests of his vassals, his sharecroppers and farmers. If pressure by the tax collectors became excessive, the lord opened his château or his fortified house to the villagers and their cattle, and received with harquebus fire the bailiffs who came to distrain their property. Against enemy attack and against the passage of soldiers, with their propensity to pillage and acts of cruelty, the lords and their men defended their *censitaires*, sometimes arming them and forming them into troops. The system was a hard one, but it seemed to involve a genuine exchange of services. In Brittany, though, an area which was always somewhat off the beaten track, always comparatively less developed than others, where, moreover, the seignorial system showed some archaic features, many lords appear to have exploited the peasants brutally. It is therefore necessary to study the exact nature and implications of the seignorial regime in each region and each district affected by the revolts with which we are concerned.

The Role of the Peasants in French
Revolts as a Whole Between 1624 and 1648

IT IS NECESSARY ALWAYS TO KEEP IN MIND first and foremost that the revolts of the peasants did not take place in isolation. The peasants revolted along with many other groups, and after a number of others had already revolted.

During the period when France was getting more and more involved in the Thirty Years' War, the king's absolute power was quite as much challenged as it was affirmed. To confine ourselves to the period of the most numerous and most serious peasant revolts, at the beginning of this period, in 1625, pamphlets entitled *Admonitio ad Regem Ludovicum XIII* and *Mysteria politica* blamed the king for his alliances with the Huguenot heretics, his war against Catholic Spain (a war "against God and in the first place against God's Church") and reminded him that he ran the risk of being excommunicated and deposed by the pope in the name of the indirect power of the sovereign pontiff over the temporal authority of kings, and that, if this were to happen, the grandees of the kingdom, and even the king's subjects as a whole, would be obliged to execute the pope's sentence; "for when a Prince takes up arms against religion, his subjects' duty is not to obey him but rather to resist him." The bishop of Chartres, Léonor d'Estampes de Valençay, had replied to this view, on behalf of the clergy of France: "It is to be understood that, in addition to the universal agreement of peoples and nations, the Prophets announce, the Apostles confirm and the Martyrs confess that Kings are ordained by God, and that is not all: Kings are themselves gods. . . ." Accordingly, one must obey them unquestioningly. "If it were permissible for subjects to question that which Princes decree, what sort of authority would magistrates enjoy? . . . Homes would be full of discord, towns would be full of sedition and provinces of brigandage, and everything would in the end collapse in tumult and confusion . . . The King has made an alliance (with the heretics) because he has chosen to do so . . . He has gone to war because to do this was just and reasonable; or, rather . . . such a war is just because the King has undertaken it." The king holds power directly from God, the pope has no authority over his temporal affairs, and it is never legitimate to rebel against the king, even in the interest of religion. But the bishop's little work, though duly printed and published, had been repudiated by the Assembly of the Clergy, in 1626, on the ground that it contained questionable formulations, and the bishop was obliged to retract. Although the clergy of France stood, indeed, for royal absolutism, and supported the king against the parlements,[1] much anxiety and confusion still prevailed in many minds regarding the precise limits of royal authority. A *dévot* party continued to exist even after the disgracing of the queen-mother and of Keeper of the Seals de Marillac, right down to the Fronde and beyond, which was opposed on religious grounds to the anti-Spanish policy of the government. We know how much importance the peasants attached to everything that affected religion.[2] What influence may these disputes have had on some of them?

The king's brother, the princes of the blood, and the grandees conspired unceasingly. They held on to the idea that royal power had been entrusted by the realm to the family of Hugh Capet, and that, therefore, the king's relations, all those who might come

---

1. P. Blet, S.J., *Le Clergé de France et la monarchie. Étude sur les assemblées générales du clergé de 1615 à 1666* (Rome, Gregorian University Press, 1959), I, pp. 335–370.

2. Y. Durand, *Cahiers de Paroisses et de châtellenies pour les états généraux de 1614–1615* (Paris, P.U.F.), 1966.

to the throne in the event of a succession of premature deaths, had the right to share power with the king, in his council. It was intolerable that the king should wield power on his own, helped by favorites of baser birth, with a chief minister like Richelieu or Mazarin and state councillors who were mere lawyers. The fact that this government of favorites and commissaries should be violating, in the name of *raison d'état*, as a result of ceaseless wars, the entire ancient customary constitution of the kingdom, neglecting to govern "by the Great Council," with the aid of the peers of the realm, of the high officers of the Crown, deliberating with the magistracy in the Parlement de Paris, with the aid of the States-General and of assemblies of notables; that it should disregard the privileges of the provinces, districts and towns, and treat with contempt the traditional powers of the corporations of officials and the established forms of justice—all this gave rise to a kind of horror, and to constant efforts to oppose all these pernicious innovations: centralization, the imposition of uniformity, the development of the modern state. Hence the ever-renewed plots, around Louis XIII's brother, Gaston d'Orléans, and the queen-mother, Marie de Médicis, to bring Gaston out of the court circle and start a civil war: Ornano's plot; the conspiracy of Chalais, in 1626; the intrigues of Marie de Médicis; the Day of Dupes, November 10, 1630; the disgracing of the queen; the exiling of her loyal supporter, Keeper of the Seals de Marillac; the arrest and sentencing to death of his brother, the army commander Marshal de Marillac, who was executed at Rueil on May 8, 1632; the flight of Gaston to Lorraine when his friends were charged with *lèse-majesté* by the royal declaration of March 30, 1631; the revolts of Henri de Montmorency, Gaston's accomplice, who tried to incite the province of Languedoc against the government, his family having been governors there for a century and having many followers, but who was defeated on September 1, 1632, at Castelnaudary, captured, condemned to death, and executed on October 30, 1632.

The flight of Gaston d'Orléans was in itself a very serious matter, since the king was accused of heresy. The Spaniards might make use of his brother to launch an invasion of France. A member of the French royal family could always gather malcontents around him who would be convinced of his right to the Crown and would bring back the state of civil war which had, in the days of the League, made possible the installation of a Spanish garrison in Paris. The danger was all the greater because the heir presumptive to the throne, at a time when Louis XIII had no son and seemed unlikely to beget one, had taken refuge at the court of Lorraine, and had there clandestinely married the duke of Lorraine's sister Marguerite. This reinforced the claim to the throne of France maintained by the Guise family who, starting with Henri le Balafré, put themselves forward as descendants of Charlemagne and regarded Hugh Capet and his successors, in particular Henry IV and his son Louis XIII, as usurpers. The marriage united the claims of the Guises with Gaston's own claims to the Crown and strengthened his own dynastic position. In fact, Gaston d'Orléans had made this marriage alliance with a dynasty hostile to the king and the realm despite the king's wish and explicit prohibition. The king, Gaston's elder brother and sovereign, ought to be regarded as father and guardian of Monsieur, the heir to his throne. When minors married without the consent of father and guardian, the law, based on the Ordinance of Blois, declared that abduction had taken place and the marriage was invalid. Accordingly the king had the Parlement announce, on March 24, 1634, that the alleged marriage between Monsieur le Duc d'Orléans, the king's only brother, and Princess Marguerite of Lorraine, had not been validly contracted, that Duke Charles of Lorraine, a vassal of the Crown, had been guilty of abduction in suborning Gaston and inducing him to do this thing, and that the duke was therefore guilty of lèse-majesté. After prolonged negotiations, the Assembly of the Clergy concurred in this view, on July 7, 1635. Having returned to France and been pardoned in October, 1634, Gaston acknowledged in August, 1635, that his marriage was null and void. It was not a moment too soon to deprive the Lorrainers and Spaniards of this weapon. On May 9, 1635, France had formally declared war on Spain. On August 15, 1636, the Spaniards took Corbie by surprise, broke through the defense line of the Somme which protected Paris, and threatened the capital of France.

However, the pope had made no statement. The nullity of the

marriage was open to doubt. The French government's discussions
with the pope dragged on. Then the unexpected birth of a dauphin,
the future Louis XIV, in 1638, rendered the problem less acute.
After Richelieu's death Louis XIII gave his consent to the
marriage, and Marguerite of Lorraine was then able to enjoy her
rights as duchess of Orleans.[3]

The reconciliation between the king and Gaston in 1634 was
only temporary. Gaston started again in 1636 to involve himself
with other princes of the blood and grandees, allies of Spain,
taking advantage of the French defeats and the threat of invasion.
At the beginning of 1637 the king was obliged to write to "his good
towns," as, for example, to Saintes on January 15, ordering them
to refuse entry to Gaston or his envoys.

In 1641, by agreement with Gaston, the comte de Soissons fled
to Sedan and there, together with the duke of Guise, the duke of
Bouillon, "and other princes and officers of the Crown," issued a
manifesto calling on the "provinces, towns and personages" of
France to revolt in order to impose a "general peace" (which at
that moment could serve only the interests of the Hapsburgs of
Spain and Austria) and "to endeavor to restore everything to its
former place, reestablishing the laws that have been overthrown,
the immunities, rights and privileges of the provinces, towns and
personages that have been violated . . . ensuring . . . respect
for churchmen and nobles, dignity to *Parlements*, prosperity to
trade, and relief from burdens to the poor . . ."[4] "To restore
everything to its former place" was the philosophy of these purely
reactionary revolts of the aristocracy, the most definite result of
which, had they succeeded, would have been to make the kingdom
incapable of carrying on the struggle to prevent Hapsburg hegemony. The comte de Soissons was defeated and killed in the fight
at La Marfée, not far from Sedan, on July 6, 1641.

The following year saw the conspiracy of the king's favorite,
Cinq-Mars, *grand écuyer de France*, with the duke of Orleans and
the duke of Bouillon. On March 13, 1641, they signed a treaty
with Spain by which they were to be supplied at Sedan with an
army of 12,000 infantry and 6,000 cavalry, the command to be

3. P. Blet, *op. cit.*, pp. 399–446.
4. Bibl. Nat., Ms. fr. 17 331, fo. 46 ro.

taken by Gaston, with Bouillon and Cinq-Mars as *maréchaux de camp*, for the purpose of a march on Paris. Spain's reward was to be peace, which she badly needed, and the restitution of France's conquests. But Cinq-Mars was detected and arrested on June 12, 1642, and the duke of Bouillon arrested while he was with the army in Italy. Gaston was unable to escape in time to safety with his Spanish friends. Cinq-Mars was beheaded at Lyons on September 12, 1642.

These risings and the manifestos which sought to justify them helped to spread the idea among the people that the king was ill-informed, that his ministers and councillors were tyrants, bringing in pernicious innovations, and that their authority, like their way of governing the country, was illegal and illegitimate.

While members of the royal family, peers of France, and high officers of the Crown were indulging in plots, plans to murder the chief minister, Richelieu, armed outbreaks and attempts to start civil war, the king's officials, his magistrates, headed by the parlements, "which had something sacred and venerable" about them, adopted as their particular form of rebellion refusal to obey, and whittled away the government's authority by continuous harsh criticism. The corporations of officials, and not only the parlements, Chambres des Comptes, and Cours des Aides but the *trésoriers de France* in every *généralité*, the *élus* in every *élection financière* (who were nominated by the king, not elected by the inhabitants), the magistrates in every *présidial*, *bailliage*, and *sénéchaussée*, considered, and told Chancellor Séguier, that while they owed the king allegiance and therefore obedience, they also owed something to their conscience, namely, respect for their professional integrity and therefore refusal to obey orders which ran contrary to this; and also something to justice, namely, respect for its dignity, and therefore maintenance of just relations between the king and his subjects, when necessary protecting the king's subjects against the king's government.[5] This conception implied that they would critically examine the edicts, declarations, letters patent, and decrees sent them by the king, thereby suspending their obedience to him, and would address observations to the king

5. R. Mousnier, "La participation des gouvernés à l'activité des gouvernants," *Études suisses d'Histoire générale*, 20 (1962–1963), pp. 212–213.

aimed at securing the withdrawal of decisions he had taken, or would put forward amendments to legislative and administrative acts and orders they had received. This was what all these bodies did every day, through the procedure of remonstrances, which formed an integral part of their function. However, this procedure was a very slow one, and the government considered that it was unacceptable in time of war. Furthermore, the parlements and other sovereign courts drew out this procedure beyond all reasonable limits of time. Normally, the official corporations would have expressed their remonstrances once, and then, if the king upheld his decision and sent his *jussion*, they would have carried out the order. Now, however, the sovereign courts resisted six, seven, or eight repeated *jussions* and went beyond the procedure of remonstrance to rebellion. The official bodies accompanied their refusals to obey with criticisms of the king's ministers and councillors, those "favorites" with usurped authority who, said the magistrates, were prolonging an unjustified war, in order to acquire importance and provide cover for their exactions, and were squandering for their own boundless luxury the money squeezed out of the people's toil, enriching an army of their creatures, financiers, and tax-farmers, leeches and harpies sucking the blood of the poor. After these acts of rebellion, these criticisms, which were printed and circulated widely on behalf of venerable bodies of magistrates who were the embodiment of the king's justice, what authority could the laws and instructions of the government retain among the people?

In addition to all this, revolts by the towns became frequent, the peasants being involved in these to a greater or lesser extent. These revolts began, in the main, in one of two circumstances: either the appointment of *élus* or the introduction or increase of indirect taxes. There were revolts when the king wished to replace the assessment and apportionment of the burden of the taille, the chief direct tax, drawn up by the provincial or local states, the assemblies of deputies of the three orders, clergy, nobility, and Third Estate, and the collection of the taille by commissaries of officials of these states by assessment, apportionment of liability, and collection carried out by royal officials, the *élus* and *receveurs*. The disadvantages that were feared, in addition to the loss of a privilege, a distinction, and an honor, were an increase in taxation (because the newly introduced officials had to be paid, and on top of their salaries these men took *"taxations"* for their services whenever they gave receipts, signed rolls, confirmed accounts, and so on) and also a reduction in the number of the richest taxpayers, because these would purchase the new offices and become exempt from the taille. This tax did not vary according to the total income of those liable to tax; it was a fixed sum assessed on a certain district, and if a taxpayer became exempt, then what he would have paid had to be made up by the rest.[6]

When the king wanted to increase indirect taxes (*aides*) or demesne taxes, or to introduce new ones, the damage done was twofold: these taxes fell upon articles of current consumption, such as wine, and affected the poor directly, in their everyday life, while indirectly, by reducing sales of their produce, they made things harder for the winegrowers and for the *seigneurs directs* of vineyards, whose rents in money were jeopardized. Moreover, these taxes seemed extraordinary, whereas the taille had become customary. Since 1439 it had also become customary for the king himself to decide when and how much should be levied. Whatever was customary was not disputed. Whatever was new, however, whether a tax or the amount of a tax, was always looked upon as extortionate, a "gabelle," as they said in the southwest. Again, the taille had been established in order to pay the soldiers. The good people did not understand why the government needed to ask for extra taxes in order to maintain its armies, not realizing that both the numbers and the equipment of the latter had greatly increased. Finally, there was a traditional notion that the king should "live of his own," meeting all state expenses from the revenues of his demesne. Any subsidy apart from that ought to be agreed to by his subjects. And it was only too true that the king imposed subsidies which had never been agreed to, and that the lawyers certified as demesne taxes exactions which seemed to the good people to have nothing to do with the royal demesne. Too often they had the feeling that wrong was being done to them.

6. See *La Nouvelle Defaitte des Croquants en Quercy par Monsieur le Maréchal de Thémines* (Paris, "chez Jean de Bordeaux, rue Daufine, au bout du Pont-Neuf, a la fleur de Lys," 1624); ed. Ed. Fournier, "Variétés historiques et littéraires," *Vu* (Paris, P. Jannet, 1857), pp. 323–330. See also *Mercure français*, 10, pp. 473–478.

Thus, in Burgundy, a *pays d'États*, it was announced in 1629 that the king intended to introduce *élus*. The assembly of estates persuaded the king to withdraw this measure in exchange for a large sum of money which they then had to collect from the people of the province. In Dijon, a town which constituted a "corporation and college," a rumor got about in 1630 that the government was going to introduce taxes on drinks. The wine-growers, who occupied an entire quarter of the town, rose in revolt on February 28 and March 1, to the sound of *Lanturelu*, and burned the king and the cardinal in effigy. The mayor, the *échevins*, and the militia did not interfere. Then, when a certain number of the rebels began sacking and pillaging houses, the militia, backed by the garrison of the castle, suppressed the disorders. The king decided not to introduce *élus*. Should we classify this revolt as an urban one, or as a peasants' revolt?

At Aix-en-Provence, Brignolles, Draguignan, and Grasse, riots occurred in 1630 for the same reason. At Aix, indeed, there was a real revolt, known as the revolt of the Cascavéoux, between September and December, 1630. The king's attempt to introduce *élus* was a breach of the privileges of the province and the treaty binding it to the Crown. The states of Provence repudiated the royal decision in April, 1630, and were supported by a strike of the consuls (or municipal magistrates), a strike of the royal officials, and a strike of the craftsmen, who shut their shops. A common front of the entire population against the king was formed. The parlement, which was also irritated because the king was showing himself difficult about renewing the *paulette* and because of the presence of an *intendant de province*, that royal commissary abhorred by the magistracy, stirred up to revolt a population which was angered by shortages and high prices due to the plague which had just ended. The officials, the advocates, and the bourgeois appeared in arms in the streets on September 19, 1630, and drew the craftsmen into their movement. The governor of the province, the duke of Guise, whom Richelieu was seeking to remove from his position as admiral of Provence, did not try to stop them. The nobility and the Third Estate resolved to take up arms to safeguard the "liberties of the country" (*pays*) and defend the "homeland" (*patrie*).

But the parlement was divided into rival groups. One of these, led by the *président* de Coriolis and his nephew Châteauneuf, formed a party which was called the Cascavéoux, from the name of their emblem, a little bell fastened by a white ribbon. They needed a fighting force. Accordingly, they resorted to demagogy, stirring up the poorer craftsmen against the *élus* and all who might become *élus*, that is, the rich. They incited a march of villagers on Aix on November 3 and 4, 1630, uniting the agricultural workers with the urban craftsmen. They organized the plundering of their opponents' houses.

These opponents gained by the fear which these proceedings aroused among the bourgeois and the well-to-do craftsmen. Another group in the parlement, together with the first consul, the baron de Bras, formed another party of Cascavéoux, the "blue ribbons." The two parties clashed in December, and the "whites," with Coriolis and Châteauneuf, were expelled. Later they came back, drove out the "blues" and, seeking allies outside the province, took up the cause of the queen-mother. However, everybody had had enough of these troubles, and the other towns failed to follow this lead. The prince de Condé arrived with soldiers and had a few poor devils executed for form's sake. The king renounced his plan to appoint *élus*, in exchange for a substantial sum, and reestablished the *paulette*. Peasants, in this instance, played the role of auxiliaries in a revolt by the entire population, launched and led by the upper classes, and, in particular, in a struggle between rival groups of officials and nobles, one of which made use of the poorer section of the people.[7]

In Languedoc, another privileged province and *pays d'États*, the king had been making, ever since 1628 and the Huguenot rising led by the prince de Rohan, repeated efforts at centralization which amounted to so many breaches of the province's privileges. He had sent in a commissary, the prince de Condé, with discretionary powers even over the governor, the duc de Montmorency. He had increased, by his sole authority, the taxes payable by the province, which should have been agreed to by the assembly of the provincial states, and apportionment of liability and collection of the taxes

7. I have here made use of a thesis written by one of my pupils, M. Pillorget, which is shortly to be published.

had been carried out by royal officials, the *trésoriers de France*, stationed at Toulouse and Béziers. Finally, in July, 1629, by the Edict of Nîmes, *élus* had been appointed for the province. The result was, on the one hand, a legal resistance in the form of opposition by the provincial states and the parlement of Toulouse, and on the other, a rebellion, stirred up by some bishops and lords of Languedoc, which involved craftsmen and *laboureurs*. The insurrection was a serious one, and looked like becoming even more so when the revolt of Gaston d'Orléans, the queen-mother, and the duc de Montmorency against the king broke out in 1632. The assembly of the estates declared for Montmorency, the governor of Languedoc, whose family had ruled the province for a century. But Montmorency was defeated and captured at Castelnaudary, on September 1, 1632, and even before this battle his escapade had embarrassed the provincial movement against centralization. The big towns and the Protestants themselves did not want to intervene in an affair between courtiers and members of the royal family. They resumed their allegiance to the king, and since the latter had the good sense to give up his plan for introducing *élus*, the people of Languedoc allowed him to reduce as he pleased the privileges of their province. In this case, well-to-do peasants followed their lords in defense of the liberties of their province against the central government.[8]

In other instances of revolt, as well, we find the peasants playing this dependent and subordinate role. This was so in revolts caused by the passage and billeting of soldiers during their route marches, or when they went into winter quarters, which was one of the calamities of the age. The soldiers lodged and lived with the local inhabitants, who had to supply *l'ustencile*, that is, "bed, table-linen, pot, bowl, glass, a place by the fire and by the candle." They had to supply provisions for which the soldiers were supposed to pay, but using money provided by the special tax, the *subsistance*, which was levied by the royal officials or by the province or municipality. In actual fact the soldiers behaved as they pleased, even making no difference between friendly and enemy territory.

8. P. Gachon, *Les États de Languedoc et l'édit de Béziers* (1632) (Paris, 1887).

The soldiers broke into larders and wardrobes; stole money, clothes, jewels, food, and wine; slaughtered the poultry, carried off the cattle, threw furniture and doors into the fire; raped women and girls; and manhandled or murdered their husbands and fathers. Walled towns defended themselves against the soldiers, but the smaller towns and villages were devastated. In 1632 the regiment of Saint-Hilaire ravaged Upper Poitou so thoroughly that 2,000 cultivators, reduced to eating grass, dragged themselves, exhausted with hunger, to the gates of Poitiers. When the regiment drew near, the suburbs of Saint-Saturnin and Montbernage threw up barricades in order not to admit them to billets. The municipal militia of Poitiers took up arms and came to the help of the people of the suburbs, and the soldiers were unable to enter. Frustrated, they burned and ravaged the entire countryside within a radius of four or five leagues around the town.

From 1627 onward, bad harvests, dearths, famines, and plagues were frequent. The peasants, ruined and famished, flocked to the towns, making their way in and swelling the numbers of the population competing for bread that was scarce and dear. They were not unaware that lords, officials, monasteries, and churchmen had secret stores of grain, and that after every good harvest old grain reappeared on the market, whereas people had died of hunger when there was a shortage. On May 25, 1630, at Poitiers, four to five thousand "beggars" and "idlers" gathered as the town council, which was trying to control the increase in the price of grain, was coming out from a meeting. The mayor, finding himself met with stones, insults, and threats, took refuge in the courthouse, under the protection of the law. The rioters then rushed to the market-place of Notre-Dame and hurled themselves on the bakers, taking bread without paying for it. Mobs, which included many women, armed with swords and halberds, attacked the houses of the rich millers, assaulted persons who were bringing grain to the mill, carried off grain and flour, and beat up two échevins who arrested a virago in her fury.[9] In this hunger riot it is impossible to

9. P. Boissonnade, "L'administration royale et les soulèvements populaires en Angoumois, en Saintonge et en Poitou, pendant le ministère de Richelieu, 1624–1642," Memoires de la Soc. des Antiquaires de l'Ouest, 2nd series, Vol. XXVI, pp. xix, xxxviii.

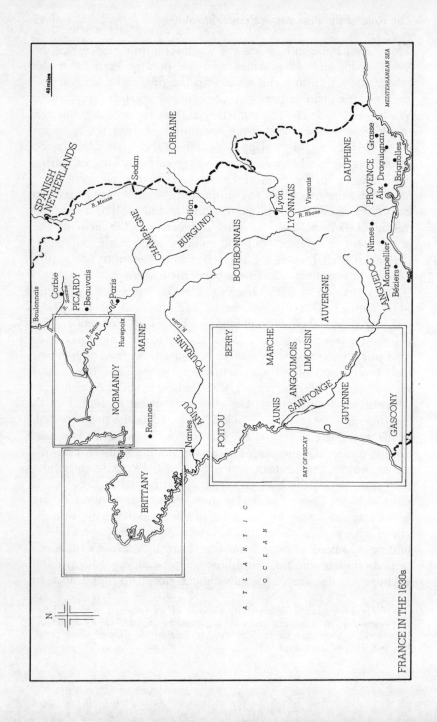

FRANCE IN THE 1630s

MEDITERRANEAN SEA

SPANISH NETHERLANDS

LORRAINE

Sedan

R. Meuse

CHAMPAGNE

BURGUNDY

Dijon

BOURBONNAIS

LYONNAIS

Lyon

R. Rhone

Vivarais

DAUPHINE

PROVENCE

Aix

Draguignan

Grasse

Brignolles

Boulonnais

Corbie

R. Somme

PICARDY

Beauvais

Paris

R. Seine

Hurepoix

MAINE

TOURAINE

R. Loire

AUVERGNE

LANGUEDOC

Nimes

Montpellier

Béziers

NORMANDY

Rennes

ANJOU

Nantes

BERRY

MARCHE

ANGOUMOIS

LIMOUSIN

R. Coronne

BRITTANY

POITOU

AUNIS

SAINTONGE

GUYENNE

GASCONY

BAY OF BISCAY

ATLANTIC OCEAN

N

40 miles

distinguish between the part played by the poor craftsmen and that played by the peasant refugees. Doubtless it was the craftsmen who were armed, but doubtless also both groups formed at one stage a single mob of hungry and angry people.

At Bordeaux in May and June, 1635, a gabelle imposed on taverns and on wine set off a revolt of tavern keepers and makers of casks which drew in many craftsmen and day-laborers, with the complicity of the majority of the bourgeois, a large number of "persons of condition," and officials of the parlement, who "regarded these rebels as their liberators." The rebels "wanted to get control of Saint Julien's Gate . . . and let in the peasants of the surrounding district, to help them. This was being loudly demanded by the peasants, who wanted to share in the plunder of the town, which they thought they had at their mercy." This was at any rate the motive ascribed to them by the secretary to the duc d'Épernon, who wrote these lines; but among these peasants there were, along with gardeners and market gardeners, also vine-growers and *laboureurs*, very seriously affected by the indirect taxes. A certain number of them managed to get into the town and take part in the revolt. The duc d'Épernon, governor of Guyenne, was unable to secure the help of the town militia or that of most of the neighboring gentry, nor was he able to raise soldiers in the usual way from his lands, among his own peasants, who hid themselves. He was reduced to a few gentlemen, a few *"honnêtes bourgeois,"* and, in the town, to a few of his former soldiers, with whose aid he either overcame the rebels or persuaded them to yield. Hardly had they been more or less quieted when "the madness extended to the peasants of the countryside. These, having, during one of the riots, managed to plunder some houses in the town, withdrew with the loot to their villages, and their neighbours were soon stirred up by their bad example to engage in plundering . . . . In a moment, all the villagers dropped their ploughs and took up arms instead: after robbing the houses in the countryside they gathered in great numbers in all the suburbs and strove to enter the town itself. The poor of the town wanted them to enter and tried to open a way for them. . . ." They assembled in the suburb of Saint-Surin, where they burned several houses. The duc d'Épernon mounted his horse and set forth at the head of

forty or fifty gentlemen of his guard. This time he secured the
support of a few companies of the town militia. The peasants
scattered. The cavalry chased them and killed forty or fifty. "The
rest of the peasants, who had been waiting to see whether these
would succeed or not, behaved themselves properly that year . . . ."
The king then granted an amnesty.[10]

The majority of the towns in the province of Guyenne, with the
exception of Montauban, followed the example of Bordeaux. At
Périgueux the people set upon the officials of the *élection*. Verta-
mon, the *intendant de justice*, prevented a massacre. The riot at
Agen on June 17 and 18, 1635, was especially violent, murderous,
and plebeian in character. The town had suffered much since 1629,
through contagious diseases, bad harvests, and famines. The
"crimson fever" had spared the rich hardly more than the poor.
The people of Agen—boatmen, wine-porters, pastry cooks, cooks,
makers of packsaddles for donkeys and mules, master glove-
makers—revolted to cries of: "Death to the *gabeleurs*! Kill the
gabeleurs! Long live the King without *gabelles*!" in order to
prevent the levying of the gabelle on wine and to prevent reinforcements to the forces of order, in the shape of the *vicesénéchal* of
the Agenais and the Condomois, with his archers, from embarking
to go to Bordeaux to help the duc d'Épernon against the rebels in
Bordeaux. The rioters in Agen acted in concert with the peasants
of the surrounding country, some of whom had entered the town
while others were active outside against all, whether royal officers
or well-to-do persons, suspected of having something to do with
the establishment and levying of the gabelle. It does not appear
that the rioters were successful in seizing the town gates and
making possible a large-scale invasion by the peasants. However,
we notice that there were "certain peasants" among those who
plundered and set on fire the house of the sieur d'Espalais,
"bourgeois of Agen." When the authorities got back the upper
hand, Councillor Méja, at the Porte du Pin, chased 120 to 140
"peasants" from Foulayronnes out of the town. Outside the town,
the peasants kept watch at the foot of the ramparts. Messire
Guillaume du Périer, a canon, being chased by a stone-throwing

10. G. Girard, *Histoire de la vie du duc d'Épernon* (Paris, chez Auguste
Courbe, 1655), Book XI, pp. 515–529.

mob, jumped over the ramparts out of the town, but broke his thighbone and was finished off with bill hooks and rods by a crowd of peasants. Others killed M. Mélot, lieutenant to the *vicesénéchal*, who had taken refuge in his country residence. The peasants hurled themselves upon the corpses of Armand Paulmier, the king's bailiff in the election, and of Maître Pierre Maury, the royal notary, whose task had been to enforce the gabelle, and who had been killed and thrown down from the walls by the townspeople. After dragging the bodies about, they eventually threw them into the Garonne. The peasants organized expeditions to go and burn down the farms of those who had been killed or plundered in the town as *gabeleurs*—David Codoing, councillor in the *élection*, Maître Jehan Raillery, the royal advocate in the *élection*, and Maître Sarrau de Redon, the royal notary in the *élection*. On Monday, June 18, "the rural parish churches for two leagues around Agen rang the alarm-bell to assemble the peasants, who marched to positions under the walls of this town." They threatened it for six months. But the magistrates of the Chamber of the Edict (of Nantes), a tribunal made up half of Catholics and half of Protestants, together with the advocates, attorneys, and consuls of Agen, a municipality composed that year of advocates, attorneys, one military man, and some bourgeois, organized a militia, erected barricades, restored order, and patrolled the town night and day, until the end of September. In August, three or four poor fellows, saddlemakers or wine-porters, were hanged for the sake of example, and then the king granted an amnesty. The barricades set up by the bourgeois were dismantled, but the "respectable people" of the town continued to carry swords all the time until the end of October. Eighteen people had been killed, nearly all of them finance officials who were alleged to be connected with the gabelle. Ten houses had been plundered in the town, and one burnt down. Outside the town, six farms had been burnt and one razed to the ground by the peasants.[11]

In these cases, which I have cited as examples, and in many

11. Magen, "Une émeute à Agen en 1635," *Recueil des travaux de la Soc. d'Agriculture, Sciences et Arts d'Agen* (1855), 1st series, Vol. VII, pp. 196–224. Agen diary of the Malebaysse family, *Revue de l'Agenais*, 20 (1893), pp. 441–451.

others, it was the townspeople who took the initiative in the
movements—sometimes the higher strata of urban society and
sometimes the lower. The peasants of the neighboring countryside
were only auxiliaries in these revolts. But there were also genuinely
rural revolts—in the first place, petty rebellions which recurred
again and again, the instigators of them apparently being country
gentlemen. There seems to have been a natural bond of interest
between those lords who belonged to the gentry and their peasants,
at least against royal taxation. Indeed, in this period of disasters
caused by the weather, harvest failures, dearths, and famines, and,
after 1630, of stagnation, followed by shrinkage, in trade with
Spain and her colonies, of ever-slower increase and then actual
decrease in the arrivals of precious metals from America, of out-
flows of gold and silver for the requirements of the armies, and of
growing scarcity of currency, the increased royal taxation, if it
were to be paid, might prevent the peasants from being able to
meet their obligations in respect of seignorial dues and ground
rent. Hence the incitements to the peasants to delay or refuse
payment which came from some of the lords, from townspeople—
royal officials, advocates, and merchants—and above all from
country squires.

In the southwest the gentry very readily went in for salt smuggling. In order to avoid the farmed-out tax called the *convoy et
comptablie de Bordeaux,* a series of tolls and taxes levied on goods
moving along the Charente, the Boutonne, the Seudre, and the
Gironde, the gentry, defying the tax-farmer's agents and guards,
sent their wine from the Garonne to Mont-de-Marsan, and there
bartered it for salt brought from Bayonne. "There are convoys of
between 300 and 400 carts escorted by 50 musketeers, led by
gentlemen of the district, so that all the guards maintained at great
expense by the tax-farmer in the Landes of Bordeaux are incapable
of preventing this abuse, and when they have tried once or twice
to stop it some of the captains of the guard and their men have
been killed, as a result of which there have been extensive investigations and sentences which it has nevertheless been impossible to carry out."[12] Between 1631 and 1644, the Cour des Aides of

12. Arch. Nat. KK 1215, fo. 323, quoted by Yves-Marie Bercé, *Soulèvements
populaires dans le Sud-Ouest* (thesis in typescript, École des Chartes, 1959),
p. 156.

Guyenne issued thirty-eight warrants for excesses and rebellion against sailors of the Garonne and boatmen of the Adour and against petty lords and their men—even, on September 23, 1631, against a baron, Baron de la Montan. These revolts developed later into risings that involved an entire district. On October 17, 1636, in the Landes of the Bazadais, the guards of the *convoy et comptablie* confiscated five oxcarts loaded with contraband salt. The alarm bell was rung in the churches of Giscos, Saint-Michel de Meilhac, and Escandes. The peasants dropped their farm implements where they stood, and took up arms. The guards managed to save their skins only by fleeing as fast as their horses could carry them. As the result of an inquiry into this affair, on December 10 the Cour des Aides called for the arrest of the treasurer and servants of the lord of Castelnau, together with the *bailli*, the registrar and the bailiff of the Castelnau court district, the curate of Giscos, and the shoemaker, the locksmith, and a dozen other inhabitants of Castelnau.[13]

All over the country the gentry, and often the royal magistrates themselves, in their capacities as lords, were accused of inciting the peasants to refuse to accept taxation in general, to refuse to pay taxes, and then to rise in armed revolt. The *intendants* of the provinces made this charge in relation to Picardy, Normandy, Champagne, Anjou, Touraine, Brittany, Poitou, Angoumois, Saintonge, Auvergne, Limousin, Bourbonnais, Périgord, Quercy, Rouergue, Guyenne, Armagnac, Languedoc, Lyonnais, Dauphiné and Provence. Here are a few examples, to illustrate the mechanism of revolts of this kind, which affected areas that, though in each case small, were numerous, and which might go on for years. The *intendant* de Corberon wrote from Limoges on August 26, 1644: "I feel obliged, therefore, to tell you that Monsieur and Madame de Pompadour—more as a result of the initiative taken by certain of their servants and officers, among others by a certain procurator-fiscal of the Treignac area, where one of the chief tax-collecting centres of the *élection* of Tulle is situated, than by any hostility they have towards the King's business—have so behaved, in the lands which they possess in great number, towards those who came to collect the taille, and have talked so arrogantly of their power

13. *Cour des Aides*, no. 55, p. 2; *ibid.*; p. 157.

and with such contempt of the authority of those who are in the
province, that it was not hard to convince the people that, since
they were under the protection of Monsieur and Madame de
Pompadour, nobody would dare to prosecute them; thanks to this
assurance the inhabitants of these lands have paid their taxes so
badly that it is a fact that since 1641 they have furnished hardly
one-third of the amount they were assessed at; this, despite the
circumstance that, while it can be said that the parishes in question
are not particularly prosperous (for there are none that come into
this category), at least they are much less wretched and more
generously relieved of burdens than the others—indeed, they were
so thoroughly relieved this year that fifty or sixty parishes of this
group were assessed at only two-thirds or less of the amount they
were charged with last year, as against two or three which were
accorded a reduction of only one-quarter. I had supposed that this
reduction, agreed with Madame de Pompadour for the well-being
of His Majesty's business in the province, through the feelings of
respect and deference I have and shall always have for *Monseigneur
le Chancelier*,[14] would result in hurrying up the despatch of the
tax-rolls for future payments and bring into the treasury money
that was due for past taxes. All that, however, failed to achieve the
effect I expected. On the contrary, it was announced in the
parishes that if the soldiers attempted to enter them (and this was
even conveyed to the officers commanding the soldiers), no one
would be able to guarantee their life and limb; the protection of
Monsieur de Pompadour being extended even to properties which
do not belong to him, and he having written letters to the officers
commanding the fusiliers[15] to make them refrain from billeting
their men in the houses of people who are only remotely within
the authority of his judges and procurators-fiscal."[16] When re-
buked by the king and the chancellor, the Pompadours, who were

14. Jean, marquis de Pompadour, lieutenant-general in the king's armies and
of Upper and Lower Limousin, was the son of Léonard-Philibert, vicomte de
Pompadour, and Marie Fabri, sister of Madeleine Fabri, wife of Chancellor
Séguier. He was thus the chancellor's nephew by marriage. Jean's wife,
mentioned here, was Marie, vicomtesse de Rochechouart, who seems to have
concerned herself very closely with her estates and her peasants.
15. Special troops with the task of ensuring the collection of taxes.
16. R. Mousnier, *Lettres et Mémoires adressés au chancelier Séguier (1633–
1649)* (Paris, P.U.F., 1964), I, no. 226, pp. 641–642.

courtiers, became more cooperative, but others continued to behave in the same way. On October 28, 1644, De Corberon asked, in a letter sent from Brive, that he be recalled from the province: "All the more because I foresee a great deal of disorder and rebellion, Monsieur le Comte de Bonneval having not only allowed his people to ill-treat some archers from the *prévôté de l'hôtel* who entered his land along with a single bailiff to collect the taille there, but having also caused to be driven away a detachment of fusiliers which I sent in subsequently to carry out distraints with more authority and compel this estate of his to pay up the taille which it owes and which it has not paid *for three years.*"[17]

It was the same in Lower Normandy. The *intendant*, du Boulay Favier, wrote from Domfront to the chancellor on February 7, 1644: "Monseigneur, I have felt obliged to take horse to endeavour to restore some degree of order in this *élection* of Domfront, where over a thousand people, from several parishes, attacked a detachment of the regiment of Le Havre and drove out, beat, stripped and despoiled the soldiers who were billeted there for the payment of taille. And as the inhabitants of Mantilly, a troublesome parish which has not made any assessment for taxes for *seven years* past, are the ringleaders of these rebels and have drawn a number of other parishes into their activities, I have to repeat the same opinion that I have already sent you, namely, that unless a memorable example is made of them, this entire *élection* will flare up in revolt." There were over 2,000 men under arms, and "the cavalry can do nothing in this district, where there are hedges everywhere and where the rebels have blocked the roads by felling trees; the rebels hold parades every day, and they have plenty of fighting men, who flock to them from every side; the adjacent parishes of Maine are beginning to feel the effects of this highly contagious poison. . . ."[18] Now here is the hidden side of this revolt, revealed in a letter from the same *intendant*, written from Alençon on January 10, 1645: "Entire *élections* would be perfectly able to pay the taxes assessed upon them if the protection furnished by the gentry did not set them in open rebellion to prevent their farmers (who are increasing the rents they pay for their farms) from paying any *taille*, or more than a very little. The

17. R. Mousnier, *op. cit.*, I, no. 234, p. 655.
18. R. Mousnier, *op. cit.*, I, no. 210, pp. 621–622.

élection of Domfront continues to be in a state of ingrained ill-will, and despite the examples that have been made and the punishment inflicted, the taxpayers persist in *a rebellion which they began seven years ago.* . . . Four or five hundred parishes pay nothing at all. . . . The people of Mantilly, about whom complaints have been addressed to you several times already, have again recently killed an archer who was distraining for taille; and no matter what I do, it is almost impossible to find out who the murderers were; the judges and the gentry ruin everything, and this district is so badly infected with rebellion that I am desperate."[19]

At the very least, the gentry helped their peasants against the bailiffs and process servers. When the men of law arrived bringing warrants to distrain the property of the peasants, the lords gathered the latter into their castles and fortified houses, together with their furniture and cattle, and if the process servers had the audacity to approach and demand entry, the lord and his men drove them off with harquebus fire. The king forbade the gentry to behave like this, by his orders of November 27, 1641, and August 22, 1642, and also by his declaration of April 16, 1643,[20] but without much result. Such things even occurred as the issue of a warrant for the arrest of Jean-Charles de Montesquieu, lord of Moncassin, baron of Secondat, an ancestor of the great jurist Montesquieu, together with his son Géraud and their accomplices, at the request of the consuls of Moncassin, on June 2, 1646, on a charge of murdering a collector of taille. Of course, I realize that the peasants were quite capable of rebelling on their own against their tax burdens. Nevertheless, the activity of the lords in this connection, and especially of the country squires, is irrefutable in many instances. Large-scale peasant revolts suggest not only a possible union of the orders against the government but also a struggle by one region against a neighboring one, or a struggle of the countryside against the towns, of the rural against the urban world. This was what happened in the case of the revolts of the *Croquants,* in Saintonge and Périgord.

19. R. Mousnier, *op. cit.,* II, no. 249, pp. 706–707.

20. P. Néron and É. Girard, *Recueil d'édits et d'ordannances royaux sur le fait de la justice* (1720), II, pp. 663, 673. *Nouveau code des tailles* (1761 ed.), I, pp. 370–406; Bibl. Nat., F. 25 566, Ch. 3.

[3]

The *Croquants* of Saintonge, Angoumois, and Poitou—1636

THE INHABITANTS OF THE ROYAL *châtellenies* in the south of Saintonge and Angoumois, bordering on the Bordeaux district, felt that they were at a disadvantage. The dues on a cask of wine carried on the river Charente were increased in 1636 to 13 livres, 10 sols on a cask valued at 20 to 24 livres, whereas in the Bordeaux district the dues on a cask transported by the Garonne—a larger cask and valued at 100 to 120 livres—were only 6 livres, 10 sols. Furthermore, being situated nearer the sea, having at their disposal a commercial organization which enabled them to sell directly to the "outside" market and to load their wines themselves in their own ships, the Bordelais sold their produce both more easily and more profitably. The people of the Charente country had to go through the agency of "outsider" commission merchants who kept most of the profit for themselves. In addition, excessively heavy dues imposed on the retail trade made the wine so expensive that the peasants could no longer sell it, and they let their vines lie untended—unless they sold their wine at a low price, to make brandy. But the needs of the stills were stripping the district of fuel, to the detriment of its metal industries. The outsider commission merchants monopolized trade, to the loss of the merchants and landowners. In a district the products of which were low in price, the charges levied by the wine and cattle brokers and by the

53

inspectors of linen weavers, carpenters, joiners, and retail traders had a paralyzing effect on business. The taille and other taxes obliged the commoners of the countryside first to borrow money and then to mortgage their property, either to townsmen or to churchmen and gentlemen. These districts, which were poorer than the Bordeaux country, suffered, in relation to the Bordelais, from a psychological complex, as an underdeveloped region.

Whereas the vines of the Bordeaux area belonged to "bourgeois" of the towns, merchants and royal officials, those of Saintonge and Angoumois belonged, as regarded either *seigneurie directe* or *seigneurie utile*, to petty nobles, or, as regarded *seigneurie utile*, to peasants. The nobles obtained their principal income from the sale of wine, either directly or through the dues they levied on their peasants. The matter became one of conflict between a country district and an urban one.

This conflict was made more acute through a bad allocation of the tax burden. Périgord and Saintonge were burdened with taille, *taillon*, and *subsistance* far in excess of their real resources, whereas the *élection* of Bordeaux district was exempt from taille; Labourd also was free from taille; and Armagnac and the viscounty of Turenne were assessed relatively lightly. Within Saintonge and Périgord a number of towns which had formerly been frontier towns, or which had shown themselves loyal to the king during the Hundred Years' War, enjoyed exemption from taille, or at least a favorable assessment.

These towns included Cognac, Marennes, Brouage, Périgueux, Bergerac, Eymet, Excideuil, and Uzeste, most of which, moreover, were in Périgord, so that the rural areas of that district were burdened all the more heavily with tax responsibilities. In addition, where the taille was *réelle*, that is, charged upon *terre roturière* in accordance with its value, and not *personnelle*, not based on the taxpayer's estimated ability to pay, the bourgeois of these "free towns" were privileged in respect of their properties in the country-side, even those distant from the towns themselves. The men of Périgueux could cultivate as many vines as they liked wherever they liked, and their farms were assessed for taille only on one-third of the value of the land they cultivated. These townsmen thus appeared as unfair competitors with the noble vinegrowers and their peasants, who were all poor men. Furthermore, the peasants, and perhaps the gentlemen too, were obliged to borrow from them, mortgaging their lands. And those bourgeois who managed the king's finances, as *trésoriers-généraux* de France, *élus*, tax collectors or tax-farmers, who grew rich by ruining the country people, were objects of general detestation.

The thing became, perhaps, a sort of continuation of the wars of religion, for these needy squires were nearly all Protestants, while the royal officials in the towns were often Catholics, and despite the "pardon" of Alais in 1629 and the confirmations of the Edict of Nantes, the king's government carried on a quiet struggle against heresy. Poitou, Angoumois, Saintonge, Quercy, Périgord, Limousin, and Auvergne had interlinked interests. Through the tax office at Tonnay-Charente passed "all the supplies destined for Saintonge and Angoumois, and the delivery that is then made from them into Limousin and in part, into Auvergne and Périgord"; the cattle trade and the large number of fairs to which the drovers and day laborers made their way, often with the sole aim of seeing people and hearing the news, made it easy for these provinces to get together. The forces of order were weak in this region: a few *vicesénéchaux*, each in command of a dozen archers, who were paid irregularly. The petty nobility, proud and even arrogant, scattered among innumerable country houses, wielded great influence over their peasants, and readily carried out judicial functions themselves. Numerous gentlemen had the reputation of each being able to assemble a sort of small private army of friends and servants, with which they engaged in private wars, smuggling, and sometimes robbery. There were a lot of them in Périgord, a wooded district where travel was difficult and the collection of taxes was always problematic. The lord of La Mothe-Hautefort, as a result of a private quarrel, had invaded the estate of Druzac, in this district, at the head of 1,200 men.[1]

So early as 1628 and 1629 the king had attempted to increase the charges on wine. At once the nobles had summoned assemblies and stirred up peasant riots against the tax collectors, the tax clerks, and the urban officials who had estates in this region. The leaders

1. Y.-M. Bercé, *op. cit.*, pp. 153–164, 185–186.

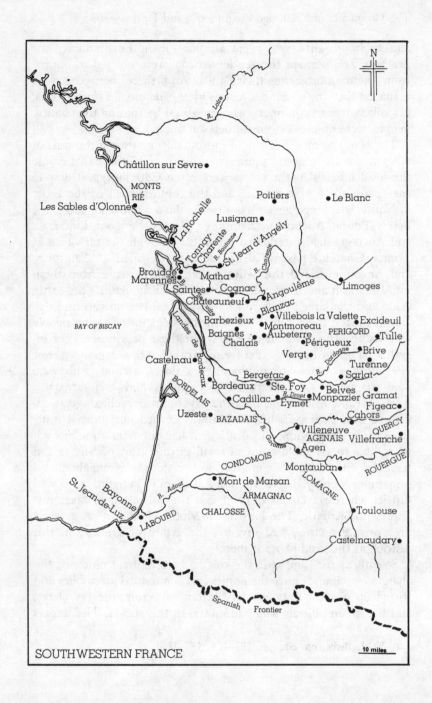

N

Châtillon sur Sevre

MONTS
RIÉ
Les Sables d'Olonne

Poitiers   Le Blanc

Lusignan

La Rochelle

Tonnay-
Charente
R. Boutonne
St. Jean d'Angély

R. Charente

Brouage
Marennes
Saintes   Matha   Cognac   Angoulême   Limoges
Châteauneuf
Blanzac
Barbezieux   Villebois la Valette   Excideuil
Montmoreau   PERIGORD
Baignes   Aubeterre   Tulle
Chalais   Périgueux   Brive
Vergt   R. Dordogne
Castelnau   Turenne
Sarlat
Bergerac
BAY OF BISCAY   Bordeaux   Ste. Foy   Belves
Cadillac   R. Dropt   Monpazier   Gramat
Eymet   Figeac
Uzeste   BAZADAIS   Cahors
R. Garonne   Villeneuve   QUERCY
AGENAIS   Villefranche
Agen
ROUERGUE
CONDOMOIS   Montauban
LOMAGNE
Bayonne   R. Adour   Mont de Marsan
St. Jean-de-Luz   ARMAGNAC
LABOURD   CHALOSSE   Toulouse

Landes de Bordeaux

BORDELAIS

Castelnaudary

Spanish   Frontier

SOUTHWESTERN FRANCE   10 miles

of the rioters were usually squireens, barbers, notaries, and "chief persons of the market-towns." As the Protestant resistance had not yet been overcome in Languedoc at that time, the king had given way and withdrawn the new charges on wine.

Things were much worse in 1636, the year following the risings which had shaken the towns along the Garonne and the peasants of their neighborhood, the terrible "year of Corbie," which was captured on August 15, 1636, when the Spaniards threatened Paris. In the spring of 1636 all the provinces between the Loire and the Garonne were in revolt. A certain number of peasants seem to have taken up arms simultaneously in Saintonge, Angoumois, Poitou, Périgord, and Guyenne. This was the revolt of the *Croquants*, which appears to have been first felt seriously in Angoumois and Saintonge. During March and April, 1636, the process servers sent out by the *élus* went through the parishes of these provinces distributing *mandes*, that is, orders to pay up. These documents bore the total of the taille, the *taillon*, and the *creue* for the garrisons, but this total was almost doubled by the addition of the sums needed to pay the charges recently assigned from the taxes to the officials, in return for payment by these officials of a special tax, representing the capital on which these charges were the interest payments. The king's government had sought in this way to obtain the money it needed in order to equip the armies for the open war now being waged against Spain.

The near-doubling of their direct taxes which resulted from this roused the indignation of the peasants of Angoumois. At the same time they learned of the increase in the charges on wine, raised to 15 livres the cask, and the reestablishment of the *"sol pour livre,"* a charge of 5 percent on all merchandise. They raised the cry of "Down with the gabelle!" and rose in revolt. On May 15, 1636, the corporation of the city of Angoulême learned that the inhabitants of the *châtellenies* of Montmoreau, La Valette, Aubeterre, Blanzac, Chalais, and Barbezieux, that is, of the south of Angoumois, the parishes which were closest to Saintonge, the Bordeaux district, and Périgord, had taken up arms and swept through the fairs massacring the so-called collectors of gabelle, the *"gabeleurs."* Soon the rising spread to Saintonge. It was a provincial revolt against "these Parisians, tax-farmers and others,

who oppress them with taxes." "So this has brought the name of
Parisian into such hatred and horror among all these people that
merely to speak it is enough to get oneself knocked down. Since
this revolt began, they have put ten or a dozen to death, and
among others, at Saint-Savinien[2] they wreaked such a frightful
fury on one of these poor tax-clerks, a native of Paris, that he was
torn alive into small pieces, and each of them took a piece to
fasten to the door of his house, where these pieces can still be
seen."[3] They decided to burst into Angoulême during the great
royal fair of May 22, 23, and 24 and there to kill all the agents of
the exchequer, *élus*, collectors, process servers, bailiffs, and tax-
farmers' clerks, and if necessary the magistrates of the Présidial,
should these try to protect the intended victims. The town corporation, having been warned, suspended the fair, thus avoiding a
concourse of peasants, mobilized the militia companies, and
erected barricades in the town. The peasants were unable to carry
out their plan. They appear to have been "dispersed" for the time
being "by the care and good order of Monsieur de Soubran,"
lieutenant to the governor of Angoumois, M. de Brassac, in the
city and castle of Angoulême.[4]

Chancellor Séguier sent a commissary, La Force, to investigate
the popular rebellions and disturbances and proceed with the collection of taxes. On June 6, however, at the fair at Blanzac, seven
to eight thousand men gathered, three or four thousand of them
being armed with harquebuses and pikes. Many of them were
former soldiers, who had served either in the king's armies against
the Protestants of La Rochelle or Saintonge, or in the Protestant
armies against the king. They were organized, "divided into twelve
or fifteen companies, led by their parish priests, all marching in
good order, to the sound of a few fifes and fiddles, for lack of
drums." They raised "a clamour and confused threats against the
lives of the *gabeleurs*, using this word to include all the collectors
of His Majesty's Taxes." They tore to pieces an unfortunate

2. In the *arrondissement* of Saint-Jean d'Angély.
3. R. Mousnier, *op. cit.*, II, app. 3, no. 2, "Account of the rising of the
peasants of Saintonge," p. 1105.
4. Letter from La Force to Séguier, June 9, 1636, in R. Mousnier, *op. cit.*,
I, p. 345.

surgeon whom they suspected of being a *gabeleur*; "after stripping
him naked and cutting off one of his arms, they made him walk all
round the fair, and then finished him off."[5]

They then proceeded to perfect their organization. The totality
of the parishes affected was constituted a "commune." Their assembly at Blanzac drew up an ordinance for these parishes, and
elected deputies to seek out the king, beg for his mercy, and convey
to him the conditions on which they would agree to submit.
Among their deputies, probably coerced into this role, were a
great noble, the sieur de Galard, brother of the comte de Brassac,
governor of Angoumois; some officials, the sieur de la Grange,
sénéchal of Barbezieux, and Sieur Gendroy, judge at Montandre;
and a "practitioner," that is, a sort of counsel, named Estancheau,
calling himself "Captain Clog" and "seneschal of the *Tiercerie*,"
who harangued the peasants from the tops of hillocks and handed
to the sieur de Galard a letter for Richelieu setting forth the conditions on which the rebels would agree to submit. At the same
time, the rebels carried out "military exercises." Not all of them
were under arms at the same time, owing to the demands of work
in the fields, but they were "enrolled and knew where they should
report at the first sound of the alarm-bell." Their number was
estimated at 40,000, a figure which could well correspond to a
population of 200,000. "On feast days they carry out military
exercises, bearing arms, which they are gradually providing themselves with as best they can—mainly in the form of swords, which
they normally wear at their sides even while ploughing their
fields."[6] They held assemblies, they had a "watchword," and they
spread the revolt and stirred up "their neighbors, by certain emissaries, to join their revolts and to furnish themselves with arms and
powder." They blockaded the towns—Cognac, Angoulême—and
did not let any provisions through to them. They threatened the
townsmen that they would burn down their country residences. La
Force was unable to find any witnesses among the king's officials or
the other townsmen. The *lieutenant-général* of the Présidial and
the mayor of Angoulême himself advised him to put off the carry-

5. *Ibid.*
6. "Account of the rising of the peasants of Saintonge," quoted in n. 3;
p. 1105.

ing out of his commissions.[7] It would be interesting to know the
precise social composition of the rebels at this stage of the revolt,
and to know whether their deputies were genuine leaders or only
men who were acting under compulsion. The documents do not
reveal as obvious rebels anyone but men of little social consequence, from the lower strata of the countryside—a practitioner,
some rural parish priests, and peasants, who, however, may have
included *laboureurs* and "cocks of the parish." One document tells
us that the judge at Montandre and the procurator-fiscal of
Châteauneuf (who was thus a seignorial official), together with
"some other leading men in the market towns," were each at the
head of a number of parishes, but the writer adds that the
peasants "force them to take on these responsibilities."[8] Thus we
see a rural commune and an army of rural commoners, with a sort
of peasant dictatorship, forcing those having the technical ability
to command and negotiate to carry out the will of the peasants.
Nevertheless, a memorandum by the *intendant* Villemontée tells
us that "the clergy and gentry connived at their political gatherings"[9]—a statement which is undoubtedly true of some of the
parish priests.

What did the *Croquants* want, at this stage of their movement,
when they could regard themselves as victors, and when we perhaps
have, for this reason, the opportunity of seeing their true mind
revealed? An anonymous manuscript memorandum, probably by
La Force, but of which only one copy survives, made for Achille de
Harlay, *premier président* of the Parlement de Paris from 1689 to
1707, seems to sum up what they were saying and to reproduce
some of their actual words.[10] They blame the excessive amount
and the ceaseless increase of taxation; for the people had paid
more during Henry IV's reign than during all the reigns of his
predecessors since the monarchy began, and yet had then gone on
to pay more in two years of Louis XIII's reign than in the whole
of Henry IV's. They blame the way taxes are collected, the distraints by bailiffs who carry off their cattle, clothes, and imple-

---

7. Letter from La Force, quoted in ns. 4 and 5.
8. "Account of the rising of the peasants of Saintonge," quoted in ns. 3
and 6; pp. 1103–1105.
9. R. Mousnier, *op. cit.*, II, app. 3, memo. no. 1, p. 1095.
10. *Ibid.*

ments, without the principal of their debts ever being reduced, because this is done merely to cover enforcement charges. The result of it all is that the peasants are ruined. They have been forced, through having been deprived of their means of work, to leave their fields untilled, even those under saffron, and, worse still, to leave their hereditary holdings and go begging for their bread. La Force echoes their complaints in his letter of June 6: "It is not, Monseigneur, that I am not, by natural feeling, touched with very great compassion when I see the extraordinary poverty in which these people live."

Furthermore, add the peasants, this expenditure to meet which they are taxed is useless. The "needs of the state" are nothing but a "pretext for enriching a few private persons . . . these tax-farmers who have brought them to despair and the extremity of poverty," "and the creatures of the man who rules the state," that is, Richelieu and his team of "faithful followers," Bouthillier, Bullion, Sublet de Noyers, etc. Courtiers' pensions, the salaries of officials newly created during Louis XIII's reign, and all the "minor charges" introduced in addition to and in excess of the taille, should be abolished. The taille, the *taillon*, and the long-established charges should be enough for the defense of the realm. The peasants pay these taxes punctually, and should they prove not to suffice, they "are willing to contribute with all that remains to them."

The only thing is that they want the present centralization of government and the present despotism to stop: "They insist that they would prefer to die rather than continue any longer under the tyranny of the Parisians. . . . The gentlemen in Paris or in the Council laugh at their sufferings." They have had to revolt in order that "their cries may reach the ears of the King himself and no longer just those of his Ministers, who advise him so badly." The ministerial regime, embodied in a favorite, whether it be Richelieu or Mazarin, was never popular. The peasants will not pay if they are taxed by "the ministers of the present state, who should no longer have the right to impose new taxes or charges on the people as they please, that being a right that ought to be reserved for use only in extreme emergencies and then by the States-General, as was the case in former times."

The peasants do not wish the king to suppose that they are

traitors or men who want to subvert the existing order. In this time of war with Spain, when the government was constantly in fear of a Spanish landing on the Atlantic coast, they "affirm that they are good Frenchmen." Similarly, in this time of revolts by the princes of the blood and the grandees, "they place on record that they will not receive into their company any prince or lord disaffected from the King's Court."

These peasants are thus people who want to see a return to the good old customs. They say explicitly that they are willing to pay the taxes which have become customary, and that they will pay fresh ones if the States-General, convened specially for this purpose, acknowledge the need for them and agree to them, as was the custom in former times. It is implied that they want a king who governs on his own, according to old custom. It is noteworthy that they do not ask for any innovation, either in the political system—such as regular meetings of the States-General, a king's council composed of members elected by the States-General, or supervision by the States-General of the government's policy and administration—or in the social system—such as an end to the principle of unequal liability to taxation, a fundamental feature of this "society of orders," or any far-reaching changes in the seignorial and feudal regimes. It is striking that there is nothing here that relates to lordships and fiefs. The only sign to be found of any desire for social change, for equality, might be that sword worn by the peasants even while at the plow—that sword which was the social symbol of the gentleman. However, this can be quite well accounted for by the state of civil war and the need to be always ready to fight. Everything indicates that these peasants were satisfied to remain within the existing social order and forms of property. Leaving aside the program, though, one article in the decisions adopted by the general assembly at Baignes on July 17, 1636, suggests that, in fact, an unknown number of peasants were no longer paying the seignorial dues to the gentry and other lords.[11] On the other hand, we do not observe any attacks on the *châteaux* and homes of the gentry.

Meanwhile, revolt was flaming up in Poitou as well. According

11. Bibl. Nat., Ms. fr. 15 530, f. 666.

to Villemontée, it started so early as the beginning of May, seven leagues from Nantes, in the marshes of Rié and Monts, and then extended over most of Poitou.[12] The trouble spread to Limousin. There were rebels in action even as far away as Le Blanc, in Berry. A rumor circulated in Paris that the royal and municipal officials in Poitiers were promoting the revolt.[13] The rebels had drawn up an "ordinance of the peasants of Poitou," copies of which were circulating widely. "The assembly of the common people, having taken counsel, has ordained the following."[14] The peasants organized a commune of all the parishes. The latter had to obey the orders of the commune on pain of being treated as refractory, and devastated—which implies that not all the parishes or all the peasants followed the rebels' lead voluntarily. The revolt was probably the work of a minority more vigorous than the generality of the peasants. All the inhabitants of each parish were obliged to possess arms and to be well furnished with powder and shot, on pain of a fine of twenty livres. The commune needed officers for its troops, and so certain copies of the ordinance include these words: "We instruct each parish to make all the gentlemen march with them and give support with their arms, on pain of having their houses burned and not receiving their rents and *agrières*," that is, their payments in kind from the harvests. This Article Five, which is absent from the oldest of the copies we have[15] and is to be found only in those made at the end of the century, gives a picture of a dictatorship of the commoners over the nobles, and use by the former of the latter, as military technicians, to serve the aims of the commoners. Should we speak of a dictatorship of the "proletarianized masses"?

The parishes were assigned the duty of stopping the *gabeleurs* from doing their work, and punishing them. This meant, first, the *élus*, who were accused of having imposed on the people, for their own profit, 60,000 livres of taxation in excess of what the king had ordered should be levied. They were to be "taken by the commune so as to have justice done to them at the commune's convenience

12. Memorandum, quoted in n. 9, p. 1096.
13. P. Boissonnade, *op. cit.*, p. xliv.
14. P. Séguier, II, pp. 1105–1107.
15. Bibl. Nat., Dupuy, 473, f. 253.

and be forced to make good the notorious thefts they have committed, with interest." The parishes were to arrest "those who are alleged to have demanded the alienated dues, the eighths at the rate of fifteen livres per cask, gabelle or other taxes *newly* imposed," that is, the new increases in the taille and in indirect taxes.

Henceforth, every parish had to apportion the burden of taille in the presence of the priest, the conscience of the parish, but without the rich being present, and to do this so as to lighten the burden on "God's poor" and lay "the taille on those who have the means to pay it," in particular the rich and their farmers, which would perhaps imply an attempt at introducing a proportional and even progressive form of tax, with reduction of liability at the lowest levels, imposed by a democratic assembly of the poorest people. The inhabitants had to reduce the taxes themselves and assess only three-quarters of the amount of the taille demanded by the king, and only "half of the *creue* for the garrisons, because this has increased by half in the last six years." This arithmetic need not, perhaps, be taken too literally.

The commune retained the tithes, but only for the benefit of the parish. The inhabitants were to levy "all the produce for the priest," and entrust it to two of the richest men of the parish, who would render a true account of it, doubtless because the custom was to appoint as churchwardens well-to-do people who, when necessary, contributed to the upkeep of the fabric out of their own pockets. The priest was to receive three hundred livres for his work, thus becoming a sort of functionary appointed by the inhabitants of the parish. The rest of the tithe "will be used for repairing the church and sustaining the poor of the parish."

In one way, the Poitevins went further than the Angoumoisins and the Saintongeais in their reforms. This people in arms, this assembly of poor men, using the gentlemen, the rich and the parish priest, in the common interest; this spontaneous reduction of the taxes; this new way of distributing the tax burden, intended to abolish the inequalities which favored the rich, and perhaps to establish a new inequality favoring the poor; this use of the tithe for the purpose of a sort of parish relief—all this is extremely democratic, in the manner of a kind of authoritarian democracy.

If these peasants of ours had raised themselves above the level of village considerations, their movements might have had far-reaching effects. They were not against religion or the ecclesiastical order, and they even reserved a place of honor for the parish priest. If, however, all the parishes of France had followed their example, all the beneficiaries of tithe—priests, bishops, or abbots—who were not resident in their parishes would have been deprived of their income from this source. A share would have been reserved for the officiating ministers and curates who performed the tasks of the nominal incumbents, or for those of the latter who actually themselves carried out these tasks in person. And the entire system that had resulted from the king's application of the Concordat of 1516, with the predominance in the church of courtiers and persons devoted to the king (more careful, doubtless, of the state's interests than of the church's) would have been transformed. And what would have happened if in all the parishes of the realm the payment of seignorial and feudal rents and dues had been made conditional on the lords carrying out the wishes expressed by the assemblies of the poorest?

However, the Poitevin peasants appear to have looked no further than their own villages. They had no plan for a hierarchy of elected democratic assemblies. One may even wonder if they ever perceived what their decisions implied—what an overturning of the social and political structure, the seignorial and feudal order, would mean. They say nothing about the monarchy or the government, about the orders and "estates" of the realm, or about the seignorial or feudal regimes. Why not? Was it because most of them were landowners, that is, possessed the *seigneurie utile* of their lands? Was it because some of them held fiefs, practically real landed estates? At all events, despite their greater boldness, these Poitevins do not seem, any more than the rest, to have envisaged a revolution in the social and political order, in the forms of property.

Meanwhile, Cardinal Richelieu, the chief minister of state, had received at Conflans the letter from Estancheau. The council discussed it. Richelieu proposed to the king, speaking on behalf of the council, on June 21 and 22, 1636, that the levying of the "alienated dues," which doubled the burden of the taille, be suspended, that a favorable reply be sent to Estancheau to calm the people's minds, and that reinforcements be despatched into

Angoumois—the regiments of La Meilleraie, of La Motte, and of Lusignan. These regiments would recruit men in Poitou and Limousin, reducing thereby the number of rebels, and then would suppress the revolt. The king approved these proposals.[16] On June 26 the king named the comte de Brassac, a member of the royal orders of chivalry and of the king's Council of State, as governor and lieutenant-general in his provinces of Saintonge and Angoumois, commanding the troops he was sending into the rebel provinces to fight against the risings and restore "complete tranquillity" and "our absolute authority."[17] On June 23 Richelieu wrote to M. Le Hauchard, *sénéchal* of Termerie, near Barbezieux, and to M. La Grange-Gendron, who had made it known that the rebels were ready to submit conditionally, that the latter must first give up their arms, go back home, and make "their supplications to His Majesty after the style of good subjects."[18]

As for the rebels, they continued to hold their assemblies, now here and now there, either in order to concentrate their forces or to exercise them. At the very moment when the king's government was making these decisions, the commune of Angoumois was meeting at the fair held in the market town of La Couronne, on June 24. The people of ten or twelve parishes of the *châtellenie* of Villebois, and of twenty other neighboring parishes, gathered at this place to the number of ten to twelve thousand men armed with muskets, pikes, scythes, and iron forks, and deliberated in a meadow in the midst of the town, until four in the afternoon. Their military organization was a very serious affair. They erected four barricades on the four main roads leading to La Couronne, and posted three hundred men to guard each one. In the meadow they formed themselves into four battalions. A sergeant of the company of the parish of Saint-Estèphe, in the *châtellenie* of Châteauneuf, killed one of his men "who did not act in accordance with his rank and offended against military discipline." Their hatred of the townsfolk had not disappeared: they killed a craftsman of Angoulême with a pistol shot.

On June 26 the rebels held a great conference and drew up the

16. Avenel, V, pp. 485 and 488.
17. Archives de la Guerre, A¹ 32, item 100.
18. Bibl. Nat., Ms. fr. 15 530, f. 665.

conditions on which they would submit: *"abolition,"* that is, an amnesty for themselves and those who had helped them, cancellation of the new taxes, handing over to them of the "abettors of the *gabeleurs"* and in particular of the *prévôt* of Saintonge, who had undertaken to raise a hundred horsemen armed with carbines in order to levy the taille and the "minor charges." "The majority of them insist that they will never submit until they have these pardons and cancellations, in proper form, in their hands."[19] Richelieu, however, required unconditional surrender. The conflict was far from over.

Meanwhile, in July, the king's forces began to arrive. Soubran, de Brassac's lieutenant, the *intendant* Villemontée, and the commissary La Force redoubled their efforts at negotiation and conciliation. The men of Blanzac, the original rebels, came to make their surrender at Angoulême and swore an oath of loyalty to the king before M. de Soubran. The peasants around Cognac calmed down and allowed provisions to enter the town. But M. de La Rochefoucauld, who by his presence and authority held the peasants of his estates in submission, left the district to go to Forges, the spa in Normandy. Immediately, their neighbors called on these peasants to take up arms. Many of them obeyed, and assembled at Matha, a market town in Saintonge, to the number of four or five thousand, shortly before July 17.[20] This was very serious. Their defection seemed to open a way for the rebellion to start spreading once more in the directions of La Rochelle and Poitiers.

In Paris, however, the comte de Brassac and the peasants' representatives had secured from the king both the amnesty and the cancellations of taxes. On July 17, 1636, a great general assembly was held at Baignes. It was attended by about 500 deputies from the *châtellenies* of Saintonge; 100 from the villages of the region of St-Jean d'Angély and Matha; and 4 deputies from Angoumois, including the parish priest of St-Laurent des Combes, a man named Galeteau who represented his parish and has left us a summary of the assembly's decisions.[21] The assembly was held

19. Letter from La Force to Séguier, June 26, 1636, P. Séguier, I, pp. 345–346.
20. Letter from La Force to Séguier, July 19, 1636, Séguier, I, p. 346.
21. Bibl. Nat., Ms. fr. 15 530, ff. 666–669.

with the permission of the comte de Jonzac. Present were the
rebels' representatives, M. de Galard and MM. the *sénéchaux* of
Barbezieux and Baignes, who had returned from Paris and spoke
on behalf of the comte de Brassac. They got the assembly to make
preparations for surrender. The assembly resolved that the provinces of Angoumois and Saintonge, which had committed the same
crime, should act together, with each of their *châtellenies* sending
one deputy. The deputies asked M. de Galard to fix a day and
hour for them to thank M. de Brassac for having obtained from
the king "pardon for the crimes that have occurred in this recent rising." Thus the rebels acknowledged their crime and the
king's mercy.

The rebels gave up all their means of action. They would never
again sound the alarm bell "to assemble the people in arms." They
would not hold any more assemblies or armed marches without
permission from the authorities. They would not henceforth
accuse anyone of being a *gabeleur* or *maltôtier*. They would allow
the tax-farmers of *"daces, gabelles, et imposts"* to rejoin their
families without fear. They would pay, as before, the seignorial
dues to the gentlemen and lords and the tithe to the churchmen.

In exchange for all this, the rebels would be allowed to present
their complaints. Each parish would draw up a list of its grievances.
The *cahiers* (mandates) of the several parishes would be consolidated into a *cahier* for each *châtellenie*. The *cahiers* of the
châtellenies would be brought together into one set for the
province of Saintonge and another for Angoumois. The levy of
the "minor charges, five *écus* per cask of wine, *daces* and *gabelles*"
was suspended. The innkeepers and tavern keepers would be compelled immediately to reduce the price of wine, since they would
no longer be paying the five *écus* per cask. The deputies held out
the hope of an abolition of taxes, of the minor charges and subsidies.

The priest Galeteau called upon his electors to send a copy of
these decisions to each of the parishes in their *châtellenie*, and one
to Châteauneuf, so that its people could do the same for their
châtellenie, with the aim of "promptly informing the men of
Blanzac and other places nearby" and ensuring that Angoumois
proceeded in step with Saintonge.

In accordance with these agreements, an assembly was held at Saintes, on August 20, 1636, with delegates from all the *châtellenies* of Saintonge and Angoumois. There, the comte de Brassac and the *intendant* Villemontée announced officially the postponement of the "alienated charges" and received the representations of the "syndics and deputies of the Third Estate."[22] It was no longer a matter of the peasants alone. If the Third Estate was really involved, then the officials, the liberal professions, the merchants, the townspeople, and some lords were included.

These representations were first and foremost a deed of surrender. Mentioning the burden of taxes which had "reduced them to such helplessness and need that at last despair drove them into commotions whereof they confess themselves greatly guilty before His Majesty," the syndics beg for the latter's mercy.

Then, however, they go on to stress with pride their vital importance for the estates of the realm and for the state itself. They are "the liver of the body politic which distributes the blood to the other organs, and so *their fortunes are inseparable from His Majesty's magnificence.*" They have indeed the justified feeling that the power of the state and the glory of the monarch depend upon them, while at the same time their destiny depends on the power and authority of the state.

Next, they explain their position. They have never refused to pay the great taille, the *taillon,* the salary of the *vicesénéchal,* or the *creue* for the garrisons, that is, the old-established taxes that have become customary. But they wish to pay them only at the level they stood at in 1610, at the end of Henry IV's reign, that is, at a very much reduced level, and they call for the remission of all their arrears of payment back to October 1, 1636. Did they appreciate that they were by implication calling for an end to the war, the abandonment of the king's entire policy, renunciation of the alliances with the Protestant states, and surrender to the Hapsburgs?

They also ask for all the "alienated minor charges" to be abolished: those who had acquired them had already recovered their investment, through their enjoyment of the income from

22. *Ibid.,* ff. 675, v. of 681.

these charges. They demand the cancellation of all the "recently introduced" taxes on livestock, both cloven-hoofed and otherwise, on fish both fresh and salted, on iron, steel, and paper, the tax of one *sol pour livre* on goods being taken to fairs, that of two *liards* per livre for the right of conveyance, the toll established at La Rochelle, the annual levy on beverages, and so on.

They justify these demands by reference to their poverty due to the taxes they have had to pay. Actually, they say, the contracts for farming the tithes in the parishes and *châtellenies* show that the king asks much more from them, in taille and other charges, than their total income amounts to. The tithe of all produce which is levied at Louzin amounts to 1,000 livres a year, so that the locality's produce is valued at 10,000 livres, and yet Louzin pays 10,000 livres in taille, "to which if we add the cost of seed, expense of cultivation, ploughing and harvesting, rents and *terrages* to the lords, and if we also take into consideration that in these parishes the ecclesiastics, gentlemen and other privileged persons have many properties which are exempt from paying the taille, although they have to pay tithes, it will be clearly seen that nothing is left to your poor suppliants, and that in order to feed themselves and be able to pay the said taille during the last ten or twelve years, *they have had to borrow and fall into debt, or mortgage their land to townspeople or to the privileged persons of the locality*; and to this must be added the great harassment they suffer from collectors, process servers and bailiffs of the taille, who take for a first summons six, seven, eight, fifteen or sixteen livres, depending on how far the commissaries are from the *élections*, although the collectors mentioned take 66 sols 6 deniers (i.e., 3 livres, 6 sols, 6 deniers) as a due which is allotted to them and included in the commissions for these summonses; and there is also the oppression by the soldiers, who live as they please, without keeping to their authorized march-routes and halting-places." And they call, of course, for the abolition of the dreadful "joint obligation," which made it permissible to compel a taxpayer, who had already paid his own share, to make up for what could not be got from insolvent taxpayers in the same area, and thereby to ruin him as well.

They stress the need to reduce the tax on each cask of wine transported by the river Charente, to the same level as that charged on the river Garonne, in the Bordeaux district. Their neighbors in fact sold their wine with greater ease and at higher prices, because the tax they paid was less heavy, they were closer to the sea, and they themselves undertook the task of selling their produce abroad, carrying it in their own ships; whereas the petitioners' wine was left on their hands, because the charges it had to bear were heavier and because the whole trade was controlled by "outsiders." The petitioners had to sell their wine at very low prices for "distilling and conversion into brandy"; the country was thereby stripped of wood for fuel and its metal industries consequently suffered; the agents of the outsiders monopolized the entire trade, to the disadvantage of the merchants and "proprietors"—a term that could mean lords as well as others.

The petitioners asked also for a reduction in the charges levied on a cask of wine when sold retail; namely, that the charge of 15 livres per cask be brought down to the level of the "one-eighth" tax, and that the "one-eighth" and "one-twenty-fourth" taxes, which had to be paid over and above the 15 livres, be consolidated and reduced to 5 livres per cask. The reason was that, on account of these charges, the peasant was left with his wine unsold, and most of the vineyards lay fallow.

The petitioners protested against the administrative centers of the demesne which, set up on the pretext of supervising trade and industry, actually paralyzed both. They wanted to see eliminated the official brokers who had been appointed to deal with the sale of wine and livestock, because, by taking 6 sols for each cask of wine, or for each mule, they brought trade to a standstill. Because it was necessary to call upon them to be present at each transaction, a possible buyer, grown weary of waiting, would often go away and the opportunity of a sale would be lost. The petitioners asked for abolition of the tax of 5 sols charged whenever the official supervisors visited a linen weaver, carpenter, joiner or "retail merchant"; they asked for a reduction in the salt tax, and for free sale and use of salt. Finally, at a time when distraint of the houses, fields, and livestock of debtors was a frequent occurrence, they asked for mitigation of the charges demanded by the commissaries who carried out these distraints and the clerks who recorded them.

These representations, which throw so vivid a light on the

economic and social state of the province, did not go anywhere near as far as the programs put forward earlier by the rebels. These are the moderate demands of defeated men. They are purely fiscal. Without this being said in so many words, they correspond to the interests not only of the peasants but also of the lords, whether gentlemen, officials, or merchants, either directly, since the lords sold the wine produced on their "home farms" without prejudice to their noble status, or indirectly, because the relief accorded to their peasants would render more certain the payment of their rents and dues. Fundamentally, it was indeed the case that the interests of the entire Third Estate were involved here, together with those of the lords. What proves this is the attitude taken up by the peasants. The king abolished the charge of a *sol pour livre*, but he left in force the "alienated minor charges" on the taille and the 15 livres per cask of wine sold retail. These were the taxes that affected the peasants above all. "Because they carried on among themselves very little trade in articles that were subject to the said *sol pour livre*, the introduction of this tax had not greatly embittered them." In the main, the abolition of the *sol pour livre* was of interest above all to the towns, to the merchants and the gentlemen who sold wholesale the produce of their "home farms" or who engaged in metalworking, activities which were not incompatible with their status as nobles. "This forced them (the peasants) to be always sounding the alarm-bell in one parish or another, in order to make the tax-collectors run away." In September, 1636, they remained "all ready to take up arms again not only as soon as they should be called upon to make payment, but even as soon as they were deprived of hope of obtaining the abolition of all the things that were harmful to them."[23] The king therefore had M. de La Rochefoucauld continue with his levying of troops, not only in order to have armed forces present in the province but also to provide a livelihood for gentlemen, in the cavalry, and for peasants and craftsmen, in the infantry; and he further excused the nobles of payment of the taxes imposed in lieu of the *arrière-ban*.

Order, however, was never fully restored. The taille was not paid. Rebellion broke out again in Saintonge, Angoumois, Aunis, and Lower Poitou, where the marshmen fell upon the *gabeleurs*.

23. Letter from La Force to Séguier, September 17, 1636, P. Séguier, I, p. 347.

In the *élections* of Les Sables d'Olonne and Mauléon (Châtillon-sur-Sèvre), the peasants refused to pay the taille. In Upper Poitou three tax-farm agents had their throats cut in a single month. The rising of the *Croquants* of Périgord in April, 1637, and their capture of Bergerac in May rekindled the revolt of the *Croquants* of Angoumois. The *intendant* Villemontée and the king's lieutenant Des Roches-Baritaud had to hasten to the rescue with their troops, the regiment of La Meilleraie and the carabiniers of Combisans. They subdued the men of the marshes of Rié and Monts in June, 1637. In November, after the defeat of the *Croquants* of Périgord, Villemontée was able to announce to the *échevins* of Poitiers that all the *Croquants* had been beaten and that the leader of those of Angoumois and Saintonge, La Feuille, had been captured, along with ten or twelve of his lieutenants. Villemontée had the chief leaders of the *Croquants* executed at Angoulême—in particular the legal practitioner d'Estancheau, who had written the letter to Richelieu and drawn up the conditions on which the peasants had agreed to submit.

Nevertheless, sporadic disturbances continued in Saintonge and Angoumois. There were still "frequent commotions, with murders of process-servers reported." In August, 1642, "the *Croquants* went and killed six process-servers in cold blood in a hostelry, and went on to besiege a certain Lambert, formerly *président* in the *élection* of Angoulême, in a house in the country," and to slaughter this unfortunate old man. Villemontée had their leader broken on the wheel in September and put forty of his accomplices in "severe imprisonment." In January, 1643, two hundred peasants assembled in arms. The comte de Jonzac and Villemontée caused them to be attacked, and captured some of them, two of these being broken on the wheel at Cognac. Thirty days before Easter, a "rabble" of two to three hundred *Croquants* attacked a force of fifty foot-soldiers and twenty carabiniers, headed by their captain, at Barbezieux; they were beaten off and "more than fifty killed on the spot."

In October, 1643, however, the regent introduced a new tax of 20 sols per hogshead of wine, known as the "*écu* per sea-cask." The nobility of Saintonge wished to hold an assembly at Saintes. The comte de Jonzac forbade the meeting, but the gentlemen gathered in the suburbs of the town and nominated twelve "wise men," including the marquis de La Caze, and a delegate to go to the Court, the sieur de Chasteaucouvert, with instructions to address himself to the comte de Brassac. Several gentlemen urged that they begin by attacking the tax office at Tonnay-Charente and seizing the money to be found there. The gentlemen of Angoumois assembled at the market town of Montignac-Charente, three leagues from Angoulême, and likewise nominated twelve "wise men," with a delegate to go to the Court. They called for abolition of the new tax and retention of the privileges of the nobility. The gentlemen of these two provinces signed a covenant (ligue) and nominated syndics with power to convoke a general assembly; each gentleman was to draw up a "list showing how many men he would be able to provide from his parish—whether on foot or on horseback, and how armed—and if need be to seize the taille money in order to pay them." Reprisals were to be taken against the intendants and governors. The gentlemen of Saintonge and Angoumois approached those of Poitou to hold an assembly on December 15, 1643, in the town of Lusignan, at which delegates from Saintonge, Angoumois, and Aunis should be present. They proposed that a general and a body of officers should be chosen by this assembly, for an army of fifteen to twenty thousand men with the task of capturing La Rochelle. Warned of this plan, the comte de Parabère prevented the holding of the intended assembly and patrolled the area with the prévôts, while Villemontée made sure of the loyalty of Poitiers with the help of the bishop (who feared a Huguenot rising), the magistrates of the Présidial and the municipality. A promise was given that the wine tax would be canceled, but a rumor got about that the government was going to impose a tax of 3 sols per bushel of grain, and levy a tithe on hay. During these events, "the Croquants revived, and killed two or three of the guards of the said sieur de Jonzac, and chased away the process-servers and tax-collectors' clerks, after mortally wounding them."[24]

It may be that the movements of the gentry and those of the

24. P. Boissonnade, op. cit., pp. xlvi–lii; Y.-M. Bercé, op. cit., pp. 219–222; letter from La Force to Séguier, from Angoulême, August 28, 1636, P. Séguier, II, pp. 296–299; memorandum by Villemontée, Séguier, II, pp. 1097–1103.

Croquants, occurring one after the other or at the same time, were unconnected—that, while the gentry and the *Croquants* gave each other incitement and encouragement by mutual example, these social strata operated independently, without any actual alliance between them. It is certainly notable that the documents do not reveal any participation by the gentry in the *Croquant* risings in 1636. However we do not find that there was any opposition by the gentry to the *Croquants,* either. This situation may be explicable as due to fear, together with a conflict of interests which was profound even though masked by the common hostility of both groups to royal taxation. But as we do not observe the *Croquants* attacking the *châteaux* or fortified houses of the gentry, their only victims being officials of the royal finances, fiscal agents, taxfarmers and their employees, or persons who had been mistaken for such, it must be admitted that the view expressed by the *intendant* Villemontée, regarding the complicity and even the participation of "many ecclesiastics and gentlemen" in these popular movements, is not without some foundation. Villemontée's motive in prosecuting only a few people of low social standing was his desire to restore tranquillity. If he had been obliged to charge numerous members of the higher orders, the provinces concerned would have been in a state of *lèse-majesté.* The punishment for that crime would be deprivation of their privileges;[25] and that would have entailed the risk of unleashing an interminable and relentless civil war.

Undoubtedly the revolt of the *Croquants* did shake the government into a state of alarm, since in 1637 there appeared declarations by its faithful subjects, published in Paris by F. Mettayer, printer in ordinary to the king, which reek of official propaganda. The "inhabitants of the town of Poitiers" denounce "the plot by the seditious commune of Périgord." "We know, as Christians and loyal Frenchmen, that the glory of Kings is to command, while the glory of subjects, whoever they may be, is to obey in all humility and willing submission . . . following God's express commandment." The entire family of a monarch—mother,

25. See *La Declaration du Roy Louis XIII contre les Criminels de Lèze-Majesté,* Saint-Germain-en-Laye, January 19, 1633; Bibl. Nat., Ms. fr. 18 424, f. 2.

brothers, sisters, uncles, aunts—must obey him, and likewise "all
princes, dukes, counts, barons and other subjects of whatever
rank." All the people of the provinces of this realm of France
declare to the king that the state has "no other life or soul" but
his. "By the superhuman decisions of your royal mind and the
miracles accomplished in your happy reign, we perceive plainly
that God holds your heart in his hand." As to "your prudent and
most eminent Council," it is "the Holy Spirit that guides it in all
situations." The rebels could thus only be tools of Satan. Finally,
the "nobility of France," it seems, caused to be printed in Paris,
by Jean Brunet, in the Rue Neufve Saint-Louys, at the Crosse
d'Or, a fine manifesto, "To The King." The nobles wished to
"ensure forever, by a triumphant victory, the conservation of the
state and the tranquillity of this realm . . . in acknowledgement
of the rights and powers that they receive from His Majesty," who
did not wish to "reduce and subject them to mechanical tasks,"
not because the nobles were "of a nobler nature," but in order that
they might apply themselves "entirely to the exercise of arms."
"So that the fact that the nobility are the creation of the sovereign
of this realm, holding from him their liberties and privileges, is
indeed the reason why they relate all their achievements to the
advantage and support of the leader from whom they derive their
essential quality and sustenance." This declaration that the nobility
did not exist of themselves but were a creation of the state cannot
have been written by a noble: it is the work of some lawyer in the
service of the council. But how frightened the government must
have been!

[4]

The *Croquants* of Périgord—1637

IN 1637 THE *Croquants* of Périgord rose, in their turn, in dangerous revolt. Why had they not risen in 1636, at the height of the revolt in Angoumois and Saintonge? Why this dispersal of effort? Possibly because the revolt in Périgord was brought about by Saintongeais who had become available for such activity. Letters from the king, dated July 20, 1637, to Villemontée and Des Roches-Baritaud tell us that a large number of peasants from Saintonge had joined the rebels in Périgord and that, after their defeat, though the majority had returned to Saintonge for the harvest, many were still absent.[1]

In Périgord, a poor district, with dense forests and winding roads, where it was hard to get about, a district scattered with castles situated in impregnable positions, and inhabited by gentlemen who were arrogant and refractory and wielded great influence over their peasants, rebellion against royal taxation was endemic. The revolt of 1637 started in a naturally rebellious region, Le Pariage, near the forest of Vergt, the inhabitants of which carried on a sort of perpetual war against the royal officials of Périgueux, both those of the *sénéchaussée* and those of the *élection*, and against the townfolk, those people who en-

1. Arch. Guerre, A¹ 38, nos. 19 and 28.

joyed exemption from paying the taille. In April, 1637, the
Croquants besieged and captured, in a castle belonging to M. de
Peiramon, Jean de Jay, esquire, sieur d'Ataux, *lieutenant particulier*
in the *sénéchaussée* and mayor of Périgueux. They then held a
great assembly at the pond of La Vernède, near Bordes, in the
commune of Grun and the canton of Vergt. A huge crowd of
peasants came from all parts of the district. They resolved to
arm themselves, take control of the province, and put an end
to the doings of the *gabeleurs*.

They then marched on Périgueux and burned, just opposite
the Taillefer gate, the house of André d'Alesme, esquire, deputy
registrar in the *élection* of Périgueux, that of Jean Vincenot
and that of Jean Salleton, collectors of taille in the *élection* of
Périgueux. Pierre de Bessot relates how—his father, inspector
in the *élection* of Périgueux, having become that year first consul
at Périgueux—"our farm buildings at Pissot were burnt down,
along with the house of the farmer at Les Landes and all
the livestock that were there."[2] Pissot is a parish in the canton
of Vergt. The *Croquants* held a second assembly at Les Terriennes,
near Périgueux, between May 1 and 6, 1637, at which seven or
eight thousand men were present. Among them, it is said, were
numerous former soldiers. They there elected as their leader
a gentleman who lived at Château-Barrière, within the city of
Périgueux, Antoine du Pruy, sieur de La Mothe La Forest. Also
among the leaders of the *Croquants* we find Léon d'Albert
de Laval, lord of Madaillan de la Sauvetat, who came of an
old family of gentlefolk going back to the 13th century. The
government regarded as one of the *Croquant* leaders Pierre
Bouchard d'Esparbès de Lussan, marquis d'Aubeterre, in Saintonge, who had already been compromised in the revolt of 1636.[3]
The *Croquants* went on to attack Périgueux, in order to get
possession of the cannon that were there. The chief finance
officials had fled. The bourgeois shut the gates and resisted
the assault, even though their houses outside the city walls had
been burnt. The peasants did not press their attack.

2. Day-book of Pierre de Bessot, 1609–1652, ed. Tamisey de Larroque, in
Bull. de la Soc. Hist. et Archéol. du Périgord, XX (1893), pp. 85, 88.
3. La Force, letter to Séguier, August 28, 1636, P. Séguier, I, p. 298.

La Mothe La Forest gave "commissions and mandates" to the parishes of all Périgord to rally on May 10 at the heath of Pleistadiou. Apparently, about 30,000 men assembled there. La Mothe La Forest retained only the best-armed of them and sent the rest home. He then, it seems, had under his command either 6,000 or 7,000 men or 15,000. With them he attacked Bergerac. On May 13, 1637, he took by surprise a town whose fortifications had been dismantled in 1630 after the defeat of the Protestants and which still felt the effects of the famine and plague of 1631, when two-thirds of the poorer people had died—a town, moreover, which was without munitions. The mayor, a nobleman, Anthoine de Gatebois, esquire, sieur de Marcilhac, had fled. The other consuls decided to stay in office, "to serve the King and do their duty." On May 14 they refused La Mothe La Forest's demand that they take up arms, join him, fortify the city, rebuild the bastions and agree to a loan for the upkeep of his army, on the grounds that "they were the King's faithful subjects . . . all this being contrary to the King's service . . . and that it was not for him (La Mothe La Forest) to relieve the oppressed people, assuming that they were oppressed." On May 15, La Mothe La Forest ordered all the inhabitants of Bergerac to go and work on the fortifications. It is said, however, that the officials and the rest of the inhabitants withdrew to a league's distance, to the marquisate of La Force, where the officials continued to carry out their responsibilities.[4]

La Mothe La Forest tried to organize the revolt by means of a series of decisions and orders dated May 15, 1637.[5] "The Commune of Périgord" first set forth the motives and aims of the revolt: "Sire . . . , we have taken an unusual step in the way we have expressed our grievances, but this is so that we may be listened to by Your Majesty, and our arms have been raised only because of the necessity that makes all things permis-

4. "La Prise de la Ville de Bergerac," Bureau d'Adresses, Bibl. Nat., L.b. 36–3117, octavo. Elie de Biran, "Soulèvement des Croquants en Périgord (1636–1637)," in *Bull. de la Soc. Hist. et Archéol. du Périgord*, IV (1877), pp. 325–341. Dupuy, 473 f., 246 recto-251 verso.

5. Ms. fr., 15, 530, f. 682 recto-689 verso.

sible . . ." The financiers "have sent among us a thousand
thieves who eat up the flesh of the poor husbandmen to the
very bones, and it is they who have forced them to take up
arms, changing their ploughshares for swords, in order to ask
Your Majesty for justice or else to die like men." It is the
taxes, first and foremost, which have caused the movement.
For the past twenty years the men have been exhausted by
"paying your tailles, which have increased to such an extraordinary extent that our small incomes are much less than the
taxes we are called upon to pay . . . . We have given more
than we are able to bear." But they cannot go on paying, owing
to the difficult economic situation: "since trade has ceased,
since cattle, wine and chestnuts have no longer had any outlet
beyond our borders, this province has been unable, in order
to continue tax payments, to change stones into bread, or ferns
into silver, or by our ceaseless toil to meet a thousand new charges
that were unknown to our fathers." This last point was as
serious as the excessive amount of the tax: the king was demanding from them something that lacked the sanction of
custom.

Besides the taxes there were the soldiers. "The soldiers . . . have
indulged in every imaginable kind of cruelty: setting fire to their
hamlets, carrying off their daughters, raping their wives before
the very eyes of the poor husbands, bound and subjected to
torture. . . . These harpies take everything, just as though this
province of yours were a conquered country."

The peasants felt their human dignity wounded. The King's
Council did not listen to their complaints: "It is as if we
were no more thought of than rubbish." The king's councillors
decided their fate, and they had "thenceforth no right to express consent to their demands." The peasants therefore humbly
begged the king: abolish these "new charges, remove from us
these finance officials, make this province a *pays d'états,*" and
allow them a syndic "to convey our grievances to Your Majesty."
These were noteworthy demands, for the idea of provincial states
taking over the responsibility of assessing and levying taxes, with
a permanent representative at the king's Court, was something
of interest to the clergy, the nobility and the entire Third Estate
no less than to the peasants themselves. Do we see here an

alliance between the peasants and the other orders, or use being made of the peasant movement by the gentlemen who perhaps had unleashed in it the first place?

The king would benefit, because the money levied would all go into his coffers, and in addition the peasants offered to serve for three months against "your enemies who have entered the Kingdom."

The revolt was organized by another decision of the commune. The general had "complete power to command" and to convene assemblies, to decide on measures to be taken and on the use of force against property and persons. The general "in his council" would judge all the "persons hostile to the people's liberty who had agreed to the general over-taxation and extraordinary and unauthorized taxes," these persons to be delivered to him by the captains of the communities. The captains would oblige their men to take an oath to serve them. All their soldiers would be "equipped and supplied with food and money, each at his own expense"—which meant that the poorer peasants would be kept out of the rebel army. The captains would take care to "keep vice out of their companies." Blasphemy would be forbidden, along with everything that might tend "against the honour and glory of God." "The priests and all the clergy will exhort the people to pray to God." An army of well-to-do peasants, disciplined and organized hierarchically, showing respect to persons and property, Christian, concerned with morality —this was what the army of the commune of Périgord ought to be.

By virtue of these decisions, La Mothe La Forest, "general of the Commune of Périgord, most humble, obedient and loyal servant of the King," issued orders, directed the communes to arm, gave safe-conducts to merchants (for example, to Jehan Mousnier and Jehan Cénémaul, merchants, of the town of Limoges, to proceed from Limoges to Bergerac and back for the purposes of their business), and invited the noblemen of Périgord to join the commune, "well knowing that the right arm in warfare is the nobility."

On May 24, 1637, extending his authority as "general of the united communes of Guyenne," he commanded fifteen designated communes, "with others bordering upon them, to arm themselves promptly in order to report to us in the town of Bergerac, within ten days, with as many men and as much provisions as they can"; he ordered their consuls "to oblige those unable to bear arms to contribute to the maintenance of the others," and all those "who possess money or grain resulting from the extraordinary taxes levied on the people during the last two years . . . to bring it to us," for the maintenance of the soldiers. Signed: "The general of the Communes of Périgord, Agenais and other communities of Guyenne and lower down, by command of my said lord, La Franchise, secretary, and alongside this sealed in red wax with the seal and armorial bearings of the said lord general."

Already, however, La Mothe La Forest had lost his nerve. Like the chief rebels of Angoumois and Saintonge, he had the grievances and wishes of the rebels set before the king by great nobles of the province, and endeavored to secure the king's mercy and alleviations of taxation. He wrote to the king on May 28, 1637, from the town of Eymet, that the communes of Guyenne "have forced me to stand at their head, in which position I have done my best to ensure that they undertook nothing contrary to Your Majesty's service." He announced that he was sending M. de Bourdeille, lord of Brantôme, governor of Périgord, uncle of the marquis, and also the Vicomte d'Aubeterre and M. de la Brosse, the *vicesénéchal*.[6] In short, he looked upon this revolt as something like the "warning strikes" called by trade union leaders in a later period.

Meanwhile, the duc d'Épernon, governor of Guyenne, was ill in his château of Cadillac. He had only three regiments at his disposal, and they were in process of reorganization. The citadel of Sainte-Foy was crammed with weapons and guns, armed with which the rebels would have been able to make themselves masters of the towns along the Garonne. D'Épernon sent there, first, a member of his guard, Codéré, and then one of his gentlemen, named Triget, with 150 soldiers. They revived the spirits of the inhabitants, who on May 15 repulsed a column of peasants sent against them by La Mothe La Forest.

The latter then tried to march down into Agenais by the valley of the Dropt. They took first Eymet, then La Sauvetat d'Eymet.

6. Arch. Aff. étr., Mem. et Doc. France, 827, f. 61 recto.

The communes of Agenais rallied to the rebels, and D'Épernon was warned that certain towns were ready to open their gates to them.

The duke called to his aid his second son, Bernard de Nogaret, duc de la Vallette, who commanded against the Spaniards, before Saint-Jean-de-Luz, the regiments of Guyenne and Mun, "made up of servants of his father the duke and of himself, and maintained by their own money," together with their cavalry company and two companies of light horse. With these scanty forces La Vallette had halted the Spaniards and prevented invasion. La Vallette went to Bordeaux to provide himself with artillery, reported to his father for orders at Cadillac, then proceeded to Marmande, where the duke had caused some troops of soldiers and some gentlemen to assemble, under the orders of the marquis de Montferrant, *maréchal de camp*, lieutenant of his company of cavalry. The vanguard of the rebels, commanded by Madaillan, was four leagues from Marmande, at La Sauvetat, where they had "enclosed themselves . . . on all sides either with walls or with stout barricades." La Vallette marched on them with 2,500 men, and, risking everything on one throw, so as not to allow the rebels time to regroup their forces, or to encourage them by seeming to show fear, he gave the order to attack without waiting for the artillery to come up, on June 1, 1637. It was a deadly conflict. La Vallette's soldiers attacked boldly, clearing "a way with their halberds, which they used instead of cannon, to overthrow the barrels and to jump over them." The rebels had no pikes, and when they had fired their muskets they were left no time to reload. The barricades were taken. From the adjoining houses, however, the rebels continued to fire on the soldiers, "with . . . slaughter and butchery of our men." Twenty-five houses had to be set on fire in order to drive the rebels out of them and enable the soldiers to press on. A thousand *Croquants* were killed, many were wounded, and only forty taken prisoner, which testifies to their courage and zeal in battle. La Vallette had two hundred dead, of whom twenty were officers, and between three and four hundred wounded. Peasants, officers, and soldiers alike were fine and brave men.

The moral effect was enormous. A column of 6,000 *Croquants*,

who were scouring the country, marched to the aid of La
Sauvetat. They arrived an hour after the battle was over and
"had not the courage to approach." For his part, La Vallette
withdrew to Mimet, "a house belonging to M. le Comte de
Curson," a league distant from La Sauvetat. Nevertheless, he
knew how to take advantage of the impression made by his
victory. On their own initiative, moreover, "their principal leaders"
offered to lay down their arms in exchange for a guarantee of
their safety.[7] La Vallette sent as his representative, to talk with
La Mothe La Forest, the Marquis de Duras, who went to and
fro several times between Mimet and Bergerac. La Mothe La
Forest was also worked upon by his prisoner Le Jay, mayor of
Périgueux. Eventually he agreed that he, his companions, and
the peasants would all go back home in exchange for the single
promise that they would not be prosecuted and that the
d'Épernons would make it their business to persuade the king
to show mercy to them. La Mothe La Forest endeavored "to
dispose his companions to this submission." Then, however,
one of them, a doctor from Périgueux named Magot, denounced
him as a "traitor and false-hearted author of their ruin and
misery, seeking to surrender their freedom to the enemy." By
his outcries and clamors he rallied over a thousand of the
Croquants to his side. He "was already barricaded with his men
in the citadel of Bergerac." La Mothe La Forest went after
him there with as many of his own friends as he could bring,
and caused him to be put to death, by means of three pistol
shots and several halberd blows. After this, he evacuated Bergerac without a fight, crossed the Dordogne, and cut the bridge:
the *Croquants* then disappeared into the forests.

This was practically the end of the great revolt. Up to
this time, the duc de La Vallette had been helped only by
a few gentlemen, MM. de Montferrant, de Calonges, de Coutures,
d'Orgueil, de Langle, the comte de Langnac, the vicomte de
Ribeyrac, to whom the king expressed, as also to the duc d'Épernon
and the duc de La Vallette, "all the satisfaction that such an

7. La Vallette, letter to Richelieu, Bergerac, June 8, 1637, Arch. Nat. KK
1216 f. 182.

important success calls for."[8] After his victory, however, La Vallette found more than three hundred of them coming to join him. Later on, when he himself was being accused of having fomented or stirred up the revolt, he ascribed the passivity of the gentry to "the fear of suffering harm and damage from those people."[9]

Madaillan had fled to Quercy with some of the *Croquants*. He seized the castles of Mercuez and Le Bas, which had been left undefended. However, the duc de La Vallette sent the comte de Maillé to lay siege to them. After two or three days' resistance, Madaillan fled from Mercuez. The castle of Le Bas held out for a few days longer. The fugitives fled to Gramat, gathered reinforcements, seized the place and sacked it, killing some persons of standing. Next they attacked Figeac, but were driven off by a sortie. Their commander, Captain Vasque, was caught and executed. Molinier de Lacau, the duc d'Épernon's lieutenant, dispersed a body of 4,000 *Croquants* assembled between Belves and Monpazier by the weaver Buffarot. The *Croquants* had intended to seize Villeneuve and Villefranche-de-Rouergue. But nothing further happened beyond a few sporadic actions here and there, some outbreaks against the *élus* at Cahors and Figeac. The *prévôts* were able to scatter the last bands. In the Forest of Vergt the *Croquant* Grelety held out with about a hundred men until 1642. It was possible to dispatch the regular troops before 1637 was over into Saintonge and Poitou, where they put down the last revolts of the *Croquants*.

On the petition of the ducs d'Épernon and La Vallette, the king granted an amnesty in June to the rebels of Périgord, which the Parlement of Bordeaux registered on August 4. Excepted from its benefits were La Mothe La Forest, people charged with common-law crimes, such as Madaillan, and those *Croquants* who had been taken in arms at La Sauvetat and elsewhere. La Vallette had asked for commissioners to be sent by the Parlement of Bordeaux to try this last group. The Parlement sent two councillors, who conducted the trial jointly with the officers of the Présidiaux. Two *Croquants* were beheaded, two

8. Arch. Guerre, A¹ 37, nos. 173, 195, June 21, 1637.
9. Manifesto of December 14, 1638, Ms. fr., 3168, f. 9 recto.

were hanged, and one was broken on the wheel. In addition, Constantin de Besson, sieur des Marais, and Jean de Fettes (known as La Mothe Grignols) were beheaded at Bergerac; Antoine de Ribeyreix, sieur de Larthège, was beheaded at Périgueux; and the marquis d'Aubeterre was prosecuted. But the Parlement of Bordeaux did not show itself in any hurry to condemn the others. It even discharged some of them, causing the king to express his displeasure to the Parlement on September 1, 1637.[10]

10. Arch. Guerre, A¹ 39, nos. 13–14. On the revolt as a whole, É. de Biran, *op. cit.* Anonymous account, Bibl. Nat., Dupuy 473, ff. 255 verso-256 verso. G. Girard, *Histoire de la vie du duc d'Épernon* (Paris, Augustin Courbe, 1655), folio, pp. 553–557. Letters from Richelieu to the King, June 13, 18, 23, 1637. Aff. étr., Memo. et Doc., France, in Avenel, *Lettres*, V, pp. 786, 788. Letters from the King to d'Épernon, La Vallette and others, Arch. Guerre, A¹ 37, 173, 193, 195, 207, 211, June 13, 1637—A¹ 39, 271, October 26, 1637. E. Cábrol, *Annales de Villefranche de Rouergue* (Villefranche, 1860), II, p. 307.

[5]

The *Nu-Pieds* of Normandy—1639

THE REVOLTS THAT occurred in Normandy took place
in a province which had been exhausted by the "contagious
disease," that is, by the plague, and by the economic crisis that
resulted from it.[1] The plague lasted from 1619 to 1639, but
was especially severe in the years immediately preceding the
great revolt, and in the areas where the rebellion was strongest—
Avranches, Coutances, Caen, Rouen. At Condé-sur-Seulle in
July, 1635, there were only two households unaffected by it;
most of the inhabitants were dead, and the rest had fled to
Rouen or Paris. In the *élection* of Caen, the parish of Cully
had lost 95 taxpayers out of 158 between 1635 and 1637. In
the parish of Moulines, in the *élection* of Falaise, in 1636,
nearly all the persons liable to pay the taille were dead. The
élection of Coutances was especially badly affected.

The first result of the plague was an agricultural crisis: in

1. For the *Nu-Pieds* I have essentially relied on an account written by my
pupil Mlle Madeleine Foisil, submitted for the specialist doctorate (3rd
cycle), together with the classical sources, *Diaire où journal de voyage du
chancelier Séguier en Normandie après la sédition des Nu-Pieds et documents
relatifs à ce voyage et à le sédition*, ed. A. Floquet (Rouen, 1842); *Memoires
du président Bigot de Monville sur la sédition des Nu-Pieds et l'interdiction
du Parlement de Normandie en 1639*, ed. vicomte d'Estaintot (Rouen,
Société de l'Histoire de Normandie, 1876). (These are referred to henceforth
as *Diaire* and Bigot respectively.)

the parish of Piron, in the *élection* of Coutances, in 1636, the
number of deaths attained "367, which is nearly half of the
parishioners, and as a result of this plague their crops were
lost in the month of August following, being left in the fields
to rot or be eaten by animals, for lack of anyone to be found
who could harvest them, the greater part of the farm animals
having been carried off in the vehemence of this affliction";
and the plague went on until 1638. The second result was the
interruption of trade through the decline of all productive activities: "At Croselles, in the *élection* of Caen, because of this
(the plague) none of the inhabitants of the parish dares go
to any market to sell his produce in order to be able to pay
what he owes"—something which brings out very well the link
between trade, the acquisition of money, and the ability to
pay taxes and rents. The third result was the overburdening
of the survivors, who had to bear the liabilities of the dead
when taxes were assessed, and their inability to pay taxes and
dues.

This province was one of the most heavily taxed in the
kingdom. Bullion, the king's superintendent of finance, declared that in Normandy "there are three *généralités* which bear
almost a quarter of the tax burden of the entire realm." The
taille had increased very much, and, what was worse, had been
imposed by the absolute authority of the king, without any
convocation of the provincial states, ever since 1635. In 1638
the taille amounted to 2,442,444 livres. In addition there were
the *creues* and *subsistances*, bringing the total to 3,485,441 livres.
The taxpayers were no longer paying up. In 1639, out of 163
parishes taxed, 82 had not paid one denier of what they
owed. The parish of Cérences, hit by the plague, had been called
upon to pay taxes in 1637 of 4,158 livres, in 1638, 8,573 livres,
and in 1639, 6,704 livres. It was in arrears to the amount of 763
livres for 1637, 8,019 livres for 1638, and its entire liability for
1639. The parish did not pay; but the impression of being
crushed beneath an unbearable burden, of oppression and injustice, was still there. And the parish was already in revolt.
Here and there all over the region, the gentry and the magistrates were encouraging the people not to pay the taille, and
preventing the collectors from taking forcible measures.

The *subsistances* affected those who were subject to taille, and also the privileged towns (*villes franches* and *villes abonnées*). The inhabitants of the towns were also subjected in 1637 to a forced loan, and in 1639 to a tax on the well-to-do. The king demanded from Rouen, a town exempt from taille, 1,249,000 livres in three years, together with royal tolls on wine, herring, salmon, sugar, and wax, and on cider and perry, the drinks of the poor folk. All the towns had to levy tolls in order to raise the money needed for the loans. The tolls harmed the townspeople by raising prices and reducing consumption, which was already low by our standards; they harmed the peasants by forcing a reduction in the purchases made from them by the towns. Avranches, Coutances, Valognes, and Carentan refused to pay the loans. At Carentan the "chief men" of the town encouraged gatherings of the poor to revolt. The war hit Normandy hard, for since 1636, the year of Corbie, it had become a frontier province. The billeting of soldiers, with their halting places and winter quarters, weighed heavily upon it In 1638 several regiments took up their quarters in Normandy. There were troops all round Coutances in November, 1638, and the Scots regiment of Douglas was at Avranches, Granville, and Gavray. The officials of the *élections* and the canons of the cathedral churches of Avranches and Bayeux were ordered to provide billets for soldiers, regardless of their privileges. It was the same with the towns and parishes by the sea, even though they were supposed to be exempt because of their responsibility for guarding the coast.

The soldiers were expensive. The states of Normandy claimed that, as a rule, in a single month a garrison cost as much as a second levy of taille. Very often, moreover, the soldiers were not paid any subsistence money, and then they committed excesses, abuses, and malpractices to which the inhabitants replied with violence against them. There were many clashes. Here are some examples. On March 4, 1638, some of the men of Alençon fought with the marquis de Praslin's companies of light horse and *arquebusiers*. On November 21, 1638, at Verneuil, the mayor and *échevins* caused the alarm to be sounded, and the people armed against Cardinal Richelieu's

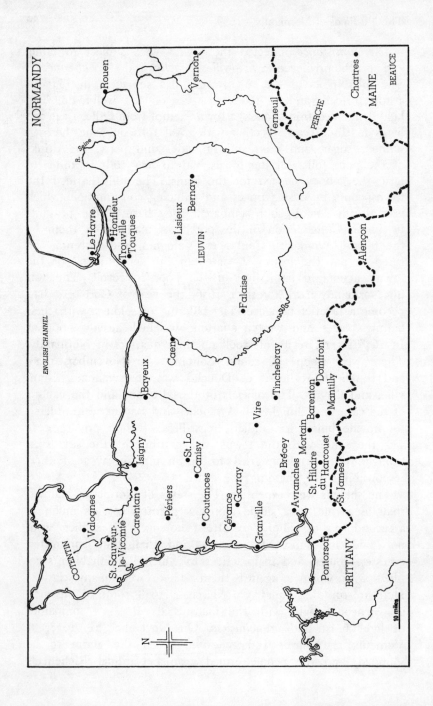

NORMANDY

Rouen

R. Seine

Vernon

Verneuil

PERCHE

Chartres
MAINE
BEAUCE

Le Havre
Honfleur
Trouville
Touques

Bernay

Lisieux

LIEUVIN

Alençon

Falaise

ENGLISH CHANNEL

Caen

Bayeux

Tinchebray

Domfront

Barenton

Mantilly

Vire

Isigny

St. Lo

Camisy

Brécey

Mortain

St. Hilaire
du Harcouet

Avranches

St. James

Périers

Coutances

Cérance

Gavray

Granville

Carentan

Valognes

COTENTIN

St. Sauveur-
le-Vicomte

Pontorson

BRITTANY

10 miles

N

company of light horse. At Périers, in the Cotentin, at the beginning of 1638, the *vicomte* of the place, that is, a royal judge equal in rank to a *prévôt*, Maître Bonaventure Leroux, incited the people of the town and those of the neighboring localities to take up arms against the companies of Hécourt and Jouy. The civilians attacked the soldiers and seized their horses and baggage. In the county of Mortain it was the gentlemen who surrounded these companies and those of Praslin.

But the province was also required actually to provide levies of troops from its own menfolk, which meant having to clothe and arm them and also to do without their labor in the fields and workshops. Caen had to raise a regiment of 1,000 men, the regiment of Matignon, and to provide it with pay and supplies. Each parish was responsible for furnishing three or four soldiers, together with their clothing and weapons. This cost each parish at least a hundred livres, and obliged them to borrow from private persons.

The nobles were affected in July, 1635, and again in January, 1639, by the summoning of the *ban* and *arrière-ban*. If a nobleman did not respond in person, he had to provide a substitute. Equipment, maintenance, and compensation amounted to a substantial sum. On another, later occasion, we hear the outcries of the Grignans and of Madame de Sévigné, who talked of becoming a bourgeoise of Paris.

Finally, in 1639 there were the Spanish prisoners. In July, between 1,000 and 1,2000 Spaniards, on their way to Flanders, were captured at sea by the Dutch fleet and put ashore in Normandy. They were dispersed to various places in Lower Normandy but guarded so carelessly that between July 3 and August 5 about six hundred of them escaped, at the very moment when Lower Cotentin revolted. We do not know whether they played any part in the events of the revolt.

The royal officials themselves were not spared by the government. There had been delay in the payment of salaries since 1636. In 1638 they were paid for only two quarters of the year, and in 1639 for only one quarter.

For the *paulette*—that annual payment, a sort of insurance premium for retention of office, which the officials considered so important—a new lease-period was announced in 1638, although the period begun in 1636 had not yet expired. In order to be allowed to pay their "premium," the officials had to advance a loan to the king, and the official valuation of all the offices, that is, the premium together with the conveyance charges, which were proportional, was raised by one quarter. The edict of August, 1638, granted the attorneys the right to bequeath their offices, but in April, 1639, the State Council sought to oblige them each to pay 1,500 livres in taxes, together with a 700-livre inheritance charge.

The officials received from the king a number of increases in salary, but these were always made conditional on their payment of corresponding taxes, which constituted the capital on which the new salaries were the interest. In short, these transactions were really so many forced loans.

Finally, the officials suffered from the creation of new offices, which reduced the value of the ones they held, since the new officials would share the "fees" and "taxations" with the old ones, and also because the cheapening of titles would reduce their prestige and dignity. The edict of September, 1635, created eight new offices in each Présidial; that of January, 1636, raised the former vicomtés to the status of vicomtés principales, with seven new officials in each. May, 1636, saw the creation of the généralité of Alençon, with fifty-seven new offices; July, 1638, that of the Cour des Aides at Caen, with ninety-three offices; and April, 1639, the élection of Saint-Lô, with forty-one offices.

The officials replied to all this by going on strike—by refusing to obey orders and rebelling. The attorneys abandoned the courts and refused to carry out their functions. They stirred up the litigants against the government. Those of Rouen took part collectively in violent acts in August, 1639, against Léonard Hugo, who was accused of being concerned in the farming of taxes imposed on them. The parlement of Rouen put off registering the edicts of September, 1635, and January, 1636, until March, 1637. It accepted only after a long delay the persons appointed to the new offices in the Présidiaux, and quite simply refused to accept those appointed to the new vicomté offices, so that the latter were unable to enter upon their duties. The old-established officials of the Présidiaux forcibly prevented the new ones from functioning. In 1639, the office for *aides* and *quatrièmes* at Rouen having been wrecked, the State Council accused the Rouen Cour des Aides of being responsible, through its hostility to the farmer of the *aides*, and on June 17 withdrew from it cognizance of all cases relating to privileges connected with drinks. The councillors of the Cour des Aides then swore to ruin the tax-farmer, and set themselves to stir up the wholesale merchants and tavern keepers.

In these circumstances there is nothing surprising in the fact that revolt was endemic in the towns and villages of Normandy, and this often at the direct instigation of the royal officials and the gentry. In 1633 an edict on hides and skins created a new office, that of an arbitrator who was to examine these materials and have them marked by an inspector, a tax being paid for this service, of course. It was a demesne due of a kind that would raise prices and put off customers. In 1634 a lieutenant of the *grand prévôt* of the king's household arrived in Rouen with the task of establishing an administrative center and a body of clerks to carry out marking and collecting of the tax. The parlement of Rouen rallied to the defense of the tanners and issued *arrêts* for these measures to be suspended. The King's Council quashed the *arrêts*. The tanners attacked the houses of the lieutenant and his archers and clerks. La Meilleraye, the governor of Rouen, was wounded.

A revolt of the playing-card makers broke out in the same year, over a tax on playing cards and tarot cards. An agent named Trotant who came to collect the tax was attacked by the mob and thrown into the Seine. Fished out, he was carried half-dead to the priory of Bonne-Nouvelle. The priory was at once besieged by a mob of men, women, and children who wanted to finish the agent off and who threatened the monks.

The prosecutions arising from these events led to sentences on a currier and a cobbler and several master tanners, but also on a wholesale merchant, Jean Le Maistre, and one of the royal officials, Philippe Vaudolle, an examiner of witnesses, who were both found guilty as ringleaders. The king granted letters of amnesty in January, 1635.

The Cour des Aides of Rouen forbade, by an *arrêt* of September 5, 1636, the levying of the *sol pour livre* as well as of the charge for stamping and marking hides and skins. Thenceforth the tanners refused to pay. It became impossible to mark a single skin. Violence was done to the inspectors, examiners, and markers, and to the process servers and bailiffs who served them. In 1637, 1638, and 1639 there were disturbances in Rouen, Caen, Vernon, and Falaise. In the last-named town the officials, some of whom were related to the master tanners, refused to give a hearing to the farmer of the inspectorate of hides and skins.

In 1637 Claude Joubert arrived, to collect the taxes imposed on the officials of the *élections principales* in exchange for the suppression of the *élections particulières*. The *élus* replied by going on strike and rioting. In Caen the *élus* stopped holding their court for disputed tax claims on market day. Everyone cried out at this. The *élus* explained that they would not hear cases so long as the royal commissaries sent to extract taxes from them had not been driven out. At once a popular riot broke out against the commissaries. At Mortain, similarly, the *élus* summoned the people to revolt, and Joubert found himself besieged by over eight hundred men, who were stopped from setting fire to the hostelry where he was staying, and roasting him alive, only by the tears of the landlady, who saw herself threatened with ruin. At Coutances, two *élus*, the brothers Jacques and Richard Delamare, stirred up "a great number of inhabitants of the parish of Monscharton," who, "armed with torches, halberds, sticks pointed at both ends," hurled themselves upon Joubert and his assistants. The officials were "beaten, outraged, knocked nearly senseless," they were robbed of their weapons, overcoats and hats, as well as of the *arrêts* of the council which they had come to put into effect, and the tax receipts they had made ready, and their horses were hamstrung. Joubert and his men got away as best they could. The rebels said "that people who came demanding money should no longer be allowed in the town." The Cour des Aides supported the *élus* and granted them replevin of the distraints carried out on their property.

When it came to levying the loan of 1637, the royal commissaries and their collection clerks complained that it was impossible to obtain payment from the officials of Falaise, Coutances, Saint-Sauveur-le-Vicomte, Avranches, Valognes, or Carentan. At Coutances, La Besnardière Poupinel, *lieutenant particulier* to the *président*, accompanied by his clerk Bertrand, patrolled the town day and night at the head of thirty to forty armed men, with drums beating. They attacked the process servers and the archers who had come to collect the money for the loan. The gentry gave shelter in their houses to the persons who had been ordered to pay the loan, together with their chattels which were threatened with distraint. At Guibray, Carentan, Vire, and Tinchebray, the officials called the poor people to revolt, and process servers, bailiffs, and commissaries were wounded.

Nobles, ecclesiastics, and members of the sovereign courts were exempt from paying the *quatrième* on drink which they obtained from their own estates for consumption by their households. However, they took to trade, and sold their drink to tavern keepers. It is therefore interesting to observe that the *élus* encouraged the tavern keepers to commit violent assaults on the tax-farmer's clerks, in order to prevent the *quatrième* from being collected, while the tavern keepers in turn stirred up the people to revolt, in 1636 and 1637, at Lisieux, Bernay, and Rouen, and the Cour des Aides issued *arrêts* in favor of exempt persons and tavern keepers against the farmer of this tax.

The gentry encouraged the peasants to refuse to pay the taille, and protected them against the collectors, process servers, and bailiffs. They rode at their head against the soldiers sent to be billeted on them. At Périers, in Cotentin, at the beginning of 1639, "*plusieurs*" gentlemen, officials, and inhabitants of this place and neighboring ones assembled on market day, summoned the people to revolt and gave them arms, and attacked the soldiers, to the sound of the alarm bell and of drums—and killed a good number. "*Plusieurs*" gentlemen of the county of Mortain assembled in arms and attacked the troops of cavalry which were taking up their quarters in the area.

These were gentlemen who took the lead in the illegal trade in salt. The greater part of the *généralités* of Rouen and

Alençon and a large part of the *généralité* of Caen were *pays de grande gabelle*, where salt was a royal monopoly, associated with heavy taxes. The Cotentin, however, with the *vicomtés* of Vire and Domfront, the enclave of Isigny and Les Veys in the *vicomté* of Mayeux, and the enclave of Touques in the area of jurisdiction of the storehouse of Honfleur, were *pays de quart-bouillon*. That is to say, the salt makers evaporated sea-water, collected the salt, handed over one-quarter of the product to the king, and sold the rest as they pleased. Their salt pans were situated around Avranches, Coutances, Carentan, Valognes, Touques, Trouville, and Isigny. This industry required a very large quantity of wood for fuel, and consequently was of interest to the owners of woods, who were usually lords, and a whole population of cutters, carters, and porters of wood.

The production of salt in this area gave rise to a considerable amount of salt smuggling. Salt was transported from the pans to where a number of dealers were waiting for it, near the frontier of the privileged area, at the edge of the parishes of the *pays de grande gabelle*, which were officially supposed to buy their salt from the royal storehouses, at much higher prices. In 1638 the illegal salt trade was carried on in the *bailliage* of Cotentin and the *vicomté* of Avranches by the three Montgomery brothers, Louis, chevalier, comte de Ducey, Pierre, chevalier, sieur de Breuil, and Jacques, esquire, sieur de Lorges. With their servants and farmers, on horseback and carrying firearms, they conducted loads of "illegal" salt, from 1629 onward, into the *pays de grande gabelle* and also across the sea to England. Where necessary they offered violent resistance to the captains and archers protecting the gabelle. On March 16, 1637, they fought with a number of carabiniers and foot-soldiers coming from Pont-d'Ouilly, in the area of jurisdiction of the salt storehouse at Falaise. Also engaged in this traffic, under similar conditions, was Laurent du Thou, sieur du Quesnay, councillor of the Présidial of Caen. The Cour des Aides was lenient with them at their trials in 1638. This resulted in an *arrêt* of the State Council on July 10, 1638, whereby the king reserved the right to hear cases of salt smuggling and forbade the Cour des Aides to deal with them, to the great indignation of the councillors of this court. The man who had been so indiscreet as to bring these matters to light was a new general clerk of the gabelle, Guillaume Dorneau. He was one of the chief victims of the Caen revolt of 1639.

These were the circumstances in which the revolt of the *Nu-Pieds* broke out. It took its name from the salt makers of the Avranches area, who walked barefoot on the sand. The revolt lasted four and a half months in this part of Normandy, and led to the formation of the "Army of Suffering." This peasant revolt was the longest and most serious of the Norman revolts of 1639, longer and more serious than that of the *Bras-Nus* of Caen or even than the troubles in Rouen. When it was crushed, though disturbances continued in a number of places, the rising in Normandy was regarded as over.

During June and the first half of July, a rumor circulated in Avranches that the gabelle was going to be introduced in Lower Normandy. There was indeed a move being made to add the *pays de quart-bouillon* to the area covered by the farm of the gabelle. This indirect fiscal reform would have ruined ten or twelve thousand peasants who lived by producing and selling fine table salt, deprived the cultivators of their customers in the salt pans, and brought down from 15 to 20 livres the acre to a mere 4 the value of the woods belonging to the churchmen and gentry. "Those who spread these rumors said openly that this change should not be tolerated, for it would bring ruin and desolation first to these *élections* and then to all Normandy: since there were ten or twelve thousand persons who neither had nor knew any other way of earning their living, and that, without the consumption of produce and wood in the salt pans, they could not make profit or sale, and the churchmen, the nobles and the people would be reduced to want and poverty, without being able to find any remedy." The people of the district, alarmed by this rumor, saw in every traveler someone who had come "to establish new charges," a "monopolist." "They appointed certain men, especially in Avranches, to call on travelers and inspect their documents; they went to the hostelries to find out who had arrived there, and in order to report to those they had chosen to command them, on what the strangers had come to do in the district, and what their business was, they carried out searches and examined their letters and papers."[2]

La Besnardière Poupinel, *lieutenant particulier* of the Présidial at Coutances, came to Avranches on Saturday, July 16, 1639, for the purpose of carrying out a commission from the parlement of Rouen which related to justice and had nothing to do with financial matters. He should have been the last to attract suspicion, since at Coutances he had himself led the revolt against the "monopolists." The men chosen to check on visitors, the priest Bastard and a certain Bonniel, went to inspect his room at the hostelry and saw "on the table the *arrêt* which he had come to execute and the commission which was attached to it." Without even reading these papers and without trying to understand them, they sent warning to the sieur de Ponthébert, a small squire who was a great talker, and a certain Champmartin, and spread the story that a commission had been issued for suppressing the salt pans of Avranches. This happened on a market day. People hastened to warn "the peasants working on table salt,"[3] the salt makers on the sands below Avranches. An hour and a half later, four hundred people, mostly salt makers and wood porters, were kicking and punching Poupinel and beating him with sticks and stones. The wretched man, his flesh in shreds, died about half past twelve noon. The spinning women put out his eyes with their spindles. The *lieutenant-général* Virieu de La Champagne took the corpse into his house. The agitation did not die down. About five in the evening a bailiff whose task was to collect the *sol pour livre*, one Saint-Martin, was attacked to shouts of "Down with the monopolist," by a crowd led by Champmartin, by the court bailiff Latour, and by Lalouey, son of a process server, all of them later leaders of the revolt.

On Sunday, July 17, the *lieutenant-général* had Poupinel buried in the nave of the cathedral, quietly, out of fear of the mob. On that day the infuriated people attacked Jean Pourcel, whose responsibility it was to collect the taxes due from officials in return for confirmation of the heritability of their offices. Jean

2. *Diaire, Pièces inédites*, 2nd document, pp. 421–422.
3. Bigot, p. 10.

Pourcel, in a very bad way, took refuge with the Capuchins, who were thus in danger in their turn. The governor of Avranches, Canisy, warned of the violence done to Pourcel and the Capuchins, sent one of his gentlemen to the scene, but did no more than that.

The agitation continued in Avranches. Nothing suspicious having been found in Poupinel's papers, another scapegoat was found, Jean Fortin, sieur de Beaupré, vicomte de Mortain, a *trésorier de France*, and councillor of the Cour des Aides at Caen. Not content with combining offices in the sphere of justice and in that of finance, he was also a tax-farmer. He had had a hand in establishing the *élection* of Saint-Lô, and that had sharply antagonized the officials of the *élection* of Coutances against him and against his brother-in-law, the sieur de Savigny. He was interested in the sale of offices in the *élection* of Saint-Lô; that is, he was one of a group of tax-farmers who had bought these offices wholesale from the king in order to sell them retail. Between July 16 and 25, the vicomte d'Avranches, Jean du Quesnoy, and the king's counsel Costardière circulated all sorts of tales concerning him. They accused him of being the only begetter and inventor of the Cour des Aides of Caen, of having contributed to the establishment of the gabelle, and of having allowed his servant Thomas Le Moyne to point out to the *intendant* Étienne d'Aligre the officials and advocates who should be taxed as being well-off. On July 25 Beaupré was warned by the marquis de La Forêt that four hundred men had set out from Avranches to murder him and raze his house to the ground. Beaupré fled at once. He went to where the king was, at Mouzon, in Lorraine, and on August 4 begged His Majesty to call off the project of introducing the gabelle in Lower Normandy.

But his foes did not give up. On August 25, at Avranches, Jean du Quesnoy, Costardière, Ponthébert, the sieur de Vauguéroult, who was a farmer of the *quatrièmes*, Chambres, who was clerk to another farmer of the *quatrièmes*, and Nicolle denounced Beaupré violently before the governor, Canisy. At Mortain, the former king's counsel Poulinier and his successor, Brilly, brought charges against Beaupré. The advocate Ménardière and his sons did everything possible to stir up the people against the judges at Mortain, who were Beaupré's brothers, and put themselves at the head of the rebels.

Furthermore, although Beaupré had secured the annulment of the gabelle, the royal officials made no effort to ensure rapid diffusion of this news, by distributing copies of the State Council's *arrêt*, which would have deprived the revolt of its pretext.

In this way, a group of officials and advocates played a part in transforming a momentary disturbance into a prolonged revolt, out of hatred and jealousy of another official and "financier" who had done too well for himself, doubtless to the disadvantage of his colleagues.

The revolt spread over two zones. The first was that of Avranches and Coutances. The boundaries of this zone ran through Pontorson, Saint-James, Coutances, and Bricey. In the *élection* of Avranches, twenty-seven out of ninety-seven parishes certainly took part in the revolt. Not all of them did this willingly: sometimes they acted under threat. The majority did not stir. Some parishes flatly refused to help, one of these being Savigny, halfway between Coutances and Saint-Lô, which had formerly been included in the *élection* of Coutances but had since April, 1639, been joined to the new *élection* of Saint-Lô, to avoid the vengeance of the *élus* and of certain officers of the Présidial. Savigny remained firmly loyal to its lord, the *noble homme* Jean-Jacques de Savigny, brother-in-law to Fortin de Beaupré, and the peasants of this parish went so far as Coutances, on September 7, to give support to the *président* of the Présidial. The town of Saint-Lô remained quiet, though the "posters" of *Jean Nu-Pieds* had been stuck up there in August, 1639.

The second rebel zone extended between Mortain and Domfront. Nine parishes in this zone were certainly involved, including Mantilly, well known for its unwillingness to pay the taille. The town of Mortain remained loyal to the king, even though Gaston d'Orléans was comte de Mortain et de Domfront.

The two rebel zones were separated by a zone of calm, around Saint-Hilaire-du-Harcouet, and the rebels were never able to organize any concerted action.

In short, the peasant revolt was clearly the work of a minority. The troubles did not even embrace the whole of the *pays du quart-bouillon*. The northern part of Cotentin, the *élections* of Carentan and Valognes, did not stir, in spite of the consequences of the plague, the burden of the taille, the excesses committed by the soldiers, and the agitation at Périers in 1638. Only the southern part of Cotentin became fully active in the rising. The north was an area with varied types of terrain and resources which were probably more diversified and more abundant. The rebel area had a granite soil, impermeable and poor. Its landscape was already that of the Bocage: small fields enclosed by dykes, that is, banks planted with trees and hedges; deeply embanked rivers; rounded ridges; deep and winding roads; country where one could not see far ahead and where it was difficult to get about. The crops were poor—rye and buckwheat. Wheat had to be bought in Brittany. Pastures and grasslands were rare and there was extensive heathland. Without the fine table salt and the fishing, this district could not survive. The peasants' holdings, which were too small and too much broken up, were always on the brink of ruin. A farm of twenty verges, a little over three hectares, divided into portions each of three or four verges, 48 to 64 ares, was regarded as normal. Productivity was low. Two poor harvests, and these cultivators were at the end of their tether. Most of them, fortunately, were also salt makers, but even so they remained below the poverty line. As the good Président Bigot de Monville wrote, they were "capable of undertaking any action, owing to their extreme wretchedness, which caused them to fear nothing worse than what they were already enduring"[4] and which made them highly susceptible to any agitation.

"Not long after, the peasants of the Vire neighborhood forcibly broke into Vire and dealt so harshly with the Sieur de la Montagne-Petouf, *président* in the *élection* of Bayeux, that they left him for dead where he lay. They also beat his son, plundered his house and thereafter kept the field like the rebels of the Avranches area."[5]

Meanwhile, the "Army of Suffering" took shape around Avranches between July 16 and 25. At the beginning of August, the countryside was divided into bailiwicks, each with a sergeant

4. *Ibid.*, p. 10.
5. Bigot, p. 11.

in charge. These bailiwicks were military districts each responsible
for providing a certain number of men. For example, Lalouey,
the process server's son, was appointed sergeant of the bailiwick
of Saint-James, which comprised 24 parishes. He was able to
raise 800 men there. The court bailiff Latour commanded 1,200
men. Here, however, just as in Périgord, it appears that these
men were not all together under arms at one time. The sergeants
each kept a nucleus of soldiers with them and reinforced this
nucleus according to need. The rest of the men stayed in their
villages, doubtless because of the requirements of their work
in the fields, and held themselves ready to answer the first
call to arms. The total number involved seems to have been
3,000 to 4,000. Hugo Grotius says 20,000. The sergeants, at the
head of groups of 40, 100, or 400 men, led out expeditions all
round Avranches. Another army was active in the area of Manteuil
and Mantilly. In training since 1638, with a view to a rising,
under the leadership of Julien Balin, sieur de Rubesnard, king's
counsel in the *élection*, it numbered not less than 800 men, commanded by a gentleman, the sieur de Reffuveille, Duplessis-
Mornay's grandson, by the sons of the advocate Ménardière,
and by the advocate Boutry.

At Coutances and at Vire we have found no evidence of
appointed leaders or methodical organization.

The rebels' general used the name Jean Nu-Pieds (John Barefoot). Their banner showed Saint John the Baptist with a motto
taken from the Gospel according to St. John: *Fuit homo missus
a Deo cui nomen erat Joannes* (There was a man sent from
God whose name was John). "Some said that this Jean Nu-Pieds
was M. Jean Morel, the curate of Saint-Saturnin, near Avranches.
Others claimed that he was the sieur de Ponthébert, a gentleman of that district, who was supposed to have disguised himself
as a peasant and held a commission from the discontented
princes and lords who had fled from France; but this is unlikely, since the disorders had no other cause than the wretchedness of a community which was tired of suffering."[6] Probably
this Jean Nu-Pieds was a collective entity. What is certain is

6. Bigot, pp. 10–11.

that four priests gave orders to the sergeants and constituted a sort of directing council: Morel, Bastard, Jean Lefebvre, and the parish priest of Saint-Senier, François Le Bonnier. Of these, Jean Morel, the priest of Saint-Gervais, a parish in Avranches, whose nickname was "Colonel Sandhills"—from the little heaps of sand which the salt makers made in order to dry them out and extract the salt—carried out the tasks of private secretary to General Jean Nu-Pieds. He countersigned the general's printed orders. He called upon the parish priests to read these orders from their pulpits. From September onward he took personal command of the sergeants and participated in the expeditions around Avranches. François Le Bonnier, the priest of Saint-Senier, raised a body of men to join forces with the rebels.

Some gentlemen attached themselves to the rebel forces, but these were "poor and of no standing." They led the troops in the expeditions. The most important of these was *not* Jean Quetil, esquire, sieur de Ponthébert, a gentleman whose nobility was of quite recent origin. His father had been ennobled, and he himself lived "in the noble manner." He owned houses in Avranches and its suburbs. He was not very rich in his own right, but his wife had brought him property. The Avranches judges were related to him by blood or by marriage. He was a profuse and very violent talker, who in this way played an important part in starting the revolt, but he had little foresight or judgment and was not at all a man of action. He deserted the revolt in September, expressing his regret at having helped to open "so great a wound."

The other gentlemen were more effectual. Pierre de Camprond, esquire, sieur de Transportière, belonged to the parish of Saint-Senier-sous-Avranches. He was an official, first king's counsel in the *vicomté* of Avranches, an attorney, and the steward of Catherine d'Orléans, duchesse de Longueville.

The three brothers Jacques, André, and Michel Richer were esquires, the two first being sieurs de Vouges and the third sieur de la Chesnaye. Their home was in the parish of Chavoy. Their family had been ennobled at the end of the fifteenth century.

Pierre de La Mothe-Bellière was brother to Étienne, the newly

made *trésorier de France* at Caen, who owed the greater part of
the price he paid for his office to Fortin de Beaupré and
did not forgive him for that. Pierre wore a sword.

Basire Basilière, or Baril de la Barillière, who became lieutenant
colonel to Jean Nu-Pieds in September, belonged to a family
which had been ennobled at the end of the fifteenth century.

The number of gentlemen who openly sided with the rebels
was very small in relation to the total number of the nobles
in the areas affected. But the others did not come to the aid
of the governor of Avranches, René Corbonnel de Canisy, marquis
du Hommet, nephew of Charles de Matignon, lieutenant-general
of Lower Normandy. Being without men, weapons, or ammunition, Canisy made no move, despite the king's orders. The
nobility were accused of complicity in the revolt. "The noblemen of the countryside allowed the alarm bell to be sounded
all day long in their parishes, to summon the rebels' assemblies,
and allowed their tenants to rise and join in this rebellion,
without taking any steps whatever to oppose them."[7]

A similar charge was brought against the officials as a body.
"In the towns, the officials tolerated the people's revolt, in
which destruction was wrought against the houses and murder
against the persons of those who were loyal to the King's
service, the collectors of the taille and other revenues of His
Majesty, and these officials did not intervene either in person
or through their friends to put a stop to a disorder which had
such dangerous results."[8]

Among the officials who were compromised as individuals
we find a number of nobles. Since Jacques du Quesnoy owned
several fiefs, which were raised to the status of knight's fee and
barony in the midst of the revolt, in August, 1639, he was therefore already an esquire, and consequently his son, Jean du
Quesnoy, as well; the latter was *vicomte* of Avranches, that is,
a judge of first instance in the king's courts, and was accused
of having spread false rumors.

Jacques de Saint-Simon, esquire, lord of Pleinmaresq, *lieutenant-
général de bailliage* for Coutances, the highest-ranking magistrate

7. *Diaire*, 5th document, p. 440.
8. *Ibid.*

there after the *bailli* himself, was charged with not preventing the raising of rebel forces at Coutances, with failing to publish the *arrêt* canceling the *gabelle*, and with other crimes. His defense was that he had been the victim of a strike by clerks of the court and process servers. He was acquitted, and kept his office. Jean de Bordes, esquire, sieur de Folligny, vicomte of Coutances, whose father had been active in the Holy League, was accused by rebels, when interrogated under torture, of having incited them to revolt, as also was the *président* of the Présidial. Altogether, though, it appears that the officials as a body sinned mainly by their passivity—and we shall never know whether it was inspired by sympathy with the rebels or by fear of them.

Certain advocates, moved by hatred of those who monopolized the offices, roused the people to revolt by their violent speeches. Jean Boutry, advocate, stirred up the people of Barenton. Along with the sieur de Reffuveille he headed the rebels in Lower Maine. The sons of the advocate La Ménardière tried to arouse Mortain.

Among the bourgeois, whose precise social position remains unclear, we find Barthélemy La Fontaine-Rigauldière, "bourgeois of Avranches." Appointed sergeant of the bailiwick of Cuves and Gavray, he took part in several expeditions. The people of Avranches cannot have been very enthusiastic, since the rebels called those "owls" who dared not come out in the daylight. We have already met, however, the son of the process server Lalouey and the bailiff Simon Dubreuil, known as Latour, who were concerned with starting the revolt and organizing the "Army of Suffering." Also taking active part in the revolt were a baker, an armorer, a carpenter, a mason, a jailer, some tanners, some shoemakers, and a day laborer. Except for the last-named we do not know whether these men were small employers or workmen.

The bulk of the soldiers of the "Army of Suffering" was, however, made up of peasants, salt makers, and wood porters. The nicknames of their leaders were borrowed from the terminology of the salt pans: *mondrins, boisdrots, sablons, plombz.*" Were there any *laboureurs* among these peasants? The different categories are not revealed. Moreover, it seems that many of the peasants joined the rebels only under coercion, forced by threats against their cattle, their money, and their houses.

To sum up, if we consider them in relation to the hierarchy of social status, we find among the rebels representatives of all three of the main orders of society, and of many "estates," many different strata of each order; never, though, the strata of highest rank within each order, such as bishops and abbots, barons, marquises and dukes, or merchants and laborers. If, however, instead of the hierarchy of status according to social esteem, we take as our yardstick the scale of wealth—the economic scale—we then perceive that we are dealing most often with people situated at the very bottom of this scale: mere curates, with only a single parish priest; impoverished gentlemen, almost none of whom had an income of as much as 500 livres, according to the records of the *ban* and *arrière-ban*, that is, 500 days' wages of a building worker; petty officials of the judiciary, with miserably small earnings; and poor wretches of peasants. This was a revolt of poor men, or men who were relatively poor, anyway, whatever might be the social esteem enjoyed by their estate.

What was the aim of the leaders of the "Army of Suffering"? To judge by their banner and their motto, Jean Nu-Pieds appears to have sought to prepare for the coming of the kingdom of Jesus Christ. According to the Acts of the Apostles, the early Christians sold their possessions and pooled the proceeds. There would therefore seem to have been a desire for some kind of egalitarian communism. But Jesus Christ said that his kingdom was not of this world, and Christians may prefer a wide variety of social and political forms.

An order by Jean Nu-Pieds was promulgated in the parishes in August, 1639, to be read out by the priests from their pulpits. The inhabitants were commanded to report in good order and properly equipped "to the place which will be assigned to them, for the defense and liberation of the fatherland, oppressed by tax-farmers and *gabeleurs*."[9] It was thus a question of liberating the land of their fathers from the burden of taxes; this libera-

9. Bibl. Nat., Ms. fr., 3833, f. 214.

tion was the aim of the antifiscal struggle carried on against the government's agents.

The document just mentioned persuades us that we ought to take seriously some others, the origin of which we do not know, but which seem to express the same sentiments with more precision and detail, and which, in particular, enable us to make out more clearly what we should understand by the "fatherland" here mentioned.

First we have the "Manifesto of the High Unconquerable Captain Jean Nu-Pieds, General of the Army of Suffering," printed at Avranches, a copy of which the marquis de La Forest handed to Fortin de Beaupré on July 25, at eleven o'clock at night.[10] It is a set of verses against the "men made rich by their taxes," who "sell their fatherland," who "run to Paris to fetch the gabelle":

And I, shall I leave a people languishing
Beneath the heel of tyranny, and allow *a crowd of outsiders*
To oppress this people daily with their tax-farms?
. . . .
I fear not their spluttered threats;
My men are good soldiers and, backing me,
Will furnish companies enough, arrayed in order,
To stand firm, helped by the peasants,
Against these gabelle-men, *real Hyrcanian tyrants,*
Who seek *to oppress peoples and nations*
By soliciting so many tyrannies,
Resisted by Normans, Poitevins, and Bretons,
. . . .
Colonel Sandhills calls on the nobility
Of every place to help us to free ourselves,
Boldly repulsing the taxes and gabelles
That everywhere they hope to make us endure.

I consider that it is clear who wrote this. "Colonel Sandhills" (*Mondrins*) was the priest Jean Morel, private secretary to Jean Nu-Pieds, and there is every reason to suppose that Jean Morel was the author of these verses. The denunciation of the "out-

10. *Diaire*, p. 406.

siders" ("*horzains*," a contemptuous term used to denote persons not Norman by birth), of the oppressors of the Norman, Poitevin, and Breton "nations," and of those who go "to fetch the gabelle" in Paris, shows clearly what is meant by the word *fatherland* (*patrie*) as used in the order by Jean Nu-Pieds: the "fatherland" is Normandy. What we have here is a particularist movement directed against centralization focused on Paris. This centralization, represented by the gabelle-collectors, is a "tyranny" —a dread word, if we recall the many apologias for tyrannicide which led to the murder of two kings of France within twenty years, Henry III and Henry IV, and which were still worrying the States-General in 1614–1615,[11] as well as the many plots to murder Richelieu. The author of the manifesto obviously sought to encourage tyrannicide: he dwelt on the theme of Caesar killed by the virtuous Brutus, and on Catiline, cut down by Cicero.

A poem entitled "To Normandy," probably by the same writer, points in the same direction:

> Help a brave *nu-pieds*,
> Show that your towns are full
> Of men of war zealous
> To fight under his banner.
> You see that everything is ready
> *For a fight to the death for freedom.*
> Like Rouen, Valognes, and Chartres,
> Since they treat you with severity,
> *If you do not defend your charters,*
> *Normans, you are men of no courage.*
>
> Go, brave colonel,
> General of the land of suffering . . .

Later on it is said of Jean Nu-Pieds:

> It is he that God has sent
> To establish in Normandy
> Perfect freedom.

11. R. Mousnier, *L'Assassinat d'Henri IV. Le Problème du tyrannicide et l'affermissement de la monarchie absolue* (Paris, Gallimard), 1964.

It is noteworthy that Jean Nu-Pieds, "general of the land of suffering," is here described as "brave colonel," if we recall that Jean Morel signed himself "Colonel Sandhills" (*Mondrins*). The famous Jean Nu-Pieds may well have been the priest of Saint-Gervais, helped by his council of other priests. It is also noteworthy that the "freedom" sought is for "Normandy" and is identified with the defense of the Norman "charters." Now, the "charter to the Normans" granted by Louis X, the Quarrelsome, on March 19, 1315, undertook that no "extraordinary levy" would be made in this province except in emergencies. What was regarded as "extraordinary" in those days was whatever did not form part of the king's demesne rights, which meant the taille and the *aides*. Since Charles VII's time the provincial states of Normandy had been the sole judges of when there was an emergency. However, Henry IV and Louis XIII had broken with precedent by not confirming, at their accessions, the "charter to the Normans," and had issued fiscal edicts on their own, to be carried out in Normandy "regardless of the Norman charter and the *clameur de haro*." The *clameur de haro* meant the privilege enjoyed by every Norman of suspending any judicial or administrative proceeding taken against him and having the case referred to the judgment of the king himself, or of his judges assigned for the purpose; this privilege was claimed by raising the cry "Haro, mon Prince! On me fait tort." ("Haro, my Prince! I am being wronged.") The provincial states of Normandy had not been called together between 1634 and 1638. Here, then, was an autonomist movement in favor of going back to the good old days of the states.

The rebels said sometimes that there should be a return to the days of good King Louis XII, and sometimes that all taxes established since the death of good King Henry must be resisted. Seditious songs acclaimed Norman particularism. The government was worried about this, "because this province had its own sovereign in former times, it is prouder of itself than other provinces; it is close to England, and it perhaps still has some inclination to have a Duke."[12] There were rumors

12. Tallemant des Reaux, *Historiettes* (Paris, La Pléiade), I, p. 268.

of an English landing in Normandy.[13] It will therefore be understood that the government may well have suspected that an insurrection like this had been stirred up by the grandees and the princes of the blood, and helped from abroad.

Not only was this a retrogressive political movement, of a particularist character, aimed against the development of the modern absolutist state, with its centralizing and unifying function; we can find no trace in this antitax struggle of any social program.

These remarks are confirmed by the results of the expeditions of the "Army of Suffering." It attacked first and foremost the finance officials, the "financiers" and those persons who were alleged to be in their service. Twenty-eight persons were the victims of these raids: a *lieutenant particulier de bailliage* at Coutances, La Besnardière Poupinel, charged with bringing in the edict on the gabelle; a *lieutenant particulier de bailliage* at Mortain, Fortin de Beaupré, charged with having taken a 29,000-livre share in the farm of the Cour des Aides at Caen; and five officials of *élections*, namely, the *président* of the *élection* of Vire, Philippe de Sarcilly, two lieutenants in the *élection* of Avranches, Delabarre and Gosselin, two Avranches *élus*, Basilly and Alibert, four collectors of taille accused of sharing in the farm of the *subsistances*—Nicolle at Coutances, Ameline and Angot de La Bretesche at Avranches, Jouvin at Vire; two farmers of the *quatrième* on salt, Vaugueboust and his clerk Blascher; two persons involved in the farm of the *aides* at Vire, Perlier, and Vincendière; etc. Nine centers for the collection of *aides* were plundered, that of the "five big tax-farms" at Pont-Saint-Gilbert, that of the *quatrième* on salt at Saint-Léonard, etc. Of the victims, two, Poupinel and Coaslin, were killed. The latter was brother-in-law to Nicolle, the collector of taille at Coutances, who was "dragged around for two or three days at the end of a horse's tail, to see all his houses set on fire, and then finished off with two pistol shots." Three were left for dead after being "stoned and beaten with sticks." The rest were threatened with death and actually had their houses sacked and burned down. Sieur Delabarre had nine houses burnt, including his own resi-

13. H. Grotius, *Letters to Oxenstierna*, 1687, nos. 1299, 1355.

dence, and in addition "seven small houses for letting" which belonged to him were ruined. Nevertheless, the château of Cresnay, at Brécé, which belonged to Fortin de Beaupré, was not destroyed, and Thomas Ier Morant, baron du Mesnil-Garnier, a treasurer of the central treasury, managed to save his château of Mesnil-Garnier, near Coutances, with the help of eighty men-at-arms. There was no attack on the châteaux of the gentry or of the *noblesse de robe*.

But the government struck back. In November, 1639, it was able to send into Normandy "the best troops of maréchal de La Meilleraye's army, under the command of the sieur de Gassion, colonel," an old soldier who had taken part in all the wars of Gustavus Adolphus, king of Sweden, and in all those of Louis XIII. He had at his disposal 4,000 men, in eight regiments of infantry and several troops of cavalry. His first move was to occupy Caen, where he disarmed the inhabitants, had the rebel *Bras-Nus* broken on the wheel, and forced the bourgeois to pay the *subsistance*. In the town and in the villages round about, his troops lived as they pleased and did "much damage." In December he marched on Avranches. The *Nu-Pieds*, caught off guard by his speed of movement, did not manage completely to regroup their men, who were scattered among the villages. Some of them went to confront de Gassion, but he outflanked them and attacked the others, on December 14, 1639, in the suburbs of Avranches. They were too few in numbers and their entrenchments were soon broken through. Latour was unable to reach Avranches in time, and fled. Lalouey succeeded in getting together only 300 out of his 800 men, arrived only a quarter of an hour before de Gassion, and appears to have fallen back without fighting. The priest Morel did not show up on the battle-field, and fled. The town of Avranches surrendered. The troops established their winter quarters there. Of the *Nu-Pieds* captured in arms, twelve were hanged and others sent to the galleys. The priest Bastard was hanged on the ramparts by order of the *intendant* Le Roy de La Potherie, on December 21, 1639.[14]

De Gassion's victory came just in time. It was said that "if he had delayed his attack, they would have swelled their num-

14. Bigot, pp. 162–167.

bers to ten thousand men, and if they had then withstood his
first onslaught, the whole region would have declared for the
revolt, for everyone expected success."[15] The whole of Normandy,
and especially the town of Rouen, had been shaken by revolt.
On December 15, 1639, King Louis XIII commissioned Messire
Pierre Séguier, chevalier, comte de Gien-sur-Loire, baron d'Autry,
chancellor of France, to proceed to Rouen for the purpose of
reestablishing His Majesty's authority. To Pierre Séguier was
delegated the king's absolute power over the armed forces and
the judiciary. On December 26, at Gaillon, he ordered that
the officials of the Présidial of Coutances be brought to trial.
These magistrates had to follow in his train to Rouen. The
chancellor entered Rouen on Monday, January 2, 1640. Next
day he informed the assembled members of the parlement of
Rouen of the king's declaration depriving them of their posts.
He ordered them to leave Rouen and report to the king. The
Cour des Aides, the *trésoriers-généraux de France*, the *échevins*,
the town councillors, and the lieutenant-general of the Présidial of
Rouen, permanent mayor of the town, were likewise deprived.
In order to save Normandy from a relapse, a royal declaration
dated January 10, 1640, rendered all the magistrates, officials,
and captains of the larger market towns and the lords of the
parishes responsible for any disorders, unless they opposed
them with all and everything that was in their charge
and under their authority. Numerous rebels were executed.
In February the chancellor moved into Lower Normandy. On
the sixteenth he entered Caen. He later spent some time in
Bayeux, then in March he went to Saint-Lô and to Coutances,
where he was met on March 4, in the suburbs of the town,
by women on their knees, crying for mercy. The prisons were
still crammed with rebels. The chancellor had a four-branched
gallows erected in the corn market of Coutances on March 6.
A number of *Nu-Pieds* had fled to the islands of Jersey and
Guernsey, among them being Ponthébert, whose house the
chancellor caused to be demolished on March 8. On that day
too the chief prisoners were tried. One was sentenced to the

15. *Diaire*, p. 441.

wheel for having helped in Coaslin's action, and the others, including the town crier, to be hanged for the disturbances in the town and the sacking of the house of Nicolle, the collector of taille. They showed "great resolution in face of death, either from insensitivity or from courage and resignation to God's will."[16] They were, however, unanimous in accusing of being "authors of or participants in the revolt" "numerous gentlemen and other persons of quality," especially the *lieutenant-général* of the Présidial, Jacques de Saint-Simon, and the *vicomte* of Coutances, the sieur Bordes. The latter was saved by the passionate intercession of the wife of Maréchal de Saint-Geran, a relation of his, and the chancellor did not persist against the others. He had a number of houses burnt or knocked down in Avranches, and ordered that the village of Cérance be razed to the ground "on account of the frequently repeated rebellions of the people of that place."[17] The *prévôt* de l'Isle, however, moved by compassion, destroyed only seven or eight houses, those belonging to the most guilty of the villagers. On March 12 and 13 the *intendant* La Potherie concluded by default the trials of those of the accused who were absent. The chancellor then returned to Paris on March 27, 1640.

Despite the harsh lesson, the covert revolt of the parlement of Rouen continued as soon as it was re-established. Nor was this the end of revolts in the parishes against taxation, instigated by the gentry, especially in the area of Mantilly and Domfront.

The good *président* of the parlement of Rouen, Bigot de Monville, offers an explanation of these events. "The discontent of the sovereign courts, of the nobility, of the richest of the towns and of the countryside would not have caused any movement. Those who have honor and property at risk do not easily undertake to disturb public order, but new taxes affecting the mass of poor people aroused their anger."[18] The facts set out above perhaps suggest that this explanation is rather limited and not altogether disinterested.

16. *Ibid.*, p. 313.
17. *Ibid.*, p. 316.
18. Bigot, pp. 4–5.

[6]

The *Torrébens* of Brittany—1675

THE NAME "the stamped-paper rebellion" commonly used to describe the revolt in Brittany in 1675 is not, perhaps, a well-chosen one, since, in Lower Brittany, the stamped-paper question played only a secondary role, whereas, on this occasion, unlike those previously discussed, we see the manor houses of the gentry being attacked, and no longer merely the *châteaux* or the houses of finance officials and "financiers," and also we find rights described as "seignorial" being challenged, with taxes not the principal issue.

Revolts continued to be numerous during the personal government of Louis XIV, between 1661 and 1675. They took place, however, in political circumstances which were rather different from those of the first half of the century. After the defeat suffered by that great attempt at a princely, aristocratic, and *parlementaire* reaction called the Fronde, there were no more rebellions by the princes of the blood and the grandees against the king. In consequence, although many gentlemen still took part in revolts, and although the gentry as a group, in parts that were out of the way, poor, and hard to move about in, like Limousin, Auvergne, and Périgord, displayed indiscipline and independence on their estates, the gentry as a whole showed more loyalty to the sovereign and more submission to his personal government. After 1675, when the kingdom had passed what the economic historians regard as the low-water mark of prices, there were indeed once more a great many disturbances and petty local revolts, but on the whole nothing very serious, if we leave aside the great Protestant rebellions like the war of the Camisards, which were wars of religion and not social struggles. Perhaps the reason for this is to be found, in spite of the burden of wars and of the great "mortalities" of 1693–1694 and 1709–1710, in the steady increase in the size of the army, the organization of the royal militias, and the development of the institution of *intendants* in the provinces. The revolts of 1675 were the last that can be considered great social and political movements.

The so-called stamped-paper revolt in Brittany was contemporary with the revolt in Bordeaux. The Girondin and Breton movements reacted on each other, turn and turn about. News of *journées* of revolt in the one area, brought by merchants on coasting vessels, stimulated *journées* in the other. On the whole, though, the Bordeaux revolt was confined to the town itself. The popular movements in the Gironde area were essentially urban and concentrated in the provincial capital. In Brittany, though the disturbances in Rennes and Nantes were serious, the peasant risings in Cornouaille and the Porhoët district seemed like a *jacquerie* or the prelude to a revolution.

The reason for this was perhaps the fact that the system of lordship in Brittany included some archaic features. There, where society had changed less rapidly than in the rest of the kingdom, the rights of justice were "inherent" in the fief. Whereas in Paris, out of 149 fiefs only 25 possessed rights of justice, in Brittany every feudal lord exercised these rights. Moreover, there were no allodial freeholds in Brittany: "All the estates in the province form part of a fief, belonging either to some lord or to the King." Every lordship was a fief. According to the rolls compiled in 1711, there were in Brittany at that time about 3,800 fiefs with rights of justice—282 ecclesiastical and 3,518 lay—which meant, on the average, two lords with rights of justice to each parish.

These fiefs varied greatly in extent. The bishop of Quimper

held in fief the town of Quimper and part of its suburbs, with
rights of temporal justice over twenty parishes. The duc de
Penthièvre held rights of justice in the town of Guingamp, with
56 parishes in his fief and power over 118 jurisdictions. The
rural jurisdiction of Largouet extended in 1665 over 17 parishes.
The majority of these rights of justice, however, were exercised
over half a parish, or a third of a parish, which might mean
several villages and hamlets in this region, with its very dispersed pattern of settlement. In fact, the lord's authority as
regards justice covered all the persons living in his lordship—
and it was very strong. In principle he should have exercised his
rights of justice only over his *directe*, that is, the lands he had
granted out as noble fiefs or as commoner's fiefs (*censives*), but
not over the lands he had retained as *domaines proches*, as
réserve seigneuriale, and which were cultivated for him by farmers
or share croppers, nor over the lands he leased out as *domaine
congéable*. Doubtless, however, because nearly every peasant
holding was made up of land belonging to all the juridical
categories, in actuality the lord exercised his right of justice
over all the land and all the people in his lordship.

This right of justice was far-reaching. The distinction between
high, middle, and low justice existed in principle, but in fact
it had been obliterated, and every lord exercised full rights of
justice, with the power of command and of "*police*," or administration, which followed from these rights. The inhabitants of
the lordship were "his men, his subjects." Whereas, in the area
in which the custom of Paris prevailed, if a lord holding rights
of justice had a dispute with one of his *censitaires* over the
payment of rents or dues, or the equivalent to be paid for
corvée, he was not allowed to bring his case before his own
judge, but had to go before one of the king's judges; in Brittany,
in a case like this, the lord had the matter decided by his
own judge. The lord possessed complete judicial power in
land questions, and so was both judge and party in his own
case. In daily life the lord's officials were in fact his servants,
employed to carry out the exploitation of the lordship. The
lord's procurator-fiscal exacted the payment of dues and the
execution of *corvées*, watched to ensure respect for the obliga-

tion to use only the lord's oven, mill, and wine-press and for the lord's monopoly of hunting and fishing, and prosecuted the peasant who cut down one of the lord's trees, or brought a few meters of heathland under cultivation without reporting the fact. The lord's seneschal became a sort of man of business, a steward or bailiff entrusted with the safeguarding of the lord's interests. He carried out purchases, had repairs done, arranged leases, collected dues, organized cartage, caused trees to be felled, and settled disputes in the lord's favor. The lord's notaries collected his *lods et ventes* and made sure that in all deeds the lands belonging to the lord and the dues owed to him were properly mentioned. The lord's bailiff performed his tasks without charge to the lord. All these officials were appointed by the lord from among the men of his lordship, sons of farmers, coppersmiths, tailors, beadles, men without special qualifications, whom he could dismiss at will. They were at his disposal. As a rule, they were not paid wages but got their remuneration in fees, which resulted in their behaving as intolerable busybodies. The lord thus had his estates managed and his fief administered free of charge and his interests protected by arbitrary justice. It was possible to appeal from the lord's justice, but in the first place this could only be an appeal to another lord. Before reaching the king's judge, it was often necessary to pass through three or four levels of jurisdiction, and through seven or eight before reaching the parlement—and even then, the parlement, filled with lords as it was, safeguarded the interests of lords. In principle, here as elsewhere, the lord who held rights of justice possessed as his private property public powers of justice and administration which he was supposed to exercise on behalf of the state and for the public weal. In reality, here more than elsewhere, private ownership had swallowed up public service, and the Breton lord used his extensive public powers for the benefit of his private interests. Did the peasant get some relief from the circumstance that a single holding of a few hectares might be made up of pieces belonging to various fiefs and several different lords?

As a rule, the Breton lord was a gentleman. As a rule also, and with some honorable exceptions, Breton gentlemen did not serve in the army, but resided on their estates. But, again as a rule, they did not manage their lordships themselves, but entrusted this task to a steward, who was often a seignorial official, and allowed him to act almost without supervision. When the lordship was a large one, they frequently farmed it out in one piece to a farmer-general who then disposed of it as he saw fit. Far from preventing the exactions of the stewards and farmers-general, the lords gave them their backing. For the peasant, the lord was above all a demanding claimant to rent from the soil, and who provided in return some inadequate services. As regards the lands of the *domaine proche*, some lords participated in their exploitation by making investments as owners of capital. Where the demesne was leased out in sharecropping tenancies, the lord advanced to the sharecropper half of the seed and half of the livestock he needed. He often did the same for his other farmers. Where the lands of his *domaine directe* were concerned, however, whether these were granted out as *censives* or as *domaine congéable*, it was unusual for the lord to invest any capital. To be sure, in every case he did provide arable soil, roads, rights of usage in the woods and heaths, and, on the *domaine proche*, farm buildings which it was his responsibility to keep in good repair.

It must be said that in general these Breton gentlemen were poor men, almost on a level with their peasants in this respect. Some of them lived like peasants, in manor houses of gray stone, with a few narrow, dark rooms, lighted only by small and infrequent windows. Some of them even had to plow their own fields. Such a lord made his way to these fields wearing his sword, "emblem and ornament of nobility," laid it down at the gate to the field, and grasped the handles of the plow. The work finished, he took up his sword again. In the diocese of Cornouaille, where the peasant revolts were most serious, Charles Colbert counted, in 1665, 28 noble families whose incomes exceeded 10,000 livres, 30 to 40 gentlemen whose incomes were under 3,000 livres, and parishes where 20 gentle families vegetated in want, some of them living on pensions granted by the provincial states.

But, it will be said, Brittany was a rich province. It exported large quantities of grain—wheat and rye—not only to the neighboring provinces but also to all the countries of Europe, even to the Baltic and the Mediterranean. Brittany wove sailcloth, linen and other fabrics, bunting and serge, knitted stockings and slippers, and sold all these products far afield, even in the Indies, both East and West. That is true. But few Bretons gained from these activities. The lords who owned extensive lordships might accumulate in their storehouses great masses of corn paid to them in seignorial dues, from 1,500 to 6,000 or 8,000 bushels of wheat or rye—and, if they were not too far from the sea, might profit by shortages elsewhere in Europe. But the lords whose lordships were of smaller size, or were farther from the sea, gained nothing in this way, in an area where transport was difficult. The peasants had no disposable surpluses in a region of poor land and in a period when fertilizers were lacking. They carried their corn to the nearest market, in order to get the little money they needed to pay the king's taxes or to pay their money-rents, which were not very high. Many peasants, true, whose holdings were too small or were on rocky soil, spent some of their time dressing hemp, spinning and weaving. Wives, daughters, and maidservants all spun. Everyone thus made a little money wherewith to pay the king's taxes, those stimulants to industry. But the profit went to the merchants, who advanced hemp and flax to the peasants, collected the fabrics they made from these materials, and exported them. Exports might increase and trade prosper, and yet the bulk of the population remain wretched.

The lords were thus driven to exact all their rights with rigor. This was doubtless even more so in the period before 1675, when the fall in prices lowered all incomes, and the shortage of currency had the same effect. In and after 1664 twelve fresh royal taxes drew money out of the province. The scarcity of coins caused farm rents and house rents to fall, and probably likewise the value of what the peasants and their lords had to sell, by a third or even a half, according to contemporaries. Everyone found himself in difficulties.[1] Certain lords and their

1. S. Ropartz, *Guingamp. Etudes pour servir à l'histoire du tiers état en Bretagne*, II, (1859), p. 118, n. 1.

procurators-fiscal or farmers-general set themselves to exact with greater strictness their seignorial rights, which, though reasonable in themselves, were felt as an unbearable burden in a period when money was tight, through the sense the peasants had of extortion and injustice and the violation of sacrosanct custom. They imposed more numerous *corvées* in order to get their corn carted to the seaports, and to repair, or even to build, manor houses and *châteaux*. They haggled over the valuation of the *corvées* in terms of money. In Cornouaille the *corvées* had been valued at 12 livres for a *feu fiscal* of six or seven tenants, by an *arrêt* of the parlement of Brittany. The gentlemen argued, however, that what was meant was 12 livres for each *feu réel*, and thus for each tenant, and they insisted on being paid this sum instead of the *corvée*. They levied new tolls on persons crossing the territory of their lordships; they demanded that rents fixed in terms of corn be paid in money, but instead of determining their value by taking the average of the three previous years or that of the last three markets, in accordance with the Breton custom, they calculated it on the basis of the moment when corn was at its dearest. They quibbled over the *champarts*, trying to get a few more sheaves for themselves. Where rents had to be paid in corn they made the measures deeper, and instead of accepting a measure full to the brim but level across the top they insisted on having it heaped up as high as possible. In 1662 the measure used by the lord of Guingamp, which in 1580 held 65 pounds of grain, had been deepened so as to take in 82 or 84 pounds even when filled only to the level of the brim, and 95 to 100 pounds when heaped up.

It was probably the *domaine congéable*, however, that offered the greatest possibilities for squeezing the peasantry. The marquis de Lavardin points to this, in a letter to Colbert, as an essential cause of the revolt. One and the same peasant holding usually included a part which was a commoner's fief, or *censive*, and a part which was leased; but, in Cornouaille, the Pohorët district, the *vicomté* of Rohan and part of the *vicomté* of Broerec, the largest part was *domaine congéable*. The *domaine congéable* was a form of property which, though it existed in the depths of the Middle Ages and is regarded by some jurists as a survival of servile tenure, had developed in Brittany during the sixteenth

century. It was not necessary to have feudal possession of a
piece of land to be able to grant it out in this way, it was
enough to be the owner of it. The *domaine congéable* seems
to have nothing feudal about it, and to correspond above all
to a situation of widespread poverty. It constituted a form of
association between a landowner without resources and a cultivator with inadequate capital, who, though he might own means
of production to a limited extent, was incapable either of being
a full-fledged landowner or of becoming a large-scale farmer, a
capitalist entrepreneur, such as was frequently to be found in
the plains round Paris. The *domaine congéable* was governed
not by the custom of Brittany but by local usages, called *usances*
or *usements,* which the parties concerned could cause to be enforced by the courts. Legal recognition was accorded to the *usances*
of Tréguier and Goello, of Léon, Broerec, Rohan, Poher, and
Cornouaille. They differed only slightly as far as the *domaine
congéable* in itself was concerned.[2] We can take as an example
the usance of Cornouaille, since it covered the entire diocese
and county of Cornouaille, except for the jurisdiction of Daoulas,
where the usance of Léon prevailed, and that of Corlay, covered by
the usance of Rohan, that is to say, practically the whole area
affected by the peasant revolts of 1675. The usance of Poher,
also covering part of the rebel area, toward Carhaix and Châteauneuf-du-Faou, differed little from that of Cornouaille. The essential feature of the *domaine congéable*[3] was the sharing of
ownership between two people. The *"seigneur foncier"* owned the
land itself, while the *"domanier"* owned the *"édifices et superfices,"* which meant the dwelling houses, barns, storehouses,
cattle sheds, stables, ovens, wells, threshing floors, walls, *"fossés"*
(dykes planted with hedges and trees), meadows, watercourses,
fruit trees, gardens, and manure spread on cultivated land. The
domanier could sell the *édifices et superfices,* and also bequeath
them, with or without making a will. Widows took their dowers
from this property.

The *domanier* had to give the *seigneur foncier* a formal state-

2. G. D'Espinay, "L'ancien droit successoral en basse Bretagne," *Nouvelle
revue historique de Droit,* 19 (1895).

3. A. Bourdot de Richebourg, *Nouveau Coutumier général* (Paris, chez
Michel Brunet, 1724), folio, IV, 1, pp. 409–410.

ment of his tenure, called *lettres recognitoires*; the lease according to the system of *domaine congéable* came up for renewal every nine years; and the *domanier* owed *cens* and seignorial and feudal dues to the *seigneur foncier*, or to the lord of the fief if this was not the same person, for the *seigneur foncier* might hold the land of a lord, as a commoner's fief or *censive*, which would not bar him from leasing it out as *domaine congéable*. The *domanier* also owed the *seigneur foncier* payment of *champart* at the rate of "the fifth sheaf," which meant 20 percent of his crops, and nine days or *corvées* each year—three performed by harnessing his horses to carts to carry wood, wine, and hay, three by providing his horses alone, and three in the form of manual work. These *corvées* had to be performed even outside the area where the *domanier* lived, "for cartage of wine and of slate for repairing the lord's house, or to convey his corn to the nearest seaport or market town." If the *seigneur foncier* undertook any building activity, these *corvées* were doubled. The *domanier* who ranked as principal tenant was obliged to collect in his turn all the payments due to the lord from the other *domaniers*. Finally, the *domanier* had to submit to the justice of the *seigneur foncier*, if the latter held rights of justice, that is, if he was lord of the fief.

On the expiration of the lease, however, the *seigneur foncier* could evict the *domanier*, reimbursing him for the *édifices et superfices*, in accordance with valuation by an expert: these payments were called *droits convenanciers où réparatoires*. The *domanier* was not allowed to build new houses without the permission of the *seigneur foncier* because he must not "encumber the land," that is, establish *édifices* which were worth more than the land itself. He could, however, construct without permission "all other *édifices* that may be useful and necessary, such as hedges, dykes, orchards, gardens and meadows." The *domaine congéable* was thus much less of an obstacle to progress than has been alleged. It was above all the poverty of the district that prevented improvements.

Every nine years the *seigneur foncier* could thus get rid of his *domaniers* and, if he was the lord of the fief, raise their rents. It may be asked whether the *seigneurs fonciers* had not done this more often before 1675. They always had an incentive to do it because, if the same *domanier* remained for forty years in a given tenancy, he thereby became "*seigneur irrévocable des édifices*," full owner without any temporal limitation. In principle, in Cornouaille, the *seigneur foncier* was not supposed to exact, in granting a fresh lease or renewing an old one, "*aucune vente*," that is, any sum of money paid over once for all and not repayable. One may wonder, however, if perhaps the *seigneurs fonciers*, when in difficulties, did exact such payments, "under the table," before 1675? An unscrupulous landlord might even go quite far in this direction. True, a *domanier* who found his tenure too heavily burdened with seignorial rent-charges might "*déguerpir*," that is, abandon it at the end of his nine-year lease, but he coud do this only by settling up all his arrears of rent and renouncing his right to reimbursement of his *droits convenanciers* for the *édifices et superfices*. It is thus clear what the lord of a fief might do: at the end of a lease under the system of *domaine congéable*, he could, making unjust use of his rights of justice, increase the seignorial and feudal rents due for the tenancy concerned; these rents might become too heavy to be borne, and nine years later the *domanier* might abandon the tenancy; the lord could then recover it without having to pay anything, and perhaps find a new *domanier* who, not having to pay for the *édifices et superfices* left by his predecessor, would agree to higher rents (hoping to be able to pay them), and even to make a substantial "under the table" payment. It would be useful to know whether this sort of operation had become common before 1675.

The *domanier*, however, might find himself unable to pay his arrears of rent and therefore unable to *déguerpir*, so that he had to remain in his "tenancy," in debt and in an impaired position, obliged to agree to sacrifices, although legally a free man. The same thing might happen to him, even if the seignorial burdens were not too heavy, if bad harvests or increased tax demands compelled him to beg the lord to postpone or reduce the payment of *champart*.

The opportunities offered by the *domaine congéable* to lords, procurators-fiscal and farmers-general who were not too scrupulous

were thus considerable. To what extent did they make use of
them? We do not know. They certainly did make some use
of them, among all the opportunities offered by the regimes
of fief and lordship, for there were complaints from the peasants
about this. Some lords answered such complaints with blows.
Charles Colbert found something more extreme than that: the
marquis de Goesbriant "sending soldiers armed with their muskets
and bandoliers, and with matches at the ready, to deliver commands and notices on his behalf to the officers of justice and
to insult those of the people whom he does not like."[4] The lords
were said to have increased the income from their lordships
by a third, in the midst of a period when prices were falling
and money was scarce.

The worsening of relations between lords and peasants must
have been felt deeply by the latter. Their human dignity and
their sense of justice and right were hurt, and they were also
affected materially. A small number of peasants, living on land
they owned themselves, laborers with plow-oxen and plows, were
well off; some of these even had large, well-appointed farms,
furniture worth 1,000 to 2,000 livres *tournois*, wardrobes, chests,
plentiful supplies of sheets, table napkins, and shirts, with
the farmer's wife owning a dozen skirts and a dozen aprons. A
large number, however, were mere *closiers*, owning a little low-
roofed house, a few bits of fields, a horse or two, and some
cows, and also *domaniers* farming a fragment of land or a little
closerie, working it with the aid of their families, and extremely poor, fortunate if their furniture was worth as much
as 200 to 300 livres. The majority were day laborers, living in
cob cottages, where they shared with their animals a single room,
with a beaten-earth floor, and were surrounded by dung heaps
and stagnant puddles. Their belongings, a bed, a cupboard, a
kneading trough, some kitchen utensils, a few old clothes, and
some animals, were worth between 20 and 100 livres. Everyone in this category put wheat and rye aside for the payment
of dues and existed on buckwheat griddle-cakes, millet gruel,
butter, and plain water. Epidemics ravaged a population of

4. Bibl. Nat., Cinq-Cents de Colbert, 291, f. 103.

human beings who were small, thin, yellow-skinned, illiterate, violent, crude, and drunk whenever possible. Beggars and vaga- bonds swarmed, plundering and burning, robbing and terrorizing anyone who possessed anything.[5] The slightest increase in their burdens upset the precarious balance of their resources. And now, when their burden was already such a heavy one, here were the provincial states of Brittany, which they looked to as their protectors, and the king, the fountain of all justice, calling for fresh efforts from them. Revolt was the consequence, and in the countryside the lords, regarded in Brittany as representatives of the king and agents of the state, were among the chief victims.[6]

The war with Holland, which Louis XIV had hoped would be brief, a "lightning war," became a long war, a "war of at- trition," when the Dutch halted the French advance and saved Amsterdam by opening the flood-gates at Muyden on July 20, 1672, when they overthrew the bourgeois government of Jan De Witt and replaced it by the aristocratic one of William of Orange, in their revolution of July–August, 1672, and when the coalition against France, formed under the leadership of the Austrian emperor in 1672, was reinforced by new allies in 1673. Louis XIV was obliged to subject to a heavy financial strain a kingdom which had not yet recovered from the "mortalities" of 1648–1653 and 1661–1662.

In Brittany, Louis XIV decided to take advantage of an investigation which had been under way since 1665, for the discovery of cases where rights of justice had been usurped. The king's legal experts having long since laid it down in principle that seignorial rights of justice were a concession from the king, a royal declaration of November 22, 1672, set up a new Chamber of the Royal Demesne at Rennes, with the task of obliging

5. Basic works: André Giffard, *Les Justices seigneuriales en Bretagne au XVIIe et XVIIIe siècles (1661–1791)* (Paris, Bibliothèque de la Fondation Thiers, 1903), fasc. I; Henri Sée, *Les Classes rurales en Bretagne du XVIe siècle à la Révolution* (Paris, 1906); Pierre Goubert, "Recherches d'Histoire rurale dans la France de l'Ouest," *Bull. de la Soc. d'Hist. mod.*, 64 (1965).
6. Basic works: Arthur de la Borderie, *La Révolte du papier timbré advenue en Bretagne, en 1675* (Saint-Brieuc, 1884); Jean Lemoine, *La Révolte dite du papier timbré ou des Bonnets rouges en Bretagne en 1675* (Paris, 1898).

the lords claiming rights of justice to show written authority from the king conceding these rights to them, duly registered by the parlement, on pain of a fine of 1,000 livres. Was a single one of the Breton lords in a position to comply? There were 3,800,000 livres to be collected for the king's treasury, less the costs of lawsuits. After the king had mitigated his demands a little, the states of Brittany, meeting in 1673, offered, in addition to 2,600,000 livres as a free gift, another sum of 2,600,000 livres in return for abolition of the Chamber of the Royal Demesne and repeal of the edicts of 1672 on the lords' rights of justice. The king agreed on December 27, 1673. But the states decided that 920,000 livres would be furnished by the nobility, lords, and officials, and the balance of 1,680,000 livres by the peasants, craftsmen, and bourgeois. The people were to pay to enable the lords to retain their fundamental privilege. The collection of the new tax began in 1675.

An edict of April, 1674, made obligatory throughout the realm the use of stamped paper for all judicial and notarial deeds. This demesne charge would increase the cost of all legal proceedings, whether agreed or disputed, and therefore would reduce the number of such transactions and the profits of all involved in the legal profession. Notaries, attorneys, process servers, and bailiffs were all bitterly opposed to the edict. They stirred up the poorer people to resist it. The magistrates supported them and did not prosecute offenders. The people were all the readier to be drawn into resistance on this issue because the cost of the stamp meant an additional demand for cash, and this was in short supply in Brittany.

An edict of September 27, 1674, reserved to the king the monopoly of the sale of tobacco. The king farmed out his tobacco business to a purchaser-general. The latter installed sub-farmers or agents everywhere and had the sale of tobacco to grocers and other petty retailers prohibited. He intended to buy up their stocks and then put these on sale at a price increased by new charges. However, his agents arrived in the provinces without sufficient funds to buy these tobacco stocks. Time went by. At last, the King's Council decided that the agents would buy up the tobacco at the prices shown on the invoices, or failing them, by weight. Now the tradesmen in question were not always in possession of invoices, and their tobacco, having dried up while in stock, had lost both bulk and weight, so that it seemed to them that their interests were suffering injury. Discontented, they stirred up their customers against the new system, finding it easy to do this because the people concerned were very angry about the interruption in the sale of tobacco and the increase in prices. They were unable to do without tobacco. Undernourished, they calmed the protests of their stomachs by means of this light narcotic, which was usually chewed and less frequently smoked in pipes.

A tax-farmer tried to oblige the craftsmen who made tinware and pewter to pay, within a period of six months, the marking charges on everything they had in their shops. This could not be done, for these goods sold slowly, and a great deal of the trade was on a credit basis. The tinware- and pewter-makers lacked cash to pay the charges. They should have been asked to pay only on what they actually sold, as they sold it. However, tinware and pewter were articles in general use, and the marking charges would raise the prices of these plates and dishes. All the poorer people felt themselves affected, and made common cause with the tinware- and pewter-makers in preventing their goods from being marked.

Finally, the king demanded new taxes from his officials, and required all commoners in possesssion of fiefs to pay frank-fee and a charge on newly acquired property.

Brittany was kept in a state of alarm by the threat of a Dutch landing on its coast. In 1674 the province was still covered with troops. At Brest 4,000 peasants, who had come from as far off as Tréguier and La Roche, were digging fortifications.[7] But although, in 1675, during the months of April, May, and June, Brittany was still threatened by De Ruyter's Dutch fleet, it was empty of troops. The king had had to reinforce his armies in Flanders, and in Alsace—where Turenne waged an overwhelming and celebrated campaign, was victorious, and then was struck down on July 27, 1675—in Germany, in Sicily, and

7. S. Ropartz, *op. cit.*, p. 120, letters from Arthur Laurence, steward to M. de Cornavallet, May 29, 1674.

in Catalonia. It had proved necessary to organize peasant militias, arm them to resist a possible enemy landing, and to resolve that the peasants were to take up arms and rally at the sound of the alarm bell. There was thus a serious risk that this defense organization might help rebels to seize a port and bring about a landing by the Dutch. The enemies of France hoped that this would happen, and rejoiced greatly over the troubles in Brittany. At the very least, they thought, the king would be forced to send an army into Brittany to subdue the rebels, thereby weakening his forces on the northern and eastern frontiers.

The revolt of the peasants in Lower Brittany started from the example set by the towns. In Rennes the grocers had obtained a hearing from the *premier président* of the parlement, sieur d'Argouges, who had shown himself favorable to their views on the tobacco question. When they heard of the disorders in Bordeaux arising from resistance to the marking of pewter, the people of Rennes, on April 18, 1675, sacked the official center for the sale of tobacco and went on to do the same to the stamped-paper centers. The events at Rennes became known in Nantes on April 20. Immediately, the mob sacked the tobacco office and the pewter-marking center, and threatened the stamped-paper center. On May 3 fresh outbreaks occurred, and this time the stamped-paper center was sacked as well.

These acts were performed by the "populace," the "rabble," but others were implicated in responsibility for them. In Nantes, though large-scale merchants remained loyal and though twenty to thirty unarmed gentlemen helped the king's lieutenant, M. de Morveau, to parley with the mob and calm them down, the bourgeois showed themselves hostile to the application of the edicts and made common cause with the rebels. When they were summoned to form companies to reestablish order, they refused to obey their captains. Suspicious "strangers" ran about the streets stirring up trouble. These were possibly beggars and vagabonds who had come in from the countryside. On May 3 a man from Lower Brittany, a potman from the neighborhood of Châteaulin, the area of the great peasant revolts, climbed the town's clock tower, sounded the alarm, and started a riot. He was sentenced to death on May 22, and hanged. On that

May 3, incidentally, the stamped-paper agents did everything they could to provoke the sacking of their office so as to be able to claim heavy compensation.

In Rennes the *journées* of June 9, 10, and 11 were provoked by Louvois, the secretary of state for war. He ordered the governor of the province, the duc de Chaulnes, to march troops into the town. The duke tried to limit the harm done by restricting the number of soldiers to be billeted to three companies. Even so, this was still a breach of the town's privileges, in defense of which all the inhabitants stood together, fearing the soldiers' plundering ways. The suburbs rose first, then the entire town, bourgeois and craftsmen alike—over 15,000 people, it was said. The governor was insulted: "great pig, great tramp, fine dog of a governor." Stones were thrown at the soldiers. The governor was helped by a family of gentlemen, the Coetlogons, loyal servants of the king, while other gentlemen, rivals of the Coetlogons, secretly encouraged the rebels. The parlement sided with the latter, issuing no *arrêt* against them and making it known by word of mouth through the attorneys and process servers that none would be issued. Going still further, the *premier président* of the parlement, d'Argouges, found this the right moment to offer his services to the governor to go to the king and ask him to withdraw the edicts on stamped paper, tobacco, the marking of pewter, frank-fees, and the taxes on officials. The duc de Chaulnes had the good sense to prevent his soldiers from opening fire. Ignoring the insults to his person, he negotiated. By showing patience, and after undertaking to promise a meeting in the near future of the provincial States, he secured agreement from the captains of the bourgeois militia that the rebels would lay down their arms on June 20.

When, however, news of the peasant risings in the Carhaix area reached Rennes, this brought about a third revolt in the town, on July 17, with another sacking of the stamped-paper centers. The duchesse de Chaulnes was insulted and put in peril of death.

Thus, in the towns, there was an alliance between the three estates, against royal taxation and in defense of local privileges.

In the countryside a rumor spread that, in addition to all the

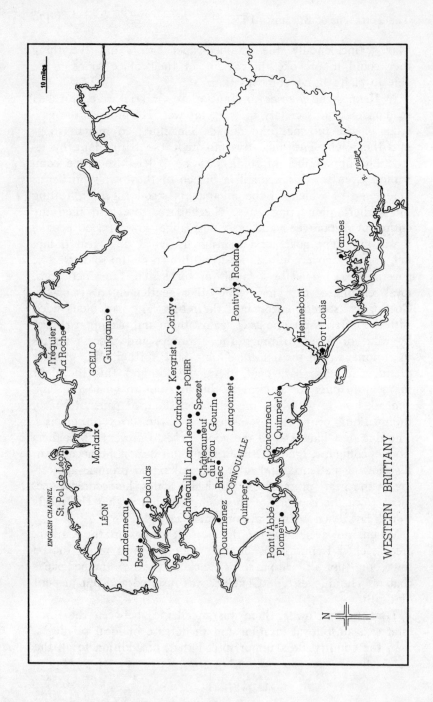

10 miles

ENGLISH CHANNEL

Tréguier
La Roche

GOELLO

Guingamp

Morlaix

St. Pol de Léon

LÉON

Landerneau

Brest

Daoulas

Châteaulin

Landeleau

Carhaix

Kergrist

Corlay

POHER

Spezet

Châteauneuf
du Faou

Gourin

Briec

CORNOUAILLE

Langonnet

Quimper

Douarnenez

Pont l'Abbé

Plomeur

Concarneau

Quimperlé

Pontivy

Rohan

Hennebont

Port Louis

Vannes

R. Vilaine

N

WESTERN BRITTANY

taxes already mentioned, the king was going to establish the gabelle in the province. Disturbances began in May and occurred almost everywhere in Lower Brittany: there were attacks on the king's officials, on tax collectors, tax-farmers, and gentlemen. Two main centers can be singled out, however—Cornouaille, between May and July, 1675, and the Carhaix area, or "Pays de Poher," between July and September. These were isolated areas: hills making a jumbled skyline, a *bocage* giving the impression of a dense forest; many woods still in existence, the remains of a former forest of beech-trees—as was shown by the frequent occurrence of the place name "Faou" (*fagus*, beech-tree); winding roads, deeply embanked by *fossés*—dykes bristling with thick hedges and trees; narrow valleys, often marshy; a soil of granitic sand or schistous clay, siliceous and poor; an abundance of broom and heather; *châteaux* and manor houses standing quite isolated, as though cut off from the world, and at the mercy of a surprise attack.

In Cornouaille the rumor circulated at the beginning of June that the marquis de La Coste, the king's lieutenant in the four dioceses of Lower Brittany—Vannes, Saint-Pol-de-Léon, Tréguier, and Quimper-Corentin (or Cornouaille)—had been given the task of introducing the gabelle. On June 9 the alarm bell was sounded at Châteaulin and in about thirty parishes around. Bands of peasants armed with guns and muskets, forks and sticks, marched on the "*grand gabeleur.*" A court bailiff presented their demands to the marquis. He behaved insolently and the marquis killed him. He and his men were then fired on, the marquis and some others being wounded. They took refuge in a house where the peasants threatened to burn them alive. To save his life the marquis had to promise them that the edicts would be withdrawn. Then he fled to Brest, where he sought treatment for his wound.

On the same day, at Briec, about halfway between Châteaulin and Quimper, fifteen or sixteen kilometers from each of them, the alarm was sounded. Two thousand peasants from more than twenty villages in the neighborhood, armed with guns, forks, and "iron-shod sticks" (probably boar-spears and pikes), gathered in the cemetery after Mass. They were addressed by Allain Le

Moign, know as "Big Moign," who was *caporal* of the *trêve* of Le Gorresquer-en-Briec, that is, of a hamlet with a chapel attached to the parish of Briec, and by Germain Balbouez, *caporal* of the *trêve* of Landudal, six or seven kilometers south of Briec. What did this title *caporal* mean? Did it mean elected leader, or was it equivalent to "cock of the parish," which would point to the activity of a peasant aristocracy, or was it a rank in the militia organized to withstand a possible landing? Led by Le Moign, Balbouez, and Laurent Le Quéau, a miller from Quéméneven, seven or eight kilometers west of Briec, the peasants, who compelled their priests, the rectors of Briec and Edern, to go with them, marched on the château of La Boissière, where they expected to find, staying with M. de Kéranstret, the marquis de La Coste and the sieur de La Garaine-Jouan, who was said to be carrying the order for establishing the gabelle. Their purpose was to slaughter all these noblemen. So far as the peasants were concerned, they were all *gabeleurs*. When they could not find the men they were looking for, they stove in some casks of wine, seized weapons and ammunition, and set fire to the château.

Informed of these events, the duc de Chaulnes on June 12 appointed the marquis de Nevet commander of the militia in the diocese of Cornouaille, issued an order forbidding gatherings of armed men, promised an amnesty, and obtained from the parlement an *arrêt* declaring the rumors about the gabelle to be false and without foundation, and decreeing penalties against those who spread such rumors. But the governor lacked troops. The peasants of the Pont-l'Abbé area now joined the "dance." On June 23 the inhabitants of "*plusieurs*" parishes sacked a local stamped-paper center, and dragged a gentleman out of church by his hair and knocked him senseless. They attacked the château of Cosquer in the parish of Combrit, sacked it and mortally wounded the castellan, Euzenou de Kersalaun. On June 24 the peasants ravaged the château of Pont-l'Abbé, burning its muniment-room. Soon afterward they attacked the Carmelite monastery of Pont-l'Abbé, which was an ecclesiastical lordship. They threatened to plunder the granaries and cellars. The monks had to sign a paper renouncing their claim to *corvées*, and are said to have signed a sort of code of peasants' rights. The peasants pushed on. In July, "certain rebels and persons who had risen in the parishes of Plomeur and Treffiagat," in the Cap-Caval district, ruined the manor house of Lestrédiagat, in Treffiagat parish, and that of Brénauvec, in the *trêve* of Plobannalec, which belonged to Messire René du Haffon, the lord of Lestrédiagat. They tore down everything, even to the slates on the roofs.[8] Everywhere the stamped-paper offices were sacked, the *châteaux* plundered. The gentry and priests took refuge in the towns, taking their chattels with them. The rebel peasants forced, by means of threats, other peasants to go along with them, parish priests to march at their head (though some priests, such as Alain Maillard, of the *trêve* of Lenviau, were genuine ringleaders), and gentlemen to put on peasant dress and take command of armed bands. Madame de Sévigné calls the rebels the "blue-caps." A blue cap was the usual headgear worn by fishermen. However, Madame de Sévigné had no bent for exactitude, and up to now we have no information enabling us to ascertain what the social groups actually were that made up these "peasant" bands. A list of rebels, mentioned by name, who were excepted from the amnesty, was drawn up by the king's authority. Research in the parish registers and what survives of notaries' records and court archives would doubtless enable us to establish who their families were and the main stages of their lives, and so to discover what sort of people we have before us.

What did these rebels want? The duc de Chaulnes sent Colbert on July 9, 1675, a "peasant code,"[9] but the copy is unfortunately no longer to be found in his correspondence. A seventeenth—or eighteenth—century copy of it, in poor condition, was found by MM. Gaultier du Mottay and Tempier in the archives of the *département* of Côtes-du-Nord, series C, 163, in 1859, and another by B. Pocquet du Haut-Jussé, which the latter assigns to the beginning of the eighteenth century. F.-M. Luzel, keeper of the records of the *département* of Finistère, searched in vain for

---

8. Daniel Bernard, "La révolte du papier timbré au pays bigouden. Nouveau documents inedits," *Mém. de la Soc. d'Hist. et d'Archéol. de Bretagne*, XLII (1962), pp. 59–67.

9. *Mélanges Colbert*, 172, f. 62.

a third copy in his depository and in the archives of the communes of his *département*. The authenticity of this "peasant code" has been questioned by MM. de La Villemarqué, Faty, and Le Men. On the other hand, MM. Gaultier du Mottay, Tempier, Luzel, de La Borderie, and B. Pocquet du Haut-Jussé are disposed to believe it authentic. Is this document a genuine one?[10]

The "peasant code" is supposed to have been drawn up and proclaimed at an assembly of delegates of fourteen parishes, held in the chapel of La Tréminon, in the parish of Plomeur, five or six kilometers southwest of Pont-l'Abbé. The title it bears is: "Copy of the statute made by the noble inhabitants of the fourteen united parishes of the land of Armorica situated between Douarnenez and Concarneau, to be inviolably observed between them until Michaelmas next, on pain of Torrében," and it is signed: "Torrében and the inhabitants." According to some scholars, Torrében means "truncheon."

The peasants declared themselves joined together "for the freedom of the province of Armorica," and declared seignorial rights abolished as being encroachments on "Armoric freedom." They resolved to send six deputies to the provincial states, providing each of them with a cap and a jacket, both red, and blue trunk-hose. Meanwhile, they laid down their arms, "by a special favor done to the gentlemen," whom they will call upon to return to their country houses as soon as possible. The peasants forbade anyone to "sound the alarm and assemble armed men without the universal consent of the said union." They abolished *champarts*, corvées, tithes, and the obligation to use the lord's mill. They reduced the charges on "foreign" wine to a hundred sols per cask and that on the wine of the province to one *écu*, and their selling price at the same time to five and three sols the pint, respectively. The money from the "old-established hearth-tax" was to be used to buy tobacco and this was to be

10. The "peasant code" has been printed three times: in Arthur de la Borderie, *Revue de Bretagne et de Vendée*, 7 (1860), pp. 92–94 (reproduced in his *Révolte du papier timbré, op. cit.*, pp. 93–98); in R. F. Le Men, *Bull. de la Soc. Archéol. et Hist. du Finistère* (1877–78), pp. 184–187; and in D. Tempier, *Mém. de la Soc. Archéol. des Côtes-du-Nord*, 2d ser. 2 (1885–86), p. 124. See also F.-M. Luzel, *Bull. de la Soc. Archéol. et Hist. du Finistère*, 14 (1887), pp. 64–67.

distributed along with the wafers at Mass in the parishes. Hunting was to be banned between March 1 and September 15. Pigeon houses were to be destroyed and pigeon shooting allowed. Parish priests were to be paid wages by their parishioners. Stamped paper was to be abolished. Justice was to be rendered by judges who would be elected and maintained by the inhabitants. "It is forbidden, on pain of being killed with pitchforks, to give shelter to the gabelle or her children, or to provide them with any food or other comfort; and, contrariwise, it is ordered that she be shot at like a mad dog." Marriage was to be allowed between gentlefolk and peasants. Women of noble status were to confer nobility on the men they married and on their posterity. Inheritances were to be divided equally. The town of Quimper and other towns were to be obliged "by force of arms" to ratify this statute, "on pain of being declared enemies of Armoric freedom." This statute was to be read out to the people from the pulpit at High Mass and posted at all crossroads.

If the "peasant code" is genuine, it calls for the following comments. The peasants were not attacking the seignorial and feudal system. Actually, *champarts*, corvées, obligations to use the lord's mill, etc., are not essentially seignorial and feudal rights but domanial ones. Shares of the crops and services, and monopolies are all forms of income of the owner of the land, which enter into land rent even if there is no lordship or fief. The tithes are church taxes, with nothing feudal about them. On the other hand, the peasants retained the two fundamentals of the seignorial and feudal regime—the *cens recognitifs* and the *lods et ventes*. Why? Perhaps because it would have been to their advantage to see the *domaine congéable* replaced everywhere by *censives* or commoner's fiefs. In reality, the peasant who possessed the *dominium utile* of a *censive* was a real landowner, who could not be dispossessed except in very precisely defined and unusual circumstances, and then only after a long procedure. An extension of the seignorial and feudal regime would have strengthened the position of the *domaniers* by making them the definitive owners of the soil itself no less than of what was on its surface.

The peasants were not attacking the structure of the society of orders and estates. They asked only for an improvement in it, namely, the opportunity to move up into the higher order by marrying a noblewoman. We should observe here that among these poor Breton gentlemen, burdened with children, marrying their daughters to peasants was probably nothing exceptional. The peasants wanted these marriages to have a consequence which they did not entail, namely, the husbands' ascent into the higher strata. But the hierarchy of orders and estates was to remain.

Finally, these peasants did not call for an overturn in the political regime. They made no demands affecting the sovereign and absolute state, the monarchical government, the existence of the provincial states. They wanted only an improvement for themselves, namely, that they be represented in the states. And on this point what they required was doubtless confined to a temporary and exceptional representation, since they say: "at the next meeting of the states, in order to explain the reasons for their uprising."

Partial improvements in their lot within the existing social and political structures was what they wished, not a radical change in these structures, not a transition from the structure of orders and estates to the structure of classes, or from the absolute monarchy to the representative or parliamentary monarchy. These rebels would seem not to have been revolutionaries.

It may be that the "peasant code" is genuine. B. Pocquet du Haut-Jussé quotes a "Code Pesovad" or "code of what is good," containing some of the demands of the "peasant code":[11] "Treaty of peace between the noble bourgeois of the town of Pont-l'Abbé and the well-intentioned persons of the neighboring parishes." The peasants lay down that champarts and corvées are to be abolished. They grant themselves permission to hunt and to kill pigeons. They forbid the use of stamped paper. They reduce the charges exacted by notaries, and command attorneys and judges to deal expeditiously with cases "and to judge them in accordance with common sense, not chicanery." This code does not go nearly as far as the "peasant code," and

11. *Histoire de Bretagne*, V (Rennes, 1913).

therefore gives rise, with all the more reason, to similar comments to those made above. It is, moreover, not impossible that our "peasant code" is the *"Code Pesovad"* touched up by some townsman at the end of the eighteenth century, or even by a romantic of the first half of the nineteenth century, who would not have been unaware of the *cahiers* of 1789, or of the way the court ridiculed the rebels and their horror of the gabelle, an echo of which we find in Madame de Sévigné.[12]

The same conclusions can be drawn from a document which, though less bold, is more certainly genuine: "The request of the people in this revolt," brought to the marquis de Nevet by "a man of the people," "on behalf of twenty parishes over Châteaulin way," and sent by the marquis to the duc de Chaulnes on July 19 and by Chaulnes to Colbert next day.[13] The peasants cry out against the judges who "lay burdens on them at every opportunity"; against the nobles, "who ill-treat us on many pretexts, for corvées or *champarts* or the obligation on us to use their mills," "who keep a great number of sheep and other livestock which cause us great losses in our crops" and "many pigeons who eat our corn," and who "threaten to have us beaten"; against "new charges which have come in during the last two years, such as the *contrôle*, the stamped-paper"; and so on. "How is it supposed that we can pay the new taxes, when those that were there already are too heavy for us to bear?" "We are ready to pay the taxes that were in being sixty years ago, and we do not object to paying anyone what he has a right to receive, and we are not arguing against anything but the new edicts and charges." And they "beg His Majesty to look upon them with compassion and to relieve them."

12. Madame de Sévigné to Madame de Grignan, Paris, Wednesday, July 24, 1675 (ed. Monmerqué, *Grands Écrivains de la France*, III, no. 419, pp. 523–524): "M. Boucherat was telling me the other day how a parish priest received, while in the presence of his parishioners, a clock which had been sent him 'from France,' as they put it. They all began shouting in their language that it was the '*gabelle*,' they could see that very well. The priest cleverly replied, in the same style: 'Not at all, my children, it is not the "*gabelle*," you don't know anything about it: it is the Jubilee.' At once they went down on their knees. What do you think of the sharp wits of those people?"

13. Quoted by B. Pocquet du Haut-Jussé, *Histoire de la Bretagne*, V, p. 505, n. 1.

These peasants did not put forward any definite remedy or
any reform. What emerged from their complaints was that
they accepted everything that was old and had become justified by
custom, that only innovations, excesses and deviations from tradition did they regard as unbearable, and that what they expected
from the king was merely the abolition of the new royal edicts
and the new land dues, together with the good functioning of
the established social and administrative institutions, which they
did not think of changing. They were angry men, but not
revolutionaries.

Here, indeed, they appear rather as the opposite of revolutionaries.

In the absence of troops, the peasant revolt seemed to enjoy
free rein. The marquis de Nevet was shut up in his château
of Lezargant. The peasants talked of capturing Quimper. They
were hostile to the towns, which to them were lairs of *gabeleurs*
and whose inhabitants seemed to them an odiously privileged lot,
since the *domaine congéable* was unknown there and all property was in the form of *censives*. The marquis de La Roche,
governor of Quimper, could not count on the bourgeois militia
and had difficulty in preventing outbreaks by the craftsmen.
But the peasants had neither a leader with sufficient experience
to coordinate their actions nor cannon they could use to attack
a town. They were not in a position to undertake a siege, for
lack of organized supply services and because they were unable
to remain together in the field. They could not capture a port
and join hands with the Dutch. Moreover, it seems that the
number of peasants who took part in the revolt reluctantly was
substantial. Indeed, the marquis de Nevet, who on July 13
had executed the murderers of the guards at the château of
La Motte, declared that this act of his "gave so much joy to
the people that there were over 2,000 people present, who called
down a thousand blessings upon me."[14] The presence of the duc
de Chaulnes at Port-Louis, from the beginning of July onward,
had a good effect. Gradually the region calmed down.

Then, however, the Pays de Poher broke out in revolt. In

14. Nevet to the duc de Chaulnes, July 15, 1675, Mélanges Colbert, 172,
f. 147.

July and August, 1675, the rebels were masters of the area of Carhaix and Gourin. Here the revolt seems to have differed from the previous one, in the first place by the presence of a leader, Sébastien Le Balp, who was the son of a miller of Kergloff, seven or eight kilometers west of Carhaix, and who himself became in 1662 the king's notary in Kergloff, one of the twenty-eight king's notaries associated with the king's court at Carhaix. Later, in this area, several priests freely became leaders of the rebels, some of them subsequently being sentenced to the galleys, like Messire Jean Dollo, of Carhaix, "proved to have been a leader of the rebels and to have made some of the inhabitants of this town sign a warrant containing his name, appointing him captain of the rebels." Five were eventually excluded from the amnesty accorded by the king. The rank-and-file priests could reproach the rectors with keeping for themselves the entire proceeds of the *droit de neume,* a ninth of the value of the chattels of a deceased person, and with taking a share of the sums given by persons who caused High Masses to be said on feast days and Sundays to the priests who said these Masses, even when these priests only, and not the rector, had been present.[15] Another factor was that the peasants in this area were practically masters of the towns, which had no walls around them—Carhaix, and, to the west, almost outside the rebel area, Pontivy, in the *vicomté* of Rohan. The peasants entered these towns freely. At Le Balp's instigation, they endeavored to take possession of some ports, so as to welcome the Dutch into Brittany. Finally, and most important, the revolt assumed more markedly in this region than elsewhere the character of a conflict between one social group and others. The red cap was the usual headgear of the peasants and had no special significance. But it does seem that it had become a social symbol. When, at Kergrist-Moëllou, about twenty kilometers east of Carhaix, on July 19, the subjects of Messire Yves de Launay, sieur de La Salle, brought together by the alarm bell, told their lord "that it was absolutely necessary that he agree to their wishes, or otherwise they would bring the *Red Caps* to come and see him,

15. See "Mémoire anonyme présenté aux États de Bretagne, vers 1655," *Bull. de la Soc. d'Hist. et d'Archéol. de Bretagne* (1931), pp. 1–5.

and they would come along with them," the "Red Caps" seeming to mean in this context an armed group of peasants, the most active of the rebels, those at the head of the revolt. Similarly, on July 23, at Maël-Carhaix, about ten kilometers east of Carhaix, at the home of Mathieu Hamon, sieur de Kerguezen, the peasants threatened the notary and the lord with the "Red Caps," who would come and put them to fire and sword. When, at the end of August, stirred up by the rebels of Poher, the southern part of Cornouaille began to move again, the parish of Combrit and some others hoisted the red flag. We do not know what this meant to them. Was it just a signal visible from afar, not a symbol? It seems nevertheless that we find this time some symbols of rebellion which testify to awareness of a social antagonism.

We find something pointing in the same direction in the deliberate attempt made by the peasants to impose their dictatorship on the other social groups. At Maël-Pestivien, ten or twelve kilometers north of Kergrist-Moëllou, on July 18, the peasants, armed with guns, muskets, and pikes, and accompanied by the rector of Pommerit, Messire Thomas Poulain, sacked the manor house of Kerbastard, belonging to the baron de Beaulieu. They announced "that the time of their absolute power had come, they mocked the king and his edicts and also the judiciary, *to all of whom they would lay down the law* and whom they would compel to acknowledge and obey them." This dictatorship had for its purpose, according to what they said, the establishment of a social order of their own, and we find further evidence of this in the way they dragged notaries about with them and forced them to draw up in due form the regulations that they obliged their lords to accept. The stamped paper played only a secondary role, since while some forbade the notaries to use it, others preferred it.

This second series of troubles began at Gourin, twenty kilometers south of Carhaix, on June 29. When they came out of church after High Mass, some peasants of Gourin, Leuhau, and Roudouallec, over two hundred persons in all, led by Guillaume Morvan, smashed with stones the gates and windows of François Jan, bailiff of the court of Carhaix, and struck him, "saying that he had the gabelle." In the cemetery of Gourin they obliged the village crier to make formal announcement that at least one person from each household must present himself the next day at Gourin equipped with weapons and means "to burn the rolls, affidavits and stamped paper." Those who failed to appear would be "burned and killed in their homes." Next day, June 30, three hundred people attended Mass and afterward went to the house of Maître François Millier, "where they seized the stamped paper and burned it publicly." Then they went to the manor house of Kerbiquet, a pretty Renaissance dwelling, on a hill six or seven kilometers southwest of Gourin. They made the sieur de Kerbiquet and the sieur de Kerstang sign "all the declarations they required of them." Struggle against the king's taxes and against the lords were closely linked in this case, perhaps because in Brittany more than elsewhere the lord was the king's representative.

On July 3 the "parishes of Cornouaille" sacked the storehouses of the tax-farmer Bigeaud at Daoulas. On the fourth these bands arrived at Landerneau, swelled their ranks with poor people of that place, and went to the building where the stamped paper was kept. They tore up and scattered to the winds as much as they could, and then proceeded to plunder and damage the house where Bigeaud lived.[16]

At Spezet, about twenty kilometers to the southwest of Carhaix, lived Henry Porcher, clerk of the court and notary in the jurisdictions of Quergorlay, Pommerit, and Lesloch, who was in charge of the rolls and affidavits of the parish of Spezet, was the sole seller of wine in Spezet, and a farmer of taxes and seignorial dues—the very model of a *gabeleur*. On Sunday, July 7, the alarm bell was rung after vespers, about three o'clock in the afternoon. Porcher was at Rennes, in connection with a case. All the parishioners came out of church and hurled themselves upon the sieur Duparc Rousel, his cousin by marriage. They forcibly deprived him of his pistols and sword, beat him with sticks and stones, and left him for dead, weltering in his own blood. They next flung themselves on Porcher's house, ate

16. A. de la Borderie, *Révolte du papier timbré* (1884), app. IV, pp. 260–268.

his bread and meat that they found there, emptied five casks of wine, used axes to break into cupboards, seized "the books of rolls and affidavits,[17] where the gabelle was written," forced the parish priest, Christophe Le Boulic, to read these out to them, and then tore them up and burned them. Next they sacked Porcher's farmhouse and drove off his livestock. Besides the peasants, a priest named Messire Jean Corbé was involved in this affair.[18]

At Carhaix, seat of the local king's court, on July 6 and 7, the peasants of twenty-one neighboring parishes, assembled by the alarm bell, sacked the offices of the "duties" of Brittany, that is, the centers for levying the taxes on drinks, and destroyed the papers they found there. They did the same, in the court registries, with the leases made between them and their lords in recent years, which were mostly *domaine congéable* leases.

The expedition which had the biggest repercussions, however, was the capture and destruction by fire of the castle of Kergoat, eight kilometers southwest of Carhaix, on July 11 and 12, 1675. This was one of the strongest castles in Brittany, a quadrilateral of walls four or five meters thick enclosing several courtyards big enough for a number of battalions to be formed in columns there. Situated at the top of a wooded hill, it dominated the roads from Carhaix to Gourin and from there to Concarneau or to Port-Louis, in one direction, and to Châteauneuf-du-Faou and from there to Châteaulin or to Quimper, in the other. It was, indeed, one of the keys of the rebel area. People said that the duc de Chaulnes was going to occupy it with 8,000 men. He would be able to house his troops in the castle and in nearby places, under the protection of the cannon of this fortress, and recover his strength. Le Balp therefore decided to capture the place. It was all the easier to draw the peasants into this enterprise because they hated the owner of the castle, the marquis Toussaint Lemoyne de Trévigny. He had made them rebuild his castle with their corvées and he had indulged in exactions at their expense.

17. That is, the record of transactions by notaries and process servers, in accordance with a scale of fees.
18. Reports of judicial inquiries and interrogations, published by F.-M. Luzel, *Bull. Soc. d'Hist. et d'Archéol. du Finistère*, 14 (1887), pp. 37 sq.

Historians have the reports of some investigations into this affair, with depositions by witnesses.[19] These proceedings were the work of the *sénéchal* of Carhaix, who acted as agent and subdelegate on behalf of the *intendant* de Marillac. The witnesses were a "*laboureur* and householder," a "housewife," a "royal and general bailiff of the royal jurisdiction of Carhaix and Duault," a "clerk of the registry of the royal court of Carhaix," a "king's notary," and so on. The peasants and notaries who gave evidence all described themselves as having been coerced by the rebels, but since they were eyewitnesses of the events and, if they had not been forced to be present they would not have been witnesses but accused, there are no grounds for accepting this assertion of theirs, which may have been inserted on his own initiative by the clerk of the court.

We learn from these depositions that as early as Thursday, July 11, the alarm bell sounded for the peasants to go and lay siege to Kergoat. Troops of peasants, armed with "iron forks" and "long sticks" (which may mean pikes, boar-spears, or guns), came from Kergloff, Saint-Hernin, Spezet, Landeleau, Gourin, Roudouallec, Lanedern, Plouyé, and Loqueffret, saying wherever they went as they marched across the country that everyone must go to Kergoat and "that whoever failed to go there would be burned before nightfall." It was Le Balp who had given the order, and if it were not carried out, "he would come *with his troops* and swoop down on the parishes." On the evening of that day, Guillaume Morvan appeared at Gourin crying that they had captured Kergoat: "We are the masters, but the parishioners of Gourin, Roudouallec, and other places must come at once with me, every one of them, or else before ten o'clock tomorrow morning we will put them to fire and sword; there are more than six thousand of us before Kergoat, who will all come here to see to that along with me; and let the alarm bell be rung for this purpose, if they wish to save their lives and property." The alarm bell rang all night.

The next day, Friday, July 22, recruitment went on, from early

19. D. Tempier, "La révolte du papier timbré en Bretagne. Nouveaux documents," *Mém. Soc. Archéol. des Côtes-du-Nord*, 2d ser. 2 (1885–86), pp. 132–143; Luzel, *Bull. Soc. Archéol. et Hist. du Finistère*, 14 (1887), pp. 37–54.

morning onward, the peasants flocking to the castle of Kergoat. It
was on that day, or perhaps the evening before, that a number of
witnesses saw arriving "the parishioners of Plounévès-du-Faou
(about twenty kilometers west of Carhaix) in large numbers, all carrying arms and marching to the sound of drums and with a flag fly-
ing, and six or seven priests, also armed with guns and long stocks,
from the said parish of Plounévès-du-Faou. When they arrived
they declared loudly to the people of the other, more distant,
parishes that everything must be burned down, and whatever
was left razed to the ground, lest soldiers come and find quarters
there and bring ruin upon the district. . . ." The castle was
easily taken. The marquis was away and there was no garrison.
Several servants were killed or wounded. The sieur de Kervilly,
steward of the castle, was killed and his body left lying in
the courtyard. The marquise made her escape and took refuge
with the Carmelites of Saint-Sauveur. Le Balp had all the deeds
and parchments burned, and removed the cannon. Some of the
peasants opened casks of wine and got drunk, while others
plundered the rooms of the castle.

M. de Kerlouet, governor of Carhaix, was informed in the
course of July 12 that peasants were besieging the castle of
Kergoat. He ordered the people to Carhaix to take up arms
in order to proceed on the following day to raise the siege.
The governor and the men of Carhaix set out next day, Saturday,
July 13, at four in the morning, by the main road from Carhaix
to Quimper-Corentin. When they reached the bridge at Kergoat
mill, however, they were halted by two peasants armed with
guns, who showed them a request signed by the marquise de
Trévigny for "two king's notaries to draw up their [the peasants']
conditions in written form." The governor decided it would
be more prudent, for the sake of Madame de Trévigny, not to
push on, but to send forward Maîtres Michel Renault and Le
Houllier, king's notaries at the royal court of Carhaix. The
two notaries, escorted by the two peasants, crossed the castle
of Kergoat. At the entrance they saw "a dead body, completely
naked"; it was the steward. In the first courtyard they saw another; "the coachman." Peasants were carrying off clothes, furniture, papers. In the rear courtyard other peasants were drinking

wine from casks, "in bowlfuls," and were mostly drunk. At the new chapel at Saint-Sauveur the notaries found the marquise de Trévigny, who "begged the witness and the said Le Houllier, in God's name, to do whatever the peasants her subjects wanted, so as to save her freedom and her life." The two notaries went with four peasants and some monks into one of the rooms in the monastery. They asked the peasants if they wanted the deed recorded on stamped paper. "They replied that they did not, and that they wanted no more stamped paper, and threatened to kill the witness and his companion if they did not do their will. And at the same moment the said Coz (one of the peasants) *took from his pocket a paper on which was written the formulation of the deed that they wanted to have* and that had to be followed as they wished, even adding some clause if they so desired." The deed was drawn up. The notary Renault "read it out aloud, from the cross in the said cemetery, to the peasants who were there, because they wished simply to know that it had been drawn up." He gave copies to "Pierre Calvé, of Kervégant, in the *trêve* of Roudouallec," nine kilometers west of Gourin and about twenty from Kergoat, to Jean Oryant and Gabriel Le Borgne, "of the village of Quernoët," perhaps Carnoët, about fifteen kilometers northeast of Carhaix, to Lorains Lorans, to Le Hairon "and others," either because their holdings were in the lordship of the marquis de Trévigny or else so that they might serve as models in their dealings with their own lords.

The Kergoat affair seems to have given a new direction to the revolt. Thenceforth the attacks were directed less against taxation offices and court registries and more against *châteaux* and manor houses. Thenceforth also there were numerous instances of deeds, authenticated by notary, being imposed on lords. Some of these have survived, and enable us to perceive clearly what the motives and aims of the peasants were. Such was the one imposed by the peasants of Tréogan and Plévin upon the Father Prior and monks of the Abbey of Langonnet, about fifteen kilometers southeast of Gourin, on July 14, 1675: abolition of "tithes of black corn," that is, buckwheat, the peasants' own food, and yearly rents paid in kind, "without power to value them"; rights of usage in the forests of the monastery, if the monks do not enclose them; return to the old *"mesure censive"* for the payment of rents, payment only of the *lods et ventes* "due in former times by right and custom"; reduction by five sols of the money equivalent of each "personal" corvée.[20] Return to what was old-established and customary, mitigation of seignorial and feudal rights, and nothing more. The seignorial and feudal regime itself was not challenged, still less the social structure. Such too was the deed imposed, on July 20, 1675, in a ground-floor room in his manor house of La Salle, upon Yves de Launay, sieur de La Salle, by a score of drunken peasants of the parish of Kergrist-Moëllou—eating and drinking, uttering violent threats, shouting that they, "like all the other peasants, intended to make new rules and oblige their master to obey the law they would impose on him": abolition of corvées and *champarts*; reduction of rents in money and in kind in proportion to the quality of the lands included in the *domaines congéables*; all the wood growing on the *fossés* to belong to the peasants, that is, the cask-wood too, that wood used for making barrel staves and other planks, which was normally reserved for the lord; permission to build houses to live in wherever they chose on their *domaine congéable*, and to erect new *fossés*, "for which," however, "they will not claim any payment or compensation should they leave the tenancy." "And the said lord shall not be able to lease out part of the *domaine congéable* but only the whole"—which meant that the lord had been reducing the extent of certain holdings in order to increase the number of his *domaniers*, thereby reducing each one's means of existence. The peasants agreed to observe their obligation to use the lord's will, but asked for scales and weights, and means of preventing fraud by the miller; it was understood that the lord would transport one millstone to the mill at his expense, and his tenant would be responsible for the other; finally, the *domaniers* might have their corn ground where they liked if the water supply was inadequate at the lord's mill in July, August, or September. In all this, as in all the other deeds, we see only partial improvements in the seignorial and feudal

20. Document sent by the duc de Chaulnes to Colbert, Bibl. Nat., Mélanges Colbert, 172, f. 149.

regime and the system of *domaine congéable*. There is no sign
of any thoroughgoing reform. It is curious that these peasants
did not even ask for the replacement of the *domaine congéable*
by the farming lease, as in the Pays de Léon, and there was
even less question of replacing the existing structures by new
ones. These peasants, who were mostly illiterate, lacked a political
and social ideology which would have provided them with
mental categories and solutions, a program for replacing the
existing social order by a fresh one. These angry men were
not revolutionaries and their outbreak was not an attempt at
revolution.

Meanwhile, Le Balp wanted to take the offensive before the
king's forces appeared on the scene, and to capture Morlaix,
so as to make contact with the Dutch fleet. For the first time,
however, he came up against the marquis de Montgaillard, who,
from his château of Le Thymeur, northwest of Carhaix, near
the road from Carhaix to Morlaix, wrote to all the gentlemen
in the area, ensuring that they held themselves in readiness
to obstruct the advance of the peasants. Intimidated by this
resistance, the poor wretches gave up their project, between
July 14 and 24.

Some days later, Le Balp had the alarm sounded again and
the peasants set out for Morlaix once more. Then, however,
the marquis de Montgaillard spread the story that 6,000 of the
king's soldiers had arrived at Morlaix. Le Balp took fright and
withdrew his men.

A few days afterward he realized that he had been tricked.
He seized the château of Le Thymeur and held the marquis
de Montgaillard prisoner there. He considered taking advantage
of a fresh rising in Cornouaille, where 4,000 rebels were besieging
Concarneau, and where the Pont-l'Abbé area had broken out
again. Le Balp decided to attack the duc de Chaulnes at Port-
Louis. He fixed Wednesday, September 3, as the date for the
rising in the Pays de Poher. On the evening of the second he
arrived at the château of Le Thymeur with 2,000 rebels, while
he had the alarm bells ringing everywhere in order to raise
30,000. He planned to take with him the marquis de Montgaillard
and his brother, hoping that he might force them to serve as

his generals. Le Balp called on the marquis's brother at midnight and threatened to kill him if he would not accompany him the next day. The sieur de Montgaillard seized his sword, killed Le Balp, and ran to the door, shouting: "Kill, kill!" The marquis de Montgaillard hurried up, followed by eighty peasants who had promised to go to their lord's help if anyone tried to kill him or burn his house down. The guard posted by Le Balp panicked and fled. The other peasants, on learning of Le Balp's death, took fright and dispersed. The death of Le Balp put an end to the great revolt.

At that moment the duc de Chaulnes had at last received reinforcements—French guards, Swiss guards, musketeers and dragoons. Over 6,000 men were concentrated at Port-Louis, Hennebont, and Quimperlé, ready to march into the rebel district. They had no need to fight. They occupied the troublesome parishes, and their billeting itself served as a harsh punishment. The parishes that surrendered in good time were pardoned. They had to give up their arms, hand over their ringleaders to justice, reestablish the king's offices, and take down the bells which had been used to sound the alarm. They had to promise to compensate their lords, but they were slow to do this, and it remains seriously doubtful whether this indemnification ever took place.

A small number of parishes resisted stubbornly, three of them around Quimper. The duke made an example of them by razing their bell towers to the ground. At Combrit fourteen peasants were hanged on an oak tree in front of the château of Cosquer. The duc de Chaulnes used an unfortunate phrase in a letter of August 18 to the governor of Morlaix: "We have executed at Quimper some of the most seditious persons in all this region, and the trees are beginning to bend, along the main roads toward Quimperlé, with the weight we have hung upon them." This was a rhetorical exaggeration. It made the duke seem a man of blood and the repression of the revolt a massacre, and the Bretons have remembered it in bitterness ever since. In reality there were few executions and these only, it seems, of persons captured arms in hand or belonging to the die-hard parishes. The other most compromised leaders of the revolt were tried by an extraordinary commission presided over by the *intendant* de Marillac, the former *intendant* of Poitou, and by the king's courts to which de Marillac delegated his authority. The usual forms of justice were observed. The prisoners were sentenced to the galleys. Most of those accused had escaped arrest.

The parlement was exiled to Vannes.

The states of Brittany, meeting in November, 1675, voted the three million livres "free gift" asked for by the king's commissaries. They were unable to prevent the dispatch of ten thousand soldiers to take up winter quarters in Brittany.

Then on February 5, 1676, the king granted the province an *abolition*—that is, a general amnesty. The parlement of Brittany registered it on March 2. One hundred and eight of the most guilty were excepted from it.

And everything seems to have returned to the same state as before.

PART TWO

RUSSIA: THE PEASANTS IN
THE REVOLTS OF THE "TIME OF
TROUBLES" AND IN THE ANABASIS
OF STENKA RAZIN

[7]

The Social Structures of Russia at the End of the Sixteenth Century

WHEN BORIS GODUNOV became tsar, in 1598, Russian society was in a deeply disturbed condition.[1] At its head was the chief of state, the tsar. He had been regarded up to that time as the hereditary proprietor of the state. Muscovy was his private patrimony, his *otchina*, hereditary in the family of Tsar Ivan Kalita. It was therefore natural for him to have an owner's absolute power over the land and all those inhabiting it. Furthermore, since the time in 1472 when Ivan III had married Zoe (Sophia) Paleologos, niece of the last emperor of Byzantium, the idea had become widespread that he was "Caesar," "czar," successor to the Byzantine emperors who were themselves successors to the Roman emperors; and therefore he was "autocrat," deriving his power only from himself, absolutely independent

1. On the general subject of this chapter, see: N. V. Riasanovsky, *A History of Russia* (New York, Oxford University Press, 1963); P. Milyukov, Ch. Seignobos, and L. Eisenmann, *Histoire de Russie*, I, *Des origines à la mort de Pierre le Grand* (Paris, Librairie Ernest Leroux, new ed. 1935); V. O. Klyuchevsky, *A History of Russia*, III, trans. C. J. Hogarth, 1911–1913; Alexandre Eck, *Le Moyen Age russe* (Paris, Maison du Livre Étranger, 1933); P. Lyashchenko, *A History of the National Economy to the 1917 Revolution*, trans. L. M. Herman (New York, Macmillan, 1949); V. T. Bill, *The Forgotten Class. The Russian Burgess from the Earliest Beginnings to 1900* (New York, Praeger, 1959); J. Blum, *Lord and Peasant in Russia*, Princeton, Princeton University Press, 1961.

and above all other mortals, even princes and kings. Finally,
the Metropolitan Zosima had written in the new Paschal canon
composed in 1492: "Two Romes have fallen, the third Rome
will be Moscow, and a fourth is not to be. . . ." Constantinople
had fallen into the hands of the Turks on account of its many
heresies. Now it was Moscow, where the true faith shone forth
in all its purity, that became the center of the Christian world.
Its tsar became, like the Roman Caesar, the "bishop from
without," the head of the church, God's vicar on earth, and
to resist his authority was to resist God himself. Joseph of
Volotsk (1440–1515), abbot of Volokolamsk, had maintained
that the tsar's power originated from God; that he was God's
representative on earth, and therefore absolute and autocratic;
that he was the natural protector of the church with all its
lands and privileges; that his authority extended to the administration of the church, which owed him all the support it could
render. His ideas had been approved by the Council of 1503
and he had himself been proclaimed a saint after his death in
1515. The raising of the metropolitan of Moscow to the rank
of patriarch, in 1589, the strengthening of the ecclesiastical
hierarchy by the appointment of metropolitans, archbishops, and
bishops, all enhanced and increased the power of the tsar.

Everyone shared these ideas. In the second half of the
sixteenth century, the Russians spoke habitually of "Holy Russia,"
and revered the autocracy. Baron von Herberstein,[2] ambassador
in Muscovy of the Holy Roman Empire of the German nation
during the reign of Vasily III (1505–1553), wrote about the
tsar: "In the sway which he holds over his people he surpasses
all the monarchs of the whole world. . . . He uses his authority
as much over ecclesiastics as laymen, and holds unlimited control over the lives and property of all his subjects; not one of
his councillors has sufficient authority to dare to oppose him,
or even differ from him on any subject. They openly confess
that the will of the prince is the will of God, and that whatever the Prince does he does by the will of God."[3] And Ivan

2. *La Moscovie du XVIe siècle, vue par un ambassadeur occidental*, S. von
Herberstein. Intro. by R. Delort (Calmann-Lévy, 1965). [*Notes Upon
Russia* . . . , Hakluyt Society Publications, 1st ser. X and XII, 1851–52.]
   3. Herberstein, pp. 30–32 [Hakluyt Society, X, pp. 30 and 32].

the Terrible wrote in 1564 to Prince Kurbsky, quoting Saint Paul: " 'Let every soul be subject unto the higher powers. For there is no power ordained that is not of God. . . . Whosoever, therefore, resisteth the power, resisteth the ordinance of God.' Think on this and reflect, that he who resists power, resists God; and who resists God is called an apostate, which is the worst sin."[4]

This autocracy, however, was hereditary in the family of Tsar Ivan Kalita; and with the death without issue of Tsar Fyodor Ivanovich, in 1598, the Kalita family was extinct. A kind of assembly of Muscovite notables, a Zemsky Sobor, elected Boris Godunov as tsar. Through his sister Irina, Fyodor's wife, he was the late tsar's brother-in-law. Fyodor, a weak man, had abandoned to this Boris, who, though almost illiterate, was vigorous and cunning, the whole of Russia's diplomacy and a large share of the task of governing the country. Boris had formed a court around himself, parallel with that of the tsar. In a country in which religious rites were regarded as having a mystical value in themselves, his accession to supreme power followed a ritual procedure, the same that Ivan the Terrible had seen fit to follow in 1564, before he applied his red-hot iron to Russia. Boris fled to a monastery; deputations from the Zemsky Sobor waited upon him there to beg him to accept the crown; he refused; the deputations came in greater numbers; he persisted for several days in his refusals; then, God's will seeming to have revealed itself plainly, he yielded. God alone named the tsar. Any elected leader, any prince nominated by the state itself, "will never be tsar." And here it was that anxiety troubled the conscience of the masses who were filled with Orthodox belief. Boris Godunov had been hailed by the clergy and the laity as "hereditary tsar," and complimented on "his *otchina*, the state." But that was all make-believe: he had in reality been elected. For the masses, an elected tsar was something as abnormal as a father or mother acquired by choice, something that seemed to be contrary to the laws of nature. The only true tsar was a "born tsar." Boris was not the tsar. But God

4. J. L. I. Fennell, *The Correspondence between Prince A. M. Kurbsky and Tsar Ivan IV of Russia (1564–1579)* (London, Cambridge University Press, 1955), p. 19.

could not leave Muscovy without a tsar, because the tsar, as lord of the land, *was* Muscovy. In the minds of the masses, who were used to seeing everything refracted through the scriptures, and were familiar with the idea of a constant recurrence of the same struggle against Satan and the spirits of darkness, until Christ should come again in power and glory, the idea of a miracle began to take shape. Either it was not Dmitri who had died at Uglich, or else something was going to happen analogous to the death of the Son who was sacrificed by the will of his Father, and then resurrected. In 1591 Tsar Fyodor's half-brother, Prince Dmitri, son of Ivan the Terrible's seventh wife, a boy nine-and-a-half years old, had been found dead with his throat cut in his house at Uglich. Whether this was an accident or a murder instigated by Boris Godunov, as many believed, he had died with God's permission, and many people were ready to believe either that God had protected him in some mysterious way or else that he might come back to life. Resurrection or miraculous protection, either way, he was going to reappear, to confound his murderers, take up his *otchina*, the state, and ensure the salvation and the well-being of the people of his patrimony. The peasants shook their heads, and obeyed Boris Godunov only with reluctance.

The well-being that the tsar should have brought, the material conditions of a true tsar's rule, were denied to the people. Ivan IV had left Muscovy in a state of ruin that Fyodor's reign had not been able to repair. Toward the end of the sixteenth century, the population of Muscovy was first and foremost a people which had been torn up by the roots, and a large number of them were actually leading a nomadic life. This was due primarily to the establishment by Ivan IV of a kind of political police, the *oprichnina*, which operated from 1566 to about 1575. The *oprichniki* shifted the princess, boyars, and influential large landowers from the center of Muscovy, removing them to the newly conquered territories on the country's borders. They broke the ties of sentiment that existed between these lords and the peasants of their estates, and put them down in isolation amid people who were unknown and alien to them. Similarly, the *oprichniki* deported townsmen and peasants, or forced the survivors to emigrate to the new territories after burning their villages, or after sacking and burning Novgorod in 1570. The second cause of this state of affairs was the long-drawn-out and unsuccessful war for Livonia, between 1558 and 1583, together with the raids by the Tatars from the Crimea, who in 1571 reached Moscow itself and burned a large part of the city. The Tatars are said to have massacred 800,000 people on their way to Moscow, and to have carried off 150,000 into captivity. The Russian peasants fled from the devastated areas. Others, whose homes were in the interior of Muscovy, overwhelmed by the increasing taxation, by the endless demands for manpower for the army, and by the exactions of the "state servitors," or *pomeshchiki*, who were paid in the form of grants of land and whose expenses increased as a result of the wars, left their holdings and moved away to the new territories. The third factor was provided by a succession of natural disasters— two epidemics, several years of bad harvests, famine. The fourth was the extension of Russia's territory itself. The Russians kept on pressing eastward and southward. New fortified lines were thrust forward, marked out by new fortress towns: in the south, Voronezh and Kursk in 1586; Oskol and Byelgorod in 1593; Valuiki in 1600. In the east, the Russians occupied the line of the Volga, took Kazan in 1552, and destroyed that Tatar Khanate; in 1556 they conquered the Tatar Khanate of Astrakhan; they founded Samara in 1586, Saratov in 1589; they overflowed into the land of the Bashkirs, where the first Russian campaign had been fought in 1468, and whose inhabitants had begun in 1557 to pay a tribute of furs to the tsar of Moscow. The Russians set up their fortress of Ufa in the Bashkir country in 1586. The peasants of Russia felt the call of these new lands and of freedom, and they moved toward light, fertile, easily worked soils, regions with temperate climates and with broad rivers that made communications simple.

Among the consequences of this uprooting of the people which had a significant bearing on the revolts were, first, the low density of the population, a dozen millions at most (and this is probably an exaggerated figure), scattered over three million square kilometers—that is, about three or four persons to one

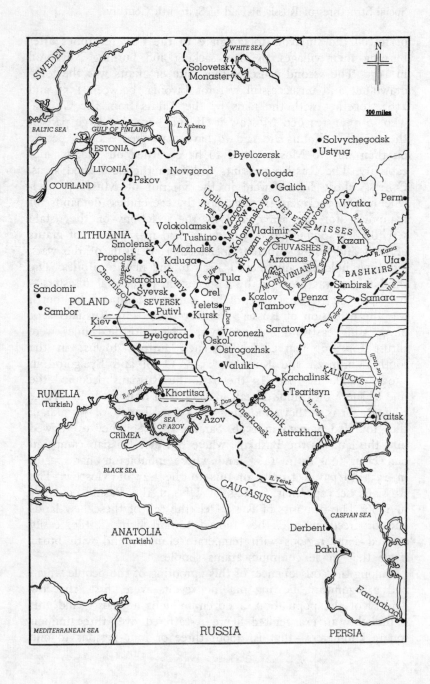

SWEDEN

WHITE SEA

Solovetsky
Monastery

BALTIC SEA

GULF OF FINLAND

L. Kubena

Solvychegodsk
Ustyug

ESTONIA

Byelozersk

LIVONIA

Novgorod

Vologda

COURLAND

Pskov

Galich

Uglich
Tver

Zagorsk

Moscow
Kolomenskoye

Vyatka

Perm

CHEREMISSES

Volokolamsk

Nizhny Novgorod

LITHUANIA

Tushino

Vladimir

Kazan

Smolensk

Mozhalsk

CHUVASHES

R. Vyatka

Propolsk

Kaluga

R. Oka

Arzamas

R. Kama

Ufa

Chernigov

R. Upa

Tula

MORDVINIANS

R. Mokcha

R. Sura

R. Syzrana

BASHKIRS

Sandomir

Starodub

Kromy

R. Dnieper

Syevsk

Orel

Kozlov

Penza

Simbirsk

Ural (or) Ural

POLAND

SEVERSK

Yelets

Tambov

Samara

Sambor

Putivl

Kursk

R. Don

Kiev

Byelgorod

Voronezh

Saratov

R. Volga

Oskol

Ostrogozhsk

Valuiki

KALMUCKS

RUMELIA
(Turkish)

R. Dnieper

Khortitsa

Kachalinsk

Tsaritsyn

R. Volga

R. Yaik (or Ural)

Yaitsk

SEA
OF AZOV

Azov

R. Don

Pagalnik

Cherkassk

CRIMEA

Astrakhan

BLACK SEA

R. Terek

CAUCASUS

CASPIAN SEA

Derbent

ANATOLIA
(Turkish)

Baku

Farahabad

MEDITERRANEAN SEA

RUSSIA

PERSIA

100 miles

N

square kilometer, whereas the kingdom of France had at this time about forty inhabitants per square kilometer. Furthermore, the country was lacking in provinces like Normandy, or *pays* (districts) such as Lieuvin, Perche, Beauce, or Hurepoix, where the population, linked with the soil for many generations, had shaped the countryside and formed those manifold ties with the soil that made it "the land of their forefathers" and impelled all social groups to defend in common the specific features of their "fatherland." Nature itself, moreover, which had broken up the land of France into small units, had left in Russia, stretching from the northwest to the southeast, broad bands of uniform vegetation—the forest zone, the black steppe zone, the white steppe zone—although around Moscow the forest had already been cleared and the soil brought under cultivation, with only scattered woods left standing. Russia lacked those strong territorial communities, little fatherlands, which in France gave a local habitation to each revolt, uniting the social groups to defend local privileges and freedoms. The great Russian revolts could unfurl themselves over vast spaces, embracing masses of people who were not greatly different from each other, though hundreds of kilometers apart.

Another result of the uprooting of the people was the formation of a "frontier," which played an important part in the revolts. In the south, in front of the fortified line, in the steppe extending between the state of Muscovy and the Tatars, were the Cossacks. The term "Cossack" was used in the sixteenth century to mean any man without a permanent home or a definite occupation, a casual worker, "free" and "idle," the equivalent of what in France was called a *sans aveu* (vagabond), *sans feu ni lieu* (without hearth or home). In both Russia and Poland, during the fifteenth century, runaway peasants had begun to take refuge in the steppelands in order to spend the summer as "Cossacks," hunting, fishing, beekeeping, fighting the Tatars and occasionally capturing some of them. In the winter they went back to the towns along the fortified lines or to the towns along the Dnieper, to sell their booty and to hire themselves out as free workers. In summer on the steppe they were obliged to go about in armed bands in order to defend themselves against the Tatars, and eventually they formed permanent communities—Christian, and above all Orthodox, but with a gradual intermingling of Turks and Tatars. Being placed in the same conditions of life as the nomads, and constantly fighting with them, they had borrowed some of their ways. By their customary law they were horsemen who, in principle, ought not to plow the land, or at least ought not to live mainly by cultivation. They should live by stockbreeding, hunting, fishing, and above all by forays against the Moslems—Turks, Tatars, Persians. Their life was a kind of continuous crusade. Every year they plundered the shores of the Crimea, of Anatolia, of Rumelia. They had their social symbols: their incisors filed to a point, their chins clean shaven. Their organization was based on principles of freedom and equality. Every slave, every serf, every subject who sought refuge among them was free and equal in rights with all the others. It was up to him to distinguish himself through his courage and his cleverness. They were divided into tens and hundreds, the leaders of these groups being sometimes elected by the groups themselves, sometimes by the general assembly of all Cossacks. Important matters were decided by the *Vyeche*, the general assembly of all the warriors of the community. They were empowered to elect a leader, or *ataman*, of all the Cossacks. In each expedition, the Cossacks who took part either put up their own *ataman* as leader or else—selected themselves for the expedition by some *ataman*—accepted his authority and acknowledged him as their leader. This was, then, an egalitarian and democratic society, a society in which talent had free rein, where a man's worth alone won him greater prestige or wealth. Some of the Cossacks were subjects of the king of Poland, others of the tsar. The kings of Poland had tried to organize them as a force against the Turks. Some thousands of Cossacks in the Polish territories along the Dnieper had agreed to be "registered," accepting pay from the Polish king and undertaking to serve him in his wars. But some "Polish" Cossacks had remained free, with a small fortified settlement on the island of Khortitsa, on the Dnieper. These were the Zaporozhian Cossacks, who carried on the fight against the Moslems on their own account.

Those Cossacks who were nominally the tsar's subjects formed free-lance squadrons in the valley of the Don. They roamed about a sort of no-man's-land between the Russian fortified lines and the realm of the Tatars. From time to time, Russian troops broke into their territory, to bring them by force under the tsar's authority. At other times the tsar negotiated with them, seeking to "register" them. Often, they organized expeditions jointly with the Zaporozhian Cossacks.

On both sides of the fortified lines, and in their vicinity, there was a floating population of runaways and renegades, who had fled from taxes, military service, seignorial dues, and labor services, and all the devastation caused by war or administration, and who hoped to recover freedom and livelihood in regions where officials were fewer and in any case busy with the struggle against the nomads. These newcomers formed a mass of people who had no legal status and an uncertain position in society, the *gulyashchie lyudi*, irregulars, marginal people, outside the law. Some of them cleared and cultivated a bit of land, others lived by casual work. On the Volga they were boatmen, boat haulers, oarsmen, porters, workers in the fisheries, the saltworks or the potash mines. But the Russian state recaptured them, little by little. More often than not it tolerated them, because it needed settlers and soldiers. The peasants could enroll among the tsar's fighting men, receiving in return the right to a piece of land, perhaps the piece they had cleared, or permission to engage in trade in the towns. But then they found themselves back in their old situation, not only as subjects of a state, but as a lord's "men." In addition to working the piece of land they were allotted, they had to cultivate the "tsar's fields," so as to provide corn for the armies. Or else their land and they themselves were soon transferred as recompense to some servant of the tsar, a *pomeshchik*, a gunner, a sapper, or a carpenter at some military post, and to him they owed dues and labor services. They found themselves again plunged into the subjection and wretchedness from which they had hoped they had escaped—and were ready to revolt.

Another result of the uprooting process was that Russia was a colonial state. From the thirteenth century onward, the Rus-

sians, in the course of their advance, had encircled a number
of seminomadic hunting tribes. These were the Mordvinians, in
the loop of the Volga, between the Sura and the Moksha; the
Cheremisses on the Vyatka; south of them, the Chuvashes;
farther eastward, on the Kama, the Bashkirs, nomadic stock-
breeders. The Mordvinians had become sedentary agriculturists
in the sixteenth century, following the Russians' example, but
they retained a sense of their individuality and had rebelled
as recently as 1580. The others were also ready for revolt, especially the Bashkirs, who had never been fully subjected. The
Russian governors obtained portions of the tribal lands by
corrupting petty princes and chieftains of the Bashkir tribes,
and deprived the Bashkirs of their grazing lands. This gave rise
to ceaseless conflicts.

A final consequence of the uprooting of the Russian people
was a lasting economic depression in the central and western
parts of the country, caused by a shortage of manpower. Ivan
IV had been obliged to resign himself to ending the Livonian
war because he could no longer raise either soldiers or revenue.
Fletcher in 1580 and Possevino in 1581 saw empty villages,
and uncultivated fields covered with scrub. In the northwest,
toward Novgorod and Pskov, in 1580, out of 34,000 holdings
counted by the census takers, 83 percent were unoccupied. Around
Moscow, circa 1586, 83 percent of the cultivable land was lying
waste. There was nothing to be surprised at in this state of
affairs, since with the prevalent level of technique the heavy
iron plow was rare, and the implements in general use were
the swing plow, without wheels and usually made of wood,
the sickle, the hoe, and the spade, and very many hours of
human labor were needed.

Productivity, too, had declined. In the first half of the sixteenth century, in the area around Moscow, the three-field
system of rotation of crops (the winter grains being rye and
wheat, and the spring grains oats, barley and millet) prevailed across 95 percent of the cultivable land. And the peasant
got by that method a return of only between three and five
for one. Over only 5 percent of the cultivable land was the
perelozhnaya applied; this was a system of cultivation in which

the fields at the center of the holding, though permanent, had no fixed rotation, but lay fallow irregularly. All around these, farther off, lay fields that were visited by the peasant only from time to time over a period of several years, to plow them and reap the crops from them, after which he abandoned them to be reoccupied by the forest. About 1580 the *perelozhnaya* had become the predominant method around Moscow. It was the rule in the south, around Tula and Orel. In the northern forest area the prevailing method was the *podsechnaya*, temporary cultivation by slashing and burning part of the forest. The meagerness of the harvests gave greater effect to the accidents of weather, in an economy which was essentially based on agriculture.

A society of uprooted people, Russia at the end of the sixteenth century was also a society in which social strata were undefined and in which social mobility was intensified. In principle, Russian society was organized and arranged in a hierarchy by the proprietor of the state, in such a way as to serve him, that is, to serve the state. Russian society was a liturgical society, a society of services, a species of the genus of societies of orders, or estates. Ivan IV had overturned this society so as to guarantee both his own authority and the defense of frontiers which had been inordinately enlarged during a century; that is, the reason for his actions was the disproportion between the state's needs and its resources.

Russian society presented some essential differences from French. In the first place, it did not know, and probably had never known, the hierarchy of feudalism. Russian society had only the domain, in which the landowner could exercise his powers as lord. The Russian state practiced the remuneration of its servants by temporarily granting them land cultivated by peasants. But the act of fealty and homage was unknown in Russia, as was the hierarchy of overlords and vassals which was the essence of the feudal system. There was no feudalism in Russia. Second, Russian society was without "intermediate bodies" such as provincial states, corporations, colleges, companies, even craft guilds. The Russia of the old regime lacked corporative organizations, doubtless because of the geographical and social fluidity of the population. Third, though the state's servitors were primarily soldiers, Russian society was not dominated, as was French in the same period, by the military and knightly ideal. No organizing principle welled up from society itself, apart from service to the state.

If a man was related to the prince, or was noble because he was a descendant of the servitors of the first princes of Moscow in olden times, or was a servitor of the tsar, he was an owner, or at least a possessor, of the chief instrument of production, the land. However, it does not seem to have been the case that belonging to the nobility implied special forms of social behavior. And even at this time, at the end of the sixteenth century, when a money economy was developing in Russia, when the lords were changing some of their dues in kind into dues payable in money, when trade, though it involved only small amounts, was active and affected every branch of the economy, travelers tell us that everyone, the tsar, the monasteries, the aristocracy, all engaged in trade, even buying in order to sell again, which is the mark of real commercial activity, it having always been allowed to lords and monasteries to sell the produce of their estates. The differentiation of social functions, the division of social labor, seems to have been less advanced than in France. It was as though everybody both cultivated the land and engaged in trade. Without the state, this society would perhaps have become, of itself, a society of classes, with disparities based on men's different relationships to the means of production, or at least would have become something close to a class society. But the state was there, and the tsar strove with all his might to emphasize this society's features as a society not of classes but of orders, existing for the good of the state.

In principle, in the Russian state, a service state, "the activities and the obligations of all subjects, from the greatest lord to the meanest peasant, were determined by the state in the pursuit of its own interests and policies."[5] The tsar laid obligations to the state upon his subjects in accordance with their respective callings, and attached everyone to certain specific functions,

5. J. Blum, op. cit., p. 150.

with the aim of maintaining and increasing the power and authority of the state. Thus, he divided the social groups not into corporations but into rungs in the ladder of service, or *chini*. The greatest lords were attached to the tasks of government, the lesser ones to those of the army and the administration; the biggest merchants were assigned to collect taxes and carry on trade for the tsar; the peasants had to be tied to their lords in order to furnish the latter with the material means to perform their state service. The aim was to fix society in a stratification of service ranks, in a hierarchy corresponding to their importance for the tsar, the proprietor of the state. If the tsar granted a privilege or a liberty, he did this not because it ensued from a right inherent in the person so favored, but because it was necessary for the task to be performed.

At the top of the ladder of the "state servitors," the highest estate of this society, were the *knyazhata*, that is, the princes of the same royal blood as the tsar. Because of their blood they would have liked to share power with the tsar and organize an aristocratic absolutism. For this very reason, since Ivan III's time, the tsar never admitted them to his privy councils. He had in fact abolished their traditional right to choose the leader, and imposed upon them a written oath to serve him and his children, to the end of their lives. Should any of these princes try to leave the tsar's service, he was arrested and charged with treason and apostasy. Ivan IV hated the *knyazhata*, and decimated them. Only a few of the old princely families remained, eaten up with grudges and hatred, and all of them ready to rebel.

Below them came the boyars. These were nobles who were not of princely extraction but had been ennobled by service to the Moscow prince. Most of them were large landowners. They ranked in the official hierarchy according to the seniority of their families in the service of the Moscow prince. The elite among them were thirty-five families who had been attached to his service since the first century of the principality's existence. Next came those whose services had begun in the time of Dmitri Donskoi (1362–1389). After them ranked the ones who had entered the service under Vasily II (1425–1462) and among whom only two families had attained a position of distinction.

All these families were enrolled in the *myestnichestvo*, or "code of precedence." When a choice had to be made among candidates for an appointment, the tsar compared the ranks of the candidates' families, and their individual places in the line of descent, and named the most senior of those whose family had held the highest rank. It meant loss of caste for a boyar to accept a position in which he would be subordinate to a man whose ancestors had been under the orders of his own. He dishonored his family by so doing, and bore responsibility for this before all his relatives and all his descendants. For this reason the boyar families compiled with care both their family trees and their records of service. In the sixteenth century the tsar had caused an official genealogical register to be drawn up. The boyars had thus acknowledged long since that it was service to the tsar that determined one's place in the aristocracy.

Among these boyars, the tsar recruited the Boyarskaya Duma, a council which, together with the Holy Synod, an assembly made up of the patriarch, the metropolitans, the archbishops and bishops, and the principal *igumeni* or abbots, formed the Tsar's Council, for the government and administration of the realm. It was among them that the tsar chose, in principle, the heads of his ministerial boards, the *prikazi*; his voivodes, or military governors of the frontier provinces; his commissaries, entrusted with all sorts of missions; and his ambassadors.

Ivan IV, however, distrusted this hereditary nobility, with their great landed estates, where they wielded the authority and influence of lords over their men. The *oprichnina* is said to have killed as many as 10,000 of them. Many of those who survived were deported from the center of Russia to the newly conquered territories. In place of their *votchini*, their ancestral lands, they had each received from the tsar a *pomestye*, an estate granted as payment for services, on a temporary basis, for only as long as these services should be rendered. The peasants who occupied these estates, or who came to occupy them, were people their lords did not know and who were not linked to them by any bonds of allegiance. The boyars' influence was diminished.

But who was to perform the services of the members of the *knyazhata* and the boyars who had disappeared? The tsar called upon medium-sized landowners, *votchinniki,* or upon state servitors who were remunerated by a temporary grant of land, or upon *pomeshchiki* of two or three generations' standing, who formed the petty nobility, the *dvoryane,* or upon men of even lower status, even peasants who had distinguished themselves as soldiers. In those days it was possible for tasks of government and administration, and civil and military functions, to be very little differentiated and to be all entrusted, as a rule, to a single person in a given place. The tsar added many different tasks to the load of one and the same individual, and there was little division of labor in the public service. Every time that a new need made itself felt, a ministerial board (*prikaz*) was set up to deal with it. The work was thus very specific and close to everyday reality. Men who were more or less illiterate might be given the power of command, with everything it implied—justice, taxation, administration. To look after the written work, keeping the records, and carrying on the correspondence, there were *dyaki,* or chief clerks, with clerks to do the actual writing under their orders. Following September 20, 1556, each *votchinnik* was obliged to provide a horseman fully armed and equipped, together with a second horse, for every three hundred *chetverti* of cultivable land, or the equivalent in money. If he failed to fulfill this obligation, he risked losing his estate. In this way the principle was established that no one could be a landowner unless he was in the service of the state. State service became the condition of landownership. To those state servitors who were not landowners, or whose estates were inadequate, or who rendered services that ought to be paid for, the tsar assigned as remuneration lands of varying extent, depending on the quality and importance of their services, and taken either from the great domains that had been confiscated from the *knyazhata* or the boyars, or from the newly conquered territories. These temporary holdings were called *pomestya,* and state servitors so remunerated were *pomeshchiki.* There were *pomeshchiki* of every rank, from members of the monarch's council to ordinary troopers and gunners. The tsar raised them up according to his favor or their merits, to be generals, heads of ministerial departments, or state councillors. He introduced them into the Boyarskaya Duma. There was thus a large-scale "call-up" from every level of the social stratification toward the top of it, an increased and relatively considerable social mobility. It did not change the social structure of orders, or estates, but it did mean a circulation and shuffling of individuals which brought groups of new men into the highest strata. These new men were not welcomed by the boyars, who could not bring themselves to regard them as equals. At the very least they wanted to retain their precedence over them in walking and sitting. Those of the new nobility who, on account of their high office, wished to precede a member of one of the old families, exposed themselves to humiliation, to being forced to acknowledge publicly their social inferiority, while anyone who accorded them the same honors as were due to the old families risked incurring punishment. Furthermore, the boyars would not agree to give up their monopoly of high office. Their resentment against the tsar and the new men degenerated into mortal hatred. There was thus a struggle between a nobility of blood and a nobility of service. The boyars were among those chiefly responsible for the "Time of Troubles."

In each territorial division the *votchinniki* and *pomeshchiki* elected ten or twenty of their number to give the necessary information about the state servitors to the officials who were charged with assigning responsibilities and estates. These elected ones were answerable to the government for providing the number of men, horses, and weapons that their division was assessed at. The state servitors in each division gave one another mutual guarantees for this service, each one having his surety, and three or four acting as surety for each other as a group.

The *votchinniki* and *pomeshchiki* elected representatives to administer the collection of taxes, supervise fortification works, be responsible for the defense of their division, watch over the fulfillment of their duties by the state servitors, sit in the voivode's council in the frontier provinces, correspond directly with the *prikazi* in the provinces of the interior, and represent the division in the Zemskie Sobori, those assemblies of notables, so to speak, which the tsars convoked to receive their decrees. The electing of these representatives did not express the idea of an individual right to be exercised, but that of an undertaking by the electors that each would fulfill his duties to the state.

Among the state servitors, both *votchinniki* and *pomeshchiki*, there were many differences of rank, depending on the importance of the tasks assigned to them and on the size of their estates, but also depending on the antiquity and reputation of their families. The extent of the *pomestya* depended on the nature and duration of the services rendered, but also on "the illustriousness of the race."[6] Hereditary dignity was one of the conditions determining degree of wealth. In the general ruin, moreover, the number of *votchini* declined, while that of the *pomestya* increased. Around Moscow, from about 1584 to 1586, 34 percent of the arable land was occupied by *pomestya*, 22 percent by *votchini*, and 36 percent by monastic estates. The farther one traveled from the center of the state, the greater the number of *pomestya*. In Ryazan, from about 1594 to 1596, 17 percent of the land was occupied by *votchini*, 13 percent belonged to monasteries, and 70 percent was held in *pomestya*. In the colonial region there were no *votchini*, only *pomestya*. But in Muscovy the *pomestye* was an old-established method of remunerating services, natural to a state in which money was little used. Since the middle of the sixteenth century it had become usual for the son or nephew of a *pomeshchik* to succeed his father or uncle when the latter was killed, or enfeebled by illness or old age. He retained the duty of service and the land that went with it: it was enough for him to be fifteen years old. In the last years of the century, moreover, even if he was not fifteen yet, he nevertheless retained part of the *pomestye*, and the same privilege was allowed to widows and daughters, until they married. The tsar even allowed a *pomestye* to be bequeathed by last will and testament. The *pomestye* was thus tending to assume in certain cases the characteristics of private property, and the state servitors best provided with land to form a sort of hereditary landed nobility.

Besides the stratification by birth and the stratification by

6. J. Mavor, *Economic History of Russia* (1925), I, p. 38.

service, an economic stratification developed among the *pomesh-chiki.* The usual size of a *pomestye* was 300 to 600 *chetverti,* corresponding to the equipment and maintenance of one or two horsemen. As a result of differences in the allotment of estates, in accordance with "race" or service, and also as a result of the fragmentation of the *pomestye* in cases of untimely death (and the wars, like the *oprichnina,* swallowed up very many *pomeshchiki*), a large number of *pomestya* were smaller than this. In Orel, in 1594–1595, 32 percent of the *pomestya* covered between 150 and 300 *chetverti* each, while 54 percent were even smaller. There were *pomestya* of 60 *chetverti*—about 15 hectares. A *pomestye* of 300 *chetverti* was worth 12 to 20 rubles at the end of the sixteenth century. The cost of equipping and maintaining a *pomeshchik* and his horse in the field was estimated at seven rubles, and prices were going up, for the growth in external trade brought in small quantities of silver which, injected into the very exiguous currency available, pro-duced inflationary effects. Thus, with only 150 *chetverti* or less, the *pomeshchik* could no longer fulfill his obligations. Either he was compelled to serve on foot, which constituted a sort of degradation, or else, and this was what happened with most, he borrowed money, frequently from monasteries but also from priests, merchants, or craftsmen. Many *pomeshchiki* fell into debt, and the rate of interest rose from 156 to 365 percent per year. With the constant wars, and especially with the flight of the peasantry toward the new lands, some *pomeshchiki* were obliged, even when of noble birth, to plow the land themselves and even to hire themselves out as agricultural workers or crafts-men. Others, when they found themselves unable to fulfill their obligations, fled to the frontiers, to settle there as peasants or join the Cossacks. Social mobility worked in both directions. There were former *pomeshchiki* among the rebels of the "Time of Troubles."

Below the state servitors came the "urban taxpayers." Russia included about two hundred and thirty towns. Moscow itself, according to Chancellor and Fletcher, covered a larger area than London of those times. Certain towns, such as Pskov and Novgorod, much declined since the sack of 1570, numbered

7,500 to 15,000 inhabitants. A larger group of towns had between 3,000 and 5,000, while the majority had about 1,000. All the towns taken together contained only a small proportion of the population, perhaps one-twenty-fifth. All of them retained a rural character. Their inhabitants grew a considerable proportion of their food within the towns' limits or just outside them. In Moscow there were large fields and meadows stretching beside the river, and there were many gardens in the city. It was surrounded by pastures where the Muscovites grazed their horses and cattle. Many small towns were nothing more than big villages, their inhabitants cultivating the fields around them. Merchants and craftsmen were also cultivators, even in sizable towns. The Russian town was rural to a much greater degree than the French of the same period.

The Russian town was above all a military and administrative center, and much less than the French town a center of trade and industry. At the heart of the Russian town was a *kreml*, a fortified enclosure which housed the soldiers who also managed the administration. Around this citadel spread the *posad*, the town of the merchants and craftsmen, still semirural. Farther out still were the "liberties," the *sloboda*, where there settled, outside the range of urban restrictions, persons who had come from afar, fugitives, or peasants sent there by the monasteries or lords who were their masters to carry on a trade.

The lower level of development of the Russian town was due, first, to a lower level of development of commerce and industry. Then, also, the best people were taken up into state service and, remunerated with land, became countryfolk or colonists. Finally, to engage in trade did not bring loss of caste. The tsar, proprietor of the state, set the example: he was the biggest merchant in his empire. A governmental board, which employed merchants as helpers, managed his business affairs. The tsar sold the products of his personal domains for 230,000 rubles a year, in Fyodor's reign. More than that, though: he bought goods in order to sell them again. He reserved for himself the monopoly of grain for export, of raw silk, caviar, potash, rhubarb, walrus tusks, and alcohol. Sometimes he stored away the entire production of some article, raised the price, and then forced the merchants to buy it from him. On other occasions he decreed an increase in prices and then forbade anyone else to sell before he had disposed of his own stock. Foreign merchants had to offer the goods they imported to the tsar's agents, who set apart what they wanted, or bought it at prices fixed by themselves, before these merchants were allowed to sell to others. Accordingly, everyone in Russia traded. The monasteries not only sold their produce but also bought to resell in other markets. The state servitors did the same. A sign of the intensity of this trade was the number of markets, held weekly in many villages, each with about a score of stalls, and also the importance of some of these markets, such as the one held at Mleva, a village in the Novgorod territory, where customers found 332 stalls awaiting them in 1551.

This trade involved only small amounts, for a number of reasons. Townsmen, big landowners, countryfolk, small peasants—all tried to be self-sufficient as to food, clothes, tools, and domestic utensils. But, owing to the small volume of currency in circulation, whoever was able to obtain a few pieces of silver—the main metal current—or a few grams of copper, acquired a comparatively large purchasing power; an increasing amount of currency was needed to pay taxes to the state and dues to the lords. Despite their own production, the big cities and the garrisons of the frontier towns needed to buy provisions. Moscow received, in winter, between 700 and 800 cartloads of grain, fish, and bacon, sent from Ryazan, Tula, and Orel. Whatever the difficulties, the peasants could not do without certain articles made by the craftsmen in the towns. The high cost of transport, especially over land, burdened as it was, moreover, by a multitude of taxes and tolls, reduced the radius within which articles of necessity were sent; it was necessary to carry out exchanges within a short radius, and therefore to multiply markets and sellers. The trading businesses were on a small scale, the shops being mere hovels in which the merchants could hardly turn around, the stalls nothing but benches hired by the craftsman, peasant, or peddler. Finally, trade was sluggish, and a merchant's capital was turned over not more than once a year, in most cases.

Everyone traded, the state servitors being also traders, craftsmen, and agriculturists, so that in Tula 30 percent of the shops
belonged to military state servitors and only 20 percent to full-
time traders. There were nevertheless merchants by profession,
dealing in salt, furs, grain, cloth, and fish, who also exploited
their own arable land, meadows, and fishponds, and were active
owners of mills, distilleries, and saltworks, as well as being pawn-
brokers and moneylenders. They were proportionately fewer than
in France, and probably less rich. They did not constitute a real
bourgeoisie. In principle, according to the official classification
of ranks, they were "urban taxpayers," on a level with the
peasants. In Moscow, however, about thirty big merchants,
honored with the title of "guests of the tsar," had the task
of managing, besides their own businesses, the personal trading
activities, both internal and external, of the tsar himself. The
richest merchants of the provincial towns, the "best men," had
to come to Moscow at certain intervals to help in the collection of taxes. In their own towns the merchants were collectively
responsible for the taxes they owed the state. From the standpoint of the official classification of ranks, we find at the top,
in the Russian towns, the state servitors, then the various
strata of merchants ("guests," "best men," "juniors"), and then
the craftsmen. If, however, we draw up an economic classification based on differences of wealth, we find the merchant strata at
the top, with the state servitors next, and the craftsmen still
at the bottom. The craftsmen did not carry the division of
social labor very far. They lacked guilds or organized corporations of any sort. The same man might be at once a shoemaker,
a joiner, and a cultivator. In Moscow itself, even, they formed
a very poor section of the population, living in shacks without
chimneys, earning little, and some of them reduced to begging.
Some craftsmen sold the finished article for not much more
than they had paid for the raw material. The tailors, shoemakers,
sawyers, and coachmen paid a tax of less than a ruble a year.
On the other hand, some workers in silver, and furriers and
carriers were worth several thousand rubles. Technique was
at a very low level. The carpenters used axes instead of saws
to cut up planks. Smelters used little bellows, hammers, and

tongs, all operated by hand. Productivity was low. The makers of luxury goods, clockmakers, painters, saddlers, lacemakers, apothecaries, and goldsmiths were foreigners, living in a special suburb of Moscow.

The "country taxpayers," the peasants, were by far the most numerous section of the population, in an economy in which large-scale trade and industry played a very secondary role. They were the main source for taxes and soldiers, and indispensable to the support of the state servitors, who were paid in land, and the great problem was to fix them to the soil when colonization was opening up ample land for them to move to. There were several categories of peasants. On those lands that were still the tsar's immediate property lived the "black peasants." It is said that for practical purposes they were already fixed to the soil at the end of the sixteenth century. On the estates of the lords, *votchinniki, pomeshchiki,* or the monasteries, were the *krestiane*, free tenants, who took the land in return for the obligation to render dues and services, and who were the only ones to pay taxes. Beneath them in the social scale of ranks were the *bobyli*, landless peasants, free agricultural workers; beneath them again the vagabonds and casual workers; and, still lower, the *kabalnye lyudi*, peasants in debt, who had given their lord an IOU, or *kabala*, for a loan of three or five rubles, to be repaid on a certain date, and who paid the interest on this loan by working on the lord's domain. These *kabalnye lyudi* often became something like peons, in bondage for life to the lord, for, since their labor went to pay the interest, they were often unable to repay the principal. The lord, their creditor, would then continue to feed and clothe them, and they were thenceforth exempt from taxes and military service. They went on working for the lord, every day of their lives, and he could, if he chose, sell their IOU to somebody else, which amounted to selling a man. All these peasants were freemen in the eyes of the law. Their lives were under the law's protection; they could own property, go to law, buy and sell, make contracts and wills. At the very bottom of the social scale were the slaves, the *kholopi*. Some lords used these as domestic servants or as cultivators. Between 9 and 15 percent of the rural holdings were cultivated by slaves. In the south, near the frontier, there were more of them. *Pomeshchiki* with small estates cultivated these by themselves or with their slaves only. About 1589, the farther one advanced into the steppes, the higher was the proportion of holdings cultivated by slaves, such holdings rising from 23 percent to 50 percent. Serfdom hardly existed.

The *krestiane* formed a community, the mir, in each village; its members were bound by mutual guarantee to pay the taxes due the state. Their assembly elected representatives and paid them. These joined with the deputies of the *votchinniki* and *pomeshchiki* in the division, or volost, for the purpose of assessing taxes on the members of the mir, in proportion to the quantity and quality of their land; they collected rents and dues; they represented the volost before the tsar's officials. Each head of a family made terms with the lord about the extent of his holding, without having to refer to the mir. In principle, the *krestiane* were free to leave both their holdings and the mir.

For the holdings they occupied, the *krestiane* owed dues in kind or in money (*obrok*) and labor services (*barshchina*). For example, in 1561, the peasants who lived in the village of Pozyrevo owed the Solovetsky Monastery, for each *vyt*, that is, for each piece of land capable of supporting a family, four *chetverti* of wheat every year, four of oats, a cheese, fifty eggs, a loaf of rye bread, a loaf of white bread, two loads of firewood, two loads of pinewood, ten fire lighters, the cultivation of two *chetverti* of the monastery's domain, and repair work on the monastic buildings.

The lot of all these peasants had grown worse at the end of the sixteenth century. The lords, hard hit by the burden of their service in the prolonged wars and by the economic crisis at the end of the century, had become more demanding. They had increased the dues they demanded, and changed *obrok* in kind into *obrok* in money, thereby forcing the peasants to trade and to make articles for sale in the towns. Soon taxes and dues absorbed the whole produce of the fields. In order to survive, the peasant had to supplement his cultivation of the land with beekeeping, hunting, fishing; the breeding of sheep, pigs, cows, and horses; even crafts of various kinds. The most serious aggravation of the peasants' lot was the tendency to transform *obrok* into *barshchina*. The latter was increased from one day a week to two or three or even more. Indeed, the lord was greatly the gainer by doing this. In 1590 the Volokolamsk Monastery obtained 71 rubles from a group of peasants as *obrok* in money. In 1591 it transformed this *obrok* into *barshchina* on the monastic domain. The rye and oats produced by this labor service in 1592 were worth 306 rubles. The monastery had thus quadrupled the income it drew from these peasants. Some lords demanded *barshchina* in the form of craftwork, themselves supplying the peasants with the raw material and themselves selling the finished products on the market. However, these changes were confined to very large estates in the Moscow region and the basin of the Kama.

The peasants, crushed by these burdens, fled to the new lands. The tsar needed their labor to support his *pomeshchiki* and *votchinniki*, and so he sought to bind them to the soil.

The *krestiane* had the right to leave their holdings and go off to find another lord. The law code of 1497 had laid down the period when they could do this: the fortnight before St. George's Day in the autumn (November 26) of each year. The peasants had to settle their outstanding dues and pay the lord a forfeit to compensate him for their departure. These provisions had been reaffirmed in the law code of 1550. While just in themselves, they had in practice restricted the peasants' freedom, because some of them lacked the necessary sum of money; others found it impossible to serve upon their lord or his steward, who made themselves scarce, the formal notice which the law insisted on of their intention to depart; others again, in debt either to the lord or to the tsar's treasury, saw themselves refused permission to leave by the lord, who was responsible for the state's taxes; still others came up against the exactions and coercion of the lords, who demanded a compensation payment of five or ten rubles, or beat, tortured, or put the peasants in chains in order to stop them from leaving. On the other hand, some monasteries and large landowners paid the debts of peasants who wanted to move, so as to attract them to their own estates. They readily went to settle on the estates of those great lords who had been granted the right to exercise the public authority of justice and administration over their peasants, because such peasants were then exempt from the state's taxation and from military service. This competition irritated the small and medium *pomeshchiki* and *votchinniki*.

Faced with the mass emigration of peasants that took place in the 1570s, Ivan IV struck back. In 1580 he forbade peasants to leave the places where they were then living, without permission from the tsar. These "prohibited years" followed one another at closer and closer intervals. As a result, in 1581 and in 1592 registers were established; in these the name of every adult male peasant was recorded, with his place of residence. Finally, a ukase of November 24, 1597, issued by Fyodor but ascribed, and correctly, to Boris Godunov, ordered that all those peasants who had fled from their lords during the previous five years be sought out and brought back, together with their families and possessions. Legally, the peasants were still not bound to the soil and its lords. In was a matter of temporary measures only, justified by the state's needs, and affecting only heads of families. Others who lived with these men could still leave as they wished. But the *krestiane* had the impression that the moment was coming when each and every one of them would be nothing but a *krepostnoi chelovek*, a bondsman, a serf.

As for the *kabalnye lyudi*, by decrees of 1586 and 1587, every *kabala* had to be recorded by a special government office. The debtor, the "*kabala* slave," no longer had the right to pay his debt or have it paid for him. He had to remain his creditor's peon till his creditor died, only after which did the debtor recover his freedom, without the possibility of the IOU being sold or bequeathed.

As regards the clergy, the bishops and other high ecclesiastics were chosen from among the higher-ranking monks. The regular clergy was very largely recruited from among the nobility. The monasteries were masters of immense estates. The bishops maintained veritable courts of secretaries, sacristans, chamberlains, majordomos, domestic servants, pages, and revenue collectors—

often amounting to about a hundred people, who were maintained by the income drawn from extensive estates and from contributions by the parish priests. The lower secular clergy, the parish priests, amounted to a hereditary group. They had the right to marry. They were considered sufficiently educated if they could read and conduct church services. In popular estimation they were on a level with the craftsmen. Those of their sons who were not attracted by the priestly calling easily became *déclassés*.[7]

Russian society thus appears before us as much less differentiated than French society of the same period. The division of social labor was less advanced. Social relationships were to a much greater degree simple relationships of coercion. Authority was derived to a much greater extent from mere ownership of the means of production. Although the tsar strove to form a society of orders, or estates, social relations in Russia were close to those of a class society. This feature of Russian society was intensified by the social upheaval that took place, with the increased geographical and social mobility that ensued.

7. F. C. Conybeare, *Russian Dissenters*, Harvard Theological Studies, X (1921), p. 21.

[8]

Peasant Revolts of the "Time of Troubles." The False Dmitris. Bolotnikov

THE DEPLORABLE situation of the petty *pomeshchiki*, craftsmen, and peasants gave rise to a permanent state of banditry. Many bands of outlaws terrorized the countryside. They sometimes numbered as many as a hundred men, organized in military fashion, each under the orders of an *ataman*. These bandits carried on methodical operations, hiding in the forests and emerging to ambush merchants, or peasants who were taking their tax money to town, or else to raid an estate and carry off the crops. The people saw these bandits as their avengers. The peasants refused to cooperate with the authorities against them. On the contrary, they acted as guides and scouts for the bandits, gave them shelter, and harbored their stolen goods for them. Sometimes an *ataman* would become a popular hero, and his legendary feats would be celebrated in songs.

Wherever the inhabitants asked for it, as a measure against brigandage, the tsar granted a *guba* charter. In the rural canton, or volost, and sometimes in the district, or *uyezd*, an assembly of the people—clergy, nobles, townsmen, peasants—by unanimous vote elected an "elder," chosen from among the nobles. The man elected went to Moscow to be sworn in at the Banditry Office and was handed an official deed. He was to fight against bandits, robbers, and murderers. He commanded a force of wardens who were peasants and craftsmen chosen and paid by the bigger taxpayers. The election was not a democratic procedure: its purpose was to ensure that every elector, by signing the record of the election, pledged himself to fulfill his obligations toward the state, and the working of the *guba* was based on the principle of mutual guarantee.[1]

However, the *guba* system proved ineffective. Banditry persisted. From time to time, sudden explosive outbreaks by the peasants occurred: by the peasants of St. Antony's Monastery in 1578, by the men whose suzerain was the Volokolamsk Monastery in 1593 and 1594.

Boris Godunov was not popular. The masses were not convinced that he was a "true tsar." The boyars were angry because he governed without them, using his own family, through an inner Duma consisting of relations of his, and because of the trials he held at which the best families of Russia were accused, with great publicity. Everyone trembled with horror as a result of his system of suspicion, informing, and torture.[2]

In the view of his contemporaries, Boris Godunov's reign was not blessed by Heaven. In 1600 the rumor spread in Moscow that Prince Dmitri Ivanovich had not died at Uglich but was still alive. Then Heaven made plain its disfavoring of the so-called Tsar Boris. The summer of 1601 saw torrential downpours of rain. The ears of corn, already full, could not ripen, the cornfields remained "green as grass." On the day of the Assumption of the Virgin Mary, August 15, a sudden frost destroyed the crops of barley and oats. Sowing had to be undertaken with frozen seed. In spring, 1602, the fields were bare. A major famine ensued. "It is not possible to buy bread for money." Hunger "carried off more victims than the plague." The authorities had to appoint special agents to remove the corpses from houses and public highways and throw them into common graves. The famine lasted all through the year 1603. The lords could no longer feed their servants and their peasants, and sent

1. J. L. H. Keep, "Bandits and the Law in Muscovy," *The Slavonic and East European Review,* 35 (1956), pp. 201–222.
2. S. Platonov, *Boris Godunov, tsar de Russie, 1598–1605,* trans. H. de Witte (Paris, Payot, 1929), pp. 243–264.

them away. These vagabonds joined the bandits, formed new bands, and carried out acts of brigandage even under the very walls of Moscow. The tsar was obliged to use his army against them. After several clashes, a pitched battle took place under the walls of the capital between the bands led by a certain Khlopko and a military force led by the boyar I. F. Basmanov. The boyar himself was killed, but his soldiers remained masters of the battlefield. Khlopko, wounded and taken prisoner, was executed and his scattered band fled southwestward, toward the Dnieper.[3]

Boris Godunov strove to combat the general distress by distributing money and promoting public works: he had stone buildings erected within the Kremlin area. But the lords, the clergy, and the peasants who were not so poor hoarded their corn away and forced the prices up. The tsar forbade large-scale purchases, had a record made of stocks, promulgated a scale of prices, made the distilling of grain and brewing of beer illegal, and decreed that corn be sold retail to small-scale purchasers. In 1601 and 1602 he allowed the peasants to leave their lords on St. George's Day in November, but restricted this right to peasants working for small landowners. Tenants of the monasteries, the boyars, the great lords, and the tsar himself were excluded from the privilege. What makeshift remedies these were! In addition, the tsar made the ukase of 1597 permanent: every year, the peasants who had run away during the previous five years were to be sought for. He dealt harshly with the Cossacks, whom he disliked. He forbade them to buy or sell even in the frontier towns. He tried to settle them permanently on Crown lands. He inflicted cruel punishments on whoever had contact with them. For the people, Boris Godunov came to embody the upholding of serfdom and the crushing of freedom.

Then it was that the Tsarevich Dmitri appeared and the great rebellion burst forth. We know about it from the letters

3. *Vosstanie I. Bolotnikova. Dokumenty i materialy* (Moscow, Publishing House for Social and Economic Literature, 1959). This publication of 451 pages includes documents on the condition of the peasantry before Bolotnikov's rising, narratives of the rising, and official texts relating to the troubles.

and financial accounts that emanated from the *prikazi*, the tsar's letters of December 2, 1606, and October 13, 1607, and the letters of Patriarch Hermogen, dated November 29, 1606. The events of this time produced chronicles which were put into ritual form in 1630, on the orders of Patriarch Filaret, father of Tsar Mikhail Romanov and head of the government, under the title of the *New Chronicler*. *Karamzin's Chronography* groups together another series of chronicles. Foreign eyewitnesses have left valuable descriptions: the Dutch merchant Isaac Massa, the German adventurer Conrad Bussow, and some Poles, who were numerous in Russia. An anonymous English account summarizes the letter from the rebel leader Bolotnikov to the inhabitants of Moscow.

Among the people of Muscovy, the affair was seen as a battle between bad angels, spirits of evil, and good angels, servants of God. God had established order in a universe full of wonders. The demons strove to reduce this to chaos. Naturally, each camp saw itself as the servant of God and the enemy as the Devil's ally. For the peasants and Cossacks, Dmitri and Bolotnikov were the party of Jesus Christ, while Godunov and Shuisky, the officially recognized tsars, belonged to Satan's troop. At the siege of Tula in 1607, when the armies of Tsar Shuisky had built a dam to drown the city, the besieged inhabitants called upon a monk who had magical powers to destroy the dam, the devil's work. The monk failed: the devils were too many. He had been able to overcome six thousand of them, but six thousand more upheld the dam. On the other side, for the tsar's party the rebels were enemies of the cross, robbers, bandits, plunderers. Their revolt was a sin against the order willed by God. Therefore, God allowed them to prosper only for a time, as a punishment, and their defeat and slaughter were mercies from God, granted by the intercession of Blessed Mary, Ever Virgin.[4]

4. See the oath of the German Friedrich Fidler, who had undertaken to poison Bolotnikov, sworn to Tsar Shuisky: "In the name of the Most Holy and Glorious Trinity, in the name of the Eternal, God the Father, God the Son and God the Holy Ghost, I, Friedrich Fidler, swear to exterminate by poison the enemy of Tsar Vasily Ivanovich of all the Russian realm, Ivan Bolotnikov. If I do this not, and betray my Sovereign, may the

Dmitri was regarded by the tsar—and has been regarded by historians—as a "false Dmitri." Godunov, and many historians after him, thought it was all an intrigue by a group of boyars, and Godunov himself suspected the Romanov family of having trained a young man to play the role of Prince Dmitri. Many historians think this was a certain Grigory Otrepev, a renegade monk who was perhaps a former servant of the Romanovs. In 1603 and 1604 he traveled through Lithuania and Poland, claiming to be the son of Ivan IV, miraculously escaped from an attempt on his life organized by Boris Godunov. In Poland he became friendly with the Jesuits, was converted by them, promised to support the Catholic cause in Russia, and informed Pope Clement VIII of his intentions in a letter of April 24, 1604. Established in the castle of Mniszek, at Sambor, he sent forth proclamations into the provinces of Muscovy, despatched emissaries to the Don Cossacks, and summoned to his side refugees from Russia. In October, 1604, he invaded Russia at the head of as many as 4,000 Cossacks who had emigrated from Russia, reinforced by Polish adventurers. Ten thousand Cossacks of the Dnieper and the Don joined him, and another Cossack force cut communications between Moscow and southern Russia.

These "Cossacks" were in fact a very motley crew. There certainly were genuine Cossacks among them. Were these the majority? In any case, they were joined by regular soldiers from the frontier, *streltsy* (musketeers), horsemen, gunners, sappers, soldiers of the supply services—all of whom were runaway peasants or their sons; they were joined, too, by peasants

---

Lord withhold heavenly bliss from me forever; may God's only Son, Jesus Christ, who shed his blood for us, deny me his mercy for eternity; may the power of the Holy Ghost cease to give me strength; may all the Angels who watch over Christians turn away from me. May the natural elements created for the good of man turn against me; may the earth swallow me up alive; may whatever grows on earth become poison for me, and no longer nourishment; may the Devil seize my body and my soul. Even should my spiritual Father release me from my oath, if I change my mind about fulfilling it, may this release be invalid. But I will keep my word and destroy with this poison Ivan Bolotnikov, relying on the help of God and the Gospels." Fidler betrayed Shuisky, handed over the poison to Bolotnikov, received a substantial gift from him and thus, says Bussow, "sold his soul to the Devil." *Vosstanie I. Bolotnikova. Dokumenty i materialy*, p. 159.

living in the forts and mobile camps of the frontier area. Peasants and slaves rallied to them as they advanced. "Cossacks" meant all those who rose in revolt for their freedom. Dmitri suffered several defeats from the army of Boris Godunov. But the presence of the Cossacks saved him, for it made him the personification of freedom. Many towns rebelled in his favor against the oppressor, the tsar, whose army had to pull back lest it be cut off from Moscow. Some boyars joined him. At last the situation was stabilized around the road junction at Kromy, which linked the various rebel areas. Fighting went on there throughout the whole winter of 1604–1605. Godunov's army proved unable to throw the Cossacks back to the South, but the Cossacks could not succeed in opening the road to Moscow. Then, just as things were turning in Godunov's favor, suddenly, on April 13, 1605, the tsar died, at the age of fifty-three.

Three weeks later, his army before Kromy went over to "the true Tsar Dmitri Ivanovich." On June 10, Godunov's wife and son were killed in Moscow, and his daughter raped and imprisoned. On June 20, 1605, Dmitri entered the capital in triumph.

Now that he had relieved them of the Godunov family, however, Dmitri was no longer of any interest to the boyars. The new tsar was surrounded by Poles, and on May 8, 1606, he married a Polish aristocrat, Marina Mniszech, who brought more Poles along with her. The Poles, as Catholics, were regarded by the Russians as heretics and as hereditary foes. The tsar dressed in the Polish fashion, and ridiculed the Russian church ritual, which was, for the Russian people, a condition necessary for maintaining the order of the universe. Prince Vasily Shuisky, Prince Vasily Golitsyn, and other boyars brought a large body of troops into Moscow during the night of May 26, 1606, took the palace by storm, captured Dmitri, and put him to death in Red Square, after the nun Martha, mother of the Prince Dmitri of Uglich, in spite of having acknowledged the other Dmitri as her son when he first arried in Moscow, had denounced him as an impostor. The boyar clique which had carried out the coup d'état presented Shuisky to the mob, which hailed him as tsar. In June, 1606, the new tsar had the Prince Dmitri who died at Uglich canonized, and brought his remains to Moscow, as confirmation that the other one had been an impostor. Nevertheless, all the objections to Godunov could be brought against Shuisky. There was soon a rumor running round Moscow that the man executed on May 27 had not been Dmitri at all but another, substituted for him. The boyars who had rallied to Dmitri shared this view, or at any rate made use of it against the Shuisky clique. One of Dmitri's supporters, Mikhail Molchanov, fled from Moscow and, on reaching Lithuania and Poland, spread the story that Tsar Dmitri was safe and sound. He looked for him—or for someone who would play his part. The ghost of Dmitri, champion of freedom, raised a fresh insurrection. Prince Grigory Shakhovskoi, one of his supporters, exiled to Putivl, was said to have made off with the golden seal of state; he spread the story everywhere that Dmitri, escaped by a miracle from his would-be murderers, was alive and with him, and announced that Dmitri was going to fetch troops from Poland. He raised the whole town in his favor. The inhabitants of Putivl assembled several thousand Cossacks and "several thousands" more princes and boyars living nearby. This army elected a commander, Istoma Pashkov, and marched on Moscow. Prince Andrei Telyatevsky did the same at Chernigov. The rebels defeated the first troops sent against them. Then Tula and Ryazan revolted. At Perm and Vyatka, regular troops mutinied. The revolt spread to the peasants and the conquered peoples. The Mordvinians, helped by Russian peasants, besieged Nizhny-Novgorod. The people and Cossacks of Astrakhan declared against the tsar. In Moscow the masses were in a great state of agitation. In order to raise troops and rally the *pomeshchiki*, Shuisky spread the story that the Crimean Tatars had invaded. Then, after admitting that the invading Tatars were a myth, he declared that the new Dmitri was an impostor who aimed at establishing paganism. At Ryazan the revolt was led by Grigory Sunbulov and by two noblemen, the brothers Prokop and Zakhary Lyapunov. They formed a militia to fight Shuisky, made up of the nobility of Ryazan, *votchinniki* and *pomeshchiki*, seasoned by a long struggle against the Tatars. At Tula the movement was led by a person of low social standing, Filipp Pashkov, a "boyar's son," that is, someone in the service of the state servitors, who nevertheless headed a militia of noblemen. These two militias marched on Moscow. Meanwhile, the alleged Dmitri was in Poland, at Sandomir. Molchanov sent Bolotnikov to him. Ivan Bolotnikov was undoubtedly a peasant, a slave of Prince Telyatevsky's. Taken prisoner by the Tatars, he had been sold to the Turks, who had set him to row in one of their galleys. Freed by a German ship and taken to Venice, he had made his way back to Russia. While passing through Poland, he made the acquaintance of Molchanov, who sent him to Prince Shakhovskoi. Bolotnikov told how he had seen Dmitri with the voivode of Sandomir, and showed the saber and the cloak that the "true tsar" had given him. Shakhovskoi appointed him supreme voivode and entrusted twelve thousand men to his command. Bolotnikov sent agents and messengers in every direction. He summoned peasants, refugees, vagabonds, and bandits to his banner. Thousands of slaves left their masters and rallied to him. Thousands of *kabala* peons did the same. A good many of them had served their masters or lords as soldiers, and knew how to use firearms and serve in the field. Bolotnikov also received *krestiane* from the upper Dnieper, near the western frontier, peasants who were obliged to provide men for the army: some of them free peasants from the "black lands," others peasants from the monastic estates, others again from the lands which had been given to Godunov and had become his private domain. This entire region had welcomed Dmitri and had been plundered by Godunov's troops. There also came to join Bolotnikov, besides Cossacks, of course, men from the suburbs of the towns, "boyars' sons," at the lowest level of the state servitors, *streltsy* (musketeers), Ukrainians, Poles. Bolotnikov crushed several detachments of Shuisky's troops, and with his bands, who devastated everything as they advanced, he linked up with the noble militias of the Lyapunovs and Pashkov. In October, 1606, they occupied the village of Kolomenskoye, under the walls of Moscow.

What did the rebel peasants really want? Most of them, seemingly, had nothing new in mind, no change in the social order, but simply wanted a return to the good old customs.

It appears that they wanted the "true tsar," the heir to Kalita, a tsar who would restore the peasants' former freedom to leave their holdings and choose a new place to live and a new lord to work for, that is, who would enable them to discuss their conditions of work: a "good tsar" who would reduce taxes and shorten military service, but who would also compel the lords to cut down the dues and services they exacted. Thus the peasants would be able to produce more for themselves and obtain a bigger surplus to sell, benefiting more from the progress of trade and money economy in Russia. They do not seem to have wanted to abolish autocratic tsarism or the domanial and seignorial order.

Did Bolotnikov bring anything new? What really was the content of his manifestos, his "Tempting Letters"? His letter to the famished people of Moscow seems to have said this: rebel against your nobles and masters, kill them, take their possessions, sack the city. But did the manifestos have nothing more in them than this brief program for a particular moment, inspired by the desire to take Moscow by provoking a rebellion? In the regions freed from Shuisky's forces the rebels organized themselves, electing voivodes, or governors, without our being able to make out what role was played by particular social groups. Bolotnikov's actions and what we know of his manifestos suggest that he was for dispossessing the nobles, boyars, *votchinniki*, and *pomeshchiki* to the advantage of the peasants and craftsmen. This dispossession would imply redistribution of the land among the peasants, probably as private property. We thus get a picture of a democracy of small peasant proprietors with elected political leaders, so that Bolotnikov would appear to have brought with him the germs of a real peasant revolution. This reconstruction of what happened remains very hypothetical, however. Bolotnikov seems to have sincerely believed that he had seen Tsar Dmitri in Poland; he seems to have "given" himself heart and soul to the "true tsar," to have awaited him trustingly from day to day, and, having taken an oath to him, to have wished to remain faithful to him to the end. A "loyal subject" of the "true tsar"—this is what Bolotnikov appears to have been above all. Allegiance to the tsar, the myth of the "good Tsar," would not seem to be logically in harmony with a program of peasant democracy; but logic does not seem to have predominated among the rebels.[5]

Historians have presumed that, had they conquered, Bolotnikov's chief associates would simply have taken the place of the nobles and there would have been no change in the social order: Peter would merely have replaced Paul. Every revolt risks being diverted in this way. But the existence of this danger does not mean that the motive and purpose of the revolt was merely to set others in the seats of the rich. What actually happens as a result of a rebellion is one thing, its driving forces and aims are quite another.

In any case, the devastations carried out by Bolotnikov's bands, his call for massacre and plundering of the nobles and the rich, alarmed his companions, Sunbulov, the Lyapunov brothers, Filipp Pashkov, and their noble militiamen. From fear of an upheaval in the social order they broke with Bolotnikov and went over to Shuisky's camp. Shuisky was also joined by the noble militias of Tver and Smolensk. On December 2, 1606, Bolotnikov was defeated, and he fled and shut himself up in Kaluga.

Meanwhile, however, the revolt of the Mordvinians spread to the Cheremisses and the Chuvashes. The siege of Nizhny-Novgorod continued. The Cossacks of the Terek, who lived near the Caucasus, rose in revolt, and brought with them their own Tsar Peter, who claimed to be a son of the last "true Tsar," Fyodor, the son and successor of Ivan the Terrible, but who was probably a Volga boatman turned Cossack. These Cossacks of the Terek joined forces with the Cossacks of the Don, and together they advanced northward, rescued Bolotnikov, and captured Tula. Shuisky suffered several defeats.

In the spring of 1607 Shuisky gathered together a large army, recruited in the north and in the Smolensk region. With this he laid siege to Tula. Shakhovskoi and Bolotnikov set their hopes on Tsar Dmitri's arriving to give fresh impetus to the rebellion. Owing, however, to the betrayal of his cause by several towns, Dmitri was unable to link up with them. Tsar

5. *Vosstanie I. Bolotnikova. Dokumenty i materialy,* pp. 154, 160–161.

Shuisky had the river Upa dammed below Tula, and the city was flooded. People had to go about in ferryboats. Provisions ceased to arrive and prices rose. A ton of rye cost 100 Polish florins, and a spoonful of salt half a thaler. Famine set in. The townspeople ate dogs, cats, horses, and the hides of oxen and cows. On October 10, 1607, Tula was obliged to surrender, after Shuisky had promised to spare the lives of the besieged. "Tsar Peter" was hanged in Moscow; Bolotnikov was carried off and drowned by Shuisky's men, after having his eyes put out; Prince Shakhovskoi was exiled to Lake Kubena. Tsar Shuisky returned to Moscow in triumph.

The Cossacks invented "false Dmitris" by the dozen. But in August, 1607, the second Dmitri appeared. Who he really was is not known. Historians have styled him the "Brigand," the "Plunderer," or the "Felon," of Tushino, after the place where he held court. The sources show him to us first in prison at Propoisk, near the Lithuanian frontier. On release, he went to Starodub and directed a companion of his to announce throughout the land of Seversk that Tsar Dmitri was alive and living at Starodub. The townspeople of Starodub, convinced by his claim, gave him money and sent messages to other towns. A small army gathered round the "Brigand"—Cossacks, vagrants, and Polish adventurers, including several generals. These men had no illusions about their figurehead, any more than he had himself: the Brigand was an impostor whom his soldiers treated as a joke. The name of Dmitri provided cover for the operations of a band of plunderers. For all the malcontents of society, however, he was the genuine Dmitri. Even Marina Mniszech recognized him as her husband, and bore him a child. The nun Martha declared that he was indeed her son. Following Bolotnikov, the second Dmitri became the totem of all the rebels, who rallied round him.

In spring 1608 the second Dmitri defeated at Bolkhov one of the armies of the Moscow tsar, commanded by the latter's brother, Prince Dmitri Shuisky, and was able to approach close to the capital and set up his headquarters at the village of Tushino. He could not capture Moscow itself, but Shuisky, for lack of money and men, was unable to dislodge him from Tushino. Muscovy thus had two centers of government, situated close to each other. At Tushino the Brigand had his Court, his boyars' Duma, and his administration. He levied taxes, dispensed justice, conferred titles, and distributed lands. The boyars shuttled clandestinely between Moscow and Tushino, some of them serving both Shuisky and the Brigand at the same time.

The second Dmitri had been, broadly speaking, accepted as tsar by the south of Russia, and now wanted to extend his authority over the north, which, moreover, had escaped so far the devastations of civil war. The Polish generals Sapieha and Lisowski led between 20,000 and 30,000 men against the monastery of the Holy Trinity and St. Sergius, at Zagorsk, the nodal point of the roads to the north. Their attack began in September, 1608. But this monastery was really a kremlin, a huge fortress, several kilometers in circumference, and well defended. The attack failed and a long, drawn-out siege began.

Nevertheless, some bands sent out by the Brigand did succeed in infiltrating into the north. At their approach, more than twenty towns, including Suzdal, Vladimir, Yaroslavl, and Vologda, acknowledged Dmitri as tsar. But he disappointed everyone. He granted country estates and towns to Polish noblemen, to heretics, apparently as fiefs. This shocked the Russians of all strata, and in particular the "black peasants," the state peasants who were, in theory at least, freemen, and who were numerous in the north. Above all, his forces plundered and ruined everything and everyone. Shuisky's generals, on the other hand, strove to preserve social order. One after the other, the towns took a stand against the Brigand. Ustyug was the first, and called upon Vologda not to swear allegiance to Dmitri, sending its militia to give support for resistance. The towns formed leagues for mutual aid. As soon as a town was cleared of the Tushino gang, its militia hastened to help the other towns. Soon Ustyug, Vologda, Vladimir, Galich, and Nizhny-Novgorod, nearly all the towns along the middle reaches of the Volga and those to the north of the river, had declared against the Brigand.

Still, the situation seemed deadlocked. Then, in February, 1609, Vasily Shuisky approached the Swedes, and obtained from them a force of 6,000 soldiers, in return for relinquishing his claims as tsar upon Livonia, ceding some Russian territory, and promising to ally with Sweden against Poland. His nephew, Prince Mikhail Vasilevich Skopin-Shuisky, a brilliant general of twenty-three, succeeded, with the help of the Swedes, in clearing the northwest of the Tushino bandits.

Meanwhile, King Sigismund of Poland invaded Russia and in September, 1609, laid siege to Smolensk, "the strategic key to the Russian lands along the Dnieper." Sigismund sent envoys to Tushino to summon the Poles who were there to join their king. Sapieha left Tushino, with all the Poles who were not noblemen. This marked the beginning of the breakup of the second Dmitri's movement. The Polish nobles remained at Tushino, but their agreement with the Russians could not last. They insulted the Brigand. The hetman Rozynski disparaged him. After several unsuccessful attempts, the Brigand managed to escape from Tushino at the end of 1609. After his departure, Tushino began to be abandoned by all. Many of the Poles joined their king before Smolensk. Others, on leaving Tushino, formed separate robber bands. The Cossacks rallied around the Brigand himself, who had gone to Kaluga. Henceforth he embodied only the people's aspirations to freedom. Other Russians went to join Shuisky and asked his forgiveness. Yet others constituted a sort of Duma at Tushino. Princes Masalsky and Khvorostinny, the nobles Pleshcheyev and Velyaminov, the clerk Gramatin, the commoners Andronov and Molchanov sent an embassy to Sigismund to offer the crown to his son Wladyslaw, and signed a treaty with the Polish king on February 4, 1610.

Skopin-Shuisky had raised the siege of the monastery of the Holy Trinity and St. Sergius at the beginning of 1610, and now turned to threaten Tushino, which was also in danger from the Brigand's forces. Hetman Rozynski then set fire to Tushino and withdrew to Volokolamsk. He died there soon after, and his men dispersed. Skopin entered Moscow in triumph in March, 1610, but died suddenly in the following May.

The tsar's brother Dmitri Shuisky tried to relieve Smolensk, but was beaten by Hetman Zolkiewski, who then marched on Moscow. The Brigand took advantage of this defeat to press on toward the capital, too, and was the first to reach it. He was at Kolomenskoye, at the gates of Moscow, while Zolkiewski was still at Mozhaisk, a hundred versts from the capital. The Brigand's approach stimulated a revolt in Moscow led by nobles of middle rank. On July 7, 1610, Zakhary Lyapunov called upon Shuisky to abdicate. When he refused, the Lyapunov brothers stirred up the people to assemble and, despite opposition by the Patriarch Hermogen and some boyars, Shuisky was deposed and imprisoned in a monastery.

Government was carried on by a Duma of seven boyars, presided over by Prince Fyodor Mstislavsky. This Duma was, however, quite without power. It was for Moscow to choose between the heretic Pole, Wladyslaw, and the personification of the people's desires, the friend and leader of the Cossacks, the Brigand. The Muscovites of the lowest social strata supported the Brigand. Once more, as in Bolotnikov's time, fear of social upheaval proved effective, and the nobility closed their ranks again. They preferred the foreigner to the Cossack, and invited Zolkiewski in. The Pole was in a position to lay down conditions: Wladyslaw must be elected tsar. On August 27 Moscow swore allegiance to the hereditary foe, provided that he became a convert to Orthodoxy. Zolkiewski then attacked the Brigand, who was forced to fall back on Kaluga. Zolkiewski cleverly exploited the nobles' fear of the Cossacks, and caused the boyars to ask for a Polish garrison. The Polish army entered Moscow.

But Sigismund III of Poland refused to accept the conversion of Wladyslaw. Actually, he wanted the throne of Russia for himself. He pressed on with the war. In Moscow, after Zolkiewski had left, the Polish army behaved as though in a conquered country. Now that Moscow had accepted Wladyslaw, Sweden declared war on Russia, threatened Novgorod, and put forward her own candidate for the Russian throne, Prince Philip. A national reaction, anti-Swedish and anti-Polish, resulted in Moscow and other places. All at once, the Brigand at Kaluga became the incarnation of Muscovy. The whole eastern part of the country swore allegiance to him. In December, 1610, however, one of his supporters murdered him, for purely personal reasons. Deprived of the man who had legitimized and unified their movement, the false Dmitri's forces dispersed. They broke up into groups of partisans who were soon hard to distinguish from the innumerable bands of outlaws who were taking advantage of the chaos to prowl, rob, and destroy. The Brigand's death marks the end of the popular risings of the "Time of Troubles."

The "Time of Troubles" itself ended with a rallying of the Russian nation. The Patriarch Hermogen declared, from Moscow, that the Russians were relieved of their allegiance to Wladyslaw. He sent envoys to all the towns and called on them to form an army and march on the capital, to liberate it from the heretic foreigner. Once again, at Ryazan, Prokop Lyapunov assembled an army, this time made up of peasants as well as nobles, and soon to be joined by the Brigand's so-called Cossacks, from Kaluga, led by Prince Dmitri Trubetskoi, and by Cossacks led by Ivan Zarutsky. This national army elected a council of representatives who acted as a national government for Muscovy.

This army blockaded the Poles in the Kremlin. But it was torn by social conflicts. The council of representatives, far from introducing popular reforms, took measures in the nobles' favor, against runaway peasants and against Cossack plundering. The Cossacks were furious, and in July, 1611, killed Prokop Lyapunov. The dead man's troops then refused to fight alongside the Cossacks, and dispersed. The first national army and its government were no more. The Cossacks remained before the Kremlin.

The Poles took Smolensk in June, 1611, and in July the Swedes took Novgorod. Neither of them, however, pressed on toward Moscow. Once again, the Patriarch Hermogen, supported by the Abbot Dionysius, of the monastery of the Holy Trinity and St. Sergius, issued a call to the nation. This time, the answer came from Nizhny-Novgorod. A butcher named Kuzma Minin emerged there as a leader of men and an organizer. His city, together with others in the northeast, raised a powerful army, commanded by Prince Dmitri Pozharsky, with Minin in charge of pay and supplies. The army was accompanied by a council of representatives elected by the various localities and which assumed the government of Muscovy.

In September, 1612, this national army reached Moscow. The Cossacks, who were still besieging the Poles in the Kremlin, broke into two groups. Some joined the national army, while the rest, led by Zarutsky, withdrew to the "frontier," persisting in their attitude of revolt, their rejection of the society of estates, of seignorial property, and of the autocratic state. In November the national army succeeded in overwhelming the Poles and liberating Moscow.

Prince Pozharsky, on behalf of the nobles, and Prince Trubetskoi, on behalf of the Cossacks, sent out letters to convoke the church leaders and the representatives of the *chini*. A Zemsky Sobor, an assembly of notables such as the tsars had formerly summoned to receive their orders and pledge to fulfill them, met at the beginning of 1613. As before, it represented the *chini*, the "service ranks," but it was broader based. For the first time, it included even the peasants. Represented in it—though not all the social strata of Russia—were the clergy, the boyars, the "state servitors," the "urban taxpayers," and certainly also the "black peasants," the state peasants of North Russia. Twelve out of 277 signatures were those of peasants; but this assembly was nevertheless an expression of the same structures of Russian society as before. The Zemsky Sobor did not elect a tsar. After fasting for three days in order to purge itself of its sins during the period of disturbances—for the assembly's forms of thought remained the same—it acknowledged and proclaimed the man who was the tsar indicated by God, because he was related to the family of the Kalita, because he was closest by birth to the old tsars, and because he was the "born tsar." It was a Don Cossack, an *ataman*, who spoke the decisive words: "The born tsar, Mikhail." Thus, on February 21, 1613, by unanimous secret vote, the "chosen of God," Mikhail Romanov, was acknowledged. The Zemsky Sobor dispatched a boyar and some churchmen to the Red Square, where thousands of townspeople were assembled. They were informed of the assembly's pronouncement, and gave it their approval, shouting with one voice: "Mikhail Fyodorovich."

Mikhail belonged to the Romanovs, an old boyar family related by blood to the line of Kalita. He was the son of the Metropolitan Filaret, grandson of Nikita Romanov, the brother of Anastasia Romanova, Ivan IV's wife. Thus, he was grandnephew by marriage to Tsar Ivan IV, whom he called his "grandfather." The Romanov family were popular. The people recalled with warmth the good Anastasia who had exercised a calming influence on Ivan the Terrible. Nikita Romanov had dared to take up the defense of some of the Terrible Tsar's victims. Filaret had not shown himself hostile to the Cossacks of Tushino, and his patriotism was proved, since the Poles had held him prisoner. Mikhail, only sixteen years old, had not had time to get on the wrong side of anyone. But while all this was important, what was decisive was that he was "the born tsar," "the chosen of God before his birth," and that the chronicler Timofeyev could place him in the succession of hereditary tsars, immediately after Fyodor and ignoring any other in between.

The peasants had their "good tsar." Would they get the rest? Mikhail took up his *otchina*, the state.

[9]

Russian Society Before the Revolt
of Stenka Razin

THE REBELLION LED by the Cossack Stenka Razin unleashed a terrible civil war which lasted through 1670 and 1671
in a large area of the basins of the Volga and the Don. These
troubles were the culmination of a reaction against the increasing despotism of a ruling circle formed around the Romanov
tsars, Mikhail (1613–1645) and Aleksei (1645–1676), against
an administrative centralization which increasingly did away
with local liberties, and also doubtless against the government's
efforts to fix the entire population of Russia, geographically and
socially, within the structures of a society of estates, in accordance
with the needs of the state and the state's service.

The growth of absolutism and the development of centralized
organs of government and administrative institutions were forced
upon Russia, as upon other European states, by the pressure
of national wars. After Mikhail Romanov had been elected
tsar it was necessary to carry on the war against the Swedes,
who were occupying Novgorod and besieging Pskov. By the peace
of Stolbovo, in 1617, Sweden gave back Novgorod but kept the
approaches to the Gulf of Finland. The Polish Prince Wladyslaw
maintained his claim to the throne of Russia and in 1618 appeared in arms under Moscow's walls, but he proved incapable

of capturing the city. An armistice which lasted fourteen and a half years was arranged at Deulino, by which the Poles kept Smolensk and Chernigov.

In 1632 the Russians tried to take advantage of the death of King Sigismund to recover the Polish-occupied territories. But their siege of Smolensk turned into a disaster and the surrender of the Russian army in 1634. The tsar had to give up even his claims to Estonia, Livonia, and Courland.

In 1654 the Cossacks of the Dnieper, in revolt against the Poles under the leadership of Bogdan Khmelnitsky, decided to become the tsar's men and swear allegiance to him. The result was a long, hard, and costly war against Poland and against the Tatars. After exhausting their financial resources, the Russians were obliged to sign in 1667 the armistice of Andrusovo with the Poles, by which they recovered Smolensk but kept, of Little Russia, only the left bank of the Dnieper, with Kiev on the right bank.

Between wars, the Russian government lived in fear of foreign aggression, on the part of the Swedes, the Poles, the Turks, and the Tatars. It had to ensure the defense of frontiers that were inordinately long, and build fortresses, the lack of which had been cruelly felt in 1634. Toward the steppe, always exposed to Tatar incursions, the government reinforced, between 1636 and 1656, a new defense line in front of the one formed by Tula, Tambov, Voronezh, Ostrogozhsk, and Byelgorod. General staffs for local defense had to be established—at Novgorod against Sweden, at Syevsk against Poland, at Byelgorod against the Crimean Tatars. They had to enlist foreign officers, and even whole regiments of Englishmen and Germans; arrange for the training in European fashion, by foreign officers, of regiments made up of petty *pomeshchiki* with insufficient land, "boyars' sons," peasants, and slaves; and develop the standing forces of musketeers, or *streltsy*, to the number of 20,000 in Moscow and as many again in the provinces. The army numbered 70,000 men in 1631, 164,000 in 1681. All these men had to be well paid—and in money. The upkeep of the army, which had demanded 250,000 rubles in 1613, absorbed 750,000 rubles, half the state's budget, in 1680. The Smolensk war cost Mikhail

570,000 rubles. Aleksei's first two years of war with Poland, in 1654 and 1655, cost over 1,400,000 rubles.

Military expenditure made it necessary to increase taxes, both in number and in amount: the general assessment (*tyaglo*), which was assessed on fiscal units, or *sochi*, and then, after 1646, on hearths—with censuses in 1619 and 1646; special taxes, "for the postal service" (for ambassadors, couriers, official journeys), "for the prisoners" (for the redemption of those in Turkish and Tatar captivity), for the musketeers or *streltsy*; customs and excise duties; in 1653, a tax of 10 percent on all merchandise; duties charged on petitions, on legal decisions, on copies of deeds made for private persons; the salt tax, increased in 1646, which led to revolts in 1648; the tobacco monopoly, established in 1634; and so on. In order to make certain the assessment and collection of all these taxes, in face of resistance, the government had to strengthen its authority, centralize administration, and bind everyone to his place of residence and his social position.

Absolutism exercised by the tsar himself, for the common good, would not perhaps have aroused great opposition. But this government was that of a clique. The two tsars both had the misfortune to come to the throne while still adolescents, only sixteen years old in each case, and not to include strong will among their personal qualities. They left the task of government to a ruling circle made up of favorites, members of their own family or of related families, or persons who were merely boyars, or even *pomeshchiki*. Under Mikhail, prominent roles were played by members of the Saltykov family, related to him through his mother, and, from 1619 to 1633, by his father Filaret, Patriarch of Moscow, the real head of the government; under Aleksei, by his guardian the boyar Boris Morozov and his father-in-law Ilya Miloslavsky, both of them attended by a clientele of followers. These coteries showed in their exercise of state power a degree of selfishness, greed, and corruption which transformed the autocracy of absolutism into despotism and tyranny. They provoked the revolt of May, 1648, in Moscow and the revolts later in that year in other towns.

The ruling group operated through the Boyarskaya Duma and the Holy Synod, which functioned as the Tsar's Council, but the makeup of this body changed. After the "Time of Troubles" little remained of the princely *knyazhata* or the great aristocratic boyar families. A small number of families still retained prestige and influence because they were related to the Romanovs or had given proof of their loyalty to the new dynasty. Little by little, however, these families died out. Under Mikhail and Aleksei, the Shuisky, Kurbsky, Mikulinsky, Penkov, Mstislavsky, Vorotinsky, and other families disappeared. The ranks of the boyars were growing thinner.

To fill the high offices of state the tsars had to call, either through favoritism or according to merit, but in any case without taking account of their lineage and of the *myestnichestvo*, upon ordinary *pomeshchiki*, sons of noblemen and churchmen, but also peasants' sons, even butchers' sons, on whom they conferred the titles of *Dumnie Dvoryane, Dumnie Dyaki, Okolnichi*: the Naryshkins, the Miloslavskys, the Lopukhins, the Boborykins, the Yazykovs, the Chaadayevs, the Chirikovs, the Tolstois, the Chitris, and so on. Some of these became princes: the Prozorovskys, the Masalskys, the Dolgorukis, the Urusovs. These "new men" wormed their way into the Boyarskaya Duma, regarded themselves as entered, by virtue of their appointment, in the *Rodoslovets*, the official register of families entitled to provide candidates for the highest positions, and demanded social recognition and precedence in accordance with their services and their merits. They clashed with the boyars. The latter continued to insist on appointments and promotions regulated by the *myestnichestvo*. They claimed that the tsar had the power to grant anything *except otechestvo*, ancestral rank or "gentility." They struggled hard to keep their rights of precedence. They literally fought with presumptuous upstarts in actual sessions of the Boyarskaya Duma. On their complaints, other such men were deprived of their rank, imprisoned, and beaten with the knout. Prince Pozharsky, who had been raised from being a mere inferior gentleman-in-waiting to the tsar to the rank of boyar, and who had done much to rescue Muscovy from the Cossacks and the Poles, having tried to walk in front of Prince Saltykov, was made to give way to him, reduced in rank, and obliged to go on foot to the Saltykovs' house and humble him-

self before them. But the persistence of the new men and
the need to replace the extinct boyar families gradually imposed acceptance of the idea that the tsar, when conferring a
high rank in his service, thereby conferred "gentility." In 1682
the *myestnichestvo* was abolished: increasingly it was present
service to the tsar that conferred noble status.

Until 1621 this central government functioned with the collaboration of the Zemsky Sobor. The latter was at first made
up of members of the Boyarskaya Duma and of the Holy
Synod. The peasants disappeared from it after 1613, but it included elected representatives of the service nobility and the
urban taxpayers. After 1621 the Zemsky Sobor was convened
no more, except irregularly, in 1632, 1637, 1642, 1648, and 1654.
Then it vanished entirely from the scene. The government was
content most of the time to consult, according to circumstances,
this or that estate of Muscovy—the service nobility, or the
urban taxpayers—or this or that section of a particular estate—
such as the merchants—depending on whether the measures
to be taken affected this particular estate, or section of an
estate, most closely, or whether its special competence made
its opinion desirable. Estates and sections of estates served to
provide counsel, but no longer shared in the government.

The Tsar's Council caused its decisions to be carried out
and current business to be dealt with by over fifty central
offices or *prikazi*, which were set up *ad hoc*, as required. It was
therefore necessary to group these under ministers. Prince Miloslavsky was at one and the same time head of the treasury, of the
offices managing the infantry, the cavalry, and the foreign troops,
and also of the office which supervised apothecaries, who were
mainly foreigners. Under Aleksei two fresh *prikazi* appeared: the
prikaz of accounts, to draw up the state budget and check
the accounts of all the other *prikazi* and all the state's agents
in the provinces, and the *prikaz* of secret affairs, made up of a
dyak and ten secretaries. The tsar used this *prikaz* for all business which he wished to deal with personally, without the
Boyarskaya Duma. He recruited commissaries from it, attaching
one of the secretaries to each Russian ambassador and each army
commander's staff in the field, in order to keep him informed
and convey his personal orders.

The wars led to the establishment in each territorial division of a single representative of the state, charged with all the functions of war, finance, justice, and administration, and with full powers in relation to each of these, the sole right to correspond with the *prikazi*, and entire responsibility toward the government. An entire provincial hierarchy came into being. At the top were large military districts, or *razryadi*, embracing several cantons, and commanded by a superior governor, or chief voivode. The cantons, or volosts, were headed, according to circumstances, either by a voivode or a *starosta*, who was elected by the communities of the canton but served as an agent of the government, possessed of the same powers, prerogatives, duties, and responsibilities as the voivode.

All the local elected bodies were subordinate to these representatives of the state. The village communities kept their elected administrations, made up of councillors and a local *starosta*. In fact, however, the voivode or the *starosta* of the volost directed the entire administration of these communities, their *starosti* and councillors becoming mere passive instruments. The *starosta* of a community received the voivode's orders and carried them out; provided him and his men with meat, fish, candles, paper, ink, everything needed for their maintenance; and also gave him and all his household presents of money on his name day. All that the communities retained was the task of collecting the taxes and regulating the crafts.

The elected officers of the *guba*, the organization intended to suppress banditry, murder, robbery, witchcraft, prostitution, gambling, heresy, sacrilege, and vice, though directly responsible to the central Banditry Office in Moscow, were in reality often subject to the voivode. In other cases, instead of being elected, the *guba* was nominated by the government. After 1667 the government sent inquisitors into the provinces, omnipotent agents of the center, with plenary powers to put down banditry, and in 1669 the *guba* elders were formally placed under the authority of these inquisitors.[1]

A hierarchical, centralized administration was thus fastened upon all Muscovy. Unknown persons, usually strangers to the

1. J. L. H. Keep, "Bandits and the Law in Muscovy," *Slavonic and East European Review*, 35 (December, 1956), p. 221.

canton, came to exact obedience to decrees drawn up in the
name of the tsar by faceless groups, legislative and regulatory
documents that were generalized, cold, and impersonal. Without
taking into account the infinite variety of particular cases, these
decrees imposed upon the people, through taxation, and also
through the extortions of the state's agents, ever new efforts,
hardships, and sorrows. All this made the Russian people feel
they were being confronted by something inhuman, and had a
lot to do with the revolts, typical of the century, which were
directed against the blind machine of the modern state in formation.

In the interests of its service, and in particular of its revenue,
the Russian state sought to define the obligations of the different
estates more precisely, to distinguish between them more sharply,
and to "fix" every subject, socially in his estate and geographically
in his town or village. This was the purpose of a wide range of
ukases issued at the request of the various *prikazi*. Their large
number and the overlapping, contradictions, and gaps between
them made necessary a recasting and codification of these
ukases. The government thought for a long time about convoking
a Zemsky Sobor for this purpose, and at last the troubles of
1648 decided it. The Zemsky Sobor met in September, 1648. A
governmental commission had drawn up a plan of work. The
government put each question to the social group most concerned.
The tsar, aided by the Boyarskaya Duma, decided each point.
The whole body of decisions was adopted by the Zemsky Sobor
in 1649 and sent to all the administrations and towns for
application. This code, the *Sobornoye Ulozhenie*, a compilation
modified and completed by the regulations in force in the different *prikazi*, gave legal backing to the social organization of
the new Russia and remained in force until replaced by the
Digest of Laws of 1833.

Its basic principle was that each estate of Russian society
was tied down, for the benefit of the state, to particular duties
which gave it its distinctive character and made it virtually a
separate species.

At the top of the social hierarchy, the first estate was that
of the state servitors, with which was associated a kind of noble

status. These people owed, on a hereditary basis, military service to the tsar from which were derived obligations to serve in civil capacities and in the courts. Service to the state was the necessary condition for possession of a landed estate. The law of February 7, 1628, ratifying practice and prevalent ideas, had definitely laid it down that, apart from ecclesiastics, only persons capable of serving the state could be landowners. All hereditary landowners, or *votchinniki*, had to serve the state or else lose their property. On the other hand, however, the *pomestya* became more and more like *votchini*. It became automatic during this century for sons under the age of fifteen of *pomeshchiki* who had died prematurely to retain part of their fathers' estates until they were old enough to begin service, and for the widows and daughters to retain part of them until they married. It was now quite common for *pomeshchiki* to bequeath their estates to their heirs, and for these estates to be exchanged one for another. But the Code of 1649 even allowed a *pomestye* to be exchanged for a *votchina*, the *votchina* becoming a *pomestye*, and vice versa. The *pomeshchiki* gave away their estates as dowries, or alienated them by deeds of gift that concealed sales. The state servitors naturally preferred to own their estates as *votchini*, and the tsar allowed them to convert part of their *pomestya* into *votchini*. The *pomeshchiki* were moving toward that complete confusion between the two types of estates that was sanctioned by decree in 1714. The state servitors became a hereditary group of landowners, a hereditary landed nobility. Nevertheless, whether transmissible tenure or hereditary property, the land was always held on condition of service. The state servitor had to provide a soldier, mounted and armed, for each 300 *chetverti* of his land. After 1620 the number of soldiers was fixed in accordance with the number of peasant holdings on the estate. In 1633 it was decided that a *pomeshchik* would be exempted from service if he had less than fifteen adult male peasants on his estate. In a further easing of his lot, the minimum was raised in 1642 to fifty. Ownership of land was no longer invariably associated with obligation to serve.

The state servitors formed social strata arranged in a hierarchy according to the importance of their function, their birth and the extent of the land they held, either as *pomestya* or as *votchini*. There were thus three grades within the estate: the state servitors with Duma rank, those with metropolitan rank, and those with provincial rank. The tsar granted, especially between 1613 and 1625, large tracts of land to "new men" in particular. In this way he created twenty-three magnates, only nine of whom were from old princely families. The biggest landowner was the tsar's uncle, I. N. Romanov, who received 7,012 peasant families. Half a century later, Natalya Naryshkina having become Tsar Aleksei's second wife, the Naryshkins were given 12,000 peasant families. While all the state servitors of Duma rank engaged in trade, profiting from the great national market constituted by the needs of the army and by centralization, some of them became large-scale traders and industrialists, exploiting their advantages of not being subject, as the merchants were, to taxes, tolls, and customs duties on their goods, and of being able to make use of a labor force of serfs. Among the most famous we find the Miloslavskys, the Trubetskois, the Odoyevskys, and above all the "great boyar" Morozov. Forcing his peasants to work, he managed seventeen enterprises each producing 100 barrels of potash for export, from which he made an annual profit of 24,000 rubles. He owned iron foundries at Pavlovsk, leatherworks, linen factories, distilleries, brickworks, flour mills, and fisheries. He exported grain to the value of 12,000 rubles a year. As a moneylender, he had debts of 80,000 rubles owing to him. The foundation of this power of his was his ownership of 300 villages and hamlets in 17 cantons, with tens of thousands of serfs and debt slaves. His was merely the most striking instance among a small handful of aristocrats. Tsars Mikhail and Aleksei themselves set the example. They had developed, to serve the needs of their army, state enterprises managed by foreign merchants and foremen—Vinius, Marceli, Akem, Roet. There were iron mines near Tula, iron and copper mines in the Urals; from 1632, foundries, arms works, cannon foundries; in 1634 a glassworks near Moscow. These enterprises had survived because the tsars had been able to draft peasants into them who were obliged to perform forced labor.

This large-scale trade and industry, often formed, moreover, by a merely commercial grouping of many petty units of production, made up only a small proportion of the trade and industry of the country as a whole. The bulk of the country's needs as regards manufactured articles was still met by craft production or by domestic industry, carried on either by the peasants or by their lords. The basis of Russia's large-scale industry remained large property, land rent, and serfdom.

The state servitors of lower standing struggled to cope with the shortage of labor. In Ryazan in 1616 the *pomestya* included twenty-two times more land lying waste than under cultivation. In the canton of Tver a state servitor had an estate of 900 *desyatini*, partly *votchina* and partly *pomestye*; of this, only 95 *desyatini* were cultivated, 20 of these by the servitor and his men, and 75 in 19 peasant holdings, each of 4.6 *desyatini*. (The situation became less disastrous as the population of the central regions recovered its numbers, growing from 700,000 in 1620 to 2,000,000 by the end of the century.) The state servitors tried to ensure their livelihood and fulfill their duties to the state by cultivating on their own, with the help of slaves, seignorial demesnes on their *pomestya* or *votchini*, and the extent of these demesnes increased continually, the development of serfdom greatly assisting the process. In the towns, they went in for trade and made their serfs work for them there. Many, however, found themselves in difficulties, some because they had too little land, sometimes merely a manor house without any land, others because they could not find the labor they needed to cultivate their land. Some of these went off to join the Cossacks; others became traders, craftsmen, even peasants; the most numerous group entered the service of boyars or monasteries, sometimes as temporary slaves. The establishment of regiments organized and trained in the European manner offered them employment, and many took service in them, as private soldiers, for the sake of the high pay. Most of these regiments, however, were dissolved after each campaign was over. Thus, the petty *votchinniki* and *pomeshchiki*, the lowest-ranking state servitors, found themselves in an awkward and precarious economic situation.

The estate of urban taxpayers comprised, first and foremost, merchants, who formed a hierarchy of three grades, according to the dimensions of their business: the "best men," the "men

of middle rank," and the "juniors." The best men had to take
turns in serving for a year in Moscow itself, to ensure the payment of taxes. Among these best men separate groups kept
emerging. At their head were the "guests," the title given to
the thirty biggest merchants in Moscow who managed the tsar's
trade, internal and external, and directed his monopolies at the
same time as they carried on their own business. The most
important of them, the Stroganov family, enjoyed the title of
"distinguished men." Below them stood the "hundred guests,"
a group of 158 merchants. Then came the "hundred clothiers."
The members of these special groups concentrated many different
enterprises under their control, so that the outlines of large-
scale industry began to appear. The Stroganovs, who were former
peasants but now themselves owned whole villages, employed
10,000 wage workers and 5,000 serfs in their saltworks, potash
mines, and iron mines, and in their metalworking establishments
along the Kama, at Perm, and in the Urals. They headed the
Russian penetration of Siberia and the fur trade. Nikitnikov owned
one-quarter of the capital of the "thirty guests." He traded in
cloth, salt, and fish. His fleet of ships sailed down the Volga
to Astrakhan. Voronin owned thirty big shops, controlled large-
scale ironworks, traded in grain, and was a shipowner, a usurer,
and a supplier of munitions. Among the "hundred guests," Ya-
Gruditsyn owned forty villages, together with fisheries, saltworks,
and a number of shops—one-twenty-third of the capital belonging
to this group.

Thanks to the state, to the unification of the markets of Russia
into a single national market, to the opportunities offered by
army supply work and participation in the collection of taxes,
and thanks also to the monopoly of foreign trade maintained by
the tsar, an economic advance certainly took place and the merchants became differentiated into richer and less rich. But the
large-scale merchants remained a mere handful. The source of
their wealth was still landed property, rent from land and the
growth of serfdom. Large-scale industry and trade continued to
account for only a very small proportion of Muscovy's trade
and industry. The crafts and domestic industry, carried on by
the peasants or by their lords, supplied the bulk of the people's

needs, and this industry continued to be based predominantly on agriculture, which provided its raw materials (except metals) and on water and wood for power and fuel. Nevertheless, craft production was carried on increasingly for the market. It nourished a petty trade carried on over a large area by tens of thousands of small sellers—the makers themselves, shopkeepers, and peddlers.

About the middle of the century, the merchants who lived in the *posad* of each town had been grouped by the state into a sort of exclusive merchant community which bore collective responsibility for the payment of taxes. Trade became a duty laid upon these men by the state. Below the level of the best men, the men of middle rank and the juniors were burdened by taxes and forced loans; mutually responsible, and suffering from competition by the state servitors who were exempt from taxes and customs dues when they traded in the surplus produce of their estates, these merchants were often in difficulties.

In the towns, below the level of the best men, the different grades of state servitors fitted in between the different grades of merchants, as regards wealth and income, though they were usually superior to them in rank. There were many different grades of state servitors, but they all carried on trade and agriculture. Well below the merchants, but above the other craftsmen, were "state servitors of the lesser *chini*," which meant craftsmen in state service: smiths, carpenters, saddlers, gunners, who were allowed to carry on their occupation in their free time without paying tax. Below them came the various grades of ordinary craftsmen.

Besides these, in the suburbs or *sloboda*, the zone of "liberties" around the cities, persons of various *chini* were settled—*streltsy* (musketeers), peasants, priests' sons, church servants. Here too were *zakladchiki*, debtors who had borrowed on the security of their work. Each was under the protection of his creditor and exempt from tax. An increasing number of these, however, were fictitious debtors who in this way acquired the status of clients and privileged persons. Some of them became rich. The common feature of all these inhabitants of the suburbs was that they carried on trades and opened shops, taking profit away from the urban taxpayers while themselves remaining free from taxation, to the greater loss of the urban taxpayers and the state. The Ulozhenie declared the position of the *zakladchiki* illegal and incorporated the population of the suburbs in the towns, subjecting all these people to the state's taxes. Then the decree of February 8, 1658, imposed the death penalty on anyone who left his own town or married someone from another town. These potential taxpayers and this labor force were henceforth unable to escape. At the same time as geographical mobility was suppressed, social mobility too was reduced, since a craftsman or a merchant was now virtually unable to move to a place where he could carry on his activities in more favorable circumstances, or change his way of life, by becoming a soldier, for instance, with hopes of acquiring a *pomestye* and rising to one of the higher grades among the state servitors. Russian society was becoming a society of closed estates at the same time as the tax burden grew heavier. There were many people who were discontented with this situation.

Because of the need to guarantee to the state servitors the labor they needed to cultivate their lands, their chief means of support, the position of the rural taxpayers undoubtedly worsened more than anyone else's. All the different categories—*krestiane*, or tenants, *bobyli*, or landless workers, *kabalnye lyudi*, or temporary debt slaves—tended to merge into a single category of serfs, bound to the soil. This resulted from a dual process— contracts between private persons, and laws imposed by the state. The indebtedness of the peasants enabled the lords to make them accept contracts of serfdom. The first of these appeared, it seems, in 1628. In order to receive a loan, a free peasant undertook "to live with my master among the peasantry and there to seek my livelihood, and not to depart from that place." About 1630 undertakings never to go away, in return for a loan, had become very frequent.

More effective than these private contracts, no doubt, were the laws and regulations of the state. Since 1627–1628 the government, when registering taxpayers, had decided that all of them had to remain in their place of residence, and any who ran away had to be brought back. Since 1614 the period during which a lord could recover a peasant who had left his holding without permission, and without paying off his dues and services, was extended to nine years. In 1642 it was further extended to ten years, and to fifteen in the case of those who had been taken away illegally by other lords. In 1646 the law laid it down that not only the head of the family but everyone who was living with him—sons, brothers, nephews—should be bound to the soil. Finally, the Sobornoye Ulozhenie not only confirmed this decision and the earlier ones, but abolished all prescriptive limits on the recovery of runaway peasants.

Henceforth the peasants of the *pomestya* were bound to the *pomeshchiki* and those of the *votchini* to the *votchinniki*. The lords were free to transfer the peasants like chattels from *pomestye* to *pomestye* and from *votchina* to *votchina*. The peasants' property belonged, in the last resort, to their lords. It was the lord who represented his peasants before the state's courts, except in cases of murder, theft, or harboring of criminals. It was the lord who collected state taxes from his serfs and paid the money to the state, or who advanced them the money to meet their taxes. The lord had jurisdiction over his serfs so far as ordinary offenses were concerned, breaches of public order like brawls, drunkenness, petty theft between serfs of the same lord, and so on. He could inflict corporal punishment on them. All that he owed his serfs was food and clothing. Nothing was laid down for the protection of the serfs from their master's will. The serf who came to the town to work continued to be legally a serf. The lord, or the village commune, could always summon him back to the village. In 1678 the government registered 888,000 peasant households or holdings; of these, only 92,000, or 10.4 percent, were free peasant holdings; the remaining 796,000, or 89.6 percent, were serf holdings, of which 507,000, or 57 percent, belonged to state servitors and the rest to the tsar's Court, to boyars (10 percent), to the church, or to monasteries. The lords were able to expand *barshchina*, though *obrok* continued to be the preponderant form of peasants' support for their lords. *Barshchina* provided a substantial proportion of the labor force for large-scale industry. It was increasingly difficult for the peasants to flee to more favorable parts of the country—where, in any case, they found representatives of the administration everywhere.

Finally, at the bottom of the social order, though only just under the vagabonds and *déclassés*, were the slaves, the *zadvornie lyudi*. The lords continued to employ these to cultivate their demesnes. In 1677 and 1688 slaves still accounted for 10 percent of the households—14 percent of those near Moscow. Only in 1680 were they subjected to taxation and merged with the serfs. A special category was that of the "free" slaves. These were men who acknowledged themselves slaves of a lord who kept them and employed them as he wished; yet the slaves could repudiate their servitude whenever they close to do so. Some boyars' sons entered the service of state servitors in this way, and formed a *chin* intermediate between them and the urban taxpayers. But these voluntary slaves were exempt from taxes and military service. Therefore the Ulozhenie formally forbade anyone to become a free slave, and this social group disappeared.

Left to itself, and given peaceful conditions, Russian society would doubtless have developed a class society, an open society in which men would have found their places at different levels of the social order in accordance with the wealth they acquired in the production of goods. By the action of the state, however, and through the necessities of war, Russian society became a society of orders or estates, with a hierarchy determined by services rendered to the state. The tsar had ossified society in rigid categories. He had reduced social mobility, while at the same time, by sharpening distinctions of function, obligation, rank, and privilege between the different estates, he had stimulated and aggravated the friction and conflict between the estates. It is to be expected that more social conflicts will occur in a society of estates than in any other. In any case it is noteworthy that in the Zemsky Sobor each group thought only of its own interests, and opposed those of all the others; that in 1642 the merchants sought to cast the burden of a possible war with the Turks for Azov upon the nobles, and the nobles upon the merchants; that in 1662 the merchants complained that trade was also carried on by the archbishops, bishops, monasteries, priests, and state servitors—all of whom were exempt from taxes and customs dues. At the same time the merchants sometimes invoked the interest of the empire as a whole and of all the *chini*.

Altogether, the intensified distinction between the estates, and the geographical and social immobilization of social groups, resulted in sharpening social conflicts.

Opposition to the state and conflicts within society were aggravated by the reforms in the Orthodox Church. From the earliest times, the parish priests had been elected by the village communities. They obeyed the wishes of the mir regarding the celebration of church services, were judged, like laymen, by the assembly of the mir, and could give up their offices only with the permission of the mir. In short, they were functionaries of the village communities. In 1652 Patriarch Nikon decided that this subordination was incompatible with the dignity of the priesthood and announced that parish priests would henceforth be appointed by their archpriests and would come under the jurisdiction of the latter. Nikon's decision took away the last autonomous right of the village communities and subjected them to an ecclesiastical centralization that was ultimately that of the state, since archbishops and bishops were appointed by the state, and the Holy Synod was a branch of the State Council. The patriarch's decision aroused violent opposition on the part of the village communities and the parish priests. The latter were also infuriated by the heavy tithes they had to pay to the bishops. They felt bitter at being subjected closely to persons who were strange to them, and looked back with nostalgia to the authority of the village elders who were their own neighbors. Protopope Neronov expressed their feelings: "The rank of priest is one and the same for all. . . . All priests are on the same footing. . . . If the archpriests are the successors of the twelve great Apostles, the priests and deacons are the successors of the seventy Apostles; and they are all brothers, servants of the same Lord." It was a sort of Russian equivalent of the ideas of Edmond Richer, the ultra-Gallican. Neronov proposed that a church council be held at which the entire priesthood would be represented, even the village priests.

Other reforms introduced by Nikon provoked the religious schism called the *Raskol*. He sought to correct the holy books of the Russians, into which many mistakes had crept, and also to make changes in ritual. For example, in Muscovy the faithful crossed themselves with two fingers, and sang hallelujah twice, whereas the Greeks used three fingers and three hallelujahs. Nikon had the Greek usages adopted in 1650. However, on the one hand, these rituals had a value for the Russians in themselves, being efficacious by virtue of the way they were performed, and linked with the entire order of the cosmos willed by God; and, on the other, the Russians were quite convinced that the Russian Church was the only Orthodox one and its distinctive practices alone interpreted correctly the dogmas of the faith. If the Greeks crossed themselves with three fingers and used three hallelujahs, that must be because they had a wrong idea of the dogma of the Holy Trinity and of the relationship between the two natures of Christ, human and divine. They were heretics, and Nikon was introducing heresy into the Russian church. Many Russians, the Old Believers, or *Raskolniki*, refused to accept the reforms, and went on crossing themselves with two fingers. They were excommunicated by the higher clergy and persecuted by the tsar. They persisted in their resistance, declared that Aleksei was "not a tsar but a tyrant," and maintained that individuals and village communities were free to choose their ritual for themselves, as in former times. They defended local and individual liberties. The Council of 1666 resolved that the Old Believers must be punished by the secular arm. Executions by the knout, the rope, and the fire began.[2]

This society, going through a process of transformation, was shaken by financial and currency crises. In 1646, the government, in desperate straits for money, listened to the advice of one Nazarei Chistoi, a former merchant who had become a *dumny dyak*, a sort of secretary of state, and raised the price of a pood of salt (40 Russian pounds, or 16 kilos) from 15 to 20 kopecks. Salt thus cost six times as much as in the nineteenth century. The Volga fishermen could no longer afford to buy salt to preserve their fish, which rotted on the banks of the river. It was this cheap fish that was the food of the masses, already exasperated by the introduction of a tobacco monopoly. These were the immediate causes of the revolts of 1648.

2. F. C. Conybeare, *Russian Dissenters*, "Harvard Theological Studies," X (1921), pp. 15–23.

In 1656, at the suggestion of the boyar Fyodor Rtishchev, in order to facilitate war preparations, the tsar ordered that copper coins be issued with the same denominations and weights as silver coins, and at the same rate as the latter. The imperial mint issued excessive quantities of these coins. Counterfeiters did the same, and prices rose rapidly. At Vologda the price of rye, which had been on the average six kopecks the *chetvert* from 1646 to 1656, rose to eight rubles, eighty kopecks in 1662. In February, 1663, it reached twenty-four rubles, and one silver ruble was worth fifteen copper ones. The people were hungry. In Little Russia the soldiers could no longer find anything to buy with their coppers. Russian trade was paralyzed for lack of silver. The country's merchants bought foreign goods with silver, sold them in Russia for copper, and then, lacking silver, could no longer replace their stocks from abroad. Large-scale merchants suffered very heavy losses, for the treasury had obliged them to sell to it, for payment made in copper, exportable goods—furs, hemp, potash, lard—which the tsar had then sold to foreigners. In July, 1662, there was a popular rising. The government resigned itself in 1663 to demonetizing the copper currency and going back to one of silver. But it went bankrupt, buying back the copper coins at the rate of one kopeck for one ruble. The impoverishment inflicted was lasting.

Finally, from 1655 onward, Russia was ravaged by epidemics. Between 1659 and 1667 probably 700,000 to 800,000 people died of sickness, a very serious loss with long-term effects in a society in which most work was done by hand and there were never enough hands.

The most immediate cause of Stenka Razin's rebellion was the Cossack crisis. The Cossacks were suffering from an increase in their numbers which outran their resources, from a tendency for social classes to appear among them, from the closure of access to the Black Sea and the Caspian, and from the onward march of the tsar's administration. Tsar Mikhail's government had found it advantageous to favor the Cossacks, whose raids against the Tatars and Turks extended the territory of Muscovy and afforded protection to Russian settlers. The government had stopped harrying the Cossacks. It had reorganized them as an

autonomous Russian colony, the "great army of the Don." It
had agreed that service in this army should of itself release
men from serfdom and slavery, and it had excluded them from
tax census. Every year it sent the Cossacks money and bread,
powder and shot. In 1615 it had granted them exemption from
duties on their trade with the frontier towns.

The result of all this was that some Cossacks came to prefer to
making forays either selling the booty brought back from such
forays, or else carrying on peaceful trade as middlemen between
Russia on the one hand and the Crimean Tatars and Persia on
the other. A differentiation occurred and became marked between 1640 and 1650. On the lower Don there flourished the
trading Cossacks, rich men, "housed Cossacks," who had become
sedentary, with their capital Cherkassk. Elsewhere, especially
to the north, near the fortified line, the poor Cossacks increased
in numbers; these were the *golutvennie kazaki*, the naked and
deprived, the "robber Cossacks," who had remained loyal to
nomadic ways, to the military life and the practice of raiding.
They were constantly being reinforced by refugees, poor *pomeshchiki*, deserters from the *streltsy* and the dragoons, and serfs.
Their number increased so much after 1636 that the economic
position of the "great army of the Don" became a very difficult
one. At that moment the various lines of access to the Black Sea
and the Caspian, the routes followed by the Cossack raids, were
closed one after another. The route down the Dnieper, where
the Don Cossacks often joined hands with the Zaporozhians,
was closed by the Poles, who feared being drawn by their Cossacks' raids into a war with the Turks. The usual route followed
by the Russian Cossacks, down the Don and across the Sea of
Azov, was also barred. In 1637 the Don Cossacks, helped by
the Zaporozhians, had taken by storm the Turkish fortress of
Azov, key to the Black Sea. They had driven off all the Turkish
attempts to retake it and in 1641 had offered Azov to the tsar.
But a Zemsky Sobor which met in 1642 did not approve, and the
sultan sent an ultimatum to the tsar. On Tsar Mikhail's orders,
the Cossacks abandoned Azov, after laying it in ruins. In 1660
the sultan sent a fleet to Azov, and had another fortress built,
of stone, and the mouth of the Don barred by an iron chain

stretched between two towers. The Cossacks were thus compelled gradually to turn away toward the Caspian, by way of the Volga. In 1650 a Don Cossack named Ivan Kondyrev went plundering the shores of the Caspian. On his return to Astrakhan he sent a supplication to the tsar, received his pardon, and regained Cherkassk with his loot. Expeditions like his became a regular thing. But the voivode of Astrakhan was under orders to arrest Cossack bands whose raids might bring about a war with the shah of Persia. Those Cossacks who ignored the ban thereby placed themselves in a state of rebellion and, the route down the Volga through Astrakhan being closed, they had no alternative but to turn toward the interior, the basin of the Volga. This was the area to which the *gulyashchie lyudi* were attracted, the marginal people who had run away to the borderlands of the empire and there lived by casual work. There were at the least several tens of thousands of them—temporary debt slaves set free on the death of their creditors, serfs taken prisoner in war who had returned to Russia of their own free will and had been manumitted for this act of loyalty, deserters, peasants on temporary leave from the monasteries, and runaway peasants, the latter being the most numerous group. They found employment as boatmen, boat haulers, oarsmen, and stevedores, for the Volga, the link between Muscovy and Central Asia, was plowed by many ships; or else they worked in the fisheries, the saltworks, or the potash mines. All these wageworkers, uprooted, undisciplined, restless, poor, and sought-after for punishment by the authorities, were ready to follow a leader of reputation.

[10]

The Revolt of Stenka Razin

THE REBELLION led by the Cossack Stepan (Stenka) Razin brought about an explosion in a population which was endemically in a state of revolt. Every year the peasants fled, often after destroying the crops, stealing the farm animals, burning down the houses, and massacring the lords with their wives and children. Here and there, local risings occurred. It would be useful to know the number of runaways and of outbreaks of this sort.[1]

Many of these peasants went to join the bandits. Among these bands—which sometimes numbered as many as a hundred men, were each commanded by an *ataman* and esauls (captains) (titles borrowed from the Cossacks, from those who, in principle, lived free and equal), and which launched armed attacks on merchant caravans, convoys of ships, pilgrims, travelers, the manor houses of *pomeshchiki,* and the offices of administrators—it is hard to distinguish the mere robbers from those who may have intended to wage a war of liberation against the state and its servants. In any case, the increase of serfdom, followed by the schism and the persecution of the Old Believers, the *Raskolniki,* brought a flood of recruits to the bandits. After 1658 bandit attacks spread from

1. Documents on Stenka Razin's revolt, in E. A. Shvetsova, *Krest'ianskaya voina pod predvoditel' stvom Stepana Razina,* I, II (Moscow, 1954, 1957).

every direction. On the southern frontier and the lower course of the Volga violent actions were unceasing. Clashes occurred between the troops and the bandit gangs. The latter grew, extending their range of operations, and destroyed whole villages and massacred their inhabitants. The peasants fed the bandits, acted as scouts for them, and concealed their movements. Nobles came to join them, while other nobles refused to hand over those who were suspected of banditry. It would be useful to know the numbers of the bandits and of their attacks.

Several serious revolts broke out in the towns before the great peasant rising began. Following the increase in the price of salt, on June 1, 2, and 3, 1648, in Moscow, a mob which even included some *streltsy* stopped the tsar's horse, demanded the dismissal of bad advisers, lynched the *dyaki* Chistoi and Pleshcheyev, and demanded and obtained the head of the *dyak* Trakhaniotov. The riots spread to all parts of Moscow. The rebels even got into the Kremlin, where, however, they were halted by the fire of the foreign detachments. At once, riots broke out in other towns. In July, at Solvychegodsk, rioters brained a tax collector; in August, at Ustyug, others plundered the state storehouses. At Pskov, the Swedes having tried to remove a consignment of corn they had bought from the government, the inhabitants set upon the foreigners and tortured them. They put up a successful resistance to the tsar's troops in 1649, and surrendered only when Patriarch Nikon intervened and the tsar promised a general amnesty. At Novgorod, when news of the events at Pskov arrived, in March, 1649, the mob seized Grab, the Danish ambassador, and accused him of carrying off the state's treasure. Then the rebels plundered the houses of the rich merchants, occupied the citadel, opened the gates of the prisons, and made the men they released their leaders. They calmed down only at the end of April, when promised an amnesty.

The copper inflation provoked a rising in 1662 in Moscow. Patriarch Nikon bore a share of responsibility for this, with a letter to the tsar in 1661 in which he denounced excessive taxes and the poverty and hunger of the people. In July, 1662, several thousand people, including priests, monks, important merchants, townsfolk, peasants, slaves, soldiers, and some officers, forced their way into the presence of Tsar Aleksei, who was seized by the buttons of his clothes and forced to swear to punish the traitors. The *streltsy* crushed the revolt; 7,000 of the rebels were put to death and 15,000 others had their hands and feet cut off, were banished, and had their property confiscated. Trade and industry were disorganized by these events.

More or less at this same time the Cossack revolts had begun. About 1660 the world of the *golutvennie kazaki* was in ferment. Food was becoming harder and harder to get, and owing to the influx to refugees and the failure of harvests, famine threatened. Insults and subversive remarks were poured out against the tsar and the state. Forays continued to be made, financed by the "Old Cossacks"—the rich who supplied capital, weapons, powder, shot, and victuals. But the tsar had closed the mouths of the Volga. So, in 1660, a band of Cossacks, reinforced by deserters from the *streltsy* and dragoons, established themselves in the marshes at the elbow of the Don, built a small fortress which they called Ryga and from there sent out expeditions to plunder all the ships coming down the Volga, over a stretch of more than 300 kilometers, between Saratov and Tsaritsyn. The Old Cossacks supplied them with munitions and received a share of the loot. This time the raids were not at the expense of infidel Turks or Tatars, and could no longer be presented as a crusade against the Moslems. This was banditry against Russians and rebellion against the state. The tsar protested to the Old Cossacks against the "robber Cossacks," and the former then helped the local voivodes against these *golutvennie kazaki*. In 1665 they advanced up the Don and burnt Ryga. The *ataman* of the "robbers" and his esauls were hanged.

Then, in desperation, the *golutvennie kazaki* resolved to appeal to the tsar. One of the bandit chieftains, Vasily, known as Vaska Us ("the moustache"), set off in 1666 at the head of about five hundred Cossacks to offer their services to the tsar in Moscow. Starting from the southern Don areas, he reached Voronezh, crossed the defense line, and arrived at Tula. All the way along he had been joined by deserters from the frontier-guard battalions and peasants escaping from the estates he traversed. Serfs and servants cut their masters' throats, drove off their cattle, and rallied to Us's band, which now numbered 3,000 men. Servants came to join him from as far away as Moscow. In the capital itself, there was dangerous talk to be heard, on the theme that the people were going to settle accounts with the lords. The tsar granted pay and food to Us's men, and called on them to go back to their homes in the Cossack communities, but required them to hand over the runaway peasants who had joined them. This went against the whole Cossack tradition, and Us refused.

He returned home, taking with him all the runaways, and others as well who joined him on the way back. Us's march was a sort of rehearsal for the anabasis of Stenka Razin.

It was in 1667 that Razin's revolt began, with an expedition to the Caspian shores. The Cossack Stepan Timofeyevich Razin belonged, apparently, to the upper class of the Old Cossacks, the "housed Cossacks" who were rich merchants. Little is known about his beginnings. In 1661 he carried out a diplomatic mission to the Kalmucks, on which he may have reported to the government in Moscow. In the autumn of 1661 he made a pilgrimage to the Solovetsky Monastery, a center of the *Raskol*, on the White Sea. He appears to have founded an almshouse there for aged or wounded Cossacks. At the start of his great adventure he was a man between forty and fifty, of average height, strongly built, of inexhaustible vigor—cruel, unscrupulous, subject to volcanic outbursts of anger, but also to bouts of remorse—and tormented by concern for the salvation of his soul.

In 1667 he got together some new Cossacks, *golutvennie kazaki*, runaway peasants, escaped serfs, some craftsmen, and petty merchants and marched on Azov and the Black Sea. He was driven off by the Turks. He then went back up the Don and established himself in the marshes at the elbow of this river, not far from the Volga. From this base he attacked all the ships sailing up or down the Volga, the tsar's treasure barge, the patriarch's own ship, the corn barges of the rich Moscow merchant Shorin. He tortured and massacred the officers of the military escorts, together with the notables he captured on these vessels, and threw their mutilated bodies into the river. But he spared and took into his own forces the *streltsy* of the escort, the oarsmen, and the convicts he liberated when he captured their boat. His forces increased in number from 700 to 1,500 and his prizes furnished him with the ships of heavy burden that he needed in order to operate in the Caspian Sea.

Then, in June, 1667, he appeared before Astrakhan. The voivode was obliged to let the Cossacks pass, for his men refused to fight or his gunners to fire. They excused themselves by claiming that their guns and muskets would not work, that the powder would not stay in the touchholes of the guns. Already a supernatural halo had formed around Stenka Razin. Forty Cossack vessels entered the Caspian, sailed up the river Yaik, or Ural, and attacked the fortress of Yaitsk. Stenka presented himself at the gates in the guise of a pilgrim, along with forty of his men, and asked to be allowed in to pray in the church. Once inside, the Cossacks massacred 166 men of the garrison. The inhabitants, the soldiers, the *streltsy*, offered no resistance. The Cossacks killed the voivode and, masters of the town, raided all around it. The tsar then offered Razin a pardon if he would submit, but the *ataman* refused this offer with scorn in November, 1667.

At the beginning of 1668 he inflicted defeat on the voivode of Astrakhan, and in March set forth into the Caspian. Behind him, a detachment of the tsar's forces recaptured Yaitsk, but the soldiers let themselves be won over by their prisoners, and entered Stenka's service. He was also joined by several hundred Don Cossacks. With his fleet he ravaged the southwestern and southern coasts of the Caspian, from Derbent to Farahabad, leaving behind him only smoking ruins. In July, 1669, he defeated the Persian fleet not far from Baku and for a moment thought of settling permanently on the Persian coast, under the shah's protection. But in August, 1669, he returned to Astrakhan, bringing back as his prisoner Khan Menedi's daughter, whom he had made his mistress.

The voivode of Astrakhan had no confidence in his troops, and, with the tsar's permission, he negotiated with Stenka. The latter agreed to hand over the loot he had taken from Russian subjects and to lower his emblem of sovereign authority, a horse tail on the point of a lance, but it was tacitly accepted that he keep his Persian loot, and he positively refused to yield the guns he had taken or to release his prisoners. From August 25 until the beginning of September, Razin and his comrades stayed in Astrakhan, where they made a profound impression on the entire population, not only on the small craftsmen and merchants, the wageworkers in the fisheries and the *streltsy*, but also on the rich merchants who bought and resold the enormous mass of loot he had acquired, in the form of products of the Caspian coast and of Persia. Stenka Razin and his Cossacks, dressed in sumptuous oriental robes and covered with jewels, strolled in the bazaars, scattering their sequins freely, selling priceless eastern silks for a few kopecks, and telling stories that were like the adventures of a paladin in a fairy tale. People said of Stenka Razin that this hero who set one dreaming had a friendly word for everyone, that his generosity gave everyone what one wanted, to one's heart's content, that he treated one like a prince, both day and night. It was whispered that he had magical powers, that javelins and bullets could not hurt him. His superhuman follies were spoken of with terror and admiration: one day he was sailing down the Volga in his ship with satin sails and silken ropes, with the lovely Persian princess at his side, gorgeously dressed. Suddenly, waking out of a daydream, the *ataman* seized his mistress and lifted her high in the air, shouting: "Take her, Mother Volga, take her. You have given me much gold and silver and all sorts of good things. What have I ever given you in return? Take, then, my greatest treasure." And he hurled the princess into the river, which swallowed her up. The little people took to calling the Cossack leader *Batyushka*, "Little Father," the title accorded to great ones, to the tsar himself. A fabulous prestige surrounded Stenka Razin like a halo.

In September, 1669, the *ataman* reappeared on the Don, after various adventures. He was greeted there even by the "established Cossacks" whom he gave their share of his loot, in return for the arms, powder, and food they had supplied. But his relations with the official *ataman* of the Cossacks, whose residence was at Cherkassk, one Kornilo Yakovlev, were far from friendly, because Stenka's escapades made difficulties between the Cossacks and the tsar. Besides, Razin set up a sort of second capital, a rival to Cherkassk, a camp on an island in the Don, near the Volga, at Kachalinsk. When he came to Cherkassk in 1670, it was to murder a special envoy from the tsar, Yevdokimov, who had arrived with a friendly message from Aleksei to Razin. During the winter of 1669–1670 partisans flocked to his camp, especially *gulyashchie lyudi, zernshchiki* (players of forbidden games of chance), tavern haunters, Volga boatmen, and fishery workers, in such numbers that the merchants complained that they could no longer find employees for their trading voyages or workers for their enterprises. But Razin was also joined by members of the clergy—perhaps schismatics, *Raskolniki*—and members of the non-Russian native races. Given the makeup of his forces and his attitude to the authorities and the notables, Stenka Razin appeared to the Russians as a defender and hero of the oppressed, possibly without intending this himself. In any case he enjoyed tremendous popularity throughout the basin of the Volga. Perhaps he became to some extent the prisoner of his own popularity, and was driven by the desire to retain his authority over his men to venture into a political and social field of action further than he would have wished.

He prepared a fresh campaign, that of 1670, which unleashed the great peasant revolt. What at that moment were the aims of his men? To judge by the depositions of Cossacks captured by the government's troops during the revolt, most of them would have liked simply to set sail again across the Caspian on another plundering expedition. But it may be that Stenka Razin already had the beginnings of a political and social program. One prisoner, the parish priest Ivanov, said that Razin had proposed to the general assembly of his Cossacks that they sail up the Volga into Russia, to combat those who were betraying the tsar—the boyars, the voivodes, the *dyaki*—and to give back freedom to the humble people. According to a number of testimonies, the Cossacks had told Stenka Razin that they were ready to set off up the Volga to serve the tsar by fighting the boyars and voivodes; to which Stenka had made answer by brandishing his saber and declaring that, if he were not ready to serve the tsar, might his head be cut off. The Cossacks then, it was said, had shouted that they were ready to die for the tsar and the Virgin Mary, ready to march against the voivodes and the boyars of the Volga, because these men were preventing them from going forth into the Caspian and causing them to die of hunger.

If we take these statements as true, we see that Razin and the Cossacks were agreed on one primary point: the tsar was not responsible for their troubles; the tsar was being betrayed by the leading state servitors. What was needed was to serve the tsar by freeing him from his criminal servants and thus allow him to let his people feel his goodwill. The Cossacks added a second idea: by doing this they would be serving the Virgin Mary. Thus, their revolt seemed to them to conform to God's will and to be destined to restore the order of things willed by God. They were the good Christians, who had taken the side of the good angels, loyal to God, and who were going to fight against the bad Christians, those who had, in practice, opted for the army of the bad angels, the devils and Satan. From that point on, there would seem to have been a difference in points of view. Stenka Razin apparently wanted to destroy the great hereditary nobility, the governors, the bureaucracy, the essential elements of the Muscovite machinery of state throughout Russia, in order to restore freedom to the humble people, which can then only have meant freeing them from serfdom, from taxes they had not agreed to, from nonelected authorities, from obligations that did not result from freely discussed contracts. He seems to have envisaged, under a patriarchal tsar, a sort of democracy of small proprietors. As for the majority of the Cossacks, they would have liked to smash the power of the boyars and voivodes in the Volga region alone, because they had to cross this in order to freely carry out their raids into the Caspian. They would have wished merely to abolish locally whatever hindered the free exercise of the nomadic and warlike mode of life that was traditional among the Cossacks. If this was indeed the case, then the idea of the Cossack majority was a utopian one, since, clearly, the entire state would have to be transformed if they were to have a chance of success. But Razin's own conception was no less utopian, for his democracy would have meant in effect the destruction of the state, and would have

handed over the Russian peasantry to the Turks, Poles, and
Swedes, who would have restored a regime similar to the previous
one. If Stenka had retained a state for Russia, in a society where
rudimentary agriculture prevailed as it did, then he would probably have had to retain more or less the same form for it, and
so merely replace Peter by Paul. The conditions for a real
revolution did not exist.

Stenka Razin was reinforced by Vaska Us. The *ataman* then
prepared an attack on the fortress of Tsaritsyn, on the Volga. His
supporters secured the inhabitants' assurance that the town
would surrender without a fight. In April, 1670, Stenka marched
on Tsaritsyn. At his approach, the "notables," priests, and craftsmen came forth from the town and offered him bread and salt
in sign of their submission. Stenka took the town without a blow
being struck. The voivode, who had taken refuge in the central
tower, was arrested and put to death. Stenka introduced forth-
with the institutions and usages of Cossackdom. He divided the
inhabitants into tens and hundreds, and appointed an *ataman*,
doubtless charged with convoking a general assembly and arrang-
ing for the election of esauls and commanders of hundreds and
tens. Tsaritsyn was to become a free Cossack republic, democratic
and egalitarian.

Stenka's Cossacks were attacked by two detachments of musket-
eers, one coming from Moscow and the other from Astrakhan.
But the Cossacks assured these *streltsy* that their revolt was not
directed against the tsar but against the boyars and the traitors.
The *streltsy* then killed their officers and rallied to Stenka Razin.
They said they were sure that Astrakhan was ready to open its
gates, and invited the Cossacks to occupy it. The voivode
Prozorovsky relied on the Irish captain Butler, the English colonel
Thomas Boyle, and some foreign gunners. The rest of the garrison, however, were seized with panic at the approach of the
miracle worker Razin. Worse still, a dense hail of meteorites
fell from a clear sky and the Metropolitan Joseph announced
God's wrath against the city: God had declared for the Cossacks.
On June 24, 1670, the Cossack onslaught overwhelmed the
ramparts. They met no serious opposition, but were received
as friends and liberators. Butler, Boyle, and the other foreigners

fled. The voivode Prozorovsky, mortally wounded, was carried to the cathedral, which was soon filled with notables and well-to-do persons. The Cossacks broke down the huge oaken doors, slaughtered the refugees, and cast their bodies into a ditch. A Cossack priest counted 441 of them. The voivode's body was thrown from the top of a tower. Then the town was plundered. All the merchandise from Russia, Persia, India, and Turkestan was heaped up in a huge pile, to be divided among the people. Astrakhan became a Cossack republic. A *vyeche*, or general assembly, proclaimed Stepan Timofeyevich Razin its *gosudar*, or "great sovereign," a title that had been borne by Patriarch Filaret and Patriarch Nikon. Ivan III had called himself *"gosudar* of all Russia." The *vyeche* elected a hierarchy of officers for the thousands, the hundreds, and the tens into which the inhabitants were divided. The rest of the well-to-do were then hunted down and killed. Their widows and daughters were given in marriage to Cossacks, with Razin's blessing. For three weeks the *gosudar* and his lieutenants drank without ceasing. Then Razin, leaving Vaska Us to hold Astrakhan with half the *streltsy* and some volunteers, left with 220 ships and about 12,000 men to set up the Cossack republic all along the Volga, after which he would march on Moscow.

One after the other, Saratov, Samara, and Simbirsk fell. The inhabitants opened their gates to Razin. At Saratov, even before he arrived, the people arrested the voivode. On August 15, 1670, the day of the Assumption of the Virgin Mary, at first light, the Cossacks arrived, and the *igumen*, or abbot, of the monastery came out to offer bread and salt to Stenka. The inhabitants surrendered the town. Stenka had the voivode and the officers of the garrison executed, and introduced Cossack institutions. At the end of August, 1670, the *ataman* took Samara. On September 4 he captured Simbirsk, where the inhabitants offered no resistance, but the officers and *streltsy* sent direct from Moscow held him at bay for twenty-four hours. Though he occupied the *posad*, he was held up before the kremlin, where the voivode, the boyar Ivan Bogdanovich Miloslavsky repulsed all his attacks.

Meanwhile, Stenka Razin was spreading far and wide his

"tempting letters." Six or seven of these have survived, only one of which emanated directly from Stenka himself. He declared: "I do not wish to be your tsar, I want to live among you like a brother." He outlined a simple program: serve God and the tsar, which humored the humble people's dream of a good tsar who would free them from their bondage and their woes; remove the traitors, punish the suckers of the people's blood—the boyars, the court nobles, the men of the *prikazi*; do away with ranks and dignities; establish the Cossack order, with its absolute equality, its freedom, its deliberative assemblies and elected leaders, throughout Muscovy. He dispatched his lieutenants or envoys in every direction, to rouse the peasants and the natives. He ordered them to kill the nobles, other than those who were ready to support the tsar and fight for the Virgin, and to send two men for each roll of taxpayers and the largest possible number of horses, to report to him before Simbirsk. He spread the story that the Tsarevich Aleksei, who in reality had died on January 17, and Patriarch Nikon, who was actually in exile in the distant monastery of Byelozersk, were going to join them, which added legitimacy to his rebellion. He got a Cossack from Cherkassk, Mukum Osipov, to play the part of the tsarevich, sailing down the Volga in a ship draped in purple.

Then, in the whole area of the loop of the middle Volga and beyond, at Nizhny-Novgorod, Tambov, and Penza, in all the towns and throughout the countryside, in September and October, 1670, a huge revolt of the peasantry and the townsfolk broke out—or rather a multitude of revolts, simultaneous but uncoordinated. The insurrection began in the towns. When they saw Stenka Razin's emblem, a horsetail on the point of a lance, brandished by a few Cossacks, the *streltsy*, craftsmen, small traders, and serfs of the suburbs killed their voivode and opened the gates to Razin's lieutenants, who took all the towns along the fortified line. The revolt soon spread to the rural areas. In all the villages the peasants rose, cut down the lords, plundered their houses, destroyed their property, and formed themselves into bands which came together; joined Stenka, or the detachments which operated in his name, and brought them supplies. Monks, priests, even abbots and bishops were for Razin and influenced the inhabitants in his favor. Some went along with him or

followed his lieutenants. The priest Nikifor Ivanov wrote manifestos for him. Were most of these men Old Believers, *Raskolniki*? We do not know. There was no overt sign of collaboration
between the Old Believers and Razin,[2] though the revolt of
the Solovetsky Monastery, on the White Sea, a center of the
Raskol, had begun in 1668 and was to continue until 1676.
The native peoples, the colonial subjects of Muscovy, the Finnish
tribes, still semipagan, the Mordvinians, the Chuvashes, and
Cheremisses, joined together as a solid mass, rich and poor together, along with the Muscovite rebels, against the colonialist
state, in order to recover their national independence. The
Cossacks served merely as the ferment of an immense insurrection of all the oppressed against the state and against the nobility.
In a band of 15,000 rebels there were only a hundred Don
Cossacks. But the Cossacks were indispensable, to give courage to
the humble folk to revolt, and to coordinate the movements. If
Stenka had lasted, he would perhaps have succeeded in uniting the
rebels and leading them all together under his command toward
a single aim, thereby giving them a chance to conquer.

Meanwhile, the Astrakhan affair, the long distances Razin
had to travel, and the tying down of his forces before the
citadel of Simbirsk by Miloslavsky's resistance gave the tsar
time to raise 70,000 men, to reconstitute the European-type
regiments, the cadres for which were always ready, and to concentrate them—a long-drawn-out business in a period when it
took eleven days (in the summer) to go from Moscow to Nizhny-
Novgorod, and between forty-seven and sixty-two to go from
Nizhny-Novgorod to Astrakhan.[3] Prince Baryatinsky, reinforced,
encountered Razin on the banks of the Sviyaga, in two bloody
battles, on October 1 and 4. Razin's bands were unable to stand
against detachments trained in the European manner. They were
finally routed and Stenka had to flee down the Volga. The
worst of it was that his prestige had gone. Samara and Saratov
refused to open their gates to the fugitive, who had to take
refuge in the Don marshes with a few hundred loyal men.

Their leader and totem gone, the rebels did not lay down

2. P. Pascal, *Avvakum et les débuts du Raskol* (1938), Ch. 13, p. 443.
3. P. Pascal, "La durée des voyages en Russie au XVII° siècle," *Revue des
Études Slaves*, 27 (1951), pp. 209–219.

their arms. But the bands did not think of uniting for common action and a concerted offensive. Their only idea was to resist on the spot where they were. They were thus unable to win any decisive success. The field of operations broke up into localized units which the tsar's generals could dispose of one after the other. In the towns, in the fortified villages, and in the forests where they made huge barriers of felled trees— erecting defenses one of which was over five kilometers wide and nearly two kilometers deep—the rebels put up a heroic resistance. Everything had to be taken by storm. Until the beginning of 1671 the outcome of the civil war was still in doubt. Eight pitched battles had to be fought. When the generals thought they had won and secured the rebels' surrender, hardly had their forces left the scene when the rebels began again, without regard to the undertakings they had given. Slowly the tsar's generals advanced southward. They employed terrorist methods. The boyar Dolgoruki recaptured Nizhny-Novgorod at the end of October. In the city he had his prisoners cut to pieces alive; outside he hanged them, or nailed them to gibbets. The line of march of the troops toward the south was marked by hundreds of villages in flames and long rows of wheels and gallows. At Arzamas 18,000 men were put to death by the executioner. The gallows carried forty or fifty headless bodies. Victims of impalement howled for three days on the stakes on which they were thrust. In these apocalyptic scenes the conquered saw the precursory signs of the end of the world and the wrath of God. Some joined the schism—the *Raskol*, the Old Believers, the true Orthodox religion, which alone ensured the salvation of souls. Others hurled themselves upon flaming pyres and burnt themselves alive, in expiation, and to fend off the reign of the Beast.

Stenka Razin, on his island in the Don, was no longer anything but a half-crazy bandit. He fed the flames of his stoves with the bodies of his prisoners. Patriarch Joseph excommunicated him. When they heard this, the established Cossacks of Cherkassk declared against him and seized him in his fortress of Kagalnik in April, 1671. Sent to Moscow, he was executed there on June 6, 1671.

At the end of August, 1671, Miloslavsky's fleet arrived before Astrakhan. Vaska Us was dead, but the Cossacks were ably commanded by the energetic Fedka Shelyudak. The Cossacks rejected all Miloslavsky's offers of pardon, with howls "like mad dogs." For three months they harried the besiegers. In frequent sorties they damaged or destroyed the high wooden towers set up by Miloslavsky. They had to yield in the end, but on November 27, 1671, they won the condition they demanded, a total amnesty. The tsar's troops entered the city preceded by clergy bearing an icon of Our Lady. Despite the tsarist general's promise, an investigation was carried out in 1672, and Shelyudak and four other ringleaders were hanged.

After Stenka Razin's revolt the former state of affairs was restored. This revolt changed nothing in the evolution of the Russian state toward a more and more absolutist government and a more, and more bureaucratic and centralized administration. It changed nothing in the evolution of Russian society toward a kind of dichotomy between a nobility, originally of service but which during the eighteenth century became an ordinary landed nobility, hereditary and privileged, on the one hand, and, on the other, a peasantry of serfs subject to increasingly heavier obligations. In the second half of the eighteenth century, the Russian state and the Russian nobility became joint beneficiaries of their domination over serfs who no longer received anything in return for their services.

PART THREE

CHINA: THE PEASANTS IN
SOME REVOLTS TOWARD THE
END OF THE MING DYNASTY

[11]

The Social Structures of China in the First Half of the Seventeenth Century

IT WAS REVOLTS by peasants, bandits, and partisan leaders of peasant origin that put an end to the Ming Dynasty in 1644, after a crisis lasting twenty years. At that time Chinese society was organized in accordance with the traditional structures which it retained, in broad outline, from the days of the Han Dynasty (221 B.C. to A.D. 200) until the Tai-ping Rebellion, and even down to the Revolution of 1911. It was a society of orders, or estates, but not one that was organized, as in France, on the principle that the profession of arms was the highest of all, and the warrior a nobleman, but on that of the superiority of a bureaucracy of magistrates, recruited by competitive examination, a bureaucracy which held all political power and derived its social position and wealth from this power. Below the emperor and his family, and a nobility composed of salaried dignitaries, there were three orders: the elite, made up of magistrates and of university graduates who intended to become magistrates; the commoners, the mass of the population who lived by respectable occupations which produced material goods—agriculturists, artisans, merchants; and finally, the "mean" people, engaged in base occupations.[1] Karl A. Wittfogel considers that we ought not to speak of China as a

1. T'ung-tsu Ch'Ü, *Law and Society in Traditional China* (Paris and The Hague, Mouton, 1961), p. 128.

society of estates because it is not a decentralized feudal society, and we do not find there any *estats*, *Stände*, estates of the realm, or any corporations, as we do in a feudal society, the Chinese state being a centralized one served by functionaries, and participation in this state authority, not private property such as a lordship, being the source of power, prestige, and wealth. Wittfogel includes Chinese society in that category of societies which the classical economists called "oriental" and which Wittfogel prefers to call "hydraulic," because he has come upon them in a large number of countries which are either arid or semiarid, or else too wet, with edible aquatic plants like rice; not only in Asia but also in America, among the Incas of Peru, in the valley of Mexico, in Arizona, and in New Mexico (the Pueblo Indians). The need for large-scale works of drainage and irrigation, he thinks, made necessary a high degree of social cooperation and so an authoritarian political organization and a stratification of society that separated the agents of the "hydraulic" government from the mass of the people.[2] Whatever the origin of China's despotic and centralized state, and of Chinese society, it seems to me that Wittfogel confuses "corporations" and "orders," social orders and the political representation of these orders. For a society to be a society of orders it is necessary and sufficient for the social stratification within it to result from a special dignity ascribed by the consensus of public opinion to social functions, or social estates, which have no direct connection with the production of material goods, and this regardless of what corporations may or may not enter into the composition of the orders, and of the presence or absence of assemblies representing them.[3] This kind of social stratification certainly obtained in China, and so China must be included in the genus of societies of orders, or estates, even if we agree that it belongs to a distinct species.

China's social stratification was justified by a philosophy in-

2. K. A. Wittfogel, "Chinese Society," *Journal of Asian Studies*, 16 (1956–57), pp. 343–365; *ibid., Oriental Despotism: A Comparative Study of Total Power* (New Haven, Yale Univ. Press, 1963).

3. R. Mousnier, J. P. Labatut, and Y. Durand, "Problèmes de stratification sociale," introduction to *Deux Cahiers de la Noblesse, 1649–1651*, Publications de la Faculté des Lettres et Sciences Humaines de Paris, Série "Textes et Documents" IX (Paris, P.U.F., 1965).

spired by contemplating a natural order over which the Chinese had little control. Their society's technical equipment was relatively slight and ineffective. Most work was carried on by hand, with tools mostly made of wood. Transport was mostly accomplished on men's shoulders. Technical knowledge was empirical and rudimentary. Agriculture was much more important than industry. Society was predominantly agricultural and concerned with the land and its problems. It was therefore necessary to observe the natural elements, follow the periodicity of their movements, adapt oneself to the processes of nature, and let oneself be carried along by them. From this arose a particular cosmology, which in turn inspired a political philosophy.

The official cosmology, which actually ruled the minds of all more or less educated people in the first half of the seventeenth century, and which had even entered the minds of the masses, was that of Chu-Hsi, who died about A.D. 1200. He had written a commentary on the sacred writings of the last of the "holy men," Confucius (551–479 B.C.), and those of the greatest of the "sages," Mencius (371–289 B.C.), and his commentary was learnt by heart in the schools, along with the original texts.[4]

According to Chu-Hsi, all nature stands through the action of a Supreme Being, Tai-Ki. The latter is eternal, immaterial, without intelligence or will, but he has a separate existence and he is the cause, the source, the ultimate principle of everything; he is the universal law, the order in which all the many and various phenomena of the universe have their place.

From all eternity, Tai-Ki works by a periodic process that governs eternal nature, both animate and inanimate. This process is a succession of activities and expansions, or Yang phases, and of rests and withdrawals, or Yin phases. Yin and Yang are two essences, one positive and the other negative: the most ethereal form of matter. When Yang reaches its zenith, the Yin phase begins, and when Yin is at its nadir, a fresh Yang phase begins.

Yin and Yang give rise to the five elements, Water, Fire, Wood, Metal, and Earth. These are not the palpable things known by these names, but five essences which are the substances

4. T. T. Meadows, *The Chinese and Their Rebellions* (London, 1856), Ch. XVIII, pp. 326–410.

constituting what we know as water, fire, wood, metal, and earth. Yin and Yang gave rise to the four seasons; not the four periods of time that divide up the year, but four forms of the ultimate principle; each of them predominates in nature in its turn, during one of the periods called spring, summer, autumn, and winter.

The transcendental union of the ultimate principle in its Yang essence with the five elements constitutes the positive essence, the masculine power, the celestial principle, Heaven, while the same union, but with the Yin essence, constitutes the negative essence, the feminine power, the terrestrial principle. By their mutual and reciprocal influence, these two principles produce everything that is visible and palpable in this world, by an alternating process of expansion and contraction, constitution, and dissolution, which goes on everlastingly.

Man results from the best part of the elements at work. He is the most intelligent of all beings. His nature is perfectly good and pure, endowed with the five virtues: Benevolence, Uprightness, Propriety, Wisdom, and Sincerity. But this pure nature is affected by the material world, and so evil makes its appearance. When man listens to the inner voice of his pure nature, and obeys it, he acts in harmony with the ultimate principle. Then harmony reigns in the universe and man's actions are good, he is virtuous and prosperous, the harvests are abundant and peace prevails. But when he allows himself to be unduly influenced by the external world, he acts in a way that differs from the ultimate principle. A discord results in the universe, and man's actions are bad; he falls into emptiness and misery, for everything is upset— the rivers overflow, the locusts come, the corn freezes in the earth or the ears fail to ripen, the enemy attacks, bandits swarm and plunder, and disorder establishes itself everywhere.

The conception of the universe is thus one of periodic, cyclical phenomena, with recurrences throughout eternity, and also one of fundamental unity of all things and all beings, so that if any of them leaves its proper place, general disorder follows. It is a kind of atheism, since Tai-Ki is regarded as being without intelligence or will, but in everyday life it can easily become a conception in which Tai-Ki is treated as a personal God, compassionate, and ready both to reward and to punish.

Given this overall view of the world, the basic political problem is a dual one: keeping men in harmony with the order of the universe; and choosing, to wield political power, men who see how the ultimate principle works and who obey it utterly, either by instinct, spontaneously, like the "holy men"—but Confucius was the last of these—or by study and effort exerted upon themselves, the "sages," of whom there are several grades. Two schools of political philosophers offered, one after the other, their solutions to this problem: the Legalists and the Confucians. Their two conceptions were eventually merged and harmonized.[5]

The Legalists formulated their political philosophy in the age of the warring states, which were at length unified by the Chin and Han dynasties. Their chief theoretician was Hsün-Tzu. They started by observing a fact: the comparative scarcity of consumer goods, which was the normal condition of mankind before the industrial era that began in England in the second half of the eighteenth century. Now, human beings all have the same needs, and these needs are great, whereas the means of satisfying them are few. Men compete with each other for these goods, and their rivalry leads to disorder, which results in distress. Food, power, and dignity cannot be distributed equally among all men: there would not be enough for everyone, and nobody would be able to ensure the coordination of efforts and the unity of mankind.

Inequality must therefore be established, with a hierarchy of ranks. The more virtue a man has, the higher his rank should be; and the higher his rank, the higher his salary. But how is respect for this social order to be ensured? By a law which is uniform and equal for all, which a whole system of rewards and punishments will compel everyone to observe, whether he be a ruler, a minister, a nobleman or a peasant. To convince men and change their hearts is too long a task. Besides, is there any difference socially between a worthy man who refrains from committing crimes out of goodness and honesty, and a rascal who is so much afraid of punishment that he dares not commit crimes? There must be severe and implacable punishment. The

5. T'ung-tsu Ch'Ü, *op. cit.*, VI, pp. 226–279.

law will also make it possible to do without a scarch for a "great man," a "sage." An ordinary man will govern well by means of the law, just as any craftsman can work well by means of the compass, square, and ruler.

The Confucians increased their influence under the Han Dynasty. Fundamentally, they retained the idea of the universal law, obligatory for everyone, and the idea of a system of rewards and punishments. . . . But they laid special emphasis on inequality and declared that it was in the nature of things. Only through harmonious cooperation between beings who are very different and very unequal can a just social order be achieved. Any attempt to establish equality is irrational. It means destroying the division of labor.

Men vary in intelligence and virtue. These differences are the criteria for the division of social labor. There are two basic types of work, mental and physical. Those who are gifted for mental work are scholars and magistrates. Their function is to study, acquire virtue and govern. They are the "big men." Those who are gifted for physical work, the "little men," must serve the "big men" and keep them. Mental work is the more respected type, and so those who do it must be accorded higher payment and the right to a higher standard of living. For those who do physical work, rough clothing, vegetable food, a cottage, and travel on foot are sufficient. This is a law of nature.

What is essential is that every man's social status be well defined. This is the purpose of *li*, the proprieties, the totality of rules of behavior, expressed in rites and ceremonies. By means of *li* the reciprocal behavior of those who occupy different positions in society is regulated. The ideal state of society is when the leader acts as leader, the minister as minister, the father as father, and so on. It is when respect is shown to the five fundamental relationships: between the noble and the humble, between the superior and the inferior, between the old and the young, between the one who is near and the one who is distant, and between friend and friend. The greatest social misfortunes occur when the young are unwilling to serve the old, the humble to serve the noble, and the unworthy to serve the virtuous. But there is also a fourth, when the virtuous man fails in his duties.

Thus, *li* are the basis of all government, more fundamental even than the law. The proprieties form the basis of the social order, existing before the law and often outside it.

In order to secure respect for the proprieties, the heart must be improved through education. It is better to persuade the people to do good than to put down evil, to foster the sense of shame rather than the sentiment of fear. The people's minds must be rectified by governing them with virtue, good example, and persuasion. Hence the confidence shown in the "great man," or at least in the man at the top, whose personality is admired and conduct imitated, and who shapes the manners of the people.

Moral influence must go before punishment and prevail over it. But legal sanctions remain necessary, as an additional aid to education. The law supplements *li* by forcibly imposing them. Since it is only the differences in their mental capacity that should cause distinctions to be made between men, it follows that everyone must be given the same chance of education. The social order is based not on birth but on merit, merit of mind and heart.

These were the fundamental conceptions that, in the first half of the seventeenth century, dominated not only the minds of magistrates and scholars but those of all Chinese, despite the influence, which was then on the decline, of Wang Yang-ming.[6]

At the head of society stood the chief of state, an emperor. As a rule, the position of emperor was hereditary in a dynasty. Since 1368 the ruling dynasty had been that of Ming; they had freed China from the yoke of the Mongols, the Yuan Dynasty. Because, however, it is for the best and wisest to rule, the emperor chose the ablest of his sons to succeed him, without concern for primogeniture, and it even sometimes happened that an emperor would choose his successor from outside his own family. The emperor was absolute, having over his people all the powers of the paterfamilias in the patriarchal family, and even, in principle, still wider powers, unlimited and despotic. In the eyes of the people, indeed, his family had received a mandate from Heaven, and he himself was the "Son of Heaven," the chosen

6. R. Mousnier, *Les XVIe et XVIIe siècles, Histoire générale des civilisations* (5th ed.; 1967), pp. 574–579.

one and vicar on earth of the Positive Essence. This quality, however, he did not derive from his birth, or from the fact that his predecessor had chosen him, it was up to him to prove that he really had been chosen from on high, through his virtue and successes. If he ruled well, in harmony with the divine principles written in the sacred books, if he ensured his people peace and prosperity, then he was indeed the mandatory of Heaven, and all obedience was due to him. His will was law, provided it accorded with the sacred writings. Thus, in principle, his power was limited by Confucian thought, as interpreted by the bureaucracy of magistrates. It was in fact not easy for him to rule in disregard of the opinion of this body of men. The emperor's power, though absolute in its own sphere—politics—did not seek to regulate the whole of men's everyday lives. A Chinese could freely choose his trade or profession, travel all across China and settle wherever he liked without being questioned by any official, and he could buy and sell landed property with facility, certainty, and security. Many villages never saw any agent of the government except the tax collector. It would therefore doubtless be better to describe the emperor's power as absolutism rather than as despotism or totalitarianism.

If epidemics, famines, earthquakes, or unusually violent storms occurred, if the magistrates were corrupt, if the expenses of the Court were excessive, if taxation crushed the taxpayers, if military disasters crowded one upon another, if bandits roamed everywhere, then there could be no doubt about it: Heaven had withdrawn its mandate, its "divine commission." The emperor was not—or was no longer—virtuous. He was no longer following "the Way of Heaven," he was no longer in harmony with the universal order. He had failed in his duties as ruler, he had not respected the proprieties, he had not conformed to *li*. Thereby he had plunged the cosmos into disorder and unhappiness. He was no longer worthy to be emperor. Mencius had written: in such a case people must revolt and·change their ruler. If the rebellion succeeds, this means that the rebels are doing Heaven's will. Periodically, at the end of each 250 to 400 years, conjunctions of circumstances of this sort recurred. It was a sign to the Chinese that not only the emperor himself but his whole family had lost the "mandate of Heaven." They regrouped themselves behind a successful leader, a pretender to the imperial throne who proceeded to found a new dynasty. The latter than continued in obedience to the traditional rules, until a similar conjuncture occurred once more. This was the "cycle of dynasties." Revolt brought about a change of ruler, but only so as to preserve the form of government and the principles on which it rested. Revolt was thus never revolution. On the contrary, it formed, in a way, part of the established order, since its function was to restore this order from time to time, in a succession of dynastic cycles, in an eternal recurrence that was appropriate to an agricultural society living according to the rhythm of the periodical recurrence of the seasons, of cycles of good harvests and bad, of favorable and unfavorable climatic periods, in the belief that these cosmic phenomena were caused by the behavior of men.[7]

Chinese society shows traces of a stratification based on birth, rank, and religious purity. There may have been a tendency in this society toward the formation of castes, a process never fully carried through. This tendency would not be in the least extraordinary in a society based on the patriarchal large family and the cult of ancestors.[8] The traces in question were the social positions inherited directly from generation to generation; the imperial family; the hereditary nobility; in some instances, inherited bureaucratic office; the claim made by the magistrates, the scholars, and the commoners to regard themselves as the "pure," in contrast to an order of "mean people," hereditarily "impure" and almost completely deprived of any opportunity to rise out of their condition. But these traces gradually diminished. Contrariwise, there were many signs of a growing tendency toward a society open to talent. As each generation of the imperial nobility gave way to the next, the heir was left a social position one degree lower down the scale. The Ming emperors limited the right to inherit directly a post in the bureaucracy.

7. T. T. Meadows, *op. cit.*, Ch. II, pp. 16–28. See also J. T. C. Liu, "An Administrative Cycle in Chinese History. The Case of the Northern Sung Emperors," *The Journal of Asian Studies*, XXI (1961–62), pp. 137–152.
8. R. Mousnier, *op. cit.*, pp. 567–570.

They reduced the number of persons "nominated by virtue of their fathers' services." In 1467 they restricted the scope of the *Yin* privilege, a privilege based on kinship which enabled men to enter the bureaucracy without passing examinations. This was henceforth confined to the magistrates of the three highest ranks, and even they could use it only in favor of one son, grandson, or male collateral. The beneficiaries, moreover, could expect to be given only an inferior post in the central administration or an appointment as prefect in the provincial administration. If they wanted to rise higher, they must pass the examinations. Except for the imperial family, part of the nobility, and most of the "mean people," social status was to an increasing extent conferred by talent, as shown through examination results and through success in office.

There were still some instances of social status directly inherited from one generation to the next: first and foremost, the imperial family. Of imperial blood were the emperor's relatives and all those descended from the same ancestors as the emperor, together with their wives and concubines, or, in the case of princesses, their husbands. All the emperor's sons bore the title of Prince Imperial, with a salary of 10,000 piculs of rice a year. The eldest bore the title of Heir Presumptive, and lived in the Imperial Palace in the capital. The others were given a territorial title and lived in their princely palaces scattered about the empire, each surrounded by a great domain with between 3,000 and 19,000 followers and tenants. The sons of each Prince Imperial became "princes of the blood of the second degree," their grandsons "princes of the blood of the third degree," and so on down to the eighth degree. There was, apparently, no degree lower than the eighth, and descendants of princes of the blood of this degree remained at this level, without losing their status as members of the imperial nobility. The imperial clan numbered over 100,000 at the end of the Ming period: a considerable number in absolute terms, but only 0.10 percent of the total population, which exceeded a hundred million. No Prince Imperial or any member of his family was allowed to exercise any judicial or administrative function. They were all merely salaried dignitaries, who crowned this society and constituted, so to speak, an ornament and model for all.

Beneath them, in the same category of directly inheritable positions, came a nobility made up largely of men who were or had been soldiers and who, in addition, were related to the emperor by marriage. This nobility bore witness to the predominant role that the army had played in China, since the peasant who had founded the Ming Dynasty had reconquered the country from the Mongol invaders who had usurped the empire. It had a hierarchy of nine degrees: dukes, marquises, counts, viscounts (who were on a level with magistrates, first class), barons (on a level with magistrates, second class), and so on. Some nobles were given military commands and some active generals were ennobled, but as a rule the nobles performed no function and were, like the princes, only salaried dignitaries, examples for society.

Next came those positions in society that are not directly inheritable. Deserving to be mentioned first, owing to the important role they played in the government, are the eunuchs.[9] Confronted by an all-powerful bureaucracy, recruited by competition, powerful in ideas and traditions, the emperors, even when capable and strong-willed men, sought to find agents who were entirely devoted to their interests and those of the imperial family, persons through whom they could both keep informed and ensure the execution of their orders. They found what they needed in the eunuchs, who had been employed since Han times as intermediaries between the emperor and the bureaucracy. Under the Ming emperors the eunuchs formed a rival power group to that of the bureaucrats. In 1644 they numbered 70,000 in the Imperial Palace and 100,000 elsewhere in the empire. The emperor recruited them in batches of 3,000. Most were men who had become eunuchs of their own free will, for the sake of a career. They came from among the impoverished peasants, the vagabonds, members of hereditary military families who sought to evade their obligations, and the "mean people." From 1426 onward, young eunuchs studied in a special school in the place.

The eunuchs carried out their official functions through a

9. Robert B. Crawford, "Eunuch Power in the Ming Dynasty," *T'oung-Pao*, 49 (1961–62), pp. 115–148.

special organization consisting of twelve directorates, four offices, and eight bureaus, in which they held grades corresponding to those of the bureaucracy, but none higher than grade 4A. Actually, the emperor used them as his advisers and commissaries. The eunuchs received memoranda and petitions, passed on orders, advised the emperor on his general policy, on his choice of men as ministers and for the highest posts in the bureaucracy, on the recommendations of the Grand Imperial Secretariat, and on proposals for laws and regulations. The emperor delegated eunuchs as his representatives at the sessions of the Grand Secretariat.

The eunuchs were in charge of the political police. In 1420 they took over the "Eastern Depot." They could investigate anyone at all throughout the empire, inform the emperor directly about what they discovered, charge and arrest any person, and themselves issue edicts which had complete force of law. They supervised the imperial guards and the imperial prisons. Since 1382 the Imperial Guard, which received its orders directly from the emperor and was independent of all military authority, had been responsible for all "inquiries and punishments" and for arrests carried out on the emperor's special orders, without any legal procedure. Sixty thousand investigators pursued inquiries on behalf of the Imperial Guard, which controlled two imperial prisons, one for the north and one for the south, where, after 1478, a person arrested by an investigator was whipped or tortured until he confessed, and then handed over to the judges.

The eunuchs accompanied military expeditions in order to keep an eye on the army and the garrisons. They spied on all the magistrates as well as on the people, but above all on the highest magistrates. The eunuchs advised on increases in taxation as well as the creation of fresh taxes. They traveled through the provinces in order to check on the levying of taxes. They supervised the palace treasury. They maintained that all the wealth of the empire was the emperor's private property and ought to come directly under the palace treasury, of which they were the masters. They supervised all the manufactories directly supplying the Court and the army, and had craftsmen and laborers at their disposal for this work, men subject to forced labor. In addition, each eunuch had the right to labor service by between twenty-five and sixty men for his personal benefit. They managed the imperial domains, and were accused of appropriating part of the revenue, illegally including private estates in the imperial domains, and taking domain lands for themselves and getting them cultivated by means of unauthorized compulsion. They received large estates as gifts from the emperor, or bought them for themselves. Some landowners even registered their estates in the eunuchs' names so as to evade the burden of taxes and services. Agents of the emperor's personal authority, the eunuchs were thus a political power and a factor in social mobility.

According to both Chinese public opinion and the law, the highest state of society was that of the civil magistrates and of the university graduates from whom this bureaucracy was recruited. It really was a bureaucracy, recruited competitively, and organized in a hierarchy, with promotion from grade to grade by seniority and selection, but its members had the powers of magistrates. The army officers, who were recruited by special examinations, were in theory above the civilians, but, owing to the predominant Confucian ideas, public opinion held the magistrates in higher esteem. This elite as a whole is sometimes called by certain historians "the gentry," by analogy with England, but it would seem one should avoid using this term, which gives a false impression. In contrast to England, it was one's office that enabled one to acquire landed property, rather than the other way round. Besides, China knew neither primogeniture nor entail. Except in the case of large patriarchal families with several generations living together, brothers parted on their father's death, and his property was divided among them. Large concentrations of landed property did not last long, posts in the bureaucracy were not transmitted by inheritance, and, as a rule, particular families did not remain in possession of offices for any length of time. China and England were really two different forms of society, and it is better not to use the word *gentry* but to speak simply of the elite.[10]

10. Robert M. Marsh, *The Mandarins: The Circulation of Élites in China* (New York: The Free Press, 1961), *passim*; E. Balazs, "The Birth of Capitalism in China," *Journal of the Economic and Social History of the Orient*, III (1960), p. 202; T'ung-tsu Ch'Ü, *op. cit.*

This civil and military bureaucracy had been elevated still further socially by the Ming rulers. According to the *Annals*, it was in 1496 that the emperor first addressed the bureaucrats, and, in general, the graduates, as "My Lords." They alone were so addressed. The great values of Chinese civilization, what the Chinese most aspired to, were a post in the imperial bureaucracy, a long life, and sons to ensure that the cult of ancestors would be carried on. Public office carried with it the highest dignity, the greatest degree of social esteem, and the largest amount of wealth, with the biggest incomes in society. It did sometimes happen that a merchant or a landed proprietor was richer than a magistrate, but his dignity, his social standing, in any case remained at a lower level.

The functionaries, both civil and military, were chosen from among scholars with university degrees. These degrees were awarded by competitive examination. Legally, the examinations were open to all male Chinese. It was a society open to talent. The Chinese were imbued with this idea, and the smallest peasant could aspire to become a minister. A popular saying ran: "Ministers and generals are not born to be such." Reality did correspond to some extent to this ideal. Study did not cost much. It was enough to possess the small set of fundamental classics, one or two historical works, and some textbooks. There were elementary schools in the villages and in the patriarchal clans. Confucian free schools, open to all and subsidized by the state, existed in the chief town of each canton and prefecture. It was fashionable for well-known scholars and high officials to give courses of public lectures in the temples and public buildings, and to open free private academies. Lesser peasants, charcoal burners, brickmakers, masons, salt workers, attended these courses and learned to recite the classics. The government awarded scholarships to promising students. However, officials' sons prepared for their tests at home, aided by tutors; they lived and conversed with scholars, they had leisure, and all the rest that gave them an advantage in the examinations.[11]

The examinations took place every three years. Essays and

11. Ping-ti Ho, "Aspects of Social Mobility in China, 1368–1911," *Comparative Studies in Society and History*, I (1958–59), p. 353.

poems had to be written on questions taken from the Four Books, or *Shu*, the "Books of the Four Philosophers": the *Lun Yü*, or "Sayings," of Confucius; the *Ta Hsiao*, the "Great Learning" of Tsang-Shan, one of Confucius' disciples; the *Chung-Yung*, the "Doctrine of the Mean," by Kung-Chi, a grandson of Confucius; and the works of Mencius. Then came questions on the Five *Ching*, or Classics, said to have been written by Confucius: *Yi*, the "Book of Changes"; *Shu*, the "Book of History"; *Shih*, the "Book of Poetry"; *Li Chi*, the "Book of Rites"; and *Ch'un Ch'iu*, "Spring and Autumn," a chronicle of events between 722 and 481 B.C. After that, the candidate had to compose dissertations on the commentaries of Chu-Hsi and on the writings of the neo-Confucians of the Sung Dynasty. Finally, he was called on to discuss in writing some current problems of civil administration and hydraulic works. All parts of the examination were in written form. The technical ability to compose was the most highly esteemed quality, regardless of specific knowledge, just as in classes of higher rhetoric in France. A rigid form of composition was laid down, "the eight-legged essay," which is not more extraordinary than the lesson that forms part of the examination for *agrégés d'histoire*, which has to consist of an .introduction, three equal parts, and a conclusion, or the lesson part of the examination for *agrégés de droit*, with an introduction and two equal parts. Every examination lays down a uniform pattern for its test papers.

The would-be bureaucrat had to climb the rungs of a hierarchy of examinations. At each level, about 1 percent of the candidates passed. First there were three preliminary examinations, which were taken in the presence of the local magistrates—the first in the chief town of the canton, the second in the chief town of the prefecture, and the third also in the chief town of the prefecture, but before the director of studies for the province. This third examination, the *Yüan*, was the decisive one. Those who were fortunate enough to pass were accorded the title of *Sheng-Yüan*, or "government student," with a modest salary. It gave them no automatic right to public office, but it did admit them to the elite, even if only at the lowest level.

The *Sheng-Yüan* then braved the examinations at provincial

level. It might happen that able students failed these examinations, for there were only 70 or 80 vacancies available for every 6,000 to 8,000 candidates. If they failed, but their high scholarly attainments were recognized, they might receive the academic title of *Kung-Sheng*, "imperial student," and be given a public appointment after all.

The candidates who were successful in the provincial examinations were called *Chü-Jen* (licentiates) and could normally expect to receive an appointment and make a career for themselves. In order, however, to have the prospect of reaching the highest positions, it was necessary to brave the examination that was held in the capital itself. Those who passed this examination had then to face the last and highest of examinations, the one held in the palace. The successful candidates became *Chin-Shih* (doctors), and could look forward to the highest destinies. On the average, each examination resulted in 276 men qualifying as *Chin-Shih* in the Ming period. During the 276 years of the Ming Dynasty, 90 of these examinations were held and 24,874 candidates altogether emerged as *Chin-Shih*. The degree of *Chü-Jen* was attained between the ages of twenty-one and forty, and that of *Chin-Shih* between those of twenty-five and forty-five. The average age, however, was twenty-four for the degree of *Sheng-Yüan*, thirty for that of *Chü-Jen*, and thirty-five for that of *Chin-Shih*—the average age for doctors of theology of the Sorbonne. Many men tried five, six, even eight times. Most of them gave up.

There were, though, easier ways to success. From time to time, in each canton, subprefecture, and prefecture, the state schools were invited by the government to send their gifted pupils to the capital, where the members of the Han-lin Academy examined them. The best of these youngsters were then sent to study at the national university, and were then apparently appointed to posts in the public service without having to undergo further examinations. The same path was open to sons of officials who had shown extraordinary merit or who had given their lives for the state. Finally, it was possible, owing to the government's financial distress, to purchase the title of "student at the Imperial College," which put one on a level with the *Sheng-*

Yüan, or that of "imperial student," *Kung-Sheng*, which could enable one to secure an appointment.

Though graduates aimed at posts in the public service, they did not automatically obtain them, for there were always many more graduates than posts available to them. One had to wait one's turn. At this point, the influence possessed by a father or an uncle who had got on in the service could be extremely useful. Magistrates' sons had an advantage. But the examinations established bonds between the people involved and led to the formation of coteries which became groups for mutual assistance. The examiners became patrons to the candidates they had passed, and the latter in turn became their faithful supporters. Those who had graduated at the same time and place became relatives, so to speak, owing assistance and support to each other, regardless of their differences of origin. Finally, a rich merchant sometimes found it possible to buy a place in the administration.[12]

The examinations were great events in Chinese life. They aroused as much interest as elections in Europe. Thousands of people gathered in the towns to hear the results. The lists of those who had passed were hawked about the streets. Even the peasants read them with attention. The relatives and friends of the successful candidates were overwhelmed with congratulations. They put up signs on their houses to show their happiness. The names of the lucky ones were passed on even as far as remote hamlets, and everyone looked upon them with admiration.

Indeed, becoming a *Sheng-Yüan* was like having holy orders conferred upon one: it meant that a man was set apart from and above others. The graduates stood at the head of the people. They had to explain to them the proprieties and the laws and teach them to follow the instructions of the magistrates, and the magistrates were obliged to consult the graduates, who had free and informal access to them. Commoners, who addressed magistrates as "Great Excellency," had to address graduates as "Excellency." Like magistrates, graduates had the right to wear buttons on their hats—silver ones for the *Sheng-Yüan*, golden ones for the *Chü-Jen* and *Chin-Shih*, with a ruby and a pearl as

12. Chung-Li Chang, *The Chinese Gentry—Studies in Their Role in Nineteenth-Century Chinese Society* (Seattle, 1955).

well in the case of a magistrate, first class. The color yellow was
reserved for their robes, as also were the richest brocades and
silks. They had precedence over ordinary people at festivals and
ceremonies, in the street, and on the roads. Graduates "could
never be humiliated." Thus, if they were insulted or wounded,
the offender was given seventy strokes with the bamboo, whereas
he would have received only ten if his victim had been a peasant.
Graduates could not be summoned as witnesses in a lawsuit by
a commoner. If a graduate was involved in a case, he would
not be obliged to appear in court, but could be represented by a
servant. A special judicial procedure was laid down for graduates,
who could in no circumstance be beaten with the bamboo.
Graduates were exempt from all manual work, and so from every
form of labor service to the state. Their property was subject
to the land tax, but they themselves were exempt from any personal taxation. Finally, the Sheng-Yüan received from the government a salary, traveling expenses and special aid when there
was famine. The graduates thus formed an estate of society
endowed with distinctions and privileges.[13]

I do not know how many graduates there were in the Ming
period. Under the Manchu Dynasty of Ching, at the beginning
of the nineteenth century, in a similar society which had merely
had Manchu racialism superimposed on it, there were 739,199
Sheng-Yüan, 527,000 civil and 213,000 military, making up altogether 0.18 percent of the population, and to them should
be added the 355,535 Chien-Sheng, those who had purchased
the title of "student at the Imperial College." The elite thus
numbered 1,094,734 persons, that is, about 0.27 percent of the
total poulation, which must have amounted to more than 300
million. Together with their families, assuming five persons to
each family, the elite must have numbered between 5 and 5½
million people, or about 1.7 percent of the total population. It
seems that at this period the elite was somewhat restricted, as
a result of a reduction in the number of places in the examinations. Under the Mings, with a population officially reckoned
at 60 million, but which must really have amounted to 150

13. Ibid., pp. 32–43.

million at the beginning of the seventeenth century, the proportion constituted by the elite was certainly higher, though of about the same order of size. Under the last of the Mings, the magistrates numbered about 15,000,[14] while the army officers were more numerous: from 16,489 in 1392 they had increased to over 100,000.

The fortunate persons chosen by the emperor for a public appointment first spent a year as observers, the *Chin-Shih* often at the Han-lin Academy, as "Han-lin bachelors." Then they entered a nine-graded hierarchy, in which each grade had two levels, A and B. Promotion was by seniority at nine-year intervals, and by selection at three-year intervals. The magistrates were subject to a whole system of inspections and reports. Every month the highest magistrate of the canton or the subprefecture submitted to the prefect a report on his subordinates; every year, the prefect submitted a report to the provincial governor; every three years, the latter reported to the central government. In addition, censors carried out inspections without warning. Every three years, the heads of all the local administrative units came together in the capital to review and classify the magistrates: on each occasion many were dismissed, compulsorily retired or transferred, and many, also, were promoted. Eight types of person were considered undesirable as magistrates: the covetous, the cruel, the capricious, the incompetent, the aged, the sick, the idle, the absent-minded. The best men of grades 1 to 9 could be given the honorific title of "Great Magistrate" or other honors; those from 1 to 5B, the titles of "Pillar of the State," "Chief Minister," or "Lord"; those of the upper level of the highest grade, 1A, the honor of being one of the "Three Dukes"—Grand Preceptor, Grand Tutor, or Grand Guardian; those of the lower level, 1B, the honor of being one of the "Three Solitaries"—Junior Preceptor, Junior Tutor, Junior Guardian.

Army officers were recruited by special examinations which were mainly concerned with technical tests, horsemanship, and

14. *Ibid.*, pp. 98–111. Ping-Ti Ho, *Studies on the Population of China (1368–1953)* (Cambridge, Harvard Univ. Press, 1959). I. B. Taeuber and Nai-chi Wang, "Population Reports in the Ch'ing Dynasty," *Journal of Asian Studies*, 19 (1959–60), pp. 403–417.

archery. Officers' sons were thereby at a substantial advantage. The army hicrarchy, less differentiated than the civil one, went from 1A to 6B. Every five years the officers were reviewed and classified. They could not be given honorific titles or other honors, but they held a quasi-monopoly on patents of nobility.

The nine grades of magistrates were distributed among the various public offices. In 1421 the seat of government had been transferred from Nanking to Peking, which was now the principal capital and the emperor's own place of residence. But Nanking retained the status of capital, and all the institutions of the central government had their replicas and duplicates in Nanking. The emperor was supposed to rule in person with the help of the Han-lin Academy. This included the best of the *Chin-Shih*, who read and explained the classics and the histories to the emperor, took part in the government's deliberations, drafted proclamations, laws, and ordinances, and edited the final tests of these, and compiled the history of the empire. They ensured the permanence of the thoughts of Confucius and Chu-Hsi in the government.[15]

Around 1382 there had emerged from the Han-lin Academy the "Grand Secretariat," *Nei-Ko*, with six posts of Grand Secretary, only three of which were filled. In principle they were dependent on the Han-lin Academy, from which they were recruited. They advised the emperor, studied the state papers that were put before them, and wrote drafts for imperial rescripts. They were helped by a large editorial staff. They were personal agents of the emperor, low in grade (5A), but high in honors, up beside the Three Dukes and the Three Solitaries. Together with the eunuchs they were regarded as belonging to the "inner Court," the emperor's entourage, always in conflict with the "outer Court," the administrative organs of the central government.

For the purpose of supervising the entire machinery of government and its personnel, the emperor had censors, "the eyes and ears of the emperor": two chief censors, two chief deputy censors, four chief assistant censors, and 110 investigating censors

15. C. O. Hucker, "Governmental Organization of the Ming Dynasty, 1368–1644," *Harvard Journal of Asiatic Studies*, 21 (Dec. 1958), pp. 11–20.

for the provinces and lower local divisions. They had direct access to the emperor himself and were directly responsible to him, receiving his special commissions, the most important of which was that of regional inspector for one year, on the basis of one to a province. The inspector questioned everyone, both magistrates and ordinary people, received complaints and petitions, verified the work of government offices, observed the people's conditions of life, checked all registers, advised and reprimanded all officials, brought, if necessary, a charge against anyone by means of a memorandum sent directly to the throne, proposed reforms to the government, was consulted by provincial authorities, and held discussions with the governor of the province. His prestige was enormous. His role was comparable to that of the *maîtres des requêtes en chevauchée* (masters of requests on circuit) or the *intendants* of the provinces of France.

Supervising secretaries, divided into six offices of superintendence, one for each ministry, examined all official documents and could veto them if they did not accord with the government's policy or seemed incorrect in any way. These secretaries were often sent by the emperor into the provinces on special missions.

The central administration properly so-called comprised six ministers. Since 1368 there had been six ministries—Personnel, Finance, Rites, War, Justice, Public Works. Each of these included several offices, usually four, but thirteen in the case of the Ministry of Justice.

The emperor was supposed to rule in person. Every magistrate, officer, or citizen could send directly to him any proposals or opinions they wished on any subject. All the ministerial reports were dispatched to the Grand Secretariat, from which they passed to the eunuchs and at length reached the emperor, with a draft for a law or imperial ordinance in each instance. The emperor summoned one or more ministers to discuss problems in "privy councils" or cabinet meetings. He thus gathered around him a kind of Imperial Council, made up of ministers, censors, grand secretaries, supervising secretaries, eunuchs and members of the Imperial Guard. For very serious decisions he convoked an enlarged council, which might include, in addition to the foregoing, the heads of the various ministerial services, the censorate, the communications service, the principal military commissaries, and representatives of the nobility. Each participant had the right to contribute to the deliberations. Unanimity was sought, and if it appeared, it bound the emperor. Otherwise, the emperor himself decided. The decision was put into the form of an imperial rescript by one of the ministries, and this was checked by the supervising secretaries, the grand secretaries, and the Hanlin Academy.[16]

The government was rigorously centralized. All the local administrative divisions, from province down to canton, were creations of the central government, which financed their budget, nominated their staff, and directed and supervised their activities. All the local magistrates and functionaries were agents of the central government. Below canton level there was no official administration in the strict sense. Villages and towns had no autonomy. The towns were first and foremost the places where the magistrates and their subordinates lived, the seats of their offices.

From 1428 onward the empire consisted of 13 provinces, divided into 159 prefectures and 240 subperfectures, and subdivided into 1,144 cantons, about a hundred of which were *Chou* and the rest *Hsien* (these were exactly the same, except that the magistrate of a *Chou* canton was higher in rank). A *Chou* or *Hsien* was between 100,000 and several hundred thousand *li* in size, and it contained between several tens of thousands and several hundreds of thousands of "hearths"; its headquarters was a walled town, surrounded by some open towns and several dozen or even hundreds of villages.

Towns and villages had no legal standing, and did not constitute official corporations or communities, though their inhabitants elected representatives to busy themselves with local affairs. The government itself organized its subjects for the requirements of its business. In order to ensure the collection of taxes, the registering of the population, and the carrying out of labor services, the government had created, in 1380, the *Li-Chia*. Each *li* contained 110 "hearths," and each *Chia* 10. The magistrate nomi-

16. C. O. Hucker, *op. cit.*

nated each year as head of the *Li-Chia* a member of the *Chia* containing the ten hearths which included the largest number of male adults and paid most in taxes, and, as his agents, one of the members of each of ten other *Chia*. These agents collected taxes, counted the members of each hearth, and ensured the fulfillment of labor services. Since the time of the Sung Dynasty the inhabitants had been grouped, for various administrative tasks, into the *Pao-Chia* system. Ten hearths constituted a *P'ai*, under the supervision of a *P'ai-chang*; ten *P'ai* formed a *Chia*, under a *Chia-chang*; ten *Chia* formed a *Pao*, under a *Pao-chang*. These *chang*, all appointed by the magistrates, had the duty of informing the magistrates about vagrancy, gaming, the harboring of criminals, counterfeiting, salt smuggling, banditry, and the presence of outsiders. They had to make a census of all persons resident in their sector.[17] The magistrates appointed an administrative agent in each village, a *Ti-Pao*, whose function was to pass on their orders and to draw up reports on all robberies, murders, brawls, fires, or cases of salt smuggling.

China's provincial and local organization was sufficiently complicated to make it preferable to present it in diagrammatic form (see page 256).

Each magistrate concentrated all forms of authority in his own hands. He was concerned at one and the same time with maintaining order, dispensing justice, and collecting taxes; he was responsible for public works, granaries, social welfare, the postal service, the salt administration, religion, and education. He had to defend the area under his care in the event of a rebellion or a foreign invasion. The magistrate in a *Hsien* or a *Chou* stood alone, a stranger, for every magistrate was necessarily appointed elsewhere than in his own province, to a place where he was ignorant of the local dialect and customs. He had to have help. He therefore hired clerks and agents who were local men, familiar with the local situation, speaking the dialect of the area and having relatives and friends in the canton. In a small *Hsien* there might be a hundred to two hundred of these men,

17. T'ung-tsu Ch'Ü, *Local Government in China under the Ch'ing* (1962). Ping-ti Ho, *Studies in the Population of China (1368–1953)*, I, pp. 5–10. I. B. Taeuber and Nai-chi Wang, *op. cit.*, p. 405.

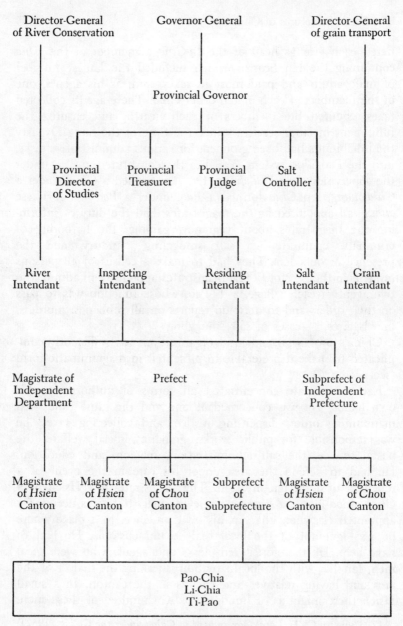

(Adapted from T'ung-tsu Chu,
Local Government in China under the Ch'ing, p. 5)

and a thousand in a large one. The clerks were recruited from among men who had taken the primary examinations, sometimes from among the *Sheng-Yüan*. They were appointed for five years, after which they could offer themselves for the practical tests of a special examination—writing a report or an administrative letter. A certain number of them thus became magistrates, but remained in the lower grades of the magistracy.

For the execution of his orders the magistrate surrounded himself with "runners": beadles, messengers, commissaries of police, jailers, archers, doorkeepers, police constables. There were several hundred, even as many as 1,500, in a *Hsien*, each appointed for a 3-year period. They were recruited from among the mean people and could never become magistrates.

The magistrate supervised the work of all these helpers of his through personal servants recruited from among the mean people, the most important of whom was his gate porter, and more especially through his private secretaries. These were technical personnel, often *Sheng-Yüan* and sometimes even *Chü-Jen*, who had had practical training by taking lessons from a professional private secretary. Experts in administration, they lived in the administrative compound, or yamen, near the magistrate, whom they provided with a sort of council or cabinet. They made all the arrangements for competitive examinations, though many of them remained, themselves, mere private secretaries all their lives. They were regarded as the equals of the magistrates and were treated with politeness and even deference. Their own magistrate addressed them as *chiao-ti*, "younger brother."

Even with all these helpers, however, the magistrate could not avoid having recourse to the advice and aid of the local elite— graduates who had not been able to get a place, retired magistrates, magistrates on leave (for example, for the three years of mourning that followed the death of one's father). The poorest of the *Sheng-Yüan*, who lived on the meager allowance they were paid, and on fees for teaching work, were included in this elite, but not, as a rule, those commoners who had risen to be landowners in the canton. Some large landowners, however, who had relatives in the magistracy, were considered as belonging to it. This elite served as guide to the commoners and the mean people, who owed obedience and respect to it and over whom it did in fact wield a very great influence. Members of the elite were regarded as being on an equality with the magistrate, to whom they had free access. Similarly, they could freely enter all the branches of the yamen and get to know the clerks and runners. The *Sheng-Yüan* were capable of inciting petitions, strikes of examination candidates (the worst possible insult to a magistrate), and even riots. The magistrate held conferences with the members of the local elite, some of whom were his superiors in the hierarchy, while others were bound to him by ties of protection and service, through having succeeded at the same examinations as himself, or by the relationship of examiner to candidate. This he did in order to obtain their views and win their support. He consulted them about public works, local defense, taxes, public assistance. The members of the elite passed on his orders and informed him of the people's reactions to them. They contributed to the building and repairing of dikes, canals, bridges, roads, fortifications, and hospitals for the poor and for widows. They formed commissions to raise funds, to take charge of public works, charitable organizations, and public granaries, and to distribute relief in times of famine or flood. They organized the local militia and took command of it. Considering themselves the guardians of Confucianism, they saw to the repair of the temples of Confucius, the examination halls, and the schools. They set up academies, managed them, and taught in them.[18]

The magistrate, his clerks, agents, and "runners," were all very badly paid. The salaries of the magistrates were not even adequate for them to be able to pay their private secretaries. Public opinion therefore accepted the fact that magistrates charged "customary fees" for every official act they performed. The magistrates kept 60 percent of this money for themselves, giving 30 percent to their staff and 10 percent to their personal servants. They paid their private secretaries well. Nevertheless, the clerks, agents, and "runners" of all kinds also levied their own "customary fees." So long as the amount remained customary, subjects of

18. T'ung-tsu Ch'Ü, *Local Government, op. cit.*, ch. X, pp. 168–190.

the administration did not complain. But the system lent itself to extortion. During periods when prices were rising, even honest magistrates were inclined to raise the rate of these "customary fees," at the time when their subjects had most difficulty in paying them. When this happened, there was murmuring, and soon riots and revolts broke out.

The bulk of the income of the elite was received as remuneration for its services to the state and to society. There was a saying: "May you be promoted in office and become rich." Income from landed property formed a much smaller part of its total revenue. It was not necessary to be a landowner in order to become one of the elite. Many of its members had no land, or very little. Newcomers to the elite were usually from families which had no land, or not much. But those numbers of the elite who were landowners owed it to their social position that they be able to draw the full rent from their lands even in times of shortage, whereas landowners who were commoners had to be satisfied in such circumstances with only part of their rent. The landowning members of the elite did not pay special taxes and were not liable for labor service. In theory they were supposed to pay the land tax, but in practice they evaded that as well. Many people registered their own lands under the name of a member of the elite in order to escape liability for taxes and labor services.

Sons and grandsons had to live with their parents and grandparents, but when these died they could separate, dividing the family's land equally. This was customary. Consequently, though there were some large landed estates, they remained few in number. Each generation had to begin afresh with a modest share.

Land was the safest investment, but it was not a very profitable one. Nevertheless, the elite was forbidden to engage in trade, especially in brokerage of all kinds, and maritime trade. The proper role for the elite was public service. Trade was regarded as a base occupation. "It would be beneath the dignity [of members of the elite] to take to trade." All the same, a few of them were allowed to carry on trade in salt, under the government's supervision, and to busy themselves with banking and money-lending, because the government's funds were deposited in private banks and pawnshops. A very small number of them engaged in maritime trade and in brokerage, under assumed names.[19]

There was much social mobility, both upward and downward. At the beginning of the Ming period the law had fixed everyone in a permanent and hereditary social position: the soldiers; the craftsmen of the lower Yangtze, hereditarily under compulsion to work for the government; the peasants; and so on. But, even at that time, provided one member of the family stayed in its legal occuption, the rest were allowed to change, and the emperor always released candidates for the public service from their hereditary obligations. Since 1550 the law on hereditary social positions had ceased to be observed.

The birth rate in families of the elite was higher than in the other social classes, and the death rate lower. As a rule, people married within their own order. It might, therefore, be supposed that the elite formed a closed, hereditary group. But the examination system corrected any such tendency. Rare were the cases in which, in the third generation, an easy life had not deprived the sons of magistrates of the energy needed for success. And, besides, cleverness appears wherever it chooses. It was very unusual for a family to be able to keep a foothold in important public office for more than two or three generations. In most cases, the grandsons and great-grandsons, finding themselves unable to get further than the first two examinations and so not succeeding in acquiring even the title of *Sheng-Yüan*, had to go to the bottom of the ladder, teach in village schools, win a little reputation, and become an agent or clerk in a yamen—and thus the family would begin its climb back up the ladder. Many preferred to become merchants and in this way provide their sons with the comfort and leisure that were so helpful when tackling the competitive examinations. There were families that are hard to categorize: some of their members were magistrates, others employees of magistrates, and yet others merchants.

Vertical mobility was comparatively great. In 1610, out of the 230 *Chin-shih* who graduated that year, 60, that is, 26 percent,

19. Chung-li Chang, *The Income of the Chinese Gentry* (Seattle, 1962), XVII, p. 369.

came from families which had not produced a single graduate during the three previous generations; 38 (16.5 percent) were from families who had had one or more *Sheng-yüan* in the three previous generations; 132 (57 percent) were from families which could show magistrates of lower or middle rank during the same period; and 18 (7.8 percent), from families which boasted high magistrates of the three topmost ranks. At that time, moreover, the order was tending to close, for during the fifteenth and sixteenth centuries the families that had never included any graduates had provided over 40 percent of the *Chin-shih*. But between 1752 and 1899, 87 percent of the British undergraduates at Cambridge, and 78 percent between 1899 and 1937, were sons of elite families. The opportunities for a boy from the lower or middle classes to obtain a university degree and enter the higher civil service of Great Britain, before 1929 and the world crisis, were probably fewer than those for a young Chinese of similar origin in the Ming period.[20]

The elite has been discussed at some length because it acted as the leaven in the mass of the population and conferred upon Chinese society its particular form and distinctive features. But it made up a very small proportion of the population. In 1880, when Chinese society, though already on the road to transformation by capitalism, retained many of its traditional aspects, the elite (magistrates and graduates) numbered 1,500,000 households, or 2 percent of the total population, the merchants and artisans 12,500,000 or 18 percent, the peasants 70 million, or 80 percent.[21] The mean people are not included in this calculation, but specialists estimate that they probably did not exceed 2 percent of the population.

If we were going to go step by step down the ladder of the legal hierarchy of orders, we ought now to deal with the peasants. Indeed, after state service, agriculture was the occupation that was regarded as most estimable and most honored. The peasant ranked as the man of greatest worth after the magistrate and

20. Ping-ti Ho, "Aspects," *op. cit.*, pp. 330–359. See also E. G. Pulleyblank, "The Ladder of Success in Imperial China," *Journal of the Social and Economic History of the Orient*, 6 (1963), pp. 330–334.
21. R. M. Marsh, *op. cit.*, pp. 13–32.

the graduate. Official writings and discourses unceasingly cited and praised him. The well-being of the peasant, the foundation of the state, seemed to be the government's principal care and concern. The magistrates seemed preoccupied solely with his happiness. Very far beneath him came the craftsmen, and right at the bottom of the social scale of the commoners were the merchants, whose profitable activities were considered base and despicable.

But social esteem did not obey the law, and it placed the rich merchants immediately after the graduates. There were merchants who had made big fortunes in the mines, the salt industry, the tea business, and in foreign trade and providing supplies for the army. All these activities, however, were state monopolies or under state supervision. The merchants engaged in them figured as auxiliaries of the public services. The state made trade more an affair of administration than of production, taking all initiative away from the merchants and preventing them from competing freely.

The mining industry was under state control. In theory, the state owned all the land and what was under it, and therefore all lodes of metal—copper and silver, for the coinage; iron, for tools and weapons; as well as all coal mines, for the fueling of the foundries. Actually, the state left private enterprise to exploit the mines, contenting itself with a percentage royalty on production. Entrepreneurs who were mining specialists by profession advanced the money needed for tools, fuel, wages, and installations. This amounted to fairly substantial sums, for, around 1600, the depth of pits exceeded 30 meters, and bamboo tubes had to be installed to drain off water, provide ventilation, and remove gases. Production was divided into three parts: 30 percent for the state, 50 percent for the entrepreneur, 20 percent for the wageworkers. The copper mines of Yunnan, so important for the currency, were developed in Ming times. Rich merchants of Kiangsu, Hupeh, Hunan, Szechwan, and Kwangtung provided the capital and hired the manager, the technicians, and foremen and workers. The last-named were poor people of these same provinces, who came to work in the mines after the harvest had been brought in. All who were employed in the mines were either paid wages or a proportion of the product, but 60 percent of the latter remained in the hands of the entrepreneurs.

It was the salt trade that offered the biggest opportunities for moneymaking. The tax on salt was one of the state's main resources. The state held the monopoly of the salt trade. Private persons, owners of salt pans, produced salt under state supervision. Merchants were given tickets by which the government authorized them to purchase salt from the producers. The victuallers who conveyed grain to the frontiers to supply the army were given these tickets as payment. Most of the salt tickets, however, were sold to registered merchants who were in a position to advance the money. It was a sort of tax-farming arrangement. In Lianghuai, an important salt-administration area, thirty large-scale merchants and two hundred petty ones carried on the salt trade in this way, but among the thirty big ones a clique of four or five held the real power. These big merchants sold the salt to the small ones, who thus became retail distributors to the public, acting as agents for the big men. Most of the merchants of Lianghuai were from Shansi Province or from Huichow, in Anhwei Province. They were famous from about 1600 on. Wretchedly dressed and eating frugally, the men from Shansi invested their money in the fisheries and in the silk and corn trades. The merchants of Huichow spent a lot on concubines and prostitutes, and on lawsuits. In the third generation, these successful merchants sought to raise themselves to the level of the elite, making up for their lack of social prestige by a luxurious style of living. They were lovers of horses, dogs, women, music, pleasure gardens. Some of them became bibliophiles, collectors, patrons of the arts. They tried to purchase university degrees or public appointments. They were obsessed by their desire to enter the elite. Their money was thus diverted from functioning as capital toward the purchase of luxury goods, or of landed property, the safest and the most prestigious form of property. Even the usurers drew 30 to 40 percent of their income from ground rent.[22]

It is problematical whether, so early as the time of the last

22. E. Balazs, *op. cit.*, pp. 196–216.

Ming emperors, commercial capitalism was coming to birth in China; whether China was not so far away as has been thought from the level of development of the West, where, long since, commercial capitalism had been in existence and growing; whether China was tending to pass, like Europe, from domanial economy to commercial capitalism, and thence to industrial capitalism. It is certain that a simple exchange economy was flourishing in China. It is certain that some regions were becoming specialized so as to feed all the rest of China. For example, Honan and Hupeh produced most of the raw cotton which was transported to Kiangnan (Anhwei and Kiangsu), manufactured into cotton goods, and then sold in markets all over China. The porcelain of Kiangsi, and the tea, silk, and iron of Kwangtung were exported on a large scale to foreign countries. There were some large industrial towns. The silk producers of Soochow, near Shanghai, operated 3,000 to 4,000 looms and employed thousands of wageworkers. The metalworking industries of Tsunhua, near Peking, employed 3,000 workers and produced 300 tons of iron a year. Metal production as a whole varied between 6,000 and 12,000 tons. In the north of Kiangsi, the demands of the government and of foreign buyers, and the investments of the merchants of Huichou, had given rise to a boom in the porcelain industry of Chingtechen. A number of porcelain kilns worked night and day and the village became a town. One even finds, at the beginning of the seventeenth century, the craftsman who saves, accumulates money, transforms it into capital, and becomes an industrialist. The small-scale weaver, Shih-Fu, became, through care, work, and saving, a capitalist owning thirty to forty looms and a business worth thousands of taels. This is no longer merely the merchant who invests in manufactories, supplying peasants and rural craftsmen with looms and raw material, and then collecting and selling the finished product; this is no longer commercial capitalism, but industrial capitalism.

However, though there were big towns like Soochow, Nanking, Sunkiang, Hangchow, Wuhu, and while in the southeast of China there were four towns with a population exceeding 50,000—one with more than 35,000 inhabitants, seven others with between 10,000 and 20,000—these towns were still first and foremost

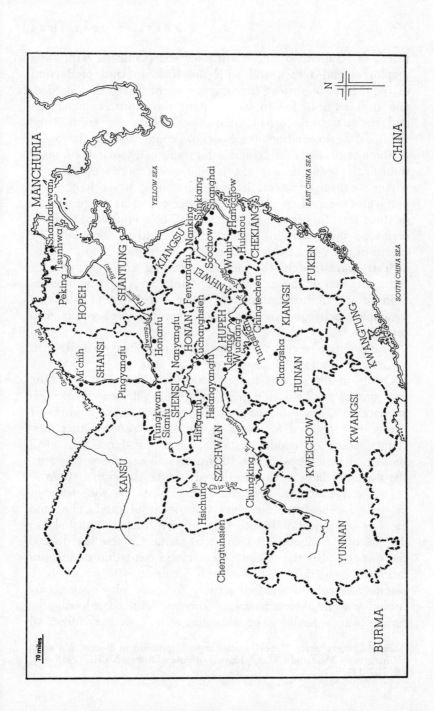

places of residence of the magistrates and graduates, with their employees and agents, and with the trade in craft production of the articles of current consumption or of luxury they needed, and it is hard to see to what extent the capitalist merchants and the wageworkers had transformed them. An entire large industrial agglomeration like Soochow could well be the result of the assembling, in a favorable location, of thousands of small individual producers, and the large number of wageworkers of whom we hear could result from the hiring by each of these petty producers of one or two journeymen, so as to group two or three men to a loom. This would still be a kind of very small, craft-type enterprise, supplying distant markets, especially by means of petty trade over a large area. We should need to know, at least approximately, the number, structure, and dimensions of the enterprises of the capitalist merchants, and to know whether Shih-Fu was an exception or not. There is a danger of mistaking a simple exchange economy for an economy of commercial capitalism.[23]

The question remains unsettled. I am inclined to believe in a Chinese commercial capitalism.

Owing to the services rendered by their fathers to the state, the sons of salt and iron merchants were allowed to take examinations in any province they chose, and a certain number of places were reserved for them in the examinations. Other merchants, those of middling status, owners of large and small shops and workshops in the towns, and those of lowest status, the mere peddlers, were not allowed to take the examinations.

In the countryside, after state service, it was the mode of property in the land, the chief instrument of production, and each person's relationship to this property, that dominated the division of the inhabitants into social strata. Chinese law divided the ownership of the soil into two levels: ownership of the surface and ownership of the subsoil. Someone who owned both surface and subsoil was full owner. Someone who owned only subsoil was an absentee owner. Someone who owned only the surface was a tenant. The absentee owners were members of

23. A. Feuerwerker, "From Feudalism to Capitalism in Recent Historical Writing from Mainland China," *Journal of Asian Studies*, XVIII (1958–59), pp. 107–115.

the elite, as well as notables from among the commoners. From these were also recruited the large landowners who exploited their estates with the aid of agricultural workers or poor tenants. These large landowners remained, however, in Ming times, excluded from the elite. Magistrates and graduates looked down on them, and it was only with the passage of time, when a member of their family had entered public service, and when marriages by other members had established a network of relationships with the elite, that they drew near to the elite and sometimes were admitted into it.[24] Beneath them, in the scale of social strata, came the peasants who were full owners, cultivating their land with the help of members of their families and a varying number of agricultural workers from outside. Then came a stratum of peasants who were partly full owners and partly tenants, some of them cultivating their land with a fairly large number of workers from outside their families, and forming a higher group within this stratum, something like farmers, while others cultivated their land with the sole aid of members of their families, supplemented by one or two servants only in case of need. Then came peasants who were mere tenants; some of these were large-scale farmers, but most had only family holdings. Next came tenants whose holdings were inadequate to support their families and who had to hire themselves out as workers to farmers or big landowners. On the same level, no doubt, should be placed the village craftsmen, who were usually also engaged in cultivation and trade. Right at the bottom of this ladder we find agricultural workers without land or implements of their own—or money.[25]

Most of these peasants were civilians under obligation to pay tax and perform labor services, the latter having largely been transformed into money payments and added to the tax, according to the system of the "single whip." Some of them, however, were hereditary military families who cultivated land assigned to them by the government and whose children were supposed to provide a substantial proportion of the men needed for an army of four million.

The peasants made up a social mass which was differentiated

24. T'ung-tsu Ch'Ü, *Law and Society, op. cit.*, pp. 133–135.
25. Robert M. Marsh, *op. cit.*, pp. 62 *et seq.*

into strata but which had its own manners and customs. For example, Chinese society was composed, in theory, of large patriarchal families embracing all the male descendants of a common ancestor in the male line. Actually there were many *tsu*, or patriarchal clans, forming a unit of mourning, made up of the "five mournings"—that is, the descendants of a great-great-grandfather down to his great-great-grandsons. The members of this *tsu* might live together, as a single religious, political, and economic unit, under the absolute authority of the male who was closest to the common ancestor. But it was above all families which included, or had included, a number of magistrates and graduates, and who were careful of their tradition and authority, that behaved in this way. Contrariwise, among the peasants especially, but also among the craftsmen and the petty and middling merchants, the family actually living together was often confined to the grandparents, their married sons, and their unmarried grandsons. When the old couple died, especially in the case of the peasants, the brothers separated, each one setting up house on his own with his wife and children. The family actually living together was then reduced to a mere nucleus, until the children, obliged by law to live with their father, married and had children of their own. Then, when their father died, the process of fragmentation was repeated. The peasant *tsu* survived as a biological and religious unit. The members chose, as did other Chinese, a leader who looked after the temple of their ancestors, the family ceremonies, and, if need be, the lands and schools of the *tsu*. But the *tsu* no longer corresponded to the family actually living together from day to day.

Similarly, marriage between persons bearing the same surname was forbidden by law, under penalty of a varying number of strokes of the bamboo, or even of beheading, depending on the seriousness of the case. Identity of surname did indeed imply a common ancestor. In fact, however, among the peasants and even among the lower levels of the commoners of the towns, marriage between persons who had the same surname, but who belonged to different *tsu*, was tolerated by public opinion. Among the peasants, even marriage between cousins in the same *tsu* was freely practiced. The magistrates would have had to annul such marriages and inflict eighty strokes of the bamboo on the guilty parties, if they had known about them, but they did not try to discover them and nobody denounced them. Among the poor peasants and townsfolk it was quite a regular thing to marry, regardless of what the law said, the widow of one's brother or cousin. The parents themselves arranged these marriages, with the complicity of the local commissary of police. In all these instances, the urge to get married, in spite of poverty, through natural need and for the sake of the help the husband and wife could give each other, broke through the law's prohibitions and caused a special morality to be adopted by the social group, through a consensus of opinion that demarcated this order from the others even more definitely than the law did.[26]

The peasants' position was a precarious one. It certainly got worse in the first half of the seventeenth century, through an imbalance between the number of inhabitants and the amount of food. The official registers of the Ming emperors show a population stationary between 1368 and 1644 at about 10½ million households and about 60 million people. Through the protection afforded by landowners who were members of the elite, and by magistrates, a large part of the population avoided registration. Sometimes ten large clans were merged into a single household, though each of them comprised a hundred separate families. The magistrates concealed part of the population in order to reduce the burden of taxes and prevent flight of taxpayers, or riots, and also to take for themselves part of what should have been paid over to the state. Finally, under the last Mings, corruption and general relaxation of discipline caused the administration to be neglected. The "Yellow Registers," which were supposed to contain lists of the entire population of China, was compiled in 1642, in advance, for 1651. In reality it must be reckoned that the population increased regularly and must have passed the figure of 150 million about 1600, to decline considerably between 1630 and 1660, during the wars, both civil and national. In 1602 the land registered as being under cultivation covered an area of 1,161,894,881 *mou*. There were

26. T'ung-tsu Ch'Ü, *Law and Society, op. cit.*, pp. 15–99.

thus 7.7 *mou* per inhabitant, and since only 4 *mou* were needed
to support one person, the situation was presumably satisfactory.
It must have become even more so during the sixteenth century,
with the introduction of new food plants. A variety of rice which
ripened in fifty days instead of needing sixty, a hundred, or a
hundred and eighty, made it possible to use the marshes before
the annual summer floods. In the Yangtze Valley the cultivator
could, by planting this quick-ripening rice, obtain two or three
crops a year. The introduction of the American plants had brought
about a revolution: maize, brought in about the middle of the
sixteenth century, became the plant that enabled use to be made of
the hills and mountainsides where the soil was too light for rice.
It was grown widely in Yunnan, Kweichow, and Szechwan. The
sweet potato, introduced into Yunnan between 1560 and 1570,
gave remarkably high returns, showed resistance to drought, proved
comparatively unattractive to locusts, could be stored easily,
was almost as nourishing as rice, and had a pleasant taste. It
began to take the place of the Chinese yam. The Chinese people
were able, under the Ming Dynasty, to apply themselves to
developing the wooded hills and forested mountains of their
country.[27] This relative prosperity did not survive the repeated
atmospheric disasters of the first half of the seventeenth century:
drought, torrential rain and floods, invasions of locusts. It may
even be that by making possible a great increase in the population the new plants rendered it more susceptible to the sudden
shortages of the last phase of the Ming era.

On the other hand, the cultivator was not in a position to get
the best price for his crop. The transport of corn, a heavy form
of merchandise, was terribly expensive. The cultivator therefore
had to sell on the local market to local merchants, who thus
held a kind of monopoly and could dictate conditions. They
offered low prices, because the cultivator lacked reserves and so
was forced to sell immediately after the harvest, at the very
moment when prices were collapsing. The ground rent he had
to pay was heavy. The tenants of Shansi Province were obliged
to pay out 60 percent of their grain crop as rent, and until

27. Ping-ti Ho, *Studies, op. cit.*, I, Ch. 1, pp. 1–23; II, Ch. 6, pp. 102–104;
Ch. VII, pp. 136, 169–195.

they had paid this they were not allowed to sow the ground afresh. In order to be able to sow, the cultivator thus usually had to borrow from the "absentee owner." A rate of interest of 25 percent was regarded as normal, and 60 percent was not unusual. Given the long period that elapses between sowing and reaping, the cultivator had to obtain long-term credit, which was all the more costly. He could not thenceforth get free of debt. After drought, locusts, and floods it was indebtedness that was a major cause of the social degradation of peasant families. Peasants had to sell their holdings and become wageworkers. Others kept their status as landowners, but in fact were simply working for their creditor. Since it was also a current practice to register one's land, or its surface at least, under the name of a large landowner who was a magistrate, in order to evade liability for taxes and services, the peasants fell under the patronage of the local elite, influential in the yamen and wielding great authority over them. The powerful position of guide to the masses which was assigned to the elite by Confucian theory and by the law was thus strengthened by the role of protector of the peasants, in relation to the magistrates, which members of the elite took upon themselves, especially when they preserved their land from taxation, either by declaring it to be theirs or by getting the magistrates to accept reduced assessments. It was likewise strengthened by their becoming creditors who could insist on work being done for them to repay debts and could use their position to bring pressure on debtors in a variety of circumstances.

Finally, at the very bottom of the social hierarchy, were the strata of mean people engaged in vile occupations. They were regarded as being "impure." A social myth explained their existence: they were descendants of criminals and unassimilated conquered peoples. In reality they were the end result of downward social mobility. But they were penned in their estate without any chance of escape. Marriage with commoners was forbidden to them. They were not allowed to purchase public appointments or university degrees. They were punished more severely than commoners for like offenses. Their "impurity," their moral defilement, together with the hereditary character of this quality, made them a caste, the only one in Chinese society. The mean people were the slaves, the prostitutes of both sexes, the singers, the musicians, the magistrates' runners; the house servants, the cooks, the porters; the laborers and odd-job men, the boatmen, fishermen, oyster gatherers, pearl fishers; the "fallen ones," sentenced for theft or murder, with degradation of their families; and the beggars. Nevertheless, slaves could be manumitted by their masters, and after the passing of three generations their descendants were regarded as commoners and were allowed to take the examinations. The mean people did not, apparently, make up more than 2 percent of the population.[28]

There is, it seems, a lack of sufficient information about the middling and petty traders, the craftsmen and the workers.

28. R. M. Marsh, *op. cit.*, pp. 58–60. Tung-tsu Ch'Ü, *Law and Society, op. cit.*, III, "The Orders," pp. 128–133.

[12]

Peasant Revolts Under the Last Mings

IT IS VERY difficult to find out about the revolts of the
Chinese peasants. China's official histories were primarily dynastic
histories. Doctors of the Han-lin Academy, as part of their
official duty, compiled chronicles for the reigning emperor. When
a dynasty came to its end, its history was written, on the basis
of these official annals, at the beginning of the next dynasty's
career, but all the material used for this history was destroyed.
This is what happened in the case of the Ming Dynasty. There
would be no means of checking the official history if local chronicles, covering provinces and cantons, had not survived, together
with local biographies, as well as chronicles and biographies that
were considered subversive and banned, but which found their
way abroad, where they were copied and eventually published.
Furthermore, chronicles and histories had to conform to Confucian standards, and for the disciples of Confucius, history
was morality in action. The chroniclers built up, consciously and
conscientiously, a corpus of precedents destined to guide future
generations of Chinese bureaucrats in the theory and practice
of administration, in accordance with the moral, social, and
political principles of Confucius. Their choice and presentation
of facts do not, therefore, inform us about *all* aspects of reality,
and they show this reality in a special light.

In these official annals, biographies take up a great deal of room: biographies of loyal magistrates and of wicked ones, of writers, hermits, virtuous wives, filial sons, faithful imperial concubines. In the *History of the Ming Dynasty* biographies take up 197 chapters out of 332, and 60 percent of the pages. The same is true of the local histories, of provinces, prefectures, and cantons. In addition, moreover, there are innumerable collections of biographies, because the Chinese were under obligation to write them as a form of funeral tribute and to contribute to the cult of ancestors, just as they sent each other birthday poems and letters. These biographies are short, between 800 and 1,000 characters in length. That of Li Tzu-cheng, the peasant who became a bandit and later emperor, which is one of the longest, contains 9,000 characters. But these biographies differ completely from Western ones. The Western biographer seeks to bring out the individuality, the personality, the unusualness of his subject. The Chinese biographer, on the contrary, tries to reduce his man to a stereotype, and fit him into a conventional mold, for the Chinese biography is either an act of social homage which must harmonize with accepted and respectable sentiments and ideas, or else an example serving to illustrate history and instruct magistrates in their responsibilities. Thus, all the biographies are alike. They contain information on the subject's family background (but usually omit the date of his birth) and they give data about his official career and quotations from his writings, together with some anecdotes, a certain number of which turn up in practically every biography. The whole thing is stereotyped and is often quite false, the construction of a type rather than the description of a man.[1]

These habits of Chinese historians are catastrophic in their consequences for our knowledge of the peasant revolts. Traditional Chinese historians were extremely hostile to the rebels because the latter disrupted the social order, and they described the rebels' deeds in accordance with recognized methods which

1. D. S. Nivison, "Aspects of Traditional Chinese Biography," and J. A. Garraty, "Chinese and Western Biography: A Comparison," in H. L. Boorman (ed.), "The Biographical Approach to Chinese History: A Symposium," *Journal of Asian Studies*, 21 (1961–62), pp. 453–489.

were aimed at discrediting them. Thus, these historians tell us
that even as children the great rebel leaders Li Tzu-cheng and
Chang Hsien-chung showed inclinations toward extreme violence.
To believe them, these men were monsters who committed
the worst of atrocities. They flayed their prisoners alive, buried
them or burned them alive, threw them into boiling water or
oil. They cut off ears, noses, hands, and feet. They tore out
eyes and teeth. They raped women and girls. They ripped open
the bellies of pregnant women. They carried out mass drownings.
They were cannibals. They forced women to prostitute themselves. They massacred women and children. They fed dogs and
fish with human flesh and blood. They were tyrants, vicious and
capricious, served by a whole network of spies, and they tortured
magistrates and rich men in order to extort money from them.
Their very faces were those of repulsive beasts, and so on.

Events are described in the same manner, in unvaryingly frightful forms. The rebels rose up in huge numbers like swarms of
bees. The corpses of their wretched victims were heaped up as
high as mountains. Entire regions were emptied of inhabitants.
No smoke from the chimneys, no dogs or chickens to be seen, but
thousands of wolves and tigers. The numbers massacred were so
great that their bodies blocked the courses of rivers and made
them overflow their banks. The waters of the rivers were reddened
with the blood of the slain. The fish and the tortoises gorged
themselves with human flesh till they themselves became unfit
to be eaten. The blood of the slain formed new rivulets.

When the reader finds the same formulations repeated again
and again throughout the history of China, he realizes that these
are merely literary clichés which he has no reason to take seriously.

Another difficulty resides in the ambiguity of the term *tsih*,
bandit. In general, every Chinese had the right to submit petitions,
but there was no legal means of combating possible acts of
tyranny by the emperor or the magistrates. The Chinese were
therefore driven to more and more illegal methods of expressing
their opposition. First, there was passive resistance, a sort of
general strike, with readiness to put up with all manner of
harassment and violence rather than give in. This sometimes
sufficed to persuade the emperor to remove unpopular mag-

istrates. If it did not, then a few men dedicated to the public
weal would sacrifice themselves. They started a local insurrection
and tried to kill certain tyrannical mandarins. Then the affair
was settled by negotiation with the government's representatives.
The authorities put an end to the exactions and violence that
had caused the trouble, and the leaders of the revolt gave
themselves up, well knowing that they would be executed in
order to save the imperial government's face. If oppression persisted, however, insurrections like these became very frequent.
The leaders became outlaws, at war with the government. They
formed bands, levied contributions from the public, attacked the
local customs offices, plundered treasuries, and forced traders to
pay taxes on their goods. Such men were called bandits or pirates.
Some were indeed from the start, or else eventually became, mere
criminals, highway robbers. But this was not true of all of them.
The word *tsih*, which is used for all of them alike, means "all
persons who set the authorities at defiance by acquisitive acts
of violence," and it is used for robbers, bandits, and rebels. Under
the Manchu Ts'ing Dynasty a section of the Chinese penal code,
constituting one-seventh of the whole, dealt with attempts
to take possession of the property of others, ranging from the
theft of a small sum of money to efforts to seize the empire
by a person who "assumes a dynastic title, enrolls troops and
perhaps styles himself a Sovereign Prince." This section as a
whole was entitled *Tsih Taou*. *Taou* meant theft and abduction,
while *tsih* embraced a wider category of crimes, including different degrees of rebellion. In a particular text, therefore, *tsih*
may mean "bandit" but it may also mean "political dissident,"
"seditious person," "rebel." It was true that citizens who took
up arms against the government and the established authorities,
and carried on a struggle in the countryside, were inexorably
driven by their need for food and security, and their determina-
tion to get their way, to commit actions which outwardly re-
sembled those of robbers and bandits, and that soon they differed from the latter only in intention.

The obscure passages in these documents and the occasions for
error on the part of the historian are thus numerous. Fortunately,
the chronicles and biographies contain, within the conventional

framework, an enormous mass of exact details on the operations of the rebel groups, the places where these occurred, the military opposition they encountered, and the fortunes of the civil war, month by month and year by year. From these it is possible to derive information, or at least hints, about the social composition of the rebel bands and their motives and aims, so that, even though these sources are very defective, they make possible at least an approximate understanding of the rebellions.[2]

The revolts of the last epoch of the Ming Dynasty broke out in a period of natural calamities, which particularly affected Shensi, where the revolts began, and also Shansi, Honan, Kweichow, and Szechwan. From 1620 onward there was a succession of droughts and famines, each worse than the last. For the second year of Emperor Ch'ung-Chen, A.D. 1637, a chronicler wrote: "In those times, drought and famine had been continual over a number of years, and yet the magistrate [of Ch'i, the birthplace of Li-Yen, a *Chü-Jen* in the service of the rebel leader Li Tzu-cheng and probable author of this passage], a certain Sung, squeezed the people relentlessly for payment of taxes."[3] Here we learn all we need to know about the circumstances of the rebellion: the coincidence of a period of shortage with a moment when taxes were heavy and implacably exacted.

Locusts devastated Honan in 1639, 1640, and 1641. Li-Yen wrote a song about them in 1640.

> In the last few years we have been suffering continuously from
> locusts and drought;
> The locusts nibble the grain shoots, leaving nothing to reap.
> The price of rice has risen several times.
> People all over the land have no way to live.
> To fill the stomach, they eat grass roots and leaves of trees.
> Children cry, looking blankly at each other.
> Pots and pans show accumulated dust. No smoke from the
> cooking stove;

2. J. B. Parsons, "Attitudes towards the late Ming rebellions," *Oriens Extremus*, 6 (1959), pp. 177–205. T. T. Meadows, *The Chinese and Their Rebellions* (London, Smith, Elder, 1856), Ch. X, pp. 116–119.
3. Quoted by V. Y. C. Shih, "Some Chinese rebel ideologies," *T'Oung Pao*, 44 (1956), p. 205.

For days, not even a meal of porridge.
The Government sends out tax-collectors, tigers to the people,
And the strong families demand debts, like wolves.

These disasters were felt even more severely in Shensi, in the northwest of the empire, where the soil was infertile.

The shortages made still worse the effects of actions which had been repeated over a long period, and caused them to be even harder to endure. Prices rose. Those for rice appear to have trebled between 1616 and 1642. The humble people were most seriously affected, but the rich and the elite suffered too, for everything seems to have got dearer. The landlords insisted more strictly on their rents, and also on presents and gifts. The peasants, in debt and ruined, sold their ownership of the surface, or of the surface and the subsoil, where they owned both. Many of them sank to the level of dayworkers, mere laborers. Relations between peasants and landowners became strained. Paradoxically, the tension grew very strong in Fukien and Kwangtung, though these were rich provinces, producing much rice. The population of these provinces was so numerous that the area of cultivable land seemed proportionately less. Rice reached the highest prices ever. Rich merchants and retired magistrates invested in land and wanted a high return on their investments. They demanded especially heavy rents for their land.[4]

In the northwest, in Shensi, the situation was so desperate that the landowners themselves appear to have been ruined. According to Fan Wen-lan, a Communist historian, in the edition of his general history of China published in 1949, this may have been one cause of the revolts, since the landowners were unable to maintain their armed bands.[5]

All over the country, landowners evaded taxation, the burden of which fell on the peasants. The largest landowners protected their peasants from the tax collectors. In a movement which spread over a wider and wider area, the peasants registered their holdings in the names of big landowners who had connections with the elite, so as to escape taxation and obtain protection from the magistrates and their employees and runners.

4. Ping-ti Ho, *Studies, op. cit.*, II, Ch. X, pp. 218–219.
5. J. B. Parsons, *op. cit.*, p. 192.

These misfortunes coincide with a great increase in the tax burden. The reasons for this are to be sought, first, in the increase of prices. Then, with the breakup of the Ming regime, the emperors, weak and impressionable men, were pulled this way and that by the empresses, the imperial concubines, and the eunuchs, so that the imperial family and the Court offered an example of luxury, excessive and useless expediture, and corruption. The princes, princesses, eunuchs, and high officials demanded presents and gifts of money from those who wished to become magistrates, from magistrates who sought promotion, and from the subjects of the administration. The eunuchs showed particular ferocity, raising illegal tolls and internal customs charges, and taxes on real or imaginary mines of silver or copper. Between 1596 and 1605 the eunuchs themselves undertook the exploitation of silver mines and used this as a means of extorting large sums. They grabbed privately owned land, made it state domain, and then had it granted to themselves or to their friends and protégés. They demanded performance of illegal labor services on their land and in their enterprises, or those of their friends and relatives. The magistrates ceased to trouble about administering honestly and efficiently and concentrated on squeezing those in their power in order to get the means of buying themselves "protection" at Court. The last Ming emperor, Ch'ung-Chen (1628–1644) started to combat the power of the eunuchs, and succeeded in eliminating a certain number of them, beginning, in 1628, with the dictator Wei Chung-hsien, master of ceremonies and head of the Eastern Depot, and the members of his clique, who dominated the bureaucracy. But the emperor was irresolute, lacking self-confidence and steadiness of opinion. He changed the men serving him too often. Between 1621 and 1644, in a period of twenty-four years, the heads of the six ministries were changed a hundred and sixteen times. In fifty-four of these cases the emperor dismissed the men concerned and in twenty-six of these he confiscated their property or had them put to death. Between 1521 and 1544 there had been no more than seven cases of dismissal and five of punishment of the heads of the six ministries. No one dared any longer to assume responsible positions, and indeed no one had the time to do this. From the top to the bottom of the hierarchy, inertia, neglect, and waste prevailed. The armies were no longer paid or supplied. The soldiers deserted, going over either to the enemy or to the bandits.[6]

Wars became continuous and unending. The Manchus intensified their attacks. Yet, in this time when the Ming government was breaking up, able generals were almost all deprived of their commands. After the arrest of General Yuan Ch'ung-huan on January 13, 1630, the Manchus found themselves up against hardly any resistance. In 1633, even, three Chinese Generals, K'ung Yu-te, Keng Chung-ming and Shen Ko-hsi, went over to their side. On two occasions, in 1629 and 1636, the Manchu armies broke through the Great Wall and reached the gates of Peking. These inroads remained short-lived however, because the Manchus did not succeed in getting control of the principal passes through the mountains. The great pass of Shanhaikwan was still held by loyal Chinese generals, who were consequently able to threaten the rear of the Manchu forces, so that the latter always had to retreat. But the war went on and on. It was accompanied, moreover, all along the frontier, by guerrilla operations and forays carried out by the nomads. In Shensi, for example, their activities had contributed to reducing the people to famine, and by making necessary the upkeep of large armed forces and the conduct of many expeditions they helped to empty the state's coffers.

The result was a continual series of additions to the tax burden. In 1639 extra taxation appears to have amounted to twenty million taels, ten times what the total income of the government, in money, had been in 1514. The burden of taxation was made still heavier by the excessive "customary fees" demanded by the magistrates, their employees, private secretaries, servants, and runners.

These excessive demands were especially suffered in Shensi. It was a remote province, far away in the northwest, to which the emperors were in the habit of sending, to fill the public offices, graduates of low achievement, incompetent and despised,

6. G. A. Kennedy, "Chu Yu-chien, Emperor Ch'ung Chen," in A. W. Hummel, *Eminent Chinese of the Ch'ing Period*, I, pp. 191–195. See also R. B. Crawford, "Eunuch Power," *op. cit.*, pp. 138–140.

incapable both of resisting the exactions of the local elite and of securing the substantial amounts due to the government. These magistrates regarded themselves as exiles, and lost no time in trying to use the opportunity to get rich.[7]

Shensi was perhaps the most backward of those provinces of the north which still depended economically on those of the south. The northern provinces received from the south, through the merchants of Fukien, Kiangsi, Chekiang, and Shanghai, their cotton and silk goods, their porcelain, tea, sugar, and salt. In return, they sent raw cotton and other raw materials. When prices rose, the northerners felt they were being exploited by the merchants from the south.

The famine of 1628 and the frontier guerrilla warfare had worn out the people of Shensi. In 1629 Emperor Ch'ung-Chen abolished the state postal system which had been set up in the time of the first emperor, in the third century B.C. This postal service cost the imperial exchequer several hundred thousand taels each year. It not only served for the transmission of official dispatches but also, in mountainous areas where main roads and navigable waterways were lacking, it provided a state transport organization. All kinds of freight were carried on the shoulders of the men who did labor service for the imperial mail. This was the means by which the province of Shensi received what it needed from outside, including corn, and sent forth its own products. The abolition of the postal service finally disorganized the province's economy, and Shensi found itself in a desperate situation. Lacking pay or supplies, the soldiers took to plundering the public granaries and treasuries. Many of them deserted. No longer receiving any corn through the postal service, the people died of hunger. When the emperor was appealed to for relief, he refused to send any money. The provincial governor, Chu Tung-meng, a greedy man and a sordid miser, insisted rigorously on the payment of taxes, and yet further payments still. All these misfortunes threw thousands of vagabonds and bandits onto the roads.[8]

7. J. B. Parsons, *op. cit.*, p. 132.
8. G. A. Kennedy, *op. cit.*, p. 195. Erich Hauer, "Li Tzu-cheng und Chang Hsien-chung," *Asia Major*, 2 (1925), pp. 436–498.

The 1630s and the beginning of the 1640s form the period
which could be called "the time of the roaming bandits," and
then, after 1640, there began, for the leading rebel chieftains,
"the time of dynastic ambitions."[9]

Broadly speaking, the revolts started in Shensi. They were
launched by deserters from the army, who were joined by peasants.
Together, these made up bands of several hundred or several
thousand men. They were mounted and could move quickly
about the country. They plundered the rural areas—peasants
as well as rich landowners being their victims. From Shensi, they
passed into neighboring Shansi, then into Honan, Hupeh, and
Szechwan, until in the end they were active in the entire region
between the Hwang-ho and the Yangtze. Sometimes they captured a town and plundered it, but had to give it up when
government troops approached. During this time of troubles there
were at least twenty-six risings in the towns, but no link can be
discovered between these movements and those of the "bandits"
before the time of the dynastic ambitions of Li Tzu-cheng.[10]

The bandits were organized on military lines. They pitched
their camp on a hillside, with a river below them for protection. Groups of sentries were posted on the top of the hill
and at the approaches to the camp. Along the roads, mounted
patrols watched the movements of the government forces as
far as over sixty kilometers away. The rebels imposed a strict
discipline on themselves.

Nevertheless, when they came up against regular troops, in
pitched battles, they were usually beaten. They then fled toward
the mountains and hid in the ravines. On many an occasion the
emperor's generals would have been able to destroy them, but
it seems that the magistrates, civil as well as military, preferred
to protract this war. It suited them better to negotiate with
the bandits and give them permission to surrender, in return for
payments of money. They granted pardons to the bandits, and

---

9. J. B. Parsons, "A case-history of revolt in China. The Late Ming rebellion
of Chang Hsien-chung," *Oriens Extremus*, 3 (1956), pp. 81–93. See also
ibid., "The Culmination of a Chinese Peasant Rebellion. Chang Hsien-chung
in Szechwan, 1644–46," *Journal of Asian Studies*, 16 (1956–57), pp. 386–
399.

10. A. Feuerwerker, *op. cit.*, p. 110.

if they caught them, set them free. Sometimes they absorbed the bandits into China's defense system. The bandits made all sorts of promises, but then, once they were free again, they resumed their activities. The magistrates excused themselves to the emperor by appealing to the compassion that should be shown to the peasants' poverty, the cause of the rebellions.

It would have been a good idea to multiply points of local resistance to banditry, but the emperor's mistrust of his subordinates prevented this from being done. In 1634 the ninth prince of T'ang, faced with the increasing bandit menace, made big contributions from his own resources to improve the defenses of Nanyang, and asked the emperor for permission to recruit 3,000 men to fight against the bandits. His request was rejected, because princes were not allowed to have more than a small bodyguard of troops under their command.[11]

In 1636 the magistrate Yang Ssu-ch'ang put forward an operational plan to finish the bandits off. This involved surrounding them with a ring of fortresses which would restrict their movements, since only one-third of the imperial forces were mounted, and the bandits' mobility was their chief trump card. Inside the fortress ring a mobile imperial force would operate actively against the bandits and destroy them. Even when he had become minister of war, Yang Ssu-ch'ang was unable to put his plan into effect, for lack of money and also because of the rivalries, quarrels, and ill will among his generals. In 1639 and 1640, though he won victory after victory, he could never annihilate the rebel bands. In the end, after a setback, he killed himself.

The bandits, whether army deserters or cultivators, were almost all of peasant origin, it seems. Can one then speak of a peasants' rising and a peasants' war? Whatever their origin, it seems that we see here men in arms to assuage their hunger by way of plunder. They appear all to have become professional bandits— peasants by origin, but by trade écorcheurs ("flayers," like the bandits in France in the period of the Hundred Years' War). We can find no traces among them of any idea of a political

11. G. A. Kennedy, "Chu Yu-chien," op. cit., I, pp. 196–198.

and social revolution, or even of reform and reorganization. During these years they made no attempt to organize a government. They did not even endeavor to unite their forces, and most of the time these bands acted in isolation. On a few occasions, two or three bands would come together in order to sweep from east to west, but these alliances were ephemeral. In 1635 the rebel leaders held a grand council in Honan in order to coordinate their attacks on the Ming forces. Their discussions and agreements had little practical effect, however. Virtually no attempt was made to overthrow the government and none to win the support of the people, whom the bandits appear simply to have regarded as material for squeezing. These bandits functioned for a long time as mere "warlords" who were preoccupied exclusively with plundering raids.

Meanwhile, the peasants seem to have shown extreme passivity. They gave no help to the emperor's forces. This attitude may be explained by a saying that dates from Ming times: "The rebels comb coarsely, but the government armies comb finely." The troops, badly paid and supplied, had little discipline and indulged in plunder and rape. From 1632 onward, the generals fairly often embezzled their soldiers' pay and, to compensate them, led them on plundering expeditions. It may be, too, that the peasants felt sympathy with the adversaries of an oppressive administration. But they do not appear to have taken any active part in the struggles waged by the bandits. The same is true of the craftsmen, the merchants, the local elite, and the towns in general. All these circles seem to have remained aloof from the bandits.[12]

Two rebel leaders eventually raised themselves above the rest and tried to take over the imperial power: Li Tzu-cheng and Chang Hsien-chung. Li Tzu-cheng was born in 1605 at Mi-Chih, in Shensi;[13] some say that he was originally a soldier at the postal station at Yin Ch'uan-i, others that he was a post courier. He had the reputation of being a good horseman and archer, but also of having a quarrelsome character. Some say that it

12. J. B. Parsons, "Attitudes," op. cit., p. 189.
13. Lien-che Tu, "Li Tzu-cheng," in W. Hummel, op. cit., I, pp. 491–493. See also E. Hauer, op. cit., pp. 437–493.

was because he had lost his livelihood through the abolition of
the imperial postal service that he became a bandit—others,
that he broke some military regulation, was sentenced to death,
and only then ran away, to become a butcher. In any case, his
family provided him with an example. In 1628, owing to famine,
his maternal uncle Kao Ying-hsiang assembled and organized an
armed band, and took the title of Ch'uang Wang, "Dashing
King." The abolition of the imperial mail and the increase
in taxation brought to his side Li Tzu-cheng, who, with his own
nephew Li-Kuo, joined Kao Ying-hsiang in 1631 and took as his
nom de guerre Ch'uang Chiang, "Dashing General."

Chang Hsien-chung was born in the north of Shensi, probably
in 1606, either in a peasant's family or in that of a petty merchant. Having become a soldier, he is said to have taken part
in a mutiny and been sentenced to death. But a senior officer,
Ch'en Hung-fan, impressed by his appearance, obtained a pardon
for him, probably about 1630.[14] Released, Chang Hsien-chung
gathered a band of several hundred men around him, mostly
deserters, and began plundering the villages of northern Shensi.

At that moment, in 1631, there were said to be in Shensi and
Shansi about three dozen different bands, embracing altogether
200,000 men, a figure which was doubtless inflated by rhetorical
exaggeration.

Chang Hsien-chung had a difficult start, suffering several heavy
defeats. Fortunately for him, at the beginning of 1632 he was
allowed to give himself up, and therefore gained a few months'
respite, after which he was able to take the field again. From
1633 onward he led his seasonal forays outside the boundaries
of Shensi. First of all, he invaded Shansi. Then after 1634 he
began plundering extensive areas of Honan, Hupeh, Szechwan,
Anhwei, and Kiangsu, reaching the sea. His entire band was
mounted and moved at a rapid pace. Each year he covered
several thousand kilometers, in three provinces at least on each
occasion. His favorite route ran southeast from Shensi, through
Honan, Hupeh, and Anhwei into Kiangsu.

His forces and his prestige alike increased. He began seizing

14. Lien-che Tu, "Chang Hsien-chung," in W. Hummel, *op. cit.*, p. 37.

walled towns. In 1635 he took Fengyangfu, in the province of Anhwei. The ancestral home of the Mings was there, and so this event made a sensation. However, he had to abandon the town when government troops drew near.

Li Tzu-cheng behaved in the same way and rose in strength and reputation similarly. In 1633, after Kao Ying-hsiang had suffered a defeat, Li broke away from him and formed a band of his own, to work for his own profit. In autumn of 1636 Kao was caught by the imperial forces and beheaded. His men chose Li Tzu-cheng to command them, and conferred on him the title of Ch'uang Wang, which Kao had borne.

The rise of these two leaders did not take place without very severe temporary setbacks. In 1634 the governor of northern Shensi, Ch'en Ch'i-yü, had been given plenary powers to put down the bandits in the provinces of Shensi, Shansi, Honan, Hukwang (i.e., Hupeh and Hunan) and Szechwan. With 36,000 men he surrounded Li Tzu-cheng and Chang Hsien-chung in a valley near Hinganfu, in the southeast of Shensi. The two rebel leaders offered to surrender. Ch'en Ch'i-yü agreed, and sent them back to their villages under guard. On the way they revolted, killed their guards, and returned to their banditry. Ch'en Ch'i-yü was dismissed and exiled, but the opportunity had been lost.[15]

In February and March of 1635, at the grand council held at Jungyanghsien, thirteen bandit chiefs met together, representing seventy-two bands; Li Tzu-cheng enthused everyone with an inflammatory speech and got agreement for China to be divided among the chiefs into separate spheres of action. He himself, with Kao Ying-hsiang and Chang Hsien-chung, was to plunder the eastern part of the country as far as the Yangtze. The decisions taken were not very well observed, but from that day forward rivalry increased between Li Tzu-cheng and Chang Hsien-chung, which became hostility after Chang had refused to hand over to Li one of his prisoners, a young imperial eunuch who was an excellent musician.

Meanwhile, with alternations of success and setback, the two leaders advanced in reputation. Chang Hsien-chung won some

15. E. Swisher, "Ch'en Ch'i-yü," in W. Hummel, *op. cit.*, p. 85.

big victories, but then, in 1638, he was severely defeated and forced to surrender. However, the government pardoned him, allowed him to keep his troops, gave him a position in the official military system, and authorized him to occupy Kucheng-hsien, in northwestern Hupeh, as representative of the government. There, Chang, having become an official personage, began entering into relations with the elite. In 1639 he resumed his rebellious activity. At Lohoushan, in the mountains of western Hupeh, he crushed the army of Tso Liang-yü, several thousand strong. It was only a fluke, and he was unable to exploit his success. In 1640, however, by means of a surprise attack, he managed to seize Hsiangyang, in the north of Hupeh, and thereby ruined the prestige of the minister of war, Yang Ssu-ch'ang, who was driven to commit suicide. For his part, Li Tzu-cheng had suffered a severe defeat in 1638, near T'ungkwan, in Shensi, at the hands of Hung Chang-chou, governor-general of the five provinces of Honan, Shensi, Shansi, Szechwan, and Hukwang (i.e., Hupeh and Hunan). Li had to flee, with a handful of men, and was obliged to hide in the mountains for over a year before he could take the field again.[16]

The year 1640 was decisive for the two rebel leaders. First, because of the intensification of social disturbances. In 1639 there was a terrible drought in Honan. Men rallied to Li Tzu-cheng in thousands, even members of the elite. In a number of places, even in rich Fukien, the peasants revolted against the large landowners. The government had to undertake bloody repressions.[17] In the Yangtze Valley discontent rose higher. In one canton, four families each employed 3,000 to 4,000 servants. When the rebels drew near, the heads of these families armed their men. But the servants turned on their masters and joined forces with the rebels.[18] The bandits ceased to be mere plunderers and became the embodiment of social opposition. Their bands became armies, armies of men in revolt against a corrupt regime and against oppression by men of privilege.

16. Chao-ying Fang, "Hung Chen-chou," in W. Hummel, op. cit., pp. 358–359.
17. Ping-ti Ho, Studies, op. cit., II, Ch. IX, pp. 218–219.
18. J. B. Parsons, "Attitudes," op. cit., p. 188.

At that period, moreover, the forces of rebellion became concentrated. In 1640 two rebel leaders, Li Tzu-cheng and Chang Hsien-chung emerged as the wielders of supreme power among the rebels. Of the other leaders, some had been killed in battle, others executed, and yet others murdered by rivals. Nearly all the remainder had accepted the supremacy of the two great leaders. A few remained independent of them, but with restricted forces.

Finally, the power and effectiveness of the rebels was growing. Li Tzu-cheng and Chang Hsien-chung had learned the art of generalship. Many Chinese now foresaw the end of the Mings, deserted by Heaven, and wanted to make sure of enjoying the favor of the possible masters of the morrow. Numerous officers of the Ming army surrendered to the rebels, accepted commands in their forces, and brought them the aid of their technical knowledge and their experience in regular warfare. They made it possible for the bands to become an army. Also, whereas, down to 1640, the elite had remained loyal to the Ming emperors, now two graduates, Li-yen, a Chü-Jen of 1627, and Nin Chin-hsing, rallied to Li Tzu-cheng and became his advisers. This was the beginning of a movement. As for Chang Hsien-chung, while he was at Kuchenghsien in 1638–1639 he had become close to at least three members of the elite, as a result of his holding an official position. He had obtained from them military intelligence, war material, and political ideas. One of the first officers of his forces, Hsieh, came from a notable family of Shansi province. His chief adviser, Wang Chao-ling, came from another notable family, from Anhwei. Chang had taken him prisoner when he was still a youngster but had already begun his studies. Chang himself had learned to read. Two Jesuit fathers, Father Gabriel de Magalhaens and Father Louis Buglio, who became close associates of his after his invasion of Szechwan in 1644, report that Chang was able to read the Christian tracts in Chinese which they had brought with them. Thus, Li and Chang acquired ideas on social and political organization, and on administration. Basically, however, the Chinese rallied in large numbers to the two leaders who happened to be already possessed of armed forces capable of opposing the government and who had proved their will to oppose it. In providing the manpower for an army for each of them, the rebel Chinese had practically forced on these bandit chiefs a role as leaders of political and social revolt which they do not seem to have thought of taking up and which was perhaps beyond them. For the requirements of their army and their policy, the need to have recourse to officers who had come over from the imperial army, and to graduate scholars, compelled Li and Chang to adopt the outlook and ideas of these graduates, that is, in the main, the spirit and teachings of Confucius and Chu-Hsi, which they believed in. In consequence, though there was certainly the possibility of a change of dynasty, there was none of revolution.

Of the two, Li Tzu-cheng, the illiterate, was the better advised and the readier to understand the advice given him. He took his stand as a zealous Confucian, bearing the mandate of Heaven. His supporters circulated the report that in 1636, in Shensi, though he plundered Michihhsien, his native place, he had said to the magistrate of the *hsien*, Pien Ta-chou: "This is my native country, do no harm to my old parents." This pattern of filial piety, the highest virtue for the Chinese and the basis of their political and social relations, in which the relationship between superior and inferior was modeled on that between the absolutist father and his subject son, had also given the magistrate money for repairing and embellishing the temple of Confucius.

Li-Yen, the Chü-Jen who became his principal adviser, suggested to him: "Anyone who wishes to take over the Empire should lay the foundations of his work in the hearts of the people."

Li-Len organized Li Tzu-cheng's propaganda. He composed songs and had them sung by children, in order to influence the people's minds. He stressed two themes: no more taxes, and land for everyone equally. One song said:

> Open the gates to welcome Prince Ch'uang [Li Tzu-Cheng].
> When Prince Ch'uang arrives
> We shall pay no more taxes

And another said:

In the morning they [the Emperor's men] demand a *sheng*
[a measure].
And in the evening they demand a *ho* [one-tenth of a *sheng*].
Nowadays it is hard for a poor fellow to stay alive.
Let us hasten to open the gate to receive Prince Ch'uang,
And all will enjoy happiness.

And another:

Shoulder to shoulder, we wait for Prince Ch'uang;
When Prince Ch'uang comes
We shall not have to pay taxes for three years.

The propagandists emphasized: Li Tzu-cheng does not kill
people, he does not love wealth, he does not insult women, he
does not loot, he buys and sells fairly, and he is going to re-
distribute the money of the rich among the people and redis-
tribute the land equally.

Li Tzu-cheng had the good sense to make his conduct conform
to these slogans. He shed as little blood as possible. During 1640
he conquered Honan Province, town after town. At the beginning of 1641 he captured Honanfu and killed the prince of
Fu, Chou Ch'ang-hsün, who was related to the imperial family. He
confiscated the prince's property and distributed it as famine
relief. He arranged distributions of corn to the people. When
he captured Yüchou he changed the name of this town to Chün-
pingchou, that is, "equitable *chou*," and everyone took this as
a symbol intended to announce the coming of a society based
on equal possession of land and equality of opportunity. In
these ways he won all hearts. The people of the countryside and
the towns flocked to join his army. The towns began to come
over to his side.

The belief became more and more widespread that he had
received the mandate of Heaven, and he believed this himself.
In 1642, after having had a narrow escape from hostile intrigues
and an attempt on his life organized by Chang Hsien-chung, Li
Tzu-cheng went through a moment of distress when he thought
of suicide. Many rebel leaders were surrendering to the govern-

ment. One of his officers, Liu Tsung-min, a smith from Lant'ien, in Shensi, the bravest of the rebels, was also thinking of giving himself up. Li Tzu-cheng went with him into a temple. He remarked: "People say that I am the son of Heaven. Why not let us divine? If the result is unfavorable, you may cut my head off and give yourself up." Liu Tsung-min agreed to this. Three times they divined, and each time they came out with the sign for "fortunate." Liu Tsung-min went back home, killed his two wives, and returned to Li Tzu-cheng to say: "I will follow you to the death." Many other men in the army, when they learned what had happened, likewise killed their wives and children, as a proof that they held as nothing their past lives and their dearest possessions and that, without looking behind them anymore, they would march with Li Tzu-cheng to victory, riches, and glory.[19]

Thus, Li Tzu-cheng was still able to reinforce or reconstitute his army. He and Chang Hsien-chung faced a tough opponent, however, in the person of the Ming general Tso Liang-yü. In 1640 and 1641 Chang was twice beaten by him, and had to make an alliance with Li Tzu-cheng, who defeated Tso Liang-yü and hurled him back in 1642 and 1643. Chang was able to plunder Honan and then, in 1643, announcing his dynastic ambitions, to declare himself "King of the West" and seize Wuchang, capital of Hupeh. However, on the one hand, Tso Liang-yü re-formed his army and returned to the attack, and on the other, Li Tzu-cheng reacted very badly to Chang's successes and his pretensions. He caused him to be told: "Death is upon you." Chang, faced with the twofold threat from the Ming general and from his rival, preferred to turn back toward Hunan and from there toward Szechwan.[20]

Meanwhile, Li Tzu-cheng marched to take over the empire. In 1643 he was able to organize a great army. His standard bore a silk pagoda and white horsetails. The battalions of his army had a white banner and yak-tails as their ensign. He conscripted all the men between fifteen and forty, and imposed an iron

19. V. Y. C. Shih, *op. cit.*, pp. 206–209.
20. Lien-che Tu, "Chang Hsien-chung," in W. Hummel, *op. cit.*, pp. 37–38; "Tso Liang-yü," *ibid.*, II, p. 761.

discipline upon them. A corporal for every ten men was in charge of weapons, fodder, and expenditure. All private gain, profit, or accumulation of money was forbidden. The most valued form of booty was horses and mules, followed by bows, arrows, shot, and firearms. Silken fabrics, pearls, and precious stones were held in little esteem. In captured towns, the soldiers did not billet themselves in houses, but remained aloof from the women and children, bivouacking in canvas tents. Deserters, "a shameful crew," were cut to pieces. Under regulations of February, 1644, any horseman whose horse left the ranks was to be beheaded. "Whoever rides over a cultivated field shall be beheaded" was a decision that went to the peasants' hearts. If a town under attack surrendered at once, everyone in it was spared. If it resisted for one day, a third of the inhabitants were massacred; if two days, two-thirds; if three, all of them, and their bodies were burned.

At Hsiangyang, in Hupeh, he organized his general staff and his government in accordance with the traditional model, having a prime minister—one Chang Kuo-shen, a magistrate, a chancellor "on his left," an *aide-de-camp* "on his right," vice-presidents, councillors and secretaries of the six boards, and commandants for the towns in his possession. As chancellor "on his left," he had Nin Chin-hsing, a graduate, who was his mentor.

He conquered Honan. He won a decisive victory over the Ming general Sun Chuan-ting, near Nanyangfu. He took up winter quarters for 1643–1644 at Sianfu, giving this town its old name from Han times, Ch'angan. This was symbolic, for the Hans were the first Chinese dynasty who united the empire. Symbolic also were the names he had adopted. In 1643 he styled himself: "the generalissimo in charge of justice by the grace of Heaven." At the end of 1643 he took the title, "The New King compliant to Heaven." He renamed his native prefecture and canton Tienpaohsien, meaning "Heaven-protected." He always paid attention to his propaganda. His supporters noised it about that Heaven had condemned the Ming Dynasty: at Peking a dust storm had arisen, yellow clouds had filled the sky, and the emperor had been very frightened. The story ran that Li Tzu-cheng was content with simple food, that he indulged in neither wine nor women, that he was a virtuous man. When he organized his first government, his prime minister, the magistrate Chang Kuo-shen, an old friend of his, had the un-lucky idea of bringing him a magistrate's wife for him to use as he pleased. Li Tzu-cheng wept, because he was going to lose a friend, and had him put to death.

He reproached his ally, Lo Jou-ts'ai, who kept several dozen wives and concubines, dressed all in white silk embroidered with flowers, and had in his camp troops of women musicians, that is, of prostitutes. He had him killed, and thereby became the direct commander of Lo's soldiers.

Names, words, and deeds were all symbolic. Li Tzu-cheng in these ways revealed his true character: he was the one who, inspired by Heaven, was going back to the most sacred tradi-tions, the one who was replacing a worn-out dynasty, deprived of the mandate of Heaven, by a new dynasty, to which the mandate of Heaven was transferred, so that it might rule in harmony with the eternal order of things. And so, during the winter of 1643 to 1644, at Sianfu, when the people saw his standard they prostrated themselves, crying: "Long live the Emperor."

Meanwhile, Li Tzu-cheng trained his forces. Rebel chiefs con-tinued to join him. He completed the conquest of Kansu and Shensi, crossed the Yellow River and took P'ingyangfu, on the left bank, so that he had a bridgehead in Shansi. He put to death 300 members of the imperial clan whom he found in the city. In this way he announced that he was waging a relentless war that could end only with the destruction of one of the two contenders, and showed his contempt for a family abandoned by Heaven. On February 8, 1644, he proclaimed himself king. He called his dynasty "Tai-shun"—that is, "great compliance" (meaning "with the will of Heaven"). He then completed the construction of his government, on the model of the one in Peking. But he did better than that: he fitted his comrades into the higher strata of the old traditional society. He re-established the five ranks of the nobility. His comrade Liu Tsung-min, the former smith who had become a general, was given the title of marquis, along with nine others. Li Tzu-cheng also named seventy-three counts, thirty viscounts, and fifty-five barons. Peter would replace Paul, but society would remain the same.

Li Tzu-cheng had at that time at his disposal, it was said,

400,000 infantry and 600,000 cavalry. He conquered all Shansi, putting to death the prince of T'ai, Chu Chuan-ch'i and all the members of the imperial clan whom he found there. Ming generals and eunuchs rallied to him. He pressed on toward Peking. On April 24, 1644, the eunuch Ts'ao Hua-chun opened the Chang-i Men gate to him, and next day Peking was his. The emperor killed himself. On June 3 Li Tzu-cheng assumed the imperial title.

But Li Tzu-cheng's power was ephemeral. On June 4 he was in flight from the capital. During the thirty-seven days of his rule there, he was preoccupied with Wu San-kwei and with the Manchus. He was unable, moreover, to do as he wished. In practice he could act only with the assent of a council made up of his principal generals. "Why don't you help me be a good emperor?" he is said to have asked them. But they wanted to profit from their victory. Li Tzu-cheng's responsibility was thus perhaps a greatly diminished one for what occurred. Nevertheless, the behavior of the victorious rebels was disappointing. Peking was treated with severity. Each rebel soldier was assigned five families whose duty it was to keep him. Plundering, rape, fires, massacres, and suicides went on all the time. Li sent the eight hundred highest Ming officials to Liu Tsung-min, who had them tortured in order to get money out of them, and then slaughtered the whole lot. However, Li retained all the rest of the higher officials, and appointed others. He preserved the entire hierarchy of the public service, which was simultaneously a social hierarchy. He kept all the existing government offices. True, he changed their names, which may have been meant to symbolize an innovation. But the new names he gave them are not known. Above all it must be pointed out that he took not the slightest step that might have indicated he was going to carry out that division of the land about which his supporters had talked so much. His government showed itself very traditionalist and conservative.

But it did not last long. Still in being was the Chinese army of General Wu San-kwei, who was defending the most important pass, Shanhaikwan, against the Manchus. Li Tzu-cheng held Wu San-kwei's father, Wu Hsiang, as hostage. But then

Wu San-kwei learned that Liu Tsung-min had carried off his favorite concubine, Ch'en-Yüan. Furious, General Wu refused to accept the new supreme authority. Li Tzu-cheng marched against him with 200,000 men. Wu San-kwei decided to appeal for help to the Manchu prince Dorgon. The Manchus and Wu's forces, together, defeated Li Tzu-cheng on May 27, 1644. Li nevertheless proclaimed himself emperor on June 3. But the Manchus were for the first time masters of the principal pass leading into China, and their rear was safe. Peking could not be defended. Li had to flee from it, setting fire as he left to part of the palace and to the towers of the nine gates. The Manchus captured Peking on June 6. There is no evidence whatsoever of any rising by the masses in favor of Li Tzu-cheng and against the foreigner, either because the people were disappointed that the new master had not divided up the land or because his defeat had revealed to them that there had been a mistake, and Li had not in fact received the mandate of Heaven. The Manchus pursued Li into Shensi, and from there into Hupeh, and in the southeast of that province, at Mount Chiukung, in the canton of T'ungshan, in June or July, 1645, he was killed, it is said, by villagers while he was looking for food, accompanied by only a score of men.[21]

Meanwhile, Chang Hsien-chung had in 1643 proclaimed himself "King of the West." He had taken Wuchang, the capital of Hupeh Province, and tried to set up a government in Hupeh and Hunan, helped by certain members of the local elite who, seeing a change of regime on the way, wished to attach themselves to a leader who might prove successful. But the fortune of battle was not favorable to him, and the imperial General Tso Liang-yü recaptured Wuchang in September, 1643.

Chang then established his headquarters at Changsha. He kept his authority over the greater part of Hunan and extended it over part of central Kiangsi. He tried to set up a government there too. His officers urged him to turn eastward and invade Chekiang and Kiangsu, which, by their wealth and situation would have been more advantageous for his dynastic ambitions.

21. E. Hauer, *op. cit.*, *passim*. See also *ibid.*, "General Wu San-Kuei," *Asia Major*, 4 (1927), pp. 563–611.

But Chang feared Tso Liang-yü, and also Li Tzu-cheng. He decided to go westward and take over Szechwan, where he was more likely to be able to remain unchallenged master.

He concentrated his forces at Yuehchou, in Hunan. They numbered more than 100,000 men. In January, 1644, he began to move up the Yangtze. At that moment Li Tzu-cheng had become a terrible threat to the Ming power, and the Ming generals, unsure of the future, preferred not to compromise themselves. They allowed Chang Hsien-chung to pass, and he encountered hardly any resistance in the Yangtze gorges near Ichang, though these could have been easily denied to him. Chang reached Chungking without difficulty. The town magistrate, Ch'en Shih-ch'i, was demoralized by the fall of Peking and the Emperor Chung-Ch'en's suicide. In July Chang laid siege to Chungking. After several days of fighting with cannon and bows, the rebels dug a large hole in the town wall, filled it with gunpowder, and blew it up by means of a flaming arrow. The town was taken on July 25, 1644.

Chang proclaimed a reign of terror against the magistrates and the elite. He announced that if the people in the various localities arrested the magistrates, seized the granaries and offered no resistance to his forces, no harm would be done to them. Such a program made his conquest of the area as easy as "splitting a bamboo."

Chang occupied Chengtuhsien on September 9, 1644, and there put to death the prince of Shou, along with a number of magistrates. Several other magistrates submitted to him and later served in the government which Chang organized. The general continued to fight against the remains of the Ming forces, the bandit gangs, and the army of a general allied to Li Tzu-cheng. At the beginning of 1645 Chang was master of most of the country between Chengtuhsien and the borders of Shensi.

Chang gave his state the name of "Great Western Country." He sought to found a dynasty. He took as the title of his reign "Tai-Shun," that is, "Great Compliance," renamed Chengtu "Hsiching," "Western Capital," and went to live in the palace of the prince of Shou. He tried to organize a government, with a minister "of the right," a minister "of the left," a Grand Secretariat, six central boards, and so on, in conformity with the traditional model. Of the nine men appointed to these positions, four were *Chin-shih* and two held lower degrees. Seven were natives of Szechwan, retired magistrates or graduates awaiting an appointment. Yen Hsi-ming, the minister "of the right" and grand secretary, was a *Chin-shih* and a former magistrate. Wu Chi-shan, the chairman of the Board of Ceremonies, was also a *Chin-shih* and had been one of the magistrates at Chengtu when it fell. Two alone did not belong to the elite: Li Shih-ying, a Taoist priest, head of the Board of Punishments, and Wang Ling-lung, a maker of arrows, head of the Board of Public Works. The man with the most influence over Chang, however, Wang Chao-ling, minister "of the left" and also grand secretary, came from an important family in Anhwei Province.

Thus, Chang governed in accordance with tradition, employing the traditional forms and members of the elite as his officials. He organized examinations, minted money, distributed degrees and titles, reestablished the *pao-chia* system, and even granted a title to the elder son of the prince of Shou. Here, too, Peter replaced Paul but Chinese society remained as before. Many magistrates, both civil and military, felt able to emerge from their hiding places and dance attendance upon Chang.

He recruited a large number of men for his army in Szechwan. He drew up grandiose plans for the conquest of all China. He covered his generals with high-sounding titles. Then, suddenly, about the middle of 1645, he made a complete turnabout and launched a reign of terror. First and foremost, he wanted to go beyond mere guerrilla warfare. He wanted to drive back the Ming generals who were in theory subordinate to a commissary sent from the Ming Court at Nanking to reestablish order, but who in fact conducted themselves as "warlords" and operated as they chose and in their own interests. The most successful of these was a certain Tseng-ying who, in the spring of 1645, recaptured Chungking and defeated one of Chang's lieutenants. Chang also resorted to terror against his opponents in the army and among the people. He wanted to be king, or, still better, emperor of China, but he could not shake off the characteristics of the bandit leader from Shensi. Within his army the highest ranks went to natives of Shensi—his adopted son Sun K'o-wang, his close followers Li Ting-kuo, Ai Neng-ch'i, and Liu Wen-hsiu, who were all made generals. The people of Szechwan felt keenly their subordination, and clashes occurred between men of Szechwan and men of Shensi. Chang was still the conquering general, exploiting a conquered country. He did not become the sovereign uniting a society in conformity with the rules of distributive justice, putting each man in the place he should occupy in accordance with his talents, for the common good.[22]

Chang's generals found his policy of terror distasteful, and advised moderation. But the evil influence of Wang Chao-ling prevailed with Chang, for religious reasons. Chang Hsien-chung was convinced that the mission of Heaven was to kill, the reason for this being that "Heaven gives men a hundred different kinds of things, and men have nothing with which to serve Heaven." Chang said that he had received this message from a divine messenger, during a dream. People also attributed this saying to him: "Heaven favors the people with a hundred grains, but man offers not a single good deed to serve Heaven. Kill, kill, kill, kill, kill, kill, kill!" Chang believed that everyone on earth was behaving criminally, and so did not deserve to live, and that he himself was the incarnation of a star sent down to earth by the Jade Emperor to kill them all. Heaven had appointed Chang as its avenger.

Chang asked Wang Chao-ling for his advice on putting an end to plots and opposition to himself. Wang replied: "These fellows who carry lances and wield spears know only whether they have food to eat and clothes to wear. They know nothing else. If you just write a few lines and make believe that these express the will of Heaven, so as to deceive them, they will submit to you." One day when the sky was full of black clouds, thunder, lightning, and torrential rain, the whole town was under three meters of water. Thousands of tents pitched on both banks of the river had been carried away by the floods. Wang Chao-ling proclaimed: "When His Majesty ascended the throne,

22. J. B. Parsons, "The Culmination," *op. cit.*

he saw the order from Heaven in which it is written: 'In this world, people are disloyal and unfilial, and have committed great crimes; the heart of man is not in accord with the mind of Heaven. The great catastrophe has arrived. There is no cause to feel pity.' This proves that when His Majesty killed the soldiers and the people, that was really the natural consequence of their own crimes, and there is no way in which they can escape punishment. His Majesty is truly acting on behalf of Heaven, so as to cause Heaven's Way to triumph. All you magistrates and people must lift up your hearts and purify your minds, in order to endure the wrath of Heaven. If in future you continue to break the law, His Majesty will exterminate you in Heaven's name, and you will have no right to feel hatred and anger." The trick worked.

Chang Hsien-chung, an officer risen from the ranks, detested the graduates. He charged them with malice, dishonesty, greed, incompetence, and bigotry. He could stand them no longer. He murdered nearly all the magistrates and graduates of Szechwan. On one occasion he killed over two hundred lowly officials at the same time. On another, he announced the holding of examinations, and then when several thousand notables of Szechwan assembled in Chengtu he had them all massacred.[23]

The entire population suffered under his rule. Some historians speak of six million victims, others of six hundred million. At the time of the census of 1578, the region contained 262,694 households and 3,102,073 persons, of whom 679,355 were subject to taxation and labor services. The census of 1720, held under the Ts'ing Dynasty, showed 634,802 households, that is, nearly 7,291,000 persons. Chang had therefore not depopulated Szechwan. It is true that under the Ts'ings, many immigrants came there from Hupeh, Hunan, Shensi, Kiangsi, and Chekiang. Ten out of twenty-four inhabitants were immigrants; at Chengtu-hsien, between 1644 and 1722, among twenty-four residents, six had come from Shensi, two from Kansu, one from Honan, and one from Kweichow. It is noteworthy, though, that the dialect of Szechwan had survived and imposed itself on all, from which

23. V. Y. C. Shih, op. cit., pp. 214–215.

we can conclude that it had always been spoken by the majority, and immigrants had never been more than a minority. It can be estimated that two-thirds or three-quarters of the people of Szechwan had survived Chang's terror, and he could not have massacred more than a million persons.

Nevertheless, his terror antagonized the people. All but three of the chief magistrates had been killed or had committed suicide. Chang had no administrators left and did not know how to replace them. In those days rebels were obliged to have recourse to graduates to carry out public duties, and these graduates brought with them the old mode of thought, the traditional conception of social relations, especially where property and relations between landowners and tenants were concerned. No revolution could be made with graduates, but no state could exist without them. In 1646 Chang Hsien-chung's government had broken down. The dream of kingship had come to an end. Food was not to be had, for the plain of Chengtu had been completely plundered and depopulated and the peasants were in flight. In the autumn of 1646 Chang left Chengtuhsien.

He planned to go back to Shensi. He came to pitch his camp at Fenghwangshan, near Hsich'ung, in the valley of the Chialing. He had dispersed his troops among several camps. He wanted to collect supplies so as to be able to invade Shensi in the following spring. But one of his officers, Liu Ching-chung, a native of Szechwan, betrayed him. Liu went over to a Manchu army commanded by Haoge, and showed them the way to Chang's camp. Haoge swept down upon Chang with 5,000 Manchu horsemen. At first Chang refused the believe the report of his approach. When the Manchus appeared he could not restrain himself, but rushed out of his tent without either helmet or breastplate, seized a spear that was stuck in the ground, and hurled himself toward the enemy, accompanied by only a handful of men. The Manchus had halted on the far bank of a small stream. Liu Ching-chung pointed Chang out to a Manchu archer, who loosed his arrow and killed him. This was in January, 1647. So died Chang Hsien-chung, in fury and recklessness, as he had lived.

His army broke up. One part, led by Sun K'o-wang and his

other adopted sons, traversed Szechwan once more and reached Kweichow. Sun K'o-wang spread his authority over Yunnan, Kwangsi, and Hunan, entered the service of the Mings, betrayed them, tried to make himself emperor, was beaten in 1657 by one of Chang Hsien-chung's old followers, Li Ting-kuo, gave himself up to the Manchus, and died as a prince in Peking in 1660. Another part of Chang's army followed the above-mentioned Li Ting-kuo, who marched into Kweichow and, after several years of victories as a free-lance "warlord," entered the Ming service and waged a national war against the Manchus. He stayed loyal to the Ming Dynasty to the very end, fighting on without discouragement in spite of reverses. He accompanied the last Ming pretender, Chu Yu-leng, and even when the latter was forced to flee into Burma in 1659, he continued to put up a desperate resistance to the Manchus who pursued him there. When he learned that the Burmese had handed Chu Yu-leng over to the Manchus and that the last of the Mings had been put to death in 1661, by Wu San-kwei, now in the Manchu service, Li Ting-kuo fell ill and died, on August 7, 1662, adjuring his son and his last general never to surrender to the Manchus.[24]

But the dynastic and national struggles of the Mings against the new Manchu Dynasty of the Ts'ings, which was destined to last until the revolution of 1911 and to be the last imperial dynasty of China, are not our subject. Nor is the insurrection of General Wu San-kwei, between 1673 and 1681, contemporaneous with the French revolts in Brittany and Bordeaux in 1675. The revolt of Wu San-kwei seems to have been that of a powerful feudatory of the Manchus who exercised royal powers and was unwilling to give them up, and not a popular movement.[25]

The Manchu Ts'ing Dynasty superimposed domination by the Manchus upon the traditional order of China, and, apart from this new racial factor, everything in China remained as though the rebellions of the first half of the century had not occurred.

24. W. Hummel, op. cit., II, p. 679; I, pp. 489–490.
25. Chao-ying Fang, "Wu San-kwei," W. Hummel, op. cit., II, pp. 877–880. See also E. Hauer, "General Wu San Kwei," Asia Major, 4 (1927), pp. 563–611.

CONCLUSION

A COMPARISON OF
THE PEASANT REVOLTS IN
FRANCE, RUSSIA, AND CHINA

In 1661, Robert Mentet de Salmonet explained the revolts of his century, referring to: "The Disobedience of the first Man which brought Disorder and Death into the World . . . Man having rebell'd against his Creator, was deprived of the Empire of the World with which he had been invested in the Earthly Paradise. Then all the Creatures rebelled against him and acknowledg'd him no more. He soon felt yet a more dangerous Revolt within himself; for that precious Gift of original Righteousness, that Curb which kept the inferior Part of his Soul subject to the Superior, having been taken off, his Passions, like Horses broke loose, no longer gave Ear to the Voice of Reason: and the Elements, whereof his Body is compos'd, and which, for his Sake, had forgotten their natural Enmity, resum'd their former Hatred, and never left off making War upon one another, till that admirable Edifice was reduc'd to Dust. 'Tis from this intestine Revolt, that Men are become like Wolves that devour one another, and, as the Apostle describes them, they are altogether unjust, covetous, wicked, Murderers, quarrelsome, deceitful and malicious; Besides they are Haters of God, Backbiters, outrageous, full of pride, Inventers of new Mischiefs, Rebels against their Fathers and Mothers, and void of natural Affection. . . ."

And he adds: ". . . As for Societies and Commonwealths, they were not form'd out of any Principle of mutual Love, but through the Fear that Men were in of one another. For as they all coveted the same Things, and likewise thought that they had an equal Right to enjoy them, from thence proceeded Quarrels and Discord. In order to remedy that, they agreed to regulate themselves by establishing certain Laws, and by a Form of Government that might secure them from the Violence and Oppression which they were mutually afraid of from their corrupt Passions, whence, says the Holy Scripture, proceed Wars and Dissensions amongst Men. However, this Policy, which they establish'd amongst themselves, did not prevent their Iniquities and Lewdness from increasing in proportion as they multiply'd upon the Earth: in so much that the World has, in a Manner, been always nothing but a horrible and bloody Theatre of their Rapine and Murders. . . ."[1]

Mentet's explanation of the origin of communities is open to doubt, since man has always existed in society and cooperation is as natural as rivalry. But his explanation of revolts is excellent. The underlying cause of seditions, and of what gives rise to them, is original sin and man's refusal to obey the commandments of God.

But understanding the "why" of phenomena does not relieve us of the task of discovering the "how."

Revolts and Circumstances

The immediate and proclaimed motive of the revolts was, in the majority of cases, in France, the burden of taxation imposed by the state. Increased taxes, new taxes, taxes collected more strictly—those provide the acknowledged reasons for rebellion. This is true, in France, of the numberless instances we know of where people refused to assess themselves or pay their taxes, the numberless acts of violence committed against tax collectors, bailiffs, process servers, their assistants, and the fusiliers sent to back them up, which constituted the first stages of revolt, the refusal to obey. Then too, for the second stage, riots, and

1. *Histoire des troubles de la Grande-Bretagne* (Paris, 1661; English trans. by Ogilvie, *The History of the Troubles of Great Britain*, London, 1735, Preface, p. i).

the third, risings in arms, in 1629, in Angoumois and Saintonge; in 1630 in Dijon, Aix-en-Provence, Brignolles, Draguignan, and Grasse; between 1629 and 1632 in Languedoc; in 1635 in Bordeaux, Périgueux, Agen; in 1636 in Saintonge, Angoumois, and Poitou, in 1637 in Périgord; in 1637, 1638, and 1639 throughout Normandy; in 1675 in Bordeaux and Brittany. In Russia state taxation was also a heavy burden and was certainly one of the underlying causes of the revolts, which were also in some cases immediately set off by some attempted fiscal trick, such as the salt outbreak in Moscow in 1648, or by a currency swindle for fiscal purposes, like the copper outbreak in Moscow in 1662. The large-scale revolts do not seem, however, to have had taxation as their immediate cause. The revolt during the Time of Troubles was due to the famine of 1601–1603, and as for the revolt of 1670, it was the anabasis of Stenka Razin that brought the people's despair and resentment to a head. In China too, increased tax burdens were a cause of revolt. It was a fiscal measure, the abolition of the postal service in 1629, that drove thousands of people to resort to banditry in Shensi, and it was the severity with which taxes were collected that intensified the revolts of 1637 and 1640, though in these instances a big part seems also to have been played by natural disasters.

The increase in the tax burden was beyond all imagining. In France, in the *généralité* of Bordeaux, the chief direct tax, the taille, rose to a million between 1610 and 1632, doubled in 1634–1635, was three times as much by 1644, and four times as much by 1648, on the eve of the Fronde. In addition, there were supplements to the *taillon* levied for the upkeep of the regiments, from 1636 onward there was the *subsistances* tax for the army, and from 1641 the *étapes* tax for the benefit of troops marching through a region—all this regardless of a deluge of indirect taxes or *aides* and an avalanche of domanial taxes. The lists that can be made from the records of these impositions on the people are still capable of causing the scholar who draws them up to clench his fists, however blasé about poverty and wretchedness he may be.

The tax burden was made still more unendurable by the way it was collected. Officially, the revenue officials were supposed to charge *taxations,* that is, sums proportional to the taxes due, and added to these. When these commissions had been levied by all the various strata of revenue officials, they amounted to 47 percent of the total amount paid by the taxpayers—or in other words, it meant that the tax was almost doubled. Records of lawsuits show that some revenue officials took even more than this in *taxations.* It must not be forgotten that the number of these officials had been greatly increased by the creation of new offices and of new revenue districts. These innovations had the double advantage of obtaining more money for the government by the sale of offices and making possible a closer watch on the taxpayer.

Faced with the resistance to the payment of taxes, the state resorted to collecting them by process of law. This meant that the charges of the bailiffs and process servers had to be met. The taxpayers were unable to pay, and so the process servers and their men carried out ruinous seizures of their goods, removing even their cattle, their plows, their doors and windows. In order to force the taxpayers to pay, the government billeted soldiers with them, which completed the taxpayers' ruin.

Phenomena comparable to these occurred in Russia, where the staff of government offices, at their various levels, gained the worst possible reputation, and in China, where the runners, the magistrates' assistants, and many of the magistrates themselves were notorious.

There seem to have been two main reasons for this increase in the pressure of taxation. The first, and by far the most important, was the frequency of national wars and the standing need to defend lengthy frontiers; very far behind came the internal troubles themselves, which necessitated keeping armies in the field. In the budgets of the period, military expenditure forms the principal item on that side, and absorbs the bulk of the state's resources. The second reason was the development of the organs of the state itself, which was becoming more and more centralized and administrative in character—the increase in the number of its agents, through whom alone it could be effective. Professor Trevor-Roper was right to see in this one of the causes of the revolts of the seventeenth century, though wrong to see in the financial burden a result of the expansion of princely courts, and in the state machine the *chief* cause both of the ruining of countries and of the revolts.[2] The expenditure of the king's Court declined in France under Louis XIII.[3] In China, under the last Ming emperors, it was certainly very much on the increase, and in Russia it also probably increased under Tsars Mikhail and Aleksei. In any case, however, this Court expenditure, though it is spectacular and strikes the imagination because it may seem to have served little useful purpose (a point open to discussion), formed only a small part of the state's total expenditure. Expenditure on the state's agents constituted but a modest proportion of this total. During the infrequent periods of peace in France, for instance in 1669, the cost of the Court and of the various royal and princely households amounted to 16 percent of the state's total expenditure, whereas expenditure on the army and navy amounted to almost half. In wartime—the normal situation—however, Court expenses made up only 5 or 6 percent of the total, while military expenditure rose to 80 percent. It should be pointed out, moreover, that a large part, sometimes three-fifths, of Court expenses went for gifts or pensions which paid for services rendered, or which kept peaceful those great lords, with their followers, who, if they had risen in revolt, would have cost the state and its subjects more than the government paid them in this way. It is hard to consider these expenses as being useless. All this relates to France. I lack information as exact as this for Russia and China, but I am inclined to think the situation was similar.

The costs of the armies were not covered by what the taxpayers provided in taxes. In France, when the troops were marching through a region, or were taking up winter quarters there, every person liable to pay the taille had to provide lodging for one or more soldiers, in proportion to the amount written against his name in the taille roll. He had to provide these soldiers

2. H. R. Trevor-Roper, "The general crisis of the seventeenth century," *Past and Present*, 16 (1959), and the discussion by R. Mousnier, J. H. Elliott, *et. al.*, in *ibid.*, 18 (1960). Reprinted in T. Aston (ed.), *Crisis in Europe (1560–1660)* (London, 1965), pp. 59 and 97.

3. R. Mousnier, *La Vénalité des offices sous Henri IV et Louis XIII* (Rouen, 1945), p. 408.

with *l'ustensile*, that is, "bed, table linen, pot, bowl, glass, room by his fire and by his candle." The soldiers were supposed to purchase the food they needed. In practice, however, the people gave them what they asked for, calculated the cost according to an official price list, and were reimbursed by the municipality, which levied a charge proportional to the taille. In practice, too, the soldiers lived at their own discretion, which meant with the uttermost indiscretion, and when their pay was late they behaved like savages. Even in friendly country they robbed, plundered, and burned. The passage of an army, or its halting for a time, was as a rule a literally devastating experience for the district concerned. Hatred of the soldiers was general. This was true also in Russia and China.

In addition, the provinces had to keep the army's storehouses supplied with food and other stores. The towns had to furnish boats, carts, horses and mules, which meant a serious drain on the productive capacity of the population. They had to look after the wounded, and the Spanish and Italian prisoners. The communities had to provide men for the militia, and every summer a contingent of soldiers was raised from the militia for the army. Bordeaux had to provide 300 men in 1638, and another 300 in 1639, which was a lot of men to be taken away from the crafts and agriculture at a time when work was carried on slowly and by hand, and every worker counted. *Bailliages* and *sénéchaussées* had to equip these men, supply their weapons and ammunition, and pay them for their first month of service. The communities thus burdened could not help falling into debt.

In those localities where the castles were that Richelieu ordered to be razed to the ground, this work of demolition was the responsibility of the local communities. In some cases, a parish had to pay three or four times as much for this purpose as the amount of their taille obligation.

It was indeed the armies that were the principal cause of the increased tax burden and brought most ruin to the places through which they passed.

This extra burden fell upon the peasants at the moment when their capacity to pay taxes was reduced. Seventeenth-century France suffered a long economic recession. Trade with Spanish

America declined more and more. The imports of precious metal from over there slowed down and by 1650 amounted to very little. Probably as a result of this, there was a slackening in the increase in prices which had gone on for a century, until 1630, then a stagnation in the general level of prices between 1630 and 1640, followed by a fall, the lowest point being reached between 1675 and 1685. The producers, peasants and craftsmen, got lower and lower prices for the goods they sold and found it harder and harder to obtain the money they needed in order to pay their taxes. Toward the end of the century we find traces of recovery, in the textile industry of Flanders and Picardy, for instance. One must avoid excessive generalization, in any case, in this conection. The regions near the sea seem to have been less affected by the recession, or even to have been spared by it. At Saint-Malô the port's activity even increased. But it also seems that the influence of the ports was little felt in the interior of the country, that a small group of merchants were the main gainers by maritime trade, and that for the peasants the recession was a reality. In Russia, on the other hand, the century seems to have been one of all-around economic growth, in production of consumer goods, and in commercial activity. But Russia was merely recovering the ground lost during the second half of the sixteenth century and in the Time of Troubles, and there is also the question of who the gainers were. With the development of serfdom, it would not seem to have been the peasants. China's trade, both external and internal, had certainly progressed during the sixteenth century, thanks to the coming of the Japanese silver brought in from Japan by the Portuguese since 1542 and the American silver which arrived by the agency of the Spaniards established at Manila. Chinese silk and gold were exchanged for Japanese silver; Chinese silk, porcelain, and rhubarb for American silver. Foreign trade increased until about from 1622 to 1624 and certainly helped in developing the Chinese merchants' corporations and bringing about the growth of the great centers where silk and porcelain were made—Soochow and Chingtechen. Later, American silver became scarcer. The struggle between the Dutch on the one hand and the Portuguese and Spaniards on the other may not, in itself, have reduced the total amount of trade, but the increasing closure of Japan to the Europeans, more or less complete by 1642, when the Dutch alone were tolerated, on the islet of Deshima, in Nagasaki Bay, brought it down to very little. Chinese junks were still allowed to frequent Japanese ports. They had always, almost from the moment when the Chinese followed the Portuguese to Japan, been more numerous there than the European vessels. But from 1622 down to about 1650 the trade carried on by the junks between China, Japan, and the Philippines slumped, while piracy increased. A period of trade depression began. For China too, moreover, the question arises of who the gainers were. The chief ones do not seem to have been the peasants and craftsmen.[4]

What was worst was the damaging effect of the large-scale atmospheric calamities, with their consequences of bad harvests, shortages, and epidemics (what the French of the time called *mortalités*), which disrupted economic life. In China between about 1622 and about 1650, famine was recurrent, population fell, and the economy was on the decline. In France the great *mortalités* were those of 1630–1632 (almost coinciding with the famines of 1628–1630 in Shensi), of 1648–1653, at the time of the Fronde, of 1661–1663, of 1693–1694, and of 1709–1710. In the intervals between them, natural calamities of a less serious or more localized character occurred. The ones that had the biggest effect were those which affected the production of grain crops, the basis of the people's food: in the case of wheat, rye, and barley, excessive rainfall in the summer months, which flattened the fields and made the grain germinate, and rotted the hay; in continental or northern climates, in Russia, excessively hard winters when the seed froze in the ground; for rice, delay in the coming of the monsoon and too dry a summer, which burned up the plants and encouraged invasion by locusts.

Let us take an example from France, from Guyenne. In 1627 the rivers overflowed. In 1628 temperatures were unusually low. Difficulties began. The winter of 1629 was hard and increased the cost of living. In March, 1630, torrential rains drowned the grain crops, and there was no harvest that year. In 1631 famine set in. It was all the more serious in the lower Garonne Valley

4. R. Mousnier, *Les XVIᵉ et XVIIᵉ Siècles* (Vol. 4, *Histoire générale des civilisations*, ed. Crouzet; 4th ed. 1965), II, 3, pp. 567–599.

because the growing of vines was already predominant there, grain and leguminous crops being relegated to the easily flooded meadows. In the Bazadais there was hardly any land in wheat. The district did not quickly recover from this, for between 1629 and 1639, hailstorms also ruined the vines, along the middle course of the Garonne and in the Charente country. The disaster had a lot to do with the way the people of Angoumois, Saintonge, and Guyenne reacted to taxation in 1635 and 1636. Spring showers ruined the land and devastated the soil in Armagnac, Lomagne, and the Condomois, where half of the inhabitants were reduced to beggary.

This famished population offered an easy prey to epidemics. Around 1625, Europe was overrun by a very serious plague. It reached Burgundy in 1626 and from there spread to the Loire Valley and Normandy, where it ravaged the areas which were to be the scene of the great revolts of 1639—Rouen (from 1630 onward), Avranches, Coutances, Caen. The plague reached the central regions of France and Languedoc in 1628, Agen and the Garonne Valley in 1629, then La Rochelle, and eventually the whole of Saintonge. The deadliest period was the summer of 1631. After that the sickness became less violent in its on-slaughts, but continued to find victims, with occasional sudden increases in intensity, and in 1652–1653 there was a new epidemic, as bad as that of 1631. These epidemics had lasting consequences. The first of them was the destruction of the producers them-selves, for the craftsmen and peasants, being less well fed, were hit harder than the other groups of society. Often, such was the shortage of men that it was no longer possible to get the harvest in, and the epidemic made famine worse, or even caused it. At Moissac the average mortality was twenty-three a year, but in the summer of 1629 there were fifty-five deaths. At Caprais-de-l'Herme about four people died in a normal year, but in 1631 there were a hundred and eighteen deaths. It was not unusual for a third of the population to be carried off during one of these *mortalités*. Another result was the interruption to trade. The well-to-do fled to their houses in the countryside. The municipali-ties banned outsiders from entering the towns, suspended fairs and markets, and refused to accept goods coming from outside. The surviving producers were unable to find outlets for their goods. Paralysis gripped the entire economy for a certain period.

Bad weather—excessively cold winters, cold and wet summers, or droughts—was so frequent in the seventeenth century that historians have wondered whether there may not have been a change in the climate. Contemporaries themselves sometimes asked this question. Shivering in June and July, 1675, the year of the stamped-paper revolts, Madame de Sévigné wrote to her daughter, Madame de Grignan, who was shivering no less in Provence, and the marquise speculated "whether the behavior of the sun and of the seasons may have changed."[5] Historians have checked this hypothesis by using three methods: studying the documents on the advance and retreat of glaciers, their advance indicating a series of cold winters; studying the proclamations by which the municipalities opened the grape-gathering season, because an unusually early start for this indicates a hot summer, and an unusually late one a cool summer—which in Western Europe means also a wet one; the study, finally, of cross sections of very old trees, because each ring corresponds to a period when the tree put forth leaves, and the larger or smaller width of the ring shows whether this period was a more or less favorable one. The outcome of these researches is that it appears that for about two millennia the climate has not changed as to its broad lines. After about 1550, however, there was a glacial spate in Europe which reached its highest point from 1599 to 1602, the time when in Russia the seed froze in the ground and when the great revolt against Boris Godunov occurred. This phenomenon continued at a high level, with spurts in 1608–1610, 1641–1644, 1664 and 1676–1679. The glaciers advanced and covered fields and meadows and even sometimes villages, which vanished from the tax rolls. These spurts followed periods when the grape harvest was late, that is, cool and wet summers, which were as unfavorable for grain crops as for vines, between 1591 and 1602 (the period which includes 1601, a "green year" in Russia, when torrential rain stopped the grain from ripening), between 1606 and 1609, between 1639 and 1644, the time of the great revolt of the *Nu-Pieds*, between 1646 and 1652, 1662 and 1663, 1672 and 1677, and especially, between 1673 and 1675, the period when the stamped-paper revolts broke out. Cold and wet summers, storms in June and July, destroyed both corn and grapes and brought shortage and dearth in their train. These periods were interrupted by series of hot, dry summers that were very favorable to grain crops and vines; in France, for example, the years 1635 to 1639. When, however, weather troubles did not spoil a "good" summer, the abundance of the harvests of corn and wine entailed a misfortune of a different kind: sale of the produce at a loss, collapse of prices, difficulty experienced by the producer in obtaining the cash needed to pay taxes and dues in money. A very favorable summer could be a cause of crisis.

Let me say that, taking a longer view, the seventeenth century does not seem to have been worse off, as regards weather, than the eighteenth or the first half of the nineteenth. The glaciers continued to be well advanced, with some big forward thrusts, the one in 1742–1745 apparently being as substantial as that of 1599–1602. After the middle of the eighteenth century the glaciers start to weaken, but they continue to be very strong, with a last general spurt between 1840 and 1850. Only after 1850 do they enter a period of large-scale retreat, which is still going on now.[6] The climate of the eighteenth century seems to some historians to have been as bad as that of the seventeenth. The effects of the "bad" years may have been greater in the seventeenth century owing to the great wars, the armies, the massive taxes which ate up reserves, the fall in prices and the economic recession. The "bad" years may have been felt less acutely in the eighteenth century because, from 1730 on, the long-term increase in prices may have revived the economy, which also benefited from colonial trade, and above all, perhaps, because less numerous and less serious wars (fought, moreover, far from the national soil) may have had less effect on the life of France. All of which is plausible, but I must say I am not convinced. During a long period, which looks rather uniform if the principal phenomena are considered from a distance, there may well occur a number of small, short-term variations which are

6. E. Leroy-Ladurie, "Histoire et climat," *Annales E.S.C.*, 13 (1959), pp. 3–35; "Climat et récoltes aux XVII° et XVIII° siècles," *ibid.*, 15 (1960), pp. 434–465.

decisive in the daily lives of the people. A few days of torrential rain or a few days of sunshine, at the moment when
the crops are coming to ripeness, are enough to make the differences between a good harvest and a bad one, or vice versa.
The summers of 1635 to 1639 were hot, and therefore favorable to
corn and vines, but the dates of the grape harvests, where these
took place, tell us nothing about the devastation of the soil by
the spring rains in Armagnac, Lomagne, and the Condomois,
which had canceled in advance the salutary effect of the "good
summer," or about the hailstorms that ruined the vines in the
Charente country. Other documentation on long-term movements leaves out too many small but repeated events which we
need to know about if we are to understand repeated crises
and revolts. Much further study will be necessary before we can
come to a definitive judgment, one way or the other, as to
whether the seventeenth century climate was worse than usual.
I think it was worse. What is certain is that it was not good for
the grain and vine-growing agriculture of those days.

Famines and epidemics coming together led to lasting impoverishment. Two or three bad harvests, and half of the inhabitants of the rural parishes, the very small peasants, were reduced to misery. Some became vagabonds and beggars. Houses
were abandoned and villages deserted. In 1634 the village of
Espaignet had only six people left. Some villages were entirely
emptied of people and left dead, at least for a time.[7] Then,
numerous bands of the people concerned made their way from
Limousin and Auvergne toward Poitou, Angoumois, and Périgord,
and from Quercy and Rouergue toward the Garonne. In 1628, six
thousand poor people who had come from Limousin crowded
at the gates of Périgueux and congested the suburbs of the town.
The land remained uncultivated and its value fell. Small landowners sold their land at ridiculously low prices. The communities got themselves into debt in their efforts to look after
the sick and feed the hungry. And these phenomena were all
the more serious, because their effects were cumulative, one

7. *Villages désertés et histoire économique, XI–XVIII° siècles* (École
Pratique des Hautes Études, VI° section, Centre de Recherches historiques,
S.E.V.P.E.N., 1965).

"mortalité" occurring before the consequences of the preceding one had been made good. From 1630 onward, France was in a situation of increasing economic difficulty. After 1662, during a period the bulk of which coincides with Colbert's ministry, there was real distress, with an actual shortage of manpower. All these misfortunes taken together lay behind the endemic condition of disturbance in which the great revolts matured. In France the troubles multiplied and intensified after 1635, with the country's entry into open war with Spain. Historians have found an increasing number of lawsuits arising from armed assaults—on tax collectors by persons subject to the taille, who also attacked persons exempt from paying taille, by entire villages on other villages alleged to be favored by the *élus* and the *trésoriers de France,* attacks on process servers and bailiffs. Gentlemen, barons, and lords were put under arrest for such actions and for having led peasants in revolt against the tax authorities. Elsewhere we find food riots of the classic kind, often spontaneous on the part of popular elements, such as craftsmen's wives, to prevent grain being sent away, or on account of the high price of bread, or for the purpose of plundering the grain stocks belonging to ecclesiastics. On other occasions there were spontaneous riots against the military and scuffles with the soldiers. On July 8, 1640, a company of light horse was proceeding at dusk near the village of Les Granges. Convinced that the soldiers intended to take up billets in the village, the peasants armed themselves with pikes and muskets and attacked them. From brawls and affrays and a state of semirevolt the people went over to open and organized revolt. In France, though there were bandits, the phenomenon of banditry does not appear to have developed on the Russian or Chinese scale. Shorter distances; a population denser than in Russia; a larger area of the land under occupation than in China, thanks to the greater use made of the mountains and forests, through the combination of agriculture and stockbreeding, almost unknown to the Chinese, who were more exclusively agriculturists, or even gardeners; above all, social and territorial structures stronger than in the two other countries, with many towns and communities, moral personalities which kept their autonomy, many intermediate strata, different cate-

gories of townspeople, a real trading *bourgeoisie*, numerous and wealthy; in the countryside of open oblong fields, a powerful stratum of *laboureurs*, farmers, and capitalist entrepreneurs who provided leadership for the peasants; a country more deeply penetrated by trade and commercial capitalism, giving rise to manufactories, with a greater number and variety of activities, more resources; the comparatively large number of royal officials, in the fields of justice and of finance, well organized in hierarchical corporations—all these factors explain the slighter development of banditry. Nevertheless, it would be interesting to see to what extent one can compare to the Russian and Chinese "bandits" those numerous gentlemen of France who practiced armed salt-smuggling at the head of groups of peasants, or those peasant leaders like the famous Grelety, of the forest of Vergt.

It will be seen how much circumstances—conjuncture in the broadest sense of the term—contribute to account for the revolts. It may even be asked if the latter was not essentially due to conjunctions of circumstances. Some historians have blamed social or political structures, the modern absolutist state, "feudal" society. Is it necessary to do this? It is noteworthy that between 1815 and 1848, when allegedly feudal society, the seignorial order, feudal rights and the absolute monarchy no longer existed, there were still peasant movements in France, in times of shortage. These movements grew less frequent during the nineteenth century, when the increase in fodder plants (which suffer no ill effects from summer rain) and the increase in stock-breeding made agriculture less susceptible to cold, wet summers; when railways and steamships, faster and with bigger carrying capacity than earlier vehicles, enabled countries where the harvest was good to come to the aid of those where it was inadequate. Technical progress improved the situation more than social changes did.[8]

8. R. Mousnier, "Recherches sur les soulèvements populaires en France, avant la Fronde," *Revue d'histoire moderne et contemporaine*, IV (1958), p. 100; "Les mouvements populaires en France au XIXe siècle," *Revue des Travaux de l'Academie des Sciences morales et politiques*, Ier trim. (1962), pp. 28–43.

If one were to say: "Circumstances suffice to explain the peasant revolts in these three countries in the seventeenth century. Similar conditions would have provoked such outbreaks in any kind of society, would have brought about crises of despair like these anywhere at all, and, consequent upon them, sudden and repeated explosions of anger; the social structures are not to blame," one would be putting forward an idea which, though perhaps mistaken, has nothing scandalous about it, and deserves careful examination.

Revolts and Social Structures

Explanations of these revolts by reference to the social and political structure have already been put forward. The British historian Trevor-Roper, considering in particular the European political revolutions between 1640 and 1660, thought that they marked the end of the Renaissance and the beginning of the Age of Enlightenment, that they were themselves the culmination of a prolonged crisis in the structures of society. The Renaissance state, with its Court and its bureaucratic apparatus of agents who were paid, to a certain extent, by what they took for themselves, weighed too heavily upon society. This burden became unbearable during the economic recession of the seventeenth century, and various social groups endeavored to get it off their backs by way of revolt and revolution. The estates rebelled against the Court. The latter tried not only to break the rebellions but also to remove the cause of them by adjusting, through mercantilism, the charges of the bureaucrats against the resources of the country. In answer to Trevor-Roper it has been pointed out that expenditure on the Court and the agents of the state was not the heaviest item of expenditure, that members of the Court and royal officials were the principal rebels, and that mercantilism was first and foremost an instrument of war against foreign states.

For Marxist-Leninist historians, whether in the U.S.S.R. or in other countries of Eastern Europe, the revolts were due to the conflict between two "class fronts." The societies where the revolts occurred were split in two. On one side were those who worked with their hands—workers and peasants, the exploited; on the other, those who had the power to command—nobles, officials, ecclesiastics, bourgeois (merchants or *rentiers*)—the exploiters, who were united under the protection of the absolute monarchy against the exploited. "Unlimited exploitation of peasant labor power" was, it appears, "the objective essence of the absolute state," the function it served. Spontaneously, the exploited masses rose up. It has been objected that the existence of "social classes" is questionable in societies of this type; that all social groups, or almost all, suffered from these periods of war and poverty; that there were rebels in all the social groups; that most of the revolts suggest a *vertical* cleavage in society, with persons of all social strata in both camps, that of rebellion and that of the government; that the cooperation between social groups seems to be more fundamental than their conflict; that the role of the absolute state was to reduce everyone, all social groups, to obedience, for the advantage of the public weal.

Many arguments have been exchanged for and against each of these theories. It seems to me that nothing is gained for our knowledge of these societies and these revolts by prolonging the polemic. I therefore content myself with a note listing the principal books and articles that may be of interest to the reader who wants to know more about this discussion.[9]

9. H. R. Trevor-Roper, *op. cit.*; and discussion of this article by R. Mousnier, J. H. Elliott *et al.*, *op. cit.*, reprinted in T. Aston (ed.), *op. cit.*; R. Mousnier, *La Vénalité*, *op. cit.*; B. Porchnev, *Les Soulèvements populaires en France de 1623 à 1648* (Russian ed., 1948; French ed., 1963; École Pratique des Hautes Etudes, VIᵉ section, Oeuvres étrangères, IV, S.E.V.P.E.N.); R. Mousnier, "Recherches," *op. cit.*, and "Les mouvements," *op. cit.*, 2e trim. (1962); *Lettres et Mémoires adressés au chancelier Séguier (1633–1649)*, Publications de la Faculté des Lettres et Sciences humaines de Paris, series "Textes et Documents," Vols. VI and VII (Paris, P.U.F., 1964), notably pp. 187–192; L. Yaresh, "The 'peasant wars' in Soviet historiography," *American Slavic and East European Review*, XVI (1957), pp. 241–259; V. V. Mavrodin, "Soviet Historical Literature and on the Peasant Wars in Russia During the 17th and 18th Centuries," trans. from *Voprosy Istorii*, 1961, No. 5, in *Soviet Studies in History* (Fall, 1962), I, 2, pp. 43–63; J. B. Parsons, "Attitudes towards the last Ming rebellions," *Oriens Extremus*, 6 (1959), pp. 177–205, notably pp. 199–205; V. Y. C. Shih, "Some Chinese rebel ideologies," *T'oung Pao*, 44 (1956), pp. 150–226, notably pp. 218–226; A. Feuerwerker, "From Feudalism to Capitalism in Recent Historical Writing from Mainland China," *Journal of Asian Studies*, XVIII (1958–1959),

*   *   *

Let us now reexamine the accounts we have given of the revolts, asking a few simple questions. First of all, who began these revolts? Did those who began them act spontaneously? A movement is spontaneous if its author acts for himself, without being forced or pushed or incited by another human will—some would even say, without the operation of his own will, but by a sort of reflex action.

The France of Henry IV, after 1598, can be regarded as being in a period of calm. Those who took up arms again, carried out a kind of secession, and reopened the civil wars were the princes, Bouillon, Longueville, Mayenne, Condé, in 1615, and then the Protestant nobility, in repeated revolts, down to the Peace of Alais in 1629, and the queen mother and her followers down to the time she was sent into exile. The Parlement de Paris, the other sovereign courts and the whole corporation of office-holders gave the example of refusal to obey, the first phase of rebellion; they were the first to cry out against the despotism and tyranny of the government, and to proclaim—beginning with the famous remonstrances of May 22, 1615—the right of the Parlement de Paris to intervene in politics and to bring together the dukes, peers, and officers of the Crown to discuss the state's affairs. It was these bodies of magistrates who proclaimed the right to resistance, stating that, while they acknowledged that they owed the king fealty and therefore obedience, as a rule, they also owed it to their consciences to show respect for their professional integrity, from which followed their right to refuse obedience to royal orders that were contrary to this; that they owed it to justice to show respect for her dignity,

---

pp. 107–115, especially pp. 110–111. See a bibliography of the polemic on the French revolts, in the review of Porchnev's book by Y. M. Bercé, *Bibliothèque de l'École de Chartes*, 122 (1964), p. 354. E. Molnar, *Les fondements économiques et sociaux de l'absolutisme* (with France as example), Comité International des Sciences Historiques, 12th International Congress of Historical Studies, Vienna, Aug. 29–Sept. 5, 1965. *Rapports, IV, Méthodologie et histoire contemporaine* pp. 115–169, Verlag Ferdinand Berger und Söhne, Horn, Vienna, Austria, 1965. In this paper there is a mistake in every line: see the criticisms in the separate volume of the transactions of the Congress (V, *Actes*, pp. 675–703).

so that it was incumbent upon them to maintain good relations between the king and his subjects, if necessary protecting the latter from the king's government. It was these bodies that multiplied the criticisms which were spread widely among the public by means of the printed word and of sermons from church pulpits, and amplified by innumerable pamphlets against the royal "favorites," ministers of state, councils, and usurpers of the royal authority; against wars which were unjustified, or worse, sacrilegious, because directed against a Spain which played the role of champion of Catholicism, and which were prolonged beyond all necessity in order to give pretexts for despotism and for the squandering, luxury, and extortions of an army of "creatures," courtiers, financiers and tax-farmers, all of them leeches and harpies sucking the people's blood. Furthermore, a great number of pamphlets and sermons had taught the French that princes and magistrates had the right to rise in revolt against a tyrant, enemy of religion and oppressor of the people, and that when this happened it was the duty of all to give them support.[10] Surrounded by these examples, offered from above, of armed revolts and refusals to obey, and this flood of criticisms of "tyranny" expressed by grave personages who had about them "something holy and venerable," with all these campaigns of incitement going on, how is it possible to affirm that a riot or revolt by peasants or craftsmen was absolutely spontaneous, even when we have no documentary evidence of immediate instigation by another social group? All the anger and resentment provoked, aroused, amplified, and given direction by this propaganda expressed itself suddenly in crises of fury, sparked off by incidents that, though sometimes trivial in themselves, were symbolic, providing an immediate cause for violent outbursts of feeling, the underlying reason for which was the association between the ideas of injustice, impiety, sacrilege, and tyranny and certain deeds of the royal agents, an association established by the propaganda of the princes, the officials, and the "good Catholics." There can therefore be no question of complete spontaneity.

In addition, moreover, in many cases the documents themselves ascribe the initiative to others than the peasants and craftsmen.

10. R. Mousnier, *L'Assassinat d'Henri IV*, collection "Trente journées qui ont fait la France" (Paris, Gallimard, 1964).

For these petty acts of resistance, refusals to pay taxes and assaults on tax collectors, which the documents suggest were numerous, though we have no actual statistics, the correspondence of the government's agents puts the blame on the gentlefolk. Throughout the kingdom, they say, it was the country gentlemen who incited the peasants to refuse to pay the taxes, who gave refuge to their flocks and chattels, when threatened with confiscation, in their castles and fortified houses, who incited the peasants to offer armed resistance, and who often themselves headed the peasants when they drove away the process servers who came, accompanied by soldiers and fusiliers, to levy taxes or billet troops.

Some important popular revolts do indeed seem to have been unleashed by the nobility and by the magistrates, both royal and municipal. During the years 1628 and 1629, in Saintonge, it was the assembled nobles who provoked the peasants' riots against tax collectors, tax-farmers' agents, and finance officials living in the towns who had estates in the countryside. The leaders of the rioters were squireens and "chief persons in the market towns." At Aix-en-Provence, in 1630, it was the king's officials and the consuls who began the troubles by going on strike, and then the officials, advocates, and bourgeois who took to the streets in arms, stirring up the craftsmen to follow them. Later, it was members of the local parlement who brought about the intervention of the peasants in the struggle. In 1637 and 1638, at Carentan, in Normandy, it was the "chief persons" of the town who incited the humble people to revolt. At Périers the royal judge urged the peasants to arm themselves and attack the soldiers. In the county of Mortain, the gentlemen surrounded the companies of soldiers. At Caen, Mortain, Coutances, the finance officers, the *élus*, started off the popular riots. At Avranches, at the time of the *Nu-Pieds* in 1639, it was a gentleman and a priest who warned the salt makers and wood carriers of the arrival of a *gabeleur*. It was the judge at Avranches, with the advocates, royal and other, who caused the people to take up arms and transformed a "disturbance" into a prolonged revolt. Even in Brittany, at Rennes, in 1675, it seems that it was the parlement and certain gentlemen who stirred up the rebels.

In other cases there is no sign of any direct participation by social groups other than the craftsmen and peasants in starting the revolt. It is noteworthy, though, that the periods of revolt nearly always began in the towns, as in Bordeaux and the towns along the Loire in 1635 and 1636. The peasants living in the surrounding district came to the aid of the rebel townsmen, and then, in 1636 and 1637, in their turn, the *Croquants* rose up. In these instances one often finds that there was a sort of complicity on the part of other social groups. The parlements and Cours des Aides refused to order action to be taken against the rioters, and the bourgeois militia to march on them. The gentlemen denied the governor their support. In Bordeaux in 1635 all the "persons of condition" were clearly on the side of the rebels. Elsewhere, even in Angoumois, Saintonge, and Périgord, the *intendants* accused the gentlefolk of "conniving" and stimulating disturbances covertly, by means of their servants. This charge may have its source in prejudice, in the ill will felt by these *hommes de robe* in relation to *hommes d'épée*. The inertia shown by the country gentlemen and the bourgeois may have been due to fear, as several documents declare. But it is not out of the question that there really was complicity, and even concealed initiative, on the part of the gentlefolk, above all when one observes that their *châteaux* were not attacked and that popular fury was wreaked only on finance officials. I recall having witnessed, a few years ago, a riot by agricultural workers in a French town which everyone knew had been set on and promoted by their employers, who outwardly had nothing to do with this "popular" movement. It seems that the revolt in Lower Brittany in 1675 is the only one of which it can be said with almost complete certainty that the peasants alone took the initiative in it, after allowing for the effect produced by the criticism of the new taxes made by the parlement of Rennes and by the example offered by the riots in the towns.

Naturally, once revolts had been started by the princes and the parlements, action and reaction ensued. It is not impossible that the popular movements may, later on, have given the princes at certain moments the idea of a possible success against a government in difficulties, and so may have become in their turn a condition for the princes' revolts and the parlements' refusal to submit. The "Lanturelu" at Dijon, the Cascavéoux at Aix, the revolt in Languedoc (these last two, moreover, themselves aristocratic in origin), and the activity of the "bands" in Poitiers in 1630—were these without any influence on the breakaway by Gaston d'Orléans and his flight to Lorraine, the queen mother's flight of July 18, 1631, and Gaston's invasion of France in 1632? Was it by chance that Gaston started to make trouble again in 1636, after the Bordeaux revolt of May–June, 1635, and the furious outbreak at Agen on June 17 and 18, 1635, and when, from the spring of 1636 onward, rebellion reigned over all the country between the Loire and the Garonne? The conspiracy of the duc de Bouillon and the comte de Soissons with Gaston in 1641, the insurrection which ended in their defeat at La Marfée on July 6, 1641, was certainly encouraged by the revolt of the *Croquants* in Périgord, since Bouillon and Soissons tried to make contact with the *Croquant* Grelety, who was still holding out in the forest of Vergt. Perhaps the same was true of the conspiracy by Cinq-Mars, Bouillon, and Gaston, who negotiated with Spain on March 13, 1642, and came to a bad end, Cinq-Mars being arrested on June 13. Did the gentlefolk themselves, moreover, take the lead in resistance to taxation after the great peasant movements of 1636 and 1637? Is it because their resistance was growing stronger, or because there were more *intendants en mission*, armed with greater powers and carrying on more extensive administrative correspondence, that we find the protection accorded by the gentry to the peasants, against the representatives of the exchequer, mentioned more often in 1643, after the death of Louis XIII, and in 1644, with indications that they had in some cases shown a similar attitude already in 1641 or 1637? We should note that a royal minority, a regency, was always a period when obedience to the law and to the government's orders became less strict. Many questions still need answering.

The familiarity I have acquired with French society as a result of forty years of work among the records enables me to go beyond superficial appearances in a number of matters even though I still need to find out a lot more than I know at present. With Russian and Chinese society, however, I have to be satisfied with the works of specialists and with published Russian documents. In Russia, in the years preceding the Time of Troubles, it was the peasants, apparently, who began the movements. Most of the bandits were of peasant origin, even though there were among them some state servitors and boyars' sons who were down on their luck. The difficulty here is the same one that always arises when people change their social position—should they be classified according to their origin or according to their new social function? Sporadic peasant revolts had broken out before the Time of Troubles. But the Time of Troubles itself was prepared by boyars hostile to Boris Godunov. It was begun by a struggle between boyar cliques. It was boyars who increased the doubt that was felt regarding Godunov's right to be tsar, and it was in all probability some of them who encouraged the "true tsar" to appear on the scene, the first false Dmitri. The peasants do not seem to have stirred until the "born tsar" showed himself. They seem to have been able to act only when led by a totem, the "true tsar." And the first people to join the false Dmitri were "Cossacks," men who had torn up their roots for the sake of freedom, together with runaway peasants and vagabonds.

Stenka Razin's revolt was prepared by urban revolts, in 1648 in Moscow, Solvychegodsk, and Ustyug; in 1649 in Pskov and Novgorod; in 1662 in Moscow. From 1658 onward it was prepared, above all, by increasing banditry, reinforced by fugitive peasants. The great rural revolts were begun by a military element, the Cossacks. In 1660 there were the Cossacks of "Ryga," the "robber Cossacks"; in 1667 there was Razin's expedition across the Caspian. Here, however, we note the discreet participation of the "trading Cossacks," the "established Cossacks," who advanced the necessary capital in the form of arms, munitions, and food supplies, and who undertook to dispose of the loot, deducting their commission. Did these capitalists merely take advantage of movements which they had not themselves initiated, or did they provoke them, while remaining ready to repudiate and oppose them if they should fail? When, in 1670, Stenka Razin, the magician, the new "totem," sailed up the Volga, revolt broke out first in the towns, among the *streltsy*, the craftsmen, the petty traders, the serfs in the suburbs. Then this revolt spread to the countryside, where the peasants, stirred up by priests and monks, rose against their lords. Here, too, the peasants followed others. But the revolt unquestionably came from the lower strata of society and "irregulars" who had broken with the law—insofar as one does not see the Cossacks as a new military aristocracy or their capitalist class as playing more than an adventitious role in the events.

In China the troubles appear to have been started, around 1628–1629, by deserters from the army, soldiers turned robbers, who formed themselves into gangs. Bandit gangs were joined by peasants and perhaps also by persons in political opposition. From 1632 onward the greater part of the regular armies were in practice not to be distinguished from bandits. The generals took the men's pay for themselves, led them on plundering expeditions, and kept a profitable rebellion going by taking care not to destroy the rebels. It may be asked whether the treason of the military elite was not the essential cause of the Chinese revolts, which were perhaps, to a greater extent than has been said, a struggle by military men against civilian society, against the civilian magistracy. The risings in the towns between the Hwang-ho and the Yangtze seem to have been started off by the actions of the bandits and soldiers. After 1640, in the great revolt against the Ming Dynasty, though members of the elite, servants, and peasants enrolled en masse in the armies of the "warlords," it was the towns that played an important and perhaps a preponderant role.

To sum up, in none of these three countries can it be said that the peasants took the initiative in these revolts. They were always begun by other elements, and, in France, a society with a greater diversity of estates than the other two, they were often begun, to a greater extent than elsewhere, by the higher social strata.

The second question we have to ask concerns the motives of the rebels—those that they expressed and those that we can deduce from their behavior.

In France it is "tyranny" that we find everywhere blamed: the king's government by means of "favorites," ministers, and state councillors, who impose their will through commissaries, in contempt of all good custom. It is the abandonment of the ideal form of government, thought of as being traditional, through a "great council," with participation several times a week by the princes of the blood, the peers, the officers of the Crown, and the parlement, with frequent consultation of assemblies of notables and meetings of the States-General. It is the contempt shown, in the name of "reasons of state," for the corporations of officials, their remonstrances, their position as magistrates and their functions, the repudiation of judicial forms, the wholesale use of commissaries of various kinds to restrict the magistrates' authority and, increasingly often, to usurp their duties. It is the violation of provincial and municipal "liberties," privileges in respect of taxation and billeting, the less and less frequent convocation of provincial states, the disappearance altogether of some of these, and the restriction of their freedom to discuss taxes.

From all this followed many innovations that were not to be borne by men imbued with the sacred character of custom and for whom every new tax, and every substantial increase in taxation, not agreed to by the States-General or the provincial states, was an exaction, a gabelle; the installation of new *élus* and new royal receivers of taxes, which meant a reduction in the number of persons liable to pay taille and at the same time an increase in the *droits et taxations* which were calculated in proportion to the taille; the introduction or increase of indirect taxes, of domanial taxes, of internal customs duties of every sort, which by reducing a consumption of goods that was already inadequate, affected everyone—peasants and craftsmen, of course, but also bourgeois and country gentlemen, owners of vineyards, who were affected either by the decline in the sale of the produce of their land or by the difficulty experienced by their peasants in paying their dues and rents. Royal taxation also had the consequence of causing antagonism between countryfolk and townsfolk, for it was in the towns that the finance officials lived, men who were unpopular because they were always obliged in the end to carry out royal edicts and commissions, because some of them were hand in glove with the tax-farmers, or were tax-farmers themselves, and also because the village communities and the peasants individually had to incur debts in order to pay their taxes and the expenses arising from the *mortalités*, and their chief creditors were these finance officials in the towns.

It was not that the latter had much joy of these circumstances. Forced loans; the creation of new offices which reduced the value of their own, and which they often had to buy back; increases in the *droits et taxations* payable to them obtained only in return for a corresponding amount of capital paid into the royal coffers—all these afflictions rained down upon them, while the new salaries and *droits et taxations* due to them amounted to little or were not in fact paid. It was a constant drain on their wealth. They too were discontented and played their part in many a revolt. But they carried the burden of peasant hatreds. One is struck by the fact that even in the *Croquant* revolts it was not the *châteaux* of the gentry that were attacked, except in some instances where the château had a strategic value and could serve as a strongpoint. It was the *châteaux*, manor houses, and farmhouses owned by the finance officials of the neighboring towns, and their relatives, that suffered. In both country and town, it was the finance officials and their families, the tax-farmers and their agents, especially if they came from Paris, who were the victims of the fury of the peasants and craftsmen. Increased royal taxes either united lords and peasants against the exchequer or else, if the tax was paid, increased the tension between peasants and lords, because royal taxes and seignorial dues got in each others' way, and in difficult years it was hard to pay both. The only instance, however, in which the peasants' revolt seemed really directed against the lords and gentlemen, when it was the *châteaux* of the gentry that were burned, and gentlemen who were massacred, was the revolt in Lower Brittany in 1675. Local scholars seem to agree in considering that in Brittany there were fewer royal officials than elsewhere and that the gentlefolk were regarded there, much more than in other parts, as the king's representatives, responsible for the new taxes and the gabelle. It is certainly beyond doubt that their exceptional justiciary powers had enabled many Breton gentlemen to squeeze their peasants in a period of economic recession.

It was thus above all royal taxation, its weight, the way it was introduced, assessed, and collected, that gave rise to the revolts, with, in many places, alliances between everyone in a given town or province against the government. Royal taxation was the way in which people were most directly made aware of the modern

state, centralizing and reducing all to equality and uniformity.
A factor common to all these revolts is the horror inspired
by the King's Council when it sought to lay down edicts, laws,
regulations, general decisions which tended to reduce the entire
kingdom to uniformity, and all the king's subjects to equality
in the service of the state, riding roughshod over local privileges,
traditional liberties, vested interests in the established hierarchies;
the horror that raised the hackles of entire groups of people
when they were confronted by the coldness of the law, of these
impersonal decisions handed down from afar, by persons unknown
to them or who were merely names, presented to them at best
by an outsider, the royal commissary, and which came to separate
the follower from his protector, the client from his patron, the
vassal from his lord, breaking the traditional bonds, which often
involved reciprocal affection and devotion and which were in
any case personal ties between man and man, something warm,
living, and human. Without intending it, probably, but pushed
forward by jurists who were imbued with ideas of equality, universal law and "reason of state,"[11] compelled above all by the
necessities of war, the king and his council were carrying forward a slow revolution which made many people feel something
like the cold hand of death upon them and provoked violent
reactions.

In Russia, a motive for all seems to have been the illegitimacy
as tsar of Boris Godunov, murderer and limb of the Devil,
unmasked by the natural calamities that afflicted his reign. For
the boyar cliques, the motives were the tyranny of the Godunov
family, with a police regime of informers and torturers, and
the monopolizing of power by favorites, in place of government
by the old hereditary nobility of service. For many of the
pomeshchiki the motive was the inadequacy of their resources
to meet the obligations of their service. For the boyars' sons
and many of the peasants the motive was the "lockout" to which
they were subjected, their dismissal by lords who, being unable
to maintain them, threw them out on to the roads. For the
mass of the peasants, the motives were the weight of taxation,

11. See R. Mousnier, *Lettres et Mémoires adressés au chancelier Séguier*,
I, pp. 65–83, on the collective mentality of the "masters of requests."

the state's efforts to bind them to the soil in service to the state servitors, so as to deprive them of power to argue about their obligations and submit them to unlimited demands. For the Cossacks, the motives were the state's attempts to extend its control over them and transform them into subjects obedient to the representatives of the administration; the bans on their free trading activity, the endeavor to bind them to the soil in the hierarchy of estates that the state wanted to establish. Here too, from the Time of Troubles onward, the development of the state appears as the basic reason for the revolts. In Russia, however, the state played a role different from that of the French state: it ossified society, immobilizing people geographically and socially, and gradually creating an estate of serfs, more and more harshly treated. It was the intensification of this tendency after the Time of Troubles, with the Cossacks enclosed and caught by the state, Russian society immobilized in the estates created for state service by the *Ulozhenie* of 1649, the serf status of the peasants completely established and legalized (except for the slaves); a tendency which began to appear to exempt certain state servitors from their service obligation, for those who possessed fewer than fifty peasant households were exempted, and thus to transform a functional estate into a class of hereditary nobles, landowners living by their ownership of means of production operated by the labor of peasants; it was all this, doubtless even more than the burden of taxes, the conscription of men, and the currency troubles, that made similar the motives of Stenka Razin and those of the rebellious craftsmen and peasants.

In China, in a period of natural calamities, the immediate motives for revolt were lack of pay, in the case of the soldiers, and taxes which had become excessively heavy, and which were implacably demanded, together with additional exactions, exceeding the capacity of the taxpayers to pay. These evils resulted to a large extent from the disorganization of the state, in a period in which the emperors, weakened by harem life, were no longer capable of controlling the intrigues of the women, eunuchs, and high officials around them, and in which ministerial instability, nepotism, favoritism, waste, and corruption made the state and its machinery a group of exploiters and no longer the corporation

uniting all wills for the common good. The state no longer regulated the working of social relations, no longer prevented the
landowners from demanding ever-greater rents, gifts, and presents
in time of shortage, but allowed conflicts between the estates
to get worse. Droughts, locusts, famines, and banditry testified
with eloquence that the dynasty no longer held the mandate of
Heaven. This judgment became in its turn a motive for revolt.

Thus, in all these countries, the action of the state is seen,
far more than social antagonisms, as the motive for the revolts.
Indeed, in Russia and China, the state seems itself to be the
generator of social antagonisms in the period under consideration.

The third question to be asked relates to the location of and
the geographical area covered by the revolts. In France, all the
revolts of the century occurred, with few exceptions, to the
west and southwest of a line through Normandy, Anjou, Touraine,
and the Bourbonnais, as far as the Dauphiné. To the north
and east of this line revolts were less frequent. The borderline
between the obedient areas and the rebellious ones coincides,
more or less, with that between the region of open, oblong
fields and that of enclosed and irregularly shaped ones. Predominant in the areas which often rose in revolt was what the
theoreticians of the second half of the eighteenth century called
petite culture (small-scale cultivation). There were holdings of
about thirty hectares, at most, frequently on sharecropping leases,
cultivated with oxen; a slow business. The *métayer* or *bordier* could
cultivate only a small part of his land, and this fraction was
still further reduced by the biannual rotation of crops: one year
of cultivation, one year of "dead" fallow. The bulk of the land
was covered with heath, either of heather or of broom. The cultivated parts were made up of irregularly shaped fields, very
often enclosed by a *fossé* (dyke), a bank of earth surmounted
by a hedge. The oxen grazed at liberty on the heathland. They
produced hardly any manure except during the winter, when
they spent more time in the cattle shed. The peasant thus had
only poor fertilizer at his disposal, and got only poor yields:
three or four for one, five or six hectoliters per hectare, sometimes five for one, nine hectoliters per hectare, but this was only

half of what the same land produced later, in 1920. There was thus little surplus for the market. Sometimes the harvest was only just big enough to keep the sharecropper and his family. Often it was not enough. The money he needed he obtained by selling stock, by selling fleeces to the clothing industry, or by some craftwork or auxiliary trade. There was a multiplicity of little holdings, individualistic and anarchic, most of which, lacking capital and reserves, provided with difficulty two successive crops and then were quickly reduced to poverty, so that the peasant found himself unable to pay his taxes and dues, and therefore rebelled. Within this region of small holdings the most disturbed areas were Périgord, Limousin, and Brittany, areas where movement about the country was difficult, which were off the beaten track, and relatively poor, so that the exchequer and the lords contended for something that was in short supply. These were areas which felt they were badly dealt with by "outsider" merchants from other provinces that were economically more developed, or, in the case of Saintonge, by the Dutch and their agents. A map of the disturbed areas coincides fairly well with those which have been the scene of peasant troubles in the twentieth century—the Poujadist agitation, for example.

To the north and east of this line was the region of what the theoreticians of the second half of the eighteenth century called *la grande culture* (large-scale cultivation). Here were holdings of 60 to 70 hectares, with open, oblong fields, situated in great plains. Plowing was carried on with teams of horses, a more rapid way of cultivating the land than with oxen. A three-year rotation of crops was observed, under which the spring grain of the second year, oats and barley, solved the problem of feeding the horses and cattle, which also grazed on the part of the land left fallow, and, after the harvest, on all the land, as "common waste." It was a system of cultivation in common of the same crop at the same time, by the same method, governed by the village community under the influence of the big farmers, the "cocks of the parish." The farms were large, with enclosures for the cattle and very long periods in stall, so that they produced much more manure, and of better quality. Yields were at the rate of nine, ten, and twelve for one, or seventeen to twenty hectoliters per hectare. The land was exploited by large farmers, capitalist entrepreneurs in their way, owners of plow-horse teams, each employing several wage-earning servants not belonging to his own family. This was a society dominated and led by these large farmers, who gave work to the poor, whose plow-teams were indispensable to the small peasants, and who often farmed the collection of seignorial dues, on behalf of the gentlemen and other lords. These large farmers probably kept their districts in submission, as a rule.[12]

It should be added that the areas where the fields were enclosed and irregularly shaped were areas of woodland, marsh, and scrub with many hedges, small copses and bushes bristling from the ground, and therefore with many places where, in summer, men could hide, creep along, move from place to place unseen, excellent country for ambushes and surprise attacks. Revolt did not find the same facilities available in the plains of the areas where the fields were open and oblong, with their distinctly defined woods, shaped like wheels, at a distance from the villages.

The areas of the north and northeast, constantly threatened by foreign invasion, were being traversed all the time by the king's armies, ready to maintain order. For the areas which were farther away, in the center and southwest of France, it was necessary to await the end of the campaigning season in order to send troops into winter quarters there. Meanwhile, revolts could spread.

The area of enclosed, irregularly shaped fields never rose as a whole, all at once. The revolts were due to a combination of many conditions and not just to the way in which the exploitation of the soil was organized and the few social relations directly governed by this fact. Besides, the form of exploitation was not imposed by geography, but itself depended on historical accidents and a certain psychology. The revolts came to birth one by one in those historical entities that formed the

12. R. Dion, *Le Val de Loire* (1933); E. Mireaux, *Une province française au Temps du Grand Roi: la Brie* (Paris, Hachette, 1957). D. Louis Merle, *La Métairie et l'évolution agraire de la Gâtine poitevine, de la fin du Moyen Age à la Révolution* (S.E.V.P.E.N., 1958).

provinces of France. But they never spread at one and the same time over the whole of even one province. Only restricted areas were affected by particular revolts. The latter were fragmented. There do not seem to have been any attempts to unite the areas in revolt, when several were up at the same time, or to spread the revolt far beyond its original center. The rebels could not see further than their own district, and so the government was able to put them down, one after the other.

In Russia, the revolt of Stenka Razin began in the Volga Valley, with the Cossacks, and also, in that country which had only recently been conquered and where security was poor, with the bandits, the plunderers of stores and sanctuaries, the individuals "obedient only to their own wills," the boatmen, the fishery and salt workers, the soldiers of the fortresses, and the monks; in areas which were constantly under threat from the nomads, and whose irregulars and fugitives were numerous. From the Time of Troubles, while revolts occurred elsewhere too, the favorite areas for them were, besides the Volga Valley up to Simbirsk and Nizhny-Novgorod, the plateau of central Russia, the plateau of the Volga, and the Don plain, that is, the wooded-steppe and steppe zones. This was a "frontier" land, still threatened by Tatar incursions, where the towns were fortresses, linked together by military posts, around which villages developed, forming "lines" supported by woods and barricades of felled trees, the farthest advanced being the line between Putivl and Simbirsk, running through Voronezh, Byelgorod, and Tambov. A land only recently settled, by refugees and uprooted people who were little disposed, either they or their sons, to accept closer control by the administration, fixation in the rigid framework of the new society of estates, or serfdom. A land of *pomeshchiki* who had difficulty in finding labor power, who demanded much from their serfs, and who often cultivated their domains with slaves, proportionately more numerous here than anywhere else. A land of cultivators who were winning excellent gray soil or "black earth" for grain, but where dust storms could destroy a crop in a few hours and spread epidemics among poorly fed peasants who were dragged down by the fatigue of harvesting, and where summer droughts brought frightful famines. A land of over-

burdened peasants who were stirred up at harvest time by a large
number of casual workers, vagabonds, and Cossacks. A land
with many non-Russian native peoples. A sort of frontier land,
less disciplined and more athirst for freedom than other parts of
Russia, more impatient of constraint, more warlike and traversed
by those tracks like the *drailles* (the sheep trails of Languedoc),
the *shlyakhi,* three of them, which, running between the heads
of ravines and rivers, converged upon Tula and were the natural
route for invading nomads, Cossacks, and rebels.

The remoteness of the country from Moscow, the time needed
to concentrate troops and bring them to where they were required, favored the outbreak of revolts, while identity of conditions of life caused them to embrace vast areas. From Astrakhan
to Simbirsk and from Astrakhan to Yelets, the revolt of Stenka
Razin developed over a territory about a thousand kilometers
wide, as the crow flies. When it came to striking the decisive
blow at Moscow, however, the distance told against the rebels.
The unity of the revolt was not genuine. When the "totem,"
Dmitri or Stenka, vanished, the revolt broke up into petty local
groups, each of which sought only to resist on the spot. Everyone
was loyal to the totem, but not to the other people of his own
condition. Everything happened as if there was no awareness
of any identity of conditions, desires, and actions, any possibility
of union and of common institutions, apart from rallying around
the person of the protector-totem.

In China the revolts spread over the whole of the region
between the Great Wall and the Yangtze. But the leaders of
the rebels came from Shensi, took refuge in Shensi after setbacks,
and recovered their strength in Shensi and the northern part of
Honan. This is the typical "yellow earth" area: plateaus cut
by labyrinths of canyons into which one descends down a succession of terraces. Land which is very fertile, but too porous,
exposed to deadly droughts caused by the desert winds, impossible to irrigate owing to the thickness of the permeable loess,
and where the population was ravaged by recurrent famines. A
region where communications were very difficult. In the loess
the only roads were narrow, deep trenches, or else watersheds
between the tangled canyons. The difficulty of communication

increased the backwardness of an area which lagged behind the rich provinces of the south. The country suffered from a "colonial"-type economy. It supplied the southern provinces with raw materials in exchange for foodstuffs and manufactured articles, and its people felt they were exploited by the southern merchants. It was also, in the eyes of Peking, a remote and unfortunate area where officials of mediocre quality were sent, who regarded it as a place of exile and thought only of enriching themselves by squeezing their subjects and then getting out as soon as possible. If a revolt broke out, it was hard for an army to move around. The army could leave the roads only with difficulty, and it could easily be brought to a standstill in the defiles or on the brink of ravines. On the other hand, handfuls of men could carry on a partisan war indefinitely in this labyrinth.

There were thus some geographical features that were common to the areas where revolts occurred most often: distance from the capital, a factor both in making revolt possible and in causing difficulties for the rebels, at a time when a column of infantry could hardly cover more than twenty-five kilometers a day, on the average, and a column of cavalry only about forty; a certain degree of isolation and difficult communications which result in an area which is relatively backward from the economic standpoint, in the feeling that it is at a disadvantage in relation to other areas and exploited by "outsiders"; a brittle economy, extremely susceptible to climatic accidents, owing to the inadequacy of the technique for exploiting the local resources, in relation to the conditions offered by the soil, the climate, and the economy in general; the demands of the state, not balanced by a firm hand on its own agents, on the lords, or on the mere entrepreneurs and landowners, because its control over these areas was feebler than elsewhere, and the strong could oppress the humble people with impunity.

Now we must consider the question of how the rebels were organized, and the progress of the revolt. There is no point in dwelling on cases where, as in Aix-en-Provence in 1630, it was gentlemen, royal officials (particularly cliques in the parlement), and bourgeois who directed the revolt. More interesting are

cases where, as at Dijon in 1630, certain elements from the lower
strata of society having begun the riot, the mayor and *échevins*
and the bourgeois militia let it proceed, allowing the king and
Cardinal Richelieu to be burned in effigy, and then when,
after two days, the riot had taken a turn toward plundering,
energetically suppressed it. Historians have concluded from this
course of events that there was a fundamental opposition between the "plebeians" and the bourgeois. A question arises: were
the plunderers at the end of the episode the same persons as the
rioters at the beginning? Did evildoers take advantage of the
troubles? Of course, some rioters might turn into evildoers without their actions incriminating the rebels as a whole. But we
are above all concerned with the peasants. Everywhere we see
the peasants forming communes of parishes. These communes
have their deliberative assemblies, their leaders, a committee of
priests in the case of the *Nu-Pieds*, a gentleman acting as general
in the case of Périgord, captains, sergeants who are priests, some
gentlemen, law officials like notaries, process servers, bailiffs,
legal practitioners—that is, "counsel," peasants, sometimes, as
with the *Nu-Pieds*, royal officials, king's advocates or judges.
The communes seem often to have been made up of well-to-do
peasants, since they had to arm, equip, and feed themselves at
their own cost. They wielded a sort of popular dictatorship: they
compelled gentlemen, priests, refractory peasants, and intractable
parishes to march, on pain of maltreatment of their persons and
burning down of their houses. In particular, they desired to have
gentlemen to command them, military technicians in the service of
the people, although the rebels must have included many former
soldiers. Probably the rebels were always in a minority. Furthermore, many of the peasants who marched did so under constraint.
Many parishes held aloof from the movements and some remained
explicitly loyal to their lords, as in Normandy. We need to know
what proportion of the peasant population participated in the
revolts, and also to what extent the other peasants looked on
the rebels with sympathy, as their own representatives, and to
what extent they were out of sympathy with them and condemned
them.

In most cases the gentlemen let the peasants get on with it, without trying to stop them. The *intendants* of the provinces declare that gentlemen, parish priests, and local notables were secretly in agreement with the movement and took a hand in the leadership of it through their servants and tenants. Some gentlemen openly rode at the head of the rebels and did not repent of this, as in Normandy, around Mantilly. Other gentlemen or priests who stood at the head of the peasants later said that they had been forced to do it. The duc de la Vallette expressed the view that the gentlemen of Périgord had not opposed the peasants because they were afraid to do so. It must be noted that, except in Lower Brittany, the peasants did not usually attack the *châteaux*, manor houses, and other residences of the gentlemen or the officers of justice. They seized, plundered, or set on fire only the properties of the finance officials and tax-farmers, or of persons who were suspected of participating in the activities of the financiers. This fact would seem to reinforce the theory of an alliance, whether open, secret, or merely tacit, between the gentry and the peasantry. It is certain, however, that the gentlemen and royal officials who openly sided with the peasants were a tiny minority. It must also be noted that, with only a few exceptions, the royal officials who directly incited the peasants to revolt and took command of them were petty officials of the judiciary, and among the poorest of these. With only a few exceptions, the gentlemen who undoubtedly did give leadership to the peasants were likewise petty gentry who, though sometimes of ancient noble origin, were extremely impecunious. In other words, broadly speaking, if we take social status as our criterion, all three estates were represented in the peasant revolts; but if we take the economic hierarchy as our criterion, then, apart from the peasants themselves, we find that it was only the poorest members of the two other estates who took part. This is at any rate the result reached in researches up to now. Further study is needed on both social structures and economic life.

If they were to succeed in their revolts, the peasants would have had to unite province with province and march on Paris, but they do not seem to have thought of doing this. They would have needed to have cannon and strongpoints, castles and towns.

They tried to capture some towns, but failed for lack of cannon. They were short of the initial "capital" needed for success, in the shape of artillery and generals.

The revolt in Lower Brittany in 1675 provides the exception. It was the only one in which the peasants attacked the *châteaux* and the persons of the gentry, and which was clearly directed against the latter. Perhaps the reasons for this are to be found in the extraordinary powers possessed by lords who all held rights of justice, in the increase in the dues and services that had to be paid to these lords, in the fact that the gentlemen who were lords, in this region where royal officials were few, themselves took on the character of representatives of the king and therefore of the royal taxation system. In short, in the archaic features of this provincial society, which perhaps gave it some resemblance to the Russian society of the same epoch.

In the Russia of the Time of Troubles it is hard to perceive any distinct peasant organization. Most of the time the peasants seem to have been led by boyars and *pomeshchiki*. In the areas liberated from Tsar Shuisky's troops the people elected voivodes, but it seems that all Shuisky's opponents participated in this, not merely the peasants. When the latter were less numerous, they had with them Cossacks who seem to have provided the peasants with leadership through Cossack institutions. During the anabasis of Vaska Us and that of Stenka Razin, the situation was different. The "peasants" (but who, precisely, from among the peasants?) massacred not only the officials and army officers, but also the well-to-do. Grouped around their emblem, the supernatural hero Stenka Razin, they adopted the democratic and egalitarian institutions of the Cossacks: the general assembly of all the people, which elects its own leaders; the division of the people into thousands, hundreds, and tens, with leaders chosen by the general assembly. But this organization remained strictly local. Peasants and Cossacks did not try to set up a hierarchy of provincial assemblies crowned by a national assembly, with a system of representation. When the hero had been beaten and was in flight, the insurrection broke up into an infinite number of disconnected local revolts.

In China there do not appear to have been any peasant or-

ganizations in the strict sense. The only organs of revolt seem
to have been bands with a military-type structure. From these
bands the warlords graduated to be commanders of armies, with
a hierarchy of officers, in no way different from the imperial
armies, and which often came to include a goodly number of
imperial officers. The only exception appears to have been the
puritan army of Li Tzu-cheng, but this was distinguished less
by its organization than by its spirit: the disdain for money,
comfort, and all pleasure, the respect for women and girls, and
for the chattels and crops of everyone, the rigorous discipline.
But this was the ideal army of the "mandatory of Heaven." Its
virtue did not survive victory. Similarly, it was not distinguished
by setting up a peasant government. The warlords organized, with
the help of graduates, over and above their councils of generals,
who were incorporated in the traditional nobility, governments
of the traditional kind, a bureaucratic hierarchy corresponding
to the traditional social hierarchy of the locality. We see nothing
that is strictly peasant in character or constitutes any sort of
innovation, apart from the change of personnel. In China alone,
of the three countries, the rebels were successful, but without
carrying out a revolution.

The last question will concern itself with what the rebels
wanted, what their program was. In France, generally speaking,
none of the rebels had a single new idea. Princes, grandees, parlements, officials, bourgeois—all wished merely to go back to
the good old customs and the traditional political constitution,
somewhat idealized. But this is equally true of the peasants. Common features appear in all their programs when analyzed. The
peasants want the abolition of government by ministers, favorites,
and courtiers, who indulge themselves and their friends. They
want respect for the traditional customs, privileges, and liberties
of the provinces and districts, a return to the old taxes, the
consent of the States-General and the provincial states as a
condition for new taxes, and the reestablishment of the provincial
states where these have been abolished. They cry out against
the tyranny of the Parisians, against the excessive centralization
of the state, the increase in taxes, the "innovations."

But that is all. The reader looks in vain for any attack on the absolute monarchy, any demand for regular meetings of the States-General, or for a King's Council elected by the States-General, or for permanent supervision of the king's policy by a standing commission derived from the States-General. He also looks in vain for anything against the inequality of the tax system or against the existing social order, which is implicitly accepted by those who call for provincial states. Even more curious to us, there is usually no demand affecting the regime of seignorial property and the feudal political system. When such demands appear, they are mere demands for reductions, mere local adjustments, but nothing is directed against the essential character of these institutions. The rebels attacked persons who seemed to them to be behaving badly, in order to correct them, and sometimes to do away with them. They did not attack the existing stratification of society, or the totality of social structures and institutions. There was, in short, no question of a struggle by one social group against another. And that was true even of the interesting Breton revolt of the Torrébens, which went further than any of the others. These rebels were very angry men. The peasants of Lower Brittany answered a cleric who was questioning them, that they were quite beside themselves, that they themselves did not understand what was driving them from within. But these crises of anger did not make revolutionaries of them. They did not have the idea of a revolution in their heads.

Why not? Doubtless because they were imbued with the omnipotence of custom, born of the community itself. From the depths of Merovingian times this idea had been handed down, reinforced during the spontaneous reconstitution of society after the invasions of the Norsemen, Magyars, and Saracens in the ninth and tenth centuries, that custom contained the authentic body of the law, above all of civil and penal law; that the king should ensure respect for custom and interfere with it as little as possible; that though he might abrogate or modify custom by law, in serious need and for the common good, he must do this only with the consent of the interested persons themselves. Our peasants do not argue about whatever is customary; it provokes neither indignation nor rebellion on their part, whatever it may be. But any violation of custom, real or imagined, even if it emanate from the king and his council and be registered by the parlement, is not law, or at least it cannot prevail against custom. All the less so, of course, if it has been forced on the parlement.

In so far as they were Christians, their Christianity did not help them accept new things. Not that Christianity is in principle bound up with any particular political or social form. And even charity ought to promote any innovation that may improve the lot of one's neighbors. But, on the other hand, since the ascension of Our Lord Jesus Christ from the top of the Mount of Olives, facing Jerusalem, and until He comes again, sitting upon the clouds in power and glory, to judge the living and the dead, the best thing a Christian can do is to remain in the place where the will of God has put him and there live in faith, hope, and charity, doing to the best of his ability all that his station in life entails, for love of Jesus Christ and of his neighbor; and it is best not to change one's station, or to change the system of stations—what is best is to live for Jesus Christ, by Jesus Christ, and in Jesus Christ. Such a state of mind does not favor willful social and political revolutions, even though it may in itself cause a revolution in mankind such as we have never yet seen. It should be added that, as a whole, the church in France, having being obliged to adapt itself to the existing political and social system, had been contaminated by it.

Finally, it is not impossible that their work as agriculturists, carried on with a technique and equipment that gave them little control over natural phenomena, the habit of bowing to natural forces which were too strong for them, the regular return of the seasons, cycles of good years and bad years, implanted in them the habit of submitting to an immutable world order that it was not possible to change in any far-reaching way, that had to be accepted and used, with which one had to use craft in order to get what advantages were possible, and continually to begin again.

The program of the Russian peasants in the Time of Troubles seems also to have been rather a return to a customary condition of things, somewhat idealized. Prisoners themselves, too, of respect for custom, and with the mentality of ritualistic cultiva-

tors, the peasants do not seem to have sought either the abolition
of tsarism or the transformation of the domanial and seignorial
regime. A "true Tsar," legitimate, chosen by God, who would
restore the country to the order willed by God; a patriarchal
"good tsar" who would reduce taxes, military service, dues and
labor services; who would restore, above all, complete freedom to
move about, to choose one's master and to settle labor conditions with him. This is apparently what everyone wanted. Did
Bolotnikov want anything more? Did he think in terms of
remodeling the Russian state and society on the basis of equal
division of the land and election of leaders by the people, under
their tsar? Perhaps, but we cannot be certain.

On the other hand, in the time of Vaska Us and Stenka Razin,
the Cossacks and peasants were, it would appear, thinking of
a revolution. There should be a good Tsar, of course, as before,
assisted by a brotherly *gosudar* (sovereign lord), but, as well, the
destruction of the entire machinery of the tsarist state—State
Council, *prikazi, dyaki,* voivodes; the disappearance of the boyars
and the *pomeshchiki;* the abolition of serfdom and slavery, the
sweeping away of the society of estates and of the fixing of people in their estates, as decreed by the *Ulozhenie.* They favored
instead an egalitarian democracy of small proprietors who, in accordance with the Cossack spirit and Cossack customs, would
elect their leaders, consent to taxation, and submit only to obligations freely discussed and accepted. Here the idea of a revolution
was indeed present.

Why was there this difference from France? Doubtless because
the French social system included many advantages for the
peasant. As *seigneur utile* of his *censive,* he too was a lord, like
the *seigneur direct.* He too owned fiefs. Provided he paid his dues
and services he was full owner of his land, with the right to
bequeath, inherit, give, or sell it; to make it produce the fruits
of his labor and to use these for himself, consuming them or
selling them for his own profit. It is noteworthy that the only
revolt that assumed the aspect of a *jacquerie,* that of the Torrébens in Brittany, occurred precisely in a region where there
were not only fiefs and *censives,* which guaranteed the peasants'
position as proprietors, but where the system of *domaine congéable*
made their share in ownership a precarious one. Where fiefs

and *censives* were predominant, the revolts do not appear to have been directed against the gentlemen or other lords. We must also recall that the Breton lord held justiciary powers which enabled him to be judge in his own case. Where the lords no longer held these powers, as in the Paris basin, or where these justiciary powers of the lords were kept in check by royal judges nearby, as in Maine and Anjou, the revolts were less numerous, less serious, or did not occur at all. The Russian peasant, however, saw his situation evolving in the opposite way to that of the French peasant. He gradually lost his rights as a landowner and his personal freedom. The advance of serfdom in Russia was an essential cause of the revolutionary spirit.

There was another one, too. This was the restriction of social mobility. French society was an open society, with social mobility going on all the time, upward and downward. Gentlemen ruin themselves by living in noble style and by service in the wars. They fall into the lower ranks of society, and vanish from our documents. Merchants, master craftsmen, and *laboureurs* have bad luck in business and lose their places in society. But others rise: peasants who carry on trade in grain or stock, *laboureurs* who farm large areas of land and the collection of seignorial dues, may acquire fiefs. They may also be able to secure some education for their sons, obtain petty offices for them, as bailiffs, process servers, attorneys, or notaries; make them tax-farmers' clerks; or launch them into commerce. The merchant who has made money, the lucky tax-farmer's clerk, or the petty judicial officer who is active and thrifty may obtain an office in the financial machinery, as *élu* or receiver, there enrich himself by *taxations* and usury, get his hands on the *censives* and fiefs of his debtors, and become a lord. These men's descendants may either live nobly, swords at their sides, on their estates, like gentlemen, and in due course secure recognition of their noble quality, or they may obtain offices in the judiciary, rise to positions in the sovereign courts, go over from there to the profession of arms, and so arrive at last by that detour at the status of *gentilshommes d'épée*. Social climbing like this could be accomplished in three or four generations. Along with many other social ties, such social mobility contributed to preventing any dichotomy appearing in French society. The peasants found it harder, perhaps, to climb the rungs of the social hierarchy in those days than in the nineteenth century; nevertheless they could climb them. They were imprisoned neither in their district nor in their "estate," nor in any particular section of this estate. They did not need to smash the existing social and political regime in order to improve their lot. If the revolt in Lower Brittany was more serious and more audacious than the others, there is every reason to suppose that social mobility was less there than elsewhere, and that the Breton peasants tried to open up possibilities for climbing the social ladder, as is suggested by their demand regarding marriage with noblewomen.

In contrast to this, the Russian state in the seventeenth century gradually imprisoned the Russian peasantry, with few exceptions. It made Russian society a closed society in which everyone was obliged to remain in his town or his village—his category, rank, order, and estate. Though not entirely abolished, social mobility was restricted more and more narrowly, and the ideal the state set before itself was that of fixing everyone where he stood. This was all the more serious a matter because in France the estates seem to have arisen spontaneously from society itself during the reorganization that followed the upheavals of the ninth and tenth centuries. It would not be true to say that the society of estates was established in France without the state playing any role, for state and society never cease to interreact; still, this order of things was the reflection of spontaneous social behavior. In Russia, it was something created by the state which violated the natural tendencies existing in Russian society to organize itself spontaneously as a class society. In combination with the lower degree of development of trade and industry in Russia, with the absence of a really substantial social group of merchants, a genuine bourgeoisie, this action by the state did indeed cut Russia in two: the serfs and slaves on the one hand, the landowning nobility on the other. In Russia there actually was a dichotomy which left no resource or hope but in an attempt at revolution. If the revolutionaries had succeeded, they would have been able to create a society without classes, a society of equal small proprietors. This society would doubtless have evolved in the direction of a class society, in which social strata would be differentiated according to wealth acquired in the production of or trade in material goods, as what was happening among the Don Cossacks inclines us to suppose. (The "Polish" Cossacks, below the rapids of the Dnieper, who were caught within a society of estates, became stratified socially in a hierarchy of orders.) But the Russian revolutionaries did not succeed. They would in any case have been tempted to occupy the places of the nobles they had conquered. And if they had remained faithful to their program, their success would doubtless have led to their ruin, for the new Russian society would have been destroyed by its neighbors, monarchial states, more centralized and more hierarchial, more capable than the new Russia of raising armies and moving them into action.

That access to property, personal freedom, and social mobility prevented revolts in societies of estates from becoming revolutionary seems confirmed by the example of China. In that country the peasants mostly had some property—either complete ownership of the soil or at least ownership of its surface, and this seems to have been guaranteed and assured them. All Chinese had the right to choose where they would live and what occupation they would follow. The system of examinations open to all, in order to recruit a bureaucracy that crowned the social hierarchy, ensured a real degree of social mobility. The peasants were fully aware of this, frequenting as they did the numerous schools and academies and taking a keen interest in the examinations and their results. The hope it made possible for everyone to cherish, either for himself or for his children, together with the respect felt for the eternal order willed by Heaven, and the devotion to ceremonies and traditions, prevented the peasants in revolt from becoming revolutionaries. They wanted an emperor mandated by Heaven, who would ensure respect for sound tradition, and the proper functioning of the same social hierarchy as before, the same bureaucracy, the same government, and the same administration. We must point out that in China the division of the land, which it was expected Li Tzu-cheng would put into effect, would not have amounted to a revolution, since the social hierarchy was based not on a hierarchy of property but on a hierarchy of dignities and offices.

It may be that societies of estates, while rarely transformed by revolutions, are disturbed more frequently than others by revolts which are aimed not at challenging the underlying principle of society and the social stratification resulting from it, but at improving the position in the hierarchy of some particular "estate" or social group. This would logically follow from a form of organization which multiplies differences between citizens, fragmenting society into many strata, groups, and bodies, all provided with functions, duties, rights, privileges, and liberties which are different and arranged hierarchically.

Thus, the revolts of the seventeenth century, in France, Russia, and China, were reactions against the state. Amid difficult economic situations, of climatic origin, the major cause of the revolts was the development of the state in France and Russia, the drive to centralization and uniformity, the whittling away of customary local privileges and liberties, even more than the burden of taxes and of service to the state, though both became heavier. In China it was, in a comparable situation, the crisis of the state provoked by the decline of a dynasty. Belief in a supernatural eternal order, respect for custom and tradition, hierarchies of orders and estates with many levels, openness of the social hierarchy in the upward direction, real social mobility, personal freedom and right to property—all these, in France and China, prevented the revolts from turning against the social and political order and becoming revolutions. In Russia, however, the state, by progressively simplifying society until it tended to become a dichotomy—fixing everyone at his given level in the framework of a society of orders which became more and more rigid, transforming the peasants into serfs deprived of property and of personal and effective freedom, and of all hope of social climbing—provoked a genuine attempt at revolution.

And now I leave it to each reader to make use of these facts and reflections to support his individual philosophy or political tendency, if he so chooses. There are better things to do, though. As a historian convinced that there is a reality outside ourselves and that we can attain to the truth about that reality by making proper use of the directing principles of knowledge, I should prefer that many readers would join in the great movement of research upon social structures, revolts, and revolutions. We all have much to learn.

Index

71 72 73 74   12 11 10 9 8 7 6 5 4 3 2 1

Revised January, 1970

haRPeR ⚜ ɔoRchbooks

American Studies: General

HENRY ADAMS Degradation of the Democratic Dogma. ‡ *Introduction by Charles Hirschfeld.* TB/1450

LOUIS D. BRANDEIS: Other People's Money, *and How the Bankers Use It. Ed. with Intro, by Richard M. Abrams* TB/3081

HENRY STEELE COMMAGER, Ed.: The Struggle for Racial Equality TB/1300

CARL N. DEGLER: Out of Our Past: *The Forces that Shaped Modern America* CN/2

CARL N. DEGLER, Ed.: Pivotal Interpretations of American History
Vol. I TB/1240; Vol. II TB/1241

LAWRENCE H. FUCHS, Ed.: American Ethnic Politics TB/1368

ROBERT L. HEILBRONER: The Limits of American Capitalism TB/1305

JOHN HIGHAM, Ed.: The Reconstruction of American History TB/1068

ROBERT H. JACKSON: The Supreme Court in the American System of Government TB/1106

JOHN F. KENNEDY: A Nation of Immigrants. *Illus. Revised and Enlarged. Introduction by Robert F. Kennedy* TB/1118

RICHARD B. MORRIS: Fair Trial: *Fourteen Who Stood Accused, from Anne Hutchinson to Alger Hiss* TB/1335

GUNNAR MYRDAL: An American Dilemma: *The Negro Problem and Modern Democracy. Introduction by the Author.*
Vol. I TB/1443; Vol. II TB/1444

GILBERT OSOFSKY, Ed.: The Burden of Race: *A Documentary History of Negro-White Relations in America* TB/1405

ARNOLD ROSE: The Negro in America: *The Condensed Version of Gunnar Myrdal's* An American Dilemma. *Second Edition* TB/3048

JOHN E. SMITH: Themes in American Philosophy: *Purpose, Experience and Community* TB/1466

WILLIAM R. TAYLOR: Cavalier and Yankee: *The Old South and American National Character* TB/1474

American Studies: Colonial

BERNARD BAILYN: The New England Merchants in the Seventeenth Century TB/1149

ROBERT E. BROWN: Middle-Class Democracy and Revolution in Massachusetts, 1691–1780. *New Introduction by Author* TB/1413

JOSEPH CHARLES: The Origins of the American Party System TB/1049

WESLEY FRANK CRAVEN: The Colonies in Transition: 1660-1712† TB/3084

CHARLES GIBSON: Spain in America † TB/3077

CHARLES GIBSON, Ed.: The Spanish Tradition in America + HR/1351

LAWRENCE HENRY GIPSON: The Coming of the Revolution: 1763-1775. † *Illus.* TB/3007

JACK P. GREENE, Ed.: Great Britain and the American Colonies: 1606-1763. + *Introduction by the Author* HR/1477

AUBREY C. LAND, Ed.: Bases of the Plantation Society + HR/1429

PERRY MILLER: Errand Into the Wilderness TB/1139

PERRY MILLER & T. H. JOHNSON, Ed.: The Puritans: *A Sourcebook of Their Writings*
Vol. I TB/1093; Vol. II TB/1094

EDMUND S. MORGAN: The Puritan Family: *Religion and Domestic Relations in Seventeenth Century New England* TB/1227

WALLACE NOTESTEIN: The English People on the Eve of Colonization: 1603-1630. † *Illus.* TB/3006

LOUIS B. WRIGHT: The Cultural Life of the American Colonies: 1607-1763. † *Illus.* TB/3005

YVES F. ZOLTVANY, Ed.: The French Tradition in America + HR/1425

American Studies: The Revolution to 1860

JOHN R. ALDEN: The American Revolution: 1775-1783. † *Illus.* TB/3011

RAY A. BILLINGTON: The Far Western Frontier: 1830-1860. † *Illus.* TB/3012

STUART BRUCHEY: The Roots of American Economic Growth, 1607-1861: *An Essay in Social Causation. New Introduction by the Author.* TB/1350

NOBLE E. CUNNINGHAM, JR., Ed.: The Early Republic, 1789-1828 + HR/1394

GEORGE DANGERFIELD: The Awakening of American Nationalism, 1815-1828. † *Illus.* TB/3061

---

† The New American Nation Series, edited by Henry Steele Commager and Richard B. Morris.
‡ American Perspectives series, edited by Bernard Wishy and William E. Leuchtenburg.
a History of Europe series, edited by J. H. Plumb.
§ The Library of Religion and Culture, edited by Benjamin Nelson.
‖ Researches in the Social, Cultural, and Behavioral Sciences, edited by Benjamin Nelson.
Σ Harper Modern Science Series, edited by James A. Newman.
° Not for sale in Canada.
+ Documentary History of the United States series, edited by Richard B. Morris.
# Documentary History of Western Civilization series, edited by Eugene C. Black and Leonard W. Levy.
Λ The Economic History of the United States series, edited by Henry David et al.
¶ European Perspectives series, edited by Eugene C. Black.
** Contemporary Essays series, edited by Leonard W. Levy.
* The Stratum Series, edited by John Hale.

CLEMENT EATON: The Freedom-of-Thought Struggle in the Old South. *Revised and Enlarged. Illus.* TB/1150

CLEMENT EATON: The Growth of Southern Civilization, 1790-1860. † *Illus.* TB/3040

ROBERT H. FERRELL, Ed.: Foundations of American Diplomacy, 1775-1872 + HR/1393

LOUIS FILLER: The Crusade against Slavery: 1830-1860. † *Illus.* · TB/3029

WILLIM W. FREEHLING: Prelude to Civil War: *The Nullification Controversy in South Carolina, 1816-1836* TB/1359

PAUL W. GATES: The Farmer's Age: *Agriculture, 1815-1860* Δ TB/1398

THOMAS JEFFERSON: Notes on the State of Virginia. ‡ *Edited by Thomas P. Abernethy* TB/3052

FORREST MCDONALD, Ed.: Confederation and Constitution, 1781-1789 + HR/1396

JOHN C. MILLER: The Federalist Era: 1789-1801. † *Illus.* TB/3027

RICHARD B. MORRIS: The American Revolution Reconsidered TB/1363

CURTIS P. NETTELS: The Emergence of a National Economy, 1775-1815 Δ TB/1438

DOUGLASS C. NORTH & ROBERT PAUL THOMAS, Eds.: *The Growth of the American Economy ot 1860* + HR/1352

R. B. NYE: The Cultural Life of the New Nation: 1776-1830. † *Illus.* TB/3026

GILBERT OSOFSKY, Ed.: Puttin' On Ole Massa: *The Slave Narratives of Henry Bibb, William Wells Brown, and Solomon Northup* ‡ TB/1432

JAMES PARTON: The Presidency of Andrew Jackson. *From Volume III of the* Life of Andrew Jackson. *Ed. with Intro. by Robert V. Remini* TB/3080

FRANCIS S. PHILBRICK: The Rise of the West, 1754-1830. † *Illus.* TB/3067

MARSHALL SMELSER: The Democratic Republic, 1801-1815 † TB/1406

JACK M. SOSIN, Ed.: The Opening of the West + HR/1424

GEORGE ROGERS TAYLOR: The Transportation Revolution, 1815-1860 Δ TB/1347

A. F. TYLER: Freedom's Ferment: *Phases of American Social History from the Revolution to the Outbreak of the Civil War. Illus.* TB/1074

GLYNDON G. VAN DEUSEN: The Jacksonian Era: 1828-1848. † *Illus.* TB/3028

LOUIS B. WRIGHT: Culture on the Moving Frontier TB/1053

American Studies: The Civil War to 1900

W. R. BROCK: An American Crisis: *Congress and Reconstruction, 1865-67* ° TB/1283

T. C. COCHRAN & WILLIAM MILLER: The Age of Enterprise: *A Social History of Industrial America* TB/1054

W. A. DUNNING: Reconstruction, Political and Economic: 1865-1877 TB/1073

HAROLD U. FAULKNER: Politics, Reform and Expansion: 1890-1900. † *Illus.* TB/3020

GEORGE M. FREDRICKSON: The Inner Civil War: *Northern Intellectuals and the Crisis of the Union* TB/1358

JOHN A. GARRATY: The New Commonwealth, 1877-1890 † TB/1410

JOHN A. GARRATY, Ed.: The Transformation of American Society, 1870-1890 + HR/1395

HELEN HUNT JACKSON: A Century of Dishonor: *The Early Crusade for Indian Reform.* † *Edited by Andrew F. Rolle* TB/3063

WILLIAM G. MCLOUGHLIN, Ed.: The American Evangelicals, 1800-1900: An Anthology ‡ TB/1382

JAMES S. PIKE: The Prostrate State: *South Carolina under Negro Government.* ‡ *Intro. by Robert F. Durden* TB/3085

FRED A. SHANNON: The Farmer's Last Frontier: *Agriculture, 1860-1897* TB/1348

VERNON LANE WHARTON: The Negro in Mississippi, 1865-1890 TB/1178

American Studies: The Twentieth Century

RICHARD M. ABRAMS, Ed.: The Issues of the Populist and Progressive Eras, 1892-1912 + HR/1428

RAY STANNARD BAKER: Following the Color Line: *American Negro Citizenship in Progressive Era.* ‡ *Edited by Dewey W. Grantham, Jr. Illus.* TB/3053

RANDOLPH S. BOURNE: War and the Intellectuals: *Collected Essays, 1915-1919.* ‡ *Edited by Carl Resek* TB/3043

A. RUSSELL BUCHANAN: The United States and World War II. † *Illus.*
Vol. I TB/3044; Vol. II TB/3045

THOMAS C. COCHRAN: The American Business System: *A Historical Perspective, 1900-1955* TB/1080

FOSTER RHEA DULLES: America's Rise to World Power: 1898-1954. † *Illus.* TB/3021

HAROLD U. FAULKNER: The Decline of Laissez Faire, 1897-1917 TB/1397

JOHN D. HICKS: Republican Ascendancy: 1921-1933. † *Illus.* TB/3041

WILLIAM E. LEUCHTENBURG: Franklin D. Roosevelt and the New Deal: 1932-1940. † *Illus.* TB/3025

WILLIAM E. LEUCHTENBURG, Ed.: The New Deal: *A Documentary History* + HR/1354

ARTHUR S. LINK: Woodrow Wilson and the Progressive Era: 1910-1917. † *Illus.* TB/3023

BROADUS MITCHELL: Depression Decade: *From New Era through New Deal, 1929-1941* Δ TB/1439

GEORGE E. MOWRY: The Era of Theodore Roosevelt and the Birth of Modern America: 1900-1912. † *Illus.* TB/3022

GEORGE SOULE: Prosperity Decade: *From War to Depression, 1917-1929* Δ TB/1349

TWELVE SOUTHERNERS: I'll Take My Stand: *The South and the Agrarian Tradition. Intro. by Louis D. Rubin, Jr.; Biographical Essays by Virginia Rock* TB/1072

Art, Art History, Aesthetics

ERWIN PANOFSKY: Renaissance and Renascences in Western Art. *Illus.* TB/1447

ERWIN PANOFSKY: Studies in Iconology: *Humanistic Themes in the Art of the Renaissance. 180 illus.* TB/1077

OTTO VON SIMSON: The Gothic Cathedral: *Origins of Gothic Architecture and the Medieval Concept of Order. 58 illus.* TB/2018

HEINRICH ZIMMER: Myths and Symbols in Indian Art and Civilization. *70 illus.* TB/2005

Asian Studies

WOLFGANG FRANKE: China and the West: *The Cultural Encounter, 13th to 20th Centuries. Trans. by R. A. Wilson* TB/1326

L. CARRINGTON GOODRICH: A Short History of the Chinese People. *Illus.* TB/3015

Economics & Economic History

C. E. BLACK: The Dynamics of Modernization: *A Study in Comparative History* TB/1321
GILBERT BURCK & EDITOR OF *Fortune:* The Computer Age: *And its Potential for Management* TB/1179
SHEPARD B. CLOUGH, THOMAS MOODIE & CAROL MOODIE, Eds.: Economic History of Europe: *Twentieth Century #* HR/1388
THOMAS C. COCHRAN: The American Business System: *A Historical Perspective, 1900-1955* TB/1180
HAROLD U. FAULKNER: The Decline of Laissez Faire, 1897-1917 Δ TB/1397
PAUL W. GATES: The Farmer's Age: *Agriculture, 1815-1860* Δ TB/1398
WILLIAM GREENLEAF, Ed.: American Economic Development Since 1860 + HR/1353
ROBERT L. HEILBRONER: The Future as History: *The Historic Currents of Our Time and the Direction in Which They Are Taking America* TB/1386
ROBERT L. HEILBRONER: The Great Ascent: *The Struggle for Economic Development in Our Time* TB/3030
DAVID S. LANDES: Bankers and Pashas: *International Finance and Economic Imperialism in Egypt. New Preface by the Author* TB/1412
ROBERT LATOUCHE: The Birth of Western Economy: *Economic Aspects of the Dark Ages* TB/1290
W. ARTHUR LEWIS: The Principles of Economic Planning. *New Introduction by the Author°* TB/1436
ROBERT GREEN MC CLOSKEY: American Conservatism in the Age of Enterprise TB/1137
WILLIAM MILLER, Ed.: Men in Business: *Essays on the Historical Role of the Entrepreneur* TB/1081
HERBERT A. SIMON: The Shape of Automation: *For Men and Management* TB/1245

Historiography and History of Ideas

J. BRONOWSKI & BRUCE MAZLISH: The Western Intellectual Tradition: *From Leonardo to Hegel* TB/3001
WILHELM DILTHEY: Pattern and Meaning in History: *Thoughts on History and Society.° Edited with an Intro. by H. P. Rickman* TB/1075
J. H. HEXTER: More's Utopia: *The Biography of an Idea. Epilogue by the Author* TB/1195
H. STUART HUGHES: History as Art and as Science: *Twin Vistas on the Past* TB/1207
ARTHUR O. LOVEJOY: The Great Chain of Being: *A Study of the History of an Idea* TB/1009
RICHARD H. POPKIN: The History of Scenticism from Erasmus to Descartes. *Revised Edition* TB/1391
MASSIMO SALVADORI, Ed.: Modern Socialism # HR/1374
BRUNO SNELL: The Discovery of the Mind: *The Greek Origins of European Thought* TB/1018

History: General

HANS KOHN: The Age of Nationalism: *The First Era of Global History* TB/1380
BERNARD LEWIS: The Arabs in History TB/1029
BERNARD LEWIS: The Middle East and the West ° TB/1274

History: Ancient

A. ANDREWS: The Greek Tyrants TB/1103

THEODOR H. GASTER: Thespis: *Ritual Myth and Drama in the Ancient Near East* TB/1281
MICHAEL GRANT: Ancient History ° TB/1190

History: Medieval

NORMAN COHN: The Pursuit of the Millennium: *Revolutionary Messianism in Medieval and Reformation Europe* TB/1037
F. L. GANSHOF: Feudalism TB/1058
F. L. GANSHOF: The Middle Ages: *A History of International Relations. Translated by Rémy Hall* TB/1411
ROBERT LATOUCHE: The Birth of Western Economy: *Economic Aspects of the Dark Ages* ° TB/1290
HENRY CHARLES LEA: The Inquisition of the Middle Ages. || *Introduction by Walter Ullmann* TB/1456

History: Renaissance & Reformation

JACOB BURCKHARDT: The Civilization of the Renaissance in Italy. *Introduction by Benjamin Nelson and Charles Trinkaus. Illus.* Vol. I TB/40; Vol. II TB/41
JOHN CALVIN & JACOPO SADOLETO: A Reformation Debate. *Edited by John C. Olin* TB/1239
FEDERICO CHABOD: Machiavelli and the Renaissance TB/1193
THOMAS CROMWELL: Thomas Cromwell: *Selected Letters on Church and Commonwealth, 1523-1540. ¶ Ed. with an Intro. by Arthur J. Slavin* TB/1462
FRANCESCO GUICCIARDINI: History of Florence. *Translated with an Introduction and Notes by Mario Domandi* TB/1470
WERNER L. GUNDERSHEIMER, Ed.: French Humanism, 1470-1600. * Illus.* TB/1473
HANS J. HILLERBRAND, Ed., The Protestant Reformation # HR/1342
JOHAN HUIZINGA: Erasmus and the Age of Reformation. *Illus.* TB/19
JOEL HURSTFIELD: The Elizabethan Nation TB/1312
JOEL HURSTFIELD, Ed.: The Reformation Crisis TB/1267
PAUL OSKAR KRISTELLER: Renaissance Thought: *The Classic, Scholastic, and Humanist Strains* TB/1048
PAUL OSKAR KRISTELLER: Renaissance Thought II: *Papers on Humanism and the Arts* TB/1163
PAUL O. KRISTELLER & PHILIP P. WIENER, Eds.: Renaissance Essays TB/1392
DAVID LITTLE: Religion, Order and Law: *A Study in Pre-Revolutionary England. § Preface by R. Bellah* TB/1418
NICCOLO MACHIAVELLI: History of Florence and of the Affairs of Italy: *From the Earliest Times to the Death of Lorenzo the Magnificent. Introduction by Felix Gilbert* TB/1027
ALFRED VON MARTIN: Sociology of the Renaissance. ° *Introduction by W. K. Ferguson* TB/1099
GARRETT MATTINGLY et al.: Renaissance Profiles. *Edited by J. H. Plumb* TB/1162
J. H. PARRY: The Establishment of the European Hegemony: 1415-1715: *Trade and Exploration in the Age of the Renaissance* TB/1045
PAOLO ROSSI: Philosophy, Technology, and the Arts, in the Early Modern Era 1400-1700. || *Edited by Benjamin Nelson. Translated by Salvator Attanasio* TB/1458
R. H. TAWNEY: The Agrarian Problem in the Sixteenth Century. *Intro. by Lawrence Stone* TB/1315

H. R. TREVOR-ROPER: The European Witch-craze of the Sixteenth and Seventeenth Centuries and Other Essays ° TB/1416
VESPASIANO: Rennaissance Princes, Popes, and XVth Century: The Vespasiano Memoirs. Introduction by Myron P. Gilmore. Illus. TB/1111

History: Modern European

MAX BELOFF: The Age of Absolutism, 1660-1815 TB/1062
D. W. BROGAN: The Development of Modern France ° Vol. I: From the Fall of the Empire to the Dreyfus Affair TB/1184 Vol. II: The Shadow of War, World War I, Between the Two Wars TB/1185
ALAN BULLOCK: Hitler, A Study in Tyranny. ° Revised Edition. Illus. TB/1123
JOHANN GOTTLIEB FICHTE: Addresses to the German Nation. Ed. with Intro. by George A. Kelly ¶ TB/1366
ALBERT GOODWIN: The French Revolution TB/1064
H. STUART HUGHES: The Obstructed Path: French Social Thought in the Years of Desperation TB/1451
JOHAN HUIZINGA: Dutch Civilization in the 17th Century and Other Essays TB/1453
JOHN MCMANNERS: European History, 1789-1914: Men, Machines and Freedom TB/1419
FRANZ NEUMANN: Behemoth: The Structure and Practice of National Socialism, 1933-1944 TB/1289
DAVID OGG: Europe of the Ancien Régime, 1715-1783 ° a TB/1271
ALBERT SOREL: Europe Under the Old Regime. Translated by Francis H. Herrick TB/1121
A. J. P. TAYLOR: From Napoleon to Lenin: Historical Essays ° TB/1268
A. J. P. TAYLOR: The Habsburg Monarchy, 1809-1918: A History of the Austrian Empire and Austria-Hungary ° TB/1187
J. M. THOMPSON: European History, 1494-1789 TB/1431
H. R. TREVOR-ROPER: Historical Essays TB/1269

Literature & Literary Criticism

JACQUES BARZUN: The House of Intellect TB/1051
W. J. BATE: From Classic to Romantic: Premises of Taste in Eighteenth Century England TB/1036
VAN WYCK BROOKS: Van Wyck Brooks: The Early Years: A Selection from his Works, 1908-1921 Ed. with Intro. by Claire Sprague TB/3082
RICHMOND LATTIMORE, Translator: The Odyssey of Homer TB/1389

Philosophy

HENRI BERGSON: Time and Free Will: An Essay on the Immediate Data of Consciousness ° TB/1021
H. J. BLACKHAM: Six Existentialist Thinkers: Kierkegaard, Nietzsche, Jaspers, Marcel, Heidegger, Sartre ° TB/1002
J. M. BOCHENSKI: The Methods of Contemporary Thought. Trans by Peter Caws TB/1377
CRANE BRINTON: Nietzsche. Preface, Bibliography, and Epilogue by the Author TB/1197
ERNST CASSIRER: Rousseau, Kant and Goethe. Intro by Peter Gay TB/1092
WILFRID DESAN: The Tragic Finale: An Essay on the Philosophy of Jean-Paul Sartre TB/1030

MARVIN FARBER: The Aims of Phenomenology: The Motives, Methods, and Impact of Husserl's Thought TB/1291
PAUL FRIEDLANDER: Plato: An Introduction TB/2017
MICHAEL GELVEN: A Commentary on Heidegger's "Being and Time" TB/1464
G. W. F. HEGEL: On Art, Religion Philosophy: Introductory Lectures to the Realm of Absolute Spirit. || Edited with an Introduction by J. Glenn Gray TB/1463
G. W. F. HEGEL: Phenomenology of Mind. ° || Introduction by eGorge Lichtheim TB/1303
MARTIN HEIDEGGER: Discourse on Thinking. Translated with a Preface by John M. Anderson and E. Hans Freund. Introduction by John M. Anderson TB/1459
F. H. HEINEMANN: Existentialism and the Modern Predicament TB/28
WERER HEISENBERG: Physics and Philosophy: The Revolution in Modern Science. Intro. by F. S. C. Northrop TB/549
EDMUND HUSSERL: Phenomenology and the Crisis of Philosophy. § Translated with an Introduction by Quentin Lauer TB/1170
IMMANUEL KANT: Groundwork of the Metaphysic of Morals. Translated and Analyzed by H. J. Paton TB/1159
IMMANUEL KANT: Lectures on Ethics. § Introduction by Lewis White Beck TB/105
QUENTIN LAUER: Phenomenology: Its Genesis and Prospect. Preface by Aron Gurwitsch TB/1169
GEORGE A. MORGAN: What Nietzsche Means TB/1198
H. J. PATON: The Categorical Imperative: A Study in Kant's Moral Philosophy TB/1325
MICHAEL POLANYI: Personal Knowledge: Towards a Post-Critical Philosophy TB/1158
WILLARD VAN ORMAN QUINE: Elementary Logic Revised Edition TB/577
JOHN E. SMITH: Themes in American Philosophy: Purpose, Experience and Community TB/1466
MORTON WHITE: Foundations of Historical Knowledge TB/1440
WILHELM WINDELBAND: A History of Philosophy Vol. I: Greek, Roman, Medieval TB/38 Vol. II: Renaissance, Enlightenment, Modern TB/39
LUDWIG WITTGENSTEIN: The Blue and Brown Books ° TB/1211
LUDWIG WITTGENSTEIN: Notebooks, 1914-1916 TB/1441

Political Science & Government

C. E. BLACK: The Dynamics of Modernization: A Study in Comparative History TB/1321
KENNETH E. BOULDING: Conflict and Defense: A General Theory of Action TB/3024
DENIS W. BROGAN: Politics in America. New Introduction by the Author TB/1469
LEWIS COSER, Ed.: Political Sociology TB/1293
ROBERT A. DAHL & CHARLES E. LINDBLOM: Politics, Economics, and Welfare: Planning and Politico-Economic Systems Resolved into Basic Social Processes TB/3037
ROY C. MACRIDIS, Ed.: Political Parties: Contemporary Trends and Ideas ** TB/1322
ROBERT GREEN MC CLOSKEY: American Conservatism in the Age of Enterprise, 1865-1910 TB/1137
JOHN B. MORRALL: Political Thought in Medieval Times TB/1076

KARL R. POPPER: The Open Society and Its Enemies *Vol. I: The Spell of Plato* TB/1101 *Vol. II: The High Tide of Prophecy: Hegel, Marx, and the Aftermath* TB/1102
HENRI DE SAINT-SIMON: Social Organization, The Science of Man, and Other Writings. || *Edited and Translated with an Introduction by Felix Markham* TB/1152
JOSEPH A. SCHUMPETER: Capitalism, Socialism and Democracy TB/3008

Psychology

LUDWIG BINSWANGER: Being-in-the-World: *Selected Papers.* || *Trans. with Intro. by Jacob Needleman* TB/1365
HADLEY CANTRIL: The Invasion from Mars: *A Study in the Psychology of Panic* || TB/1282
MIRCEA ELIADE: Cosmos and History: *The Myth of the Eternal Return* § TB/2050
MIRCEA ELIADE: Myth and Reality TB/1369
MIRCEA ELIADE: Myths, Dreams and Mysteries: *The Encounter Between Contemporary Faiths and Archaic Realities* § TB/1320
MIRCEA ELIADE: Rites and Symbols of Initiation: *The Mysteries of Birth and Rebirth* § TB/1236
SIGMUND FREUD: On Creativity and the Unconscious: *Papers on the Psychology of Art, Literature, Love, Religion.* § *Intro. by Benjamin Nelson* TB/45
J. GLENN GRAY: The Warriors: *Reflections on Men in Battle. Introduction by Hannah Arendt* TB/1294
WILLIAM JAMES: Psychology: *The Briefer Course. Edited with an Intro. by Gordon Allport* TB/1034
KARL MENNINGER, M.D.: Theory of Psychoanalytic Technique TB/1144

Religion: Ancient and Classical, Biblical and Judaic Traditions

MARTIN BUBER: Eclipse of God: *Studies in the Relation Between Religion and Philosophy* TB/12
MARTIN BUBER: Hasidism and Modern Man. *Edited and Translated by Maurice Friedman* TB/839
MARTIN BUBER: The Knowledge of Man. *Edited with an Introduction by Maurice Friedman. Translated by Maurice Friedman and Ronald Gregor Smith* TB/135
MARTIN BUBER: Moses. *The Revelation and the Covenant* TB/837
MARTIN BUBER: The Origin and Meaning of Hasidism. *Edited and Translated by Maurice Friedman* TB/835
MARTIN BUBER: The Prophetic Faith TB/73
MARTIN BUBER: Two Types of Faith: *Interpenetration of Judaism and Christianity* ° TB/75
MALCOLM L. DIAMOND: Martin Buber: *Jewish Existentialist* TB/840
M. S. ENSLIN: Christian Beginnings TB/5
M. S. ENSLIN: The Literature of the Christian Movement TB/6
HENRI FRANKFORT: Ancient Egyptian Religion: *An Interpretation* TB/77
ABRAHAM HESCHEL: God in Search of Man: *A Philosophy of Judaism* TB/807
ABRAHAM HESCHEL: Man Is not Alone: *A Philosophy of Religion* TB/838
T. J. MEEK: Hebrew Origins TB/69
H. J. ROSE: Religion in Greece and Rome TB/55

Religion: Early Christianity Through Reformation

ANSELM OF CANTERBURY: Truth, Freedom, and Evil: *Three Philosophical Dialogues. Edited and Translated by Jasper Hopkins and Herbert Richardson* TB/317
JOHANNES ECKHART: Meister Eckhart: *A Modern Translation by R. Blakney* TB/8
EDGAR J. GOODSPEED: A Life of Jesus TB/1
ROBERT M. GRANT: Gnosticism and Early Christianity TB/136
ARTHUR DARBY NOCK: St. Paul ° TR/104
GORDON RUPP: Luther's Progress to the Diet of Worms ° TB/120

Religion: The Protestant Tradition

KARL BARTH: Church Dogmatics: *A Selection. Intro. by H. Gollwitzer. Ed. by G. W. Bromiley* TB/95
KARL BARTH: Dogmatics in Outline TB/56
KARL BARTH: The Word of God and the Word of Man TB/13
WILLIAM R. HUTCHISON, Ed.: American Protestant Thought: *The Liberal Era* ‡ TB/1385
SOREN KIERKEGAARD: Edifying Discourses. *Edited with an Intro. by Paul Holmer* TB/32
SOREN KIERKEGAARD: The Journals of Kierkegaard. ° *Edited with an Intro. by Alexander Dru* TB/52
SOREN KIERKEGAARD: The Point of View for My Work as an Author: *A Report to History.* § *Preface by Benjamin Nelson* TB/88
SOREN KIERKEGAARD: The Present Age. § *Translated and edited by Alexander Dru. Introduction by Walter Kaufmann* TB/94
SOREN KIERKEGAARD: Purity of Heart. *Trans. by Douglas Steere* TB/4
SOREN KIERKEGAARD: Repetition: *An Essay in Experimental Psychology* § TB/117
WOLFHART PANNENBERG, et al.: History and Hermeneutic. *Volume 4 of* Journal for Theology and the Church, *edited by Robert W. Funk and Gerhard Ebeling* TB/254
F. SCHLEIERMACHER: The Christian Faith. *Introduction by Richard R. Niebuhr.*
Vol. I TB/108; Vol. II TB/109
F. SCHLEIERMACHER: On Religion: *Speeches to Its Cultured Despisers. Intro. by Rudolf Otto* TB/36
PAUL TILLICH: Dynamics of Faith TB/42
PAUL TILLICH: Morality and Beyond TB/142

Religion: The Roman & Eastern Christian Traditions

A. ROBERT CAPONIGRI, Ed.: Modern Catholic Thinkers II: *The Church and the Political Order* TB/307
G. P. FEDOTOV: The Russian Religious Mind: *Kievan Christianity, the tenth to the thirteenth Centuries* TB/370
GABRIEL MARCEL: Being and Having: *An Existential Diary. Introduction by James Collins* TB/310
GABRIEL MARCEL: Homo Viator: *Introduction to a Metaphysic of Hope* TB/397

Religion: Oriental Religions

TOR ANDRAE: Mohammed: *The Man and His Faith* § TB/62
EDWARD CONZE: Buddhism: *Its Essence and Development.* ° *Foreword by Arthur Waley* TB/58

EDWARD CONZE et al, Editors: Buddhist Texts through the Ages   TB/113
H. G. CREEL: Confucius and the Chinese Way   TB/63
FRANKLIN EDGERTON, Trans. & Ed.: The Bhagavad Gita   TB/115
SWAMI NIKHILANANDA, Trans. & Ed.: The Upanishads   TB/114

Religion: Philosophy, Culture, and Society

NICOLAS BERDYAEV: The Destiny of Man TB/61
RUDOLF BULTMANN: History and Eschatology: The Presence of Eternity °   TB/91
LUDWIG FEUERBACH: The Essence of Christianity. § Introduction by Karl Barth. Foreword by H. Richard Niebuhr   TB/11
ADOLF HARNACK: What Is Christianity? § Introduction by Rudolf Bultmann   TB/17
KYLE HASELDEN: The Racial Problem in Christian Perspective   TB/116
IMMANUEL KANT: Religion Within the Limits of Reason Alone. § Introduction by Theodore M. Greene and John Silber   TB/67
H. RICHARD NIEBUHR: Christ and Culture TB/3
H. RICHARD NIEBUHR: The Kingdom of God in America   TB/49

Science and Mathematics

W. E. LE GROS CLARK: The Antecedents of Man: An Introduction to the Evolution of the Primates. ° Illus.   TB/559
ROBERT E. COKER: Streams, Lakes, Ponds. Illus.   TB/586
ROBERT E. COKER: This Great and Wide Sea: An Introduction to Oceanography and Marine Biology. Illus.   TB/551
F. K. HARE: The Restless Atmosphere   TB/560
WILLARD VAN ORMAN QUINE: Mathematical Logic   TB/558

Science: Philosophy

J. M. BOCHENSKI: The Methods of Contemporary Thought. Tr. by Peter Caws   TB/1377
J. BRONOWSKI: Science and Human Values. Revised and Enlarged. Illus.   TB/505
WERNER HEISENBERG: Physics and Philosophy: The Revolution in Modern Science. Introduction by F. S. C. Northrop   TB/549
KARL R. POPPER: Conjectures and Refutations: The Growth of Scientific Knowledge   TB/1376
KARL R. POPPER: The Logic of Scientific Discovery   TB/576

Sociology and Anthropology

REINHARD BENDIX: Work and Authority in Industry: Ideologies of Management in the Course of Industrialization   TB/3035
BERNARD BERELSON, Ed., The Behavioral Sciences Today   TB/1127
KENNETH B. CLARK: Dark Ghetto: Dilemmas of Social Power. Foreword by Gunnar Myrdal   TB/1317

KENNETH CLARK & JEANNETTE HOPKINS: A Relevant War Against Poverty: A Study of Community Action Programs and Observable Social Change   TB/1480
LEWIS COSER, Ed.: Political Sociology   TB/1293
ALLISON DAVIS & JOHN DOLLARD: Children of Bondage: The Personality Development of Negro Youth in the Urban South ‖ TB/3049
ST. CLAIR DRAKE & HORACE R. CAYTON: Black Metropolis: A Study of Negro Life in a Northern City. Introduction by Everett C. Hughes. Tables, maps, charts, and graphs
    Vol. I TB/1086; Vol. II TB/1087
PETER F. DRUCKER: The New Society: The Anatomy of Industrial Order   TB/1082
CHARLES Y. GLOCK & RODNEY STARK: Christian Beliefs and Anti-Semitism. Introduction by the Authors   TB/1454
ALVIN W. GOULDNER: The Hellenic World   TB/1479
R. M. MACIVER: Social Causation   TB/1153
GARY T. MARX: Protest and Prejudice: A Study of Belief in the Black Community   TB/1435
ROBERT K. MERTON, LEONARD BROOM, LEONARD S. COTTRELL, JR., Editors: Sociology Today: Problems and Prospects ‖
    Vol. I TB/1173; Vol. II TB/1174
GILBERT OSOFSKY, Ed.: The Burden of Race: A Documentary History of Negro-White Relations in America   TB/1405
GILBERT OSOFSKY: Harlem: The Making of a Ghetto: Negro New York 1890-1930   TB/1381
TALCOTT PARSONS & EDWARD A. SHILS, Editors: Toward a General Theory of Action: Theoretical Foundations for the Social Sciences   TB/1083
PHILIP RIEFF: The Triumph of the Therapeutic: Uses of Faith After Freud   TB/1360
JOHN H. ROHRER & MUNRO S. EDMONSON, Eds.: The Eighth Generation Grows Up: Cultures and Personalities of New Orleans Negroes ‖   TB/3050
ARNOLD ROSE: The Negro in America: The Condensed Version of Gunnar Myrdal's An American Dilemma. Second Edition TB/3048
GEORGE ROSEN: Madness in Society: Chapters in the Historical Sociology of Mental Illness. ‖ Preface by Benjamin Nelson   TB/1337
PHILIP SELZNICK: TVA and the Grass Roots: A Study in the Sociology of Formal Organization   TB/1230
PITIRIM A. SOROKIN: Contemporary Sociological Theories: Through the First Quarter of the Twentieth Century   TB/3046
MAURICE R. STEIN: The Eclipse of Community: An Interpretation of American Studies   TB/1128
FERDINAND TONNIES: Community and Society: Gemeinschaft und Gesellschaft. Translated and Edited by Charles P. Loomis TB/1116
W. LLOYD WARNER and Associates: Democracy in Jonesville: A Study in Quality and Inequality ‖   TB/1129
W. LLOYD WARNER: Social Class in America: The Evaluation of Status   TB/1013
FLORIAN ZNANIECKI: The Social Role of the Man of Knowledge. Introduction by Lewis A. Coser   TB/1372

6